Don't Spoil
My Beautiful Face

Media, Mayhem and
Human Rights in the Pacific

David Robie

Foreword by Kalafi Moala

The author's previous titles include:
Eyes of Fire: The Last Voyage of the Rainbow Warrior (1986)
Och Världen Blundar ... Kampen för frihet i Stilla Havet (Swedish, translated by Margareta Eklöf) (1989)
Blood on their Banner: Nationalist Struggles in the South Pacific (1989)
Tu Galala: Social Change in the Pacific (editor) (1992)
Nius Bilong Pasifik: Mass Media in the Pacific (editor) (1995)
*The Pacific Journalist: A Practical Guide (*editor) (2001)
Mekim Nius: South Pacific media, politics and education (2004)
Eyes of Fire: The Last Voyage of the Rainbow Warrior (Memorial Edition) (2005)

Copyright © 2014 David Robie

David Robie asserts the moral rights to be identified
as the author of this work.
The copyright of the Foreword belongs to Kalafi Moala (2014).

Published by Little Island Press in association with the Pacific Media Centre.

National Library of New Zealand Cataloguing-in-publication data
Robie, David, 1945–
Don't Spoil My Beautiful Face: Media, Mayhem and Human Rights in the Pacific
Bibliography, index.
Mass media—Oceania, 2. Mass media—Social aspects, 3. Mass media—Political aspects, 4. Press and politics—Oceania, 5. Journalism—Oceania, 6. Political studies—Oceania, 7. Human rights I. Title.

ISBN 978 1 877 484 25 4

Front cover photograph: A Nuclear-free and Independent Pacific rally "no nukes" placard in Port Vila, 1983 © David Robie.

Frontispiece cartoon: © Rod Emmerson

Backcover photograph of the author: © Alyson Young

Internal design and layout: WordsAlive Ltd

Don't Spoil
My Beautiful Face

Media, Mayhem and
Human Rights in the Pacific

David Robie

Foreword by Kalafi Moala

little island press

To my wife, Del, for her commitment to human rights.

Contents

Ngā iwi e! Ngā Iwi e!
Kia kotahi ra te Moana-nui-a-Kiwa
E-i-a-i-e

All you people! All you people!
Be united as one like the Pacific Ocean

Taura Eruera, Hirini Melbourne, Robin Mohi,
Mereana Pitman, Jules Topp, Linda Topp, Kui Wano

"We, the people of the Pacific, have been victimised too long by
foreign powers ... Alien colonial, political and military domination
persists as an evil cancer in some of our native territories, such as
Tahiti-Polynesia, Kanaky, Australia and Aotearoa/New Zealand.
Our environment continues to be despoiled by foreign powers
developing nuclear weapons for a strategy of warfare that has no
winners, no liberators and imperils the survival of mankind ..."

From the Preamble to the *People's Charter for a Nuclear-Free*
and Independent Pacific – Port Vila, 1983

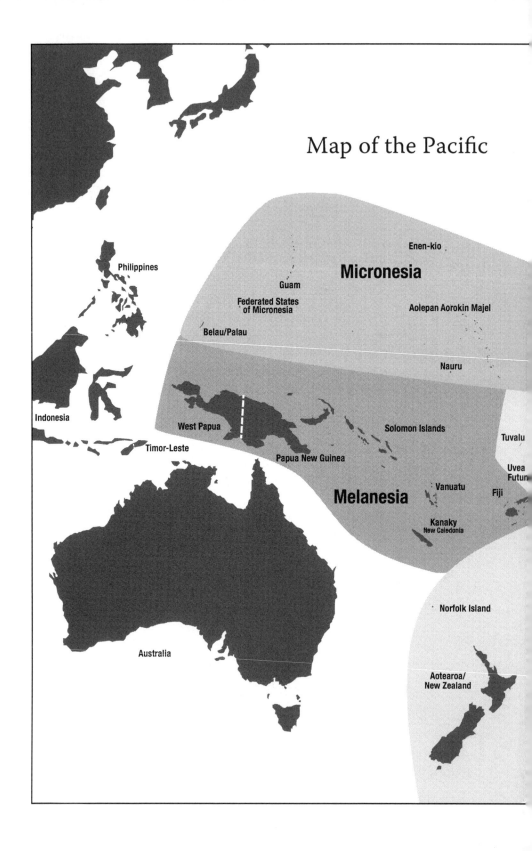

Map of the Pacific

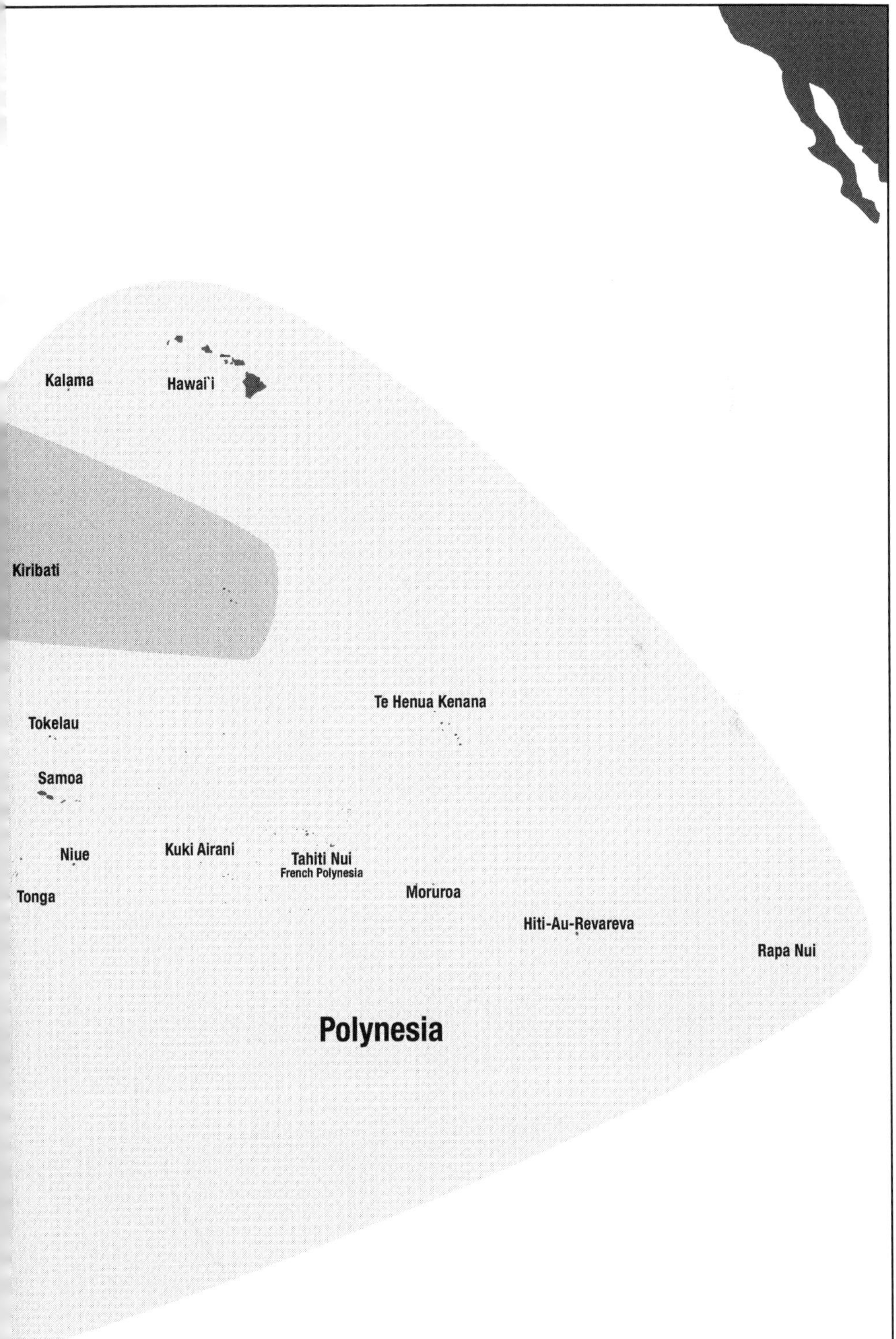

Kalama

Hawai`i

Kiribati

Te Henua Kenana

Tokelau

Samoa

Niue   Kuki Airani   Tahiti Nui
French Polynesia

Tonga   Moruroa

Hiti-Au-Revareva

Rapa Nui

Polynesia

Acknowledgements

THIS BOOK, in a sense, is a sequel to both my 1989 book *Blood on the Banner: Nationalist Struggles in the South Pacific* and my 1992 edited collection *Tu Galala: Social Change in the Pacific*. The earlier work was drawn from my journalism in early years reporting the Asia-Pacific region. *Don't Spoil My Beautiful Face* draws on both my journalism and educational philosophy since embarking on a Pacific media education career at the University of Papua New Guinea in 1993. Many people have contributed generously to this journey.

The title is based on a photograph of a young ni-Vanuatu girl with a painted face and her appealing "no nukes" placard at the third Nuclear Free and Independent Pacific (NFIP) conference in Port Vila, Vanuatu, in July 1983. She was then about the same age as my granddaughter Manon Urumahora and I have often wondered where she may be today.

Firstly, many thanks to my mentors Kalafi Moala, the doyen of Pacific press freedom champions, and John Pilger who have been inspirations. Also, to Mark Revington, as a *NZ Listener* journalist, and the Campaign Against Foreign Control of Aotearoa/New Zealand's (CAFCA) Murray Horton, who both wrote profiles of my Pacific journalism that were in various ways the genesis of this work. I am indebted to Tony Murrow, Evotia Tamua and Robyn Bern of Little Island Press, who supported and encouraged this project from the start. The editor, Mike Wagg, carried out a meticulous job on the manuscript, and Amy Tansell designed the book.

Haumani-Kay Trask's book *From a Native Daughter* offered some initial ideas about an approach to this work, and Ngapuhi photographer John Miller has always provided a benchmark for my work, and many excellent photographs for various projects over many years, including of the late Wilfred Burchett while in Auckland, on page 21 and of the *Rainbow Warrior* on page 261 and page 264 in this book. The East Sepik mask cartoon used as the frontispiece was originally drawn by the *New Zealand Herald's* Rod Emmerson for my 2005 article titled "Pacific solutions" in the Australian Journalists Association *Walkley magazine*.

Alan Robson of the Australian National University was the catalyst for my transition from journalism to media education. Thanks also to then Auckland University of Technology's Pro-Vice-Chancellor Research, Professor Richard Bedford, who assisted this project with a welcome grant in 2012 through AUT's Pacific Media Centre (PMC). Also, I am indebted to the support of the PMC, notably board chairs and members Selwyn Manning, John Utanga, Isabella Rasch, Tui O'Sullivan, Dr Camille Nakhid, Kitea Tipuna, and Professor Marilyn Waring and the Professor of Pacific Studies, Tagaloatele Peggy Fairbairn-Dunlop; Dr Heather Devere of the National Centre for Peace and Conflict Studies at Otago University; Shailendra Singh of the University of the South Pacific; and colleagues at the Asia-Pacific Human Rights Coalition in Auckland.

Many journalists, academics, advocates, activists and photographers have contributed to shaping my approach to journalism and philosophy of media education, and provided insights over many years and, in some cases, have contributed materially to this book. These people include William Akel, Sony Ambudi, Colin and Yvonne Amery, Hilari Anderson, Alexandra Arnassalon, Reverend George Armstrong, Professor Wendy Bacon, Alex Balyut, Rita BauaAlister Barry, May Bass, José Belo, Ben Bohane, Joyce Brown, Wilfred Burchett, Dr Philip Cass, Nick Chesterfield, Adilsonio da Costa Junior, Ruth Coombes, Pat Craddock, Peter Cronau, Associate Professor Trevor Cullen, Jone Dakuvula, Bengt and Marie-Therese Danielsson, Graham Davis, Patrick Decloitre, Mark Derby, Susan Detera, Jean-Pierre Deteix, Juvinal Dias, Kunda Dixit, Barbara Dreaver, Sue Elliott, Cora Fabros, Mariano Fereira, Professor Stewart Firth, Ed Garcia, Pierre Gleizes, Martin Gotje, Christine Gounder, Celestino Gusmao, Professor John Henningham, Dr Helen Hill, Bob Howarth, Vikki John, Giff Johnson, Tarcisius Kabutaulaka, Sandra Kailahi, Maire Leadbeater, Hilda Lini, Lora Lini, Keith Locke, Bunny McDiarmid, Joan Macdonald, Professor Judy McGregor, Mathew McKee, Annie McKillop, Peter Magubane, Associate Professor Tony Maniaty, Irene Manueli, Briar March, Leigh Martin, Ines Martins, Dr Anthony Mason, Barry Middlemiss, Margaret Mills, John Minto, Jale Moala, Professor Chris Nash, Nikhil Naidu, Richard Naidu, Tom Newnham, Associate Professor Levi Obijiofor, Susanna Ounei, Robin Osborne, Associate Professor Evangelia Papoutsaki, Joel Paredes, Professor Mark Pearson, Fernando Pereira, Mark Perkins, Alex Perrottet, Eddy Pinto, 'Akilisi Pohiva, Cristina Prata, Rod Prosser, John Pulu, Ed Rampell, John Richardson, John Ringer, Dr Sitiveni Ratuva, Mark Roach, Professor Robert Robertson, Amelia Rokotuivuna, Dr Angela Romano, Rex Rumakiek, Leo Santiago, Joel Saracho, Steve Sawyer, Charles Scheiner, Lopeti Senituli, Phil Shingler, Seona Smiles, Shailendra

Singh, Elaine Shaw, Max Stahl, Jon Stephenson, Dr Joseph Sukwianomb, Akosita Tamanisau, Oauline Tangiora, Mike Treen, Denys Trussell, Adi Asenaca Uluiviti, Professor Daya Thussu, Professor Crosbie Walsh, Owen Wilkes and Peter Willcox, and Barry Wilson.

Most importantly, many thanks for the never-wavering commitment, dedication, guidance, mentoring and love of my *asawa* Del, since her activist teacher days when we first met in the post-Marcos Philippine Peace Brigade in 1989. This was the year of first publication of *Blood on their Banner* and two years before the Filipino edition was published in Manila by Malaya Books.

David Robie
Auckland, January 2014

Glossary

ABC   Australian Broadcasting Corporation

ACIJ   Australian Centre for Independent Journalism

AGA   Applied Geology Associates Limited

AMIC   Asian Media Information and Communication Centre

AUT   Auckland University of Technology

CAFCA   Campaign Against Foreign Control of Aotearoa

CCF   Citizens' Constitutional Forum (Fiji)

CDRC   Citizens Disaster Rehabilitation Centre

CMATS   Certain Maritime Arrangements for the Timor Sea Treaty

BCL   Bougainville Copper Limited

BRA   Bougainville Revolutionary Amy

brousse   the bush (in New Caledonia)

broussard   European bush settler

CAFGU   Paramilitary Citizens Armed Forces Geographical Unit (Philippines)

CIGN   Special forces in the French *Gendarmerie Nationale*

FI   *Front Indépendantiste*

FLNKS   *Front de Libération Nationale Kanak et Socialiste*—Kanak Socialist National Liberation Front

Falintil   Armed Forces for the National Liberation of Timor-Leste (with the restoration of Independence in 2002 this became F-FDTL, the Defence Forces of Timor-Leste)

Fretilin   Revolutionary Front for an Independent Timor-Leste

FULK   United Kanak Liberation Front

GABRIELA   General Assembly Binding Women for Reforms, Integrity, Equality, Leadership, and Action

GATT   General Agreement on Tariffs and Trade; replaced by the World Trade Organisation (WTO) in 1995

IB   *Islands Business*

IDP   Internally displaced people

IFJ   International Federation of Journalists

indépendantiste   independence supporter in French-governed territories

IPBN Indigenous Peoples' Biodiversity Network

KNPB West Papuan National Committee

métis mixed race

MSG Melanesian Spearhead Group

NFIP Nuclear-Free and Independent Pacific movement

OPM Free Papua Movement

PACMAS Pacific Media Assistance Scheme

PCRC Pacific Concerns Resource Centre

PFF Pacific Freedom Forum (Cook Islands-based)

PASIMA Pasifika Media Association (Samoa-based)

PER Public Emergency Regulations (Fiji)

PIF Pacific Islands Forum

PIM *Pacific Islands Monthly*

PINA Pacific Islands News Association (Fiji-based)

PIMA Pacific Islands Media Association (New Zealand-based)

PJR *Pacific Journalism Review*

PMC Pacific Media Centre (AUT University)

PMCF Pacific Media and Communications Facility

PMI Pacific Media Initiative

PMW Pacific Media Watch

RAFI Rural Advancement Foundation International

RNZI Radio New Zealand International

RAM Reform the Armed Forces of the Philippines Movement

RSF *Reporters Sans Frontières* – Reporters Without Borders

UNDP United Nations Development Programme

UNESCO United Nations Educational, Scientific and Cultural Organisation

UNMISET United Nations Mission of Support in East Timor

UNTAET United Nations Transitional Administration in East Timor

UNHCR Office of the United Nations High Commissioner for Refugees

UNTL National University of Timor-Leste

UPNG University of Papua New Guinea

USP University of the South Pacific

USTKE *Union des Syndicats des Travailleurs Kanaks et des Exploités*—United Union of Kanak and Exploited Workers

wantok One who speaks the same language (Tok Pisin)

WHO World Health Organisation

WPMA West Papua Media Alerts

WTO World Trade Organisation

Foreword

Kalafi Moala

WHEN I was jailed in Tonga in 1996 for contempt of Parliament, together with my deputy editor, Filo `Akau`ola, and MP pro-democracy leader `Akilisi Pohiva, we were not allowed pen and paper or any reading material except a prison Bible. We were incarcerated in the maximum-security cells of Hu`atolitoli Prison on Tongatapu Island. For a period of 26 days, before our release, we were cut off from any kind of reliable communication with the outside world, other than occasional visits from immediate family members, and our lawyer.

We did not know what was going on outside the cells, despite the bits and pieces of local news. It was not until we were released that we found out how strong the international support for us had been.

One of the main drivers behind the protest against our imprisonment was a man who at that stage I had known more by reputation than personally. He is award-winning journalist David Robie, author of nine books, journalism professor, and an analyst and Pacific news reporter for more than three decades.

Not only did he write about our story and distribute it to his network of media in the Pacific, but news agencies from outside the region picked up the stories and drew international attention.

David, together with Pacific Media Watch colleague Peter Cronau, helped draw up a petition that was organised and sent to the King of Tonga by the Australian Centre for Independent Journalism appealing for our release. More than 170 academics, journalists, and media commentators signed the petition.

Amnesty International declared us "prisoners of conscience" and wrote a letter to the king, calling for our release "immediately and unconditionally". The world's largest association of journalists, the International Federation of Journalists (IFJ), with a membership of 400,000 journalists in 95 countries, also appealed for our release.

Without David's involvement, the story and reaction to our imprisonment would not have been so widely known.

Over the years since my 1996 imprisonment, I have watched David evolve as one of the Pacific region's most respected journalists and journalism educators *par excellence*. I don't know of anyone more committed to developing quality journalism in the Pacific and especially in developing a special "Pacific brand" of journalism with in-depth understanding of the issues—including understanding of the geopolitics of the various cultures. Above all he was committed to an untiring service to train and advance Pacific Islanders to the forefront of journalism.

David's earlier book *Mekim Nius* is very helpful and practical for Pacific journalists. I was privileged to launch that book in Suva, Fiji, in 2004, while I was there as keynote speaker at the Journalism Education Association of Australia, New Zealand and the Pacific conference organised by the University of the South Pacific. In 2005, the Pacific Islands Media Association (PIMA) awarded David the media freedom prize for services to journalism education and a free press. I had previously won this award two years in a row.

David, director of the Pacific Media Centre, is a leader in investigative journalism. He has been at the centre of reporting quite a number of the serious conflicts in the region, writing stories with detailed accuracy and depth of insight. Some of these stories are covered in this incredibly suspenseful book. The extent to which this volume covers different island states with their issues, especially political and media challenges, is quite fascinating.

From the Kanak and French standoff in New Caledonia, the French nuclear testing in Moruroa, French Polynesia; the nuclear-free and peace movement in the Pacific, to the coverage of four military coups in Fiji, the East Timor struggles and independence, West Papuan conflicts, and the Philippines human rights movement, and, of-course, the media freedom issues in Tonga—David has covered these and much more.

He was on the *Rainbow Warrior* the night before the fatal bombing of the environmental, nuclear-free ship in Auckland, New Zealand, by French secret agents on 10 July 1985 after being on board the ship on assignment to the Marshall Islands. He details what happened and the issues surrounding this state terrorist attack in one of the chapters.

This is a book that will go in the "must have" section of my personal library. It is not only a great read, but will also act as a reference book on the past four decades of news and current affairs reporting in the Asia-Pacific region.

I recommend this book to every working and aspiring journalist; and for anyone interested in Pacific media and politics, it is essential reading.

Kalafi Moala
Deputy Chair, Pasifika Media Association (Pasima)
Nuku`alofa, Tonga
6 January 2014

1

Introduction: Trust and transparency

Reporting in West Papua is a highly risky business. Journalists, Papuan
and outsiders alike, are under constant threat for reporting West Papua,
with four journalists dying in suspicious circumstances in 2010 alone.
Anywhere journalists report fearlessly, they are the targets.
West Papua Media editor Nick Chesterfield

ONCE I worked with a Kenyan chief editor, George Githii of the *Daily*
Nation, who observed wryly about media freedom in developing nations:

> For governments which fear newspapers, there is one consolation:
> We have known many instances where governments have taken over
> newspapers, but we haven't known of a single incident in which a
> newspaper has taken over a government.[1]

George, always dressed in a dapper bow tie, no matter what the emergency—
such as a senior reporter being abducted before dawn by secret police
because of a front-page exposé on a pharmaceuticals corruption case—had
impeccable credentials politically. He was former press secretary for then
President Jomo Kenyatta, founding father of Kenya. His comment stuck
with me for a long time, and at one stage I used the quote as a personal
email signature. The notion that newspapers might take over a government
or two seemed laughable.[2]

But these days the notion isn't quite so absurd. Take Italy, for example.
Italian media tycoon Silvio Berlusconi, controlling shareholder in the
Mediaset empire and personally reputedly worth $5.9 billion, planned on
making a bid to become Prime Minister of his country for a fifth time in
early 2013. Never mind the sex scandals—along with the euro crisis—that
forced him to resign almost two years earlier. Nor the fact that he failed
to distance himself from his media dominance when in power previously;
he simply shrugged off his election promises to sell off his assets in the
country's largest broadcaster to avoid a conflict of interest.

"I have always behaved correctly, both in private and in public," he told the Italian edition of *The Huffington Post*. "I have never done anything against the law, nor against morality. All the rest is disinformation and defamation."[3] Berlusconi was subsequently found guilty of tax fraud by a lower court in Milan on 26 October 2012 and sentenced to four years in prison, reduced to one year under a law aimed at reducing overcrowding jails. On 24 June 2013, he was convicted for paying an underage prostitute, and of abusing his powers in a cover-up.[4]

Berlusconi went on holiday during 2012 in an attempt to revitalise his political career—ironically, in Kenya. But in February 2013, his centre-right coalition was defeated by the centre-left coalition Italy Common Good. In July, the Supreme Court upheld his one-year commuted prison sentence and he has now been banned from public office for life. However, the 76-year-old billionaire, regarded as the "Harry Houdini of Italian politics", is unlikely to actually be jailed because of his age. He claims he has been victimised by the bias of "uncontrollable judges" and has cited 577 visits by police and paying out more than 174 million euros in legal fees.[5]

However, in November 2013, the Italian Senate voted to expel Berlusconi over his tax fraud conviction in what he described as a "bitter day, a day of mourning for democracy".[6] The expulsion triggered speculation that he may face judicial action under a cloud of criminal trials and investigations.

But powerful as Berlusconi had seemed, and as dominating as his media empire may have been in Italy for two decades, this is nothing compared to the News Corporation tentacles wrapped around political power in Australia, Britain and the US. Rupert Murdoch's personal wealth may be marginally greater than Berlusconi's at $6 billion, according to Sydney media educator David McKnight in his inquiry, *Rupert Murdoch: An Investigation of Political Power*, but News Corporation itself is worth more than $30 billion.[7]

As McKnight says, "as well as being a money spinner, it is a crusading corporation, a media institution with a mission". And in spite of the phone-hacking scandal in 2011 and the closure of the world's largest newspaper, the red-topped tabloid *News of the World* (*NOTW*), News Corp hasn't really taken much of a beating in the stock market—its share price rose by about 50 percent in the past year, "thanks to a US$10 billion share buy-back and its decision to split into two".[8] "Today News Corporation is a powerful political presence in Australia, the United Kingdom and the United States," writes McKnight.[9] "And while the power of Rupert Murdoch and News Corporation is expressed most clearly in its campaigning on major issues, such as the invasion of Iraq [in 2003] and the denial of global warming, it extends far wider."

David McKnight's book showed this to a devastating degree. And this was also echoed in the 2013 Australian federal election with Murdoch's blatantly one-sided *Daily Telegraph* coverage.[10]

In 2011, Murdoch's newspaper *NOTW* was shown to have systematically broken the law by "hacking phones on an industrial scale as well as bribing police. The resulting scandal led to a crisis within News Corp, which is not over yet."[11] There have been more than 100 arrests since 2011 as the result of three separate police investigations. An Alan Moir cartoon depicting the News Corp train crashing off the rails with Murdoch at the controls was published on the cover of the October 2012 edition of *Pacific Journalism Review*, along with an overview of the ethical and legal issues.[12]

Britain's inquiry into media standards by Lord Justice Leveson, which recommended a form of statutory control on the media rather than the traditional self-regulatory regime, was delivered in November 2012.[13] Key recommendations included establishment of an independent regulatory body for the media, which would take an active role in promoting high standards, including having the power to investigate serious breaches and sanction newspapers, and legislation to enshrine for the first time a legal duty on the government to protect freedom of the press. But even before the ink on the report was dry, there were already concerns from critics that the media had started soft-pedalling on the issue.

"We have had an inquisition into every nook and cranny of newspaper culture, an audit greater than any press inquiry in the past and one that has genuinely opened the eyes of the public to the murkier machinations of the Fourth Estate," wrote commentator Ian Burrell in *The Independent*. "And yet, just as the judge prepares to present his hotly anticipated findings, things have gone strangely quiet. Even the recent court appearance of Rebekah Brooks [a former editor of *NOTW*] and Andy Coulson [also a former editor of *NOTW*], who denied phone-hacking charges, attracted less attention in the written media than their former colleagues at News International had been expecting."[14] Former News International chief executive Brooks was subsequently charged in June 2013 with three alleged criminal conspiracies over the phone-hacking affair and went on trial. Coulson, a former spin doctor for Prime Minister David Cameron, faced similar charges in the scandal.

The controversy was aptly summarised in a *PBS Frontline* report, "Murdoch's scandal", that investigated the struggle over the future of News Corporation:

> PRESENTER [voice-over]: Tonight on *Frontline*, Rupert Murdoch and his son engulfed in scandal. How did the owner of the Fox network,

Fox news channel, the movie studio, *The Wall Street Journal*, and a worldwide media empire come to be hounded by the press and haunted by the death of a teenager [Milly Dowler, murdered at the age of 13]?

FEMALE VOICE: That's what absolutely turned the whole thing into a complete nightmare for Rupert Murdoch.

Labour MP TOM WATSON [chair of the Culture, Media and Sport Select Committee]: Mr Murdoch, at what point did you find out that criminality was endemic at *News of the World*?

MURDOCH: Endemic is a very hard, very wide-ranging word.

PRESENTER [voice-over]: Tonight, *Frontline* correspondent Lowell Bergman goes inside the phone-hacking scandal ...

LABOUR MP CHRIS BRYANT: They hacked my phone and they ran some pretty hideous stories about my sexuality.

ANDREW NEIL, FORMER *LONDON SUNDAY TIMES* EDITOR [and thus a former Murdoch employee]: They hacked my messages between myself and the chief executive.

PRESENTER [voice-over]: ... that rocked a government ...

NICK DAVIES [the journalist on *The Guardian* who exposed the scandal]: This is becoming a very, very big scandal, the biggest news organisation in the country is in trouble, the biggest police force in the country is in trouble and furthermore, the Prime Minister's right-hand man is in trouble.

PRESENTER [voice-over] ... and shook the media ...

MURDOCH: This is the most humble day of my life.

ANDREW NEIL: There is a Shakespearean tragedy in that what has happened, what has created him now looks like it can destroy him.[15]

But by early 2014, *The Guardian*'s Media Blog was declaring the Rupert Murdoch era as "all but over" with the reconfiguring of his empire.[16] The October 2012 edition of *Pacific Journalism Review* (*PJR*), a research journal for which I am founding editor, featured the Murdoch phone-hacking scandal and its consequences. The issue was dedicated to the tumultuous events in journalism over the previous year, including the Leveson Inquiry; in Australia, the Finkelstein and Convergence inquiries; and also the New Zealand Law Commission proposal for a super media regulator.

Increasingly, the newspaper industry in many Western countries is failing and the hunt is on for an elusive "new business model". But *PJR* also raised the question in an editorial: "Are media proprietors paying enough attention to the fact that the business model is built on the public trusting the journalistic practices that sit at the heart of the media brands? ... [Retaining] public trust in journalism and to rebuild lost trust becomes as important as the quest to make online journalism pay."[17]

There is a critical Pacific connection over this media "trust and transparency" issue. More than a decade before the closure of the *News of the World*, another Murdoch newspaper, *The Fiji Times*, founded in 1869 and owned by the Australian-based subsidiary News Limited, was embroiled in a major controversy.[18] That time it was over its reportage of the May 2000 coup led by maverick businessman George Speight—now in prison for life for treason along with his media minder Jo Nata—and renegade counter-revolutionary gunmen. Ten years later, News Limited was forced to sell the title by a draconian post-coup Media Decree.[19]

The Motibhai era at *The Fiji Times*, billed as "formidable" but marred by self-censorship.

Mahendra "Mac" Patel, chairman and chief executive of the Motibhai Group, operating a chain of businesses such as Fiji Foods and the Proud duty-free stores with an 80-year history in Fiji, declared that a marriage of his company and *The Fiji Times* would be a "formidable combination".[20] But in spite of being a long-standing local director on the *Times*, he was immediately embroiled in clashes with the military-backed regime, including claims of self-censorship and being jailed for a year for alleged corruption.[21] The longest-serving editor of the *Times*, Vijendra Kumar, now retired in Brisbane, said the "daunting task" for Patel was to mend fences with the regime in the post-censorship era leading to the elections in 2014. But the newspaper would need to retain the crucial role it had played in the history of Fiji: "When there was no postal service in Fiji during the early days of *The Fiji Times*, some bright mind decided to use pigeons to carry dispatches between Suva and Levuka. Patel will need similar ingenuity to take the paper to new heights."[22]

As both a journalism educator and a researcher, my student journalists and I were involved at the heart of this crisis,[23] just as I have been as a journalist covering stories such as independence or self-determination for indigenous minorities in Kanaky/New Caledonia—where I reported on the mid-1980s conflict, and the struggles in Timor-Leste and West Papua. In fact, the human rights atrocities and threats facing the media in West Papua are now the most urgent problem confronting the Pacific, yet it remains virtually ignored by international and regional media. The nature of my journalism career, for many years working in developing countries and for two global news agencies, has shaped and influenced my journalism, my teaching and my research trajectory. Social justice and ethical frameworks have provided the foundation; and also an independent commitment to media freedom. My 1996 documentary *Fri Pres* (*Free Press*) was broadcast on Fiji Television and EM TV in Port Moresby to highlight issues of censorship, self-censorship and a threatened draconian media licensing law. Sadly, not a lot has changed since:

Kanak broadcaster, political activist and musician Jacques "Kiki" Kare featured in the 1996 University of Papua New Guinea documentary *Fri Pres*.

Fri Pres/ABC/UPNG

ITEM 1: Shouts by French CRS riot police as they attack peaceful Kanak protesters holding balloons and sitting in the Place des Cocotiers in central Nouméa, New Caledonia … Sounds of truncheons crashing on sitting protesters …

ITEM 2: Shouts as Papua New Guinea police fire teargas canisters into protesting students at the national University of Papua New Guinea and also assault a journalist …

NEWS READER: The situation at Waigani as the University of Papua New Guinea students protest against the user-pays policy. [Scenes of brutality by police and firing of teargas into students; a journalist is attacked.]

ITEM 3: PNG FORESTS MINISTER TIM NEVILLE [in a studio radio interview]: He was approached by four Malaysians and they said, "You're Greg Neville, the brother of the Minister of Forests, Tim Neville." And he said, "That's correct, what's it to you?"

And their remark, warning or threat to him was that, "You had better warn your brother, the minister, he had better back off on the forest policy issues, or you and your family are as good as dead."

NARRATOR DAVID ROBIE [with *Fri Pres* title and media freedom cartoon frames as background]: Across the South Pacific today, the news media are under siege as never before. In some countries, journalists face brutal assaults, arbitrary imprisonment, gaggings, threats, defamation cases, with the threat of bankruptcy and vilification.

And they also face mounting pressure from governments to be "accountable" and to "report the truth". But whose truth and accountability to whom?

As Pacific journalists and news media become more professional and probing on the dilemmas of development, economic and social policy, and issues such as corruption and [climate change], there is a danger that some politicians want to restrict the media from reporting in the public interest.[24]

This half-hour documentary was researched and scripted by me, with University of Papua New Guinea students Stevenson Liu of Vanuatu and Priscilla Raepom of Papua New Guinea conducting the interviews on camera. Both went on to become accomplished journalists in their respective countries: Liu for Television Blong Vanuatu; and Raepom, initially with the *Post-Courier* in Port Moresby and then as founding editor of that title's innovative *New Age Woman* magazine. The extraordinary thing is that the dire freedom of the press straitjacket has remained much the same in the Pacific for almost three decades; only the specific flashpoints have changed.

Several profiles have been written about both my journalism and media education in the Asia-Pacific region, notably by CACFA's Murray Horton in *New Zealand Monthly Review*, who concluded: "David has never shied from controversy, whether with reactionary authorities ... or apologists",[25] and David McLoughlin in the *Dominion Post*, who noted my comment: "Although there are many capable, talented and courageous journalists in the region, the poor pay undermines the independence and integrity of the Fourth Estate."[26] But the most perceptive was by Mark Revington, editor of *Te Karaka*, the voice of Ngāi Tahu. Then writing in the *New Zealand Listener*, he wrote that power in Fiji doesn't always "come from the barrel of a gun. All it takes is the threat."[27] He profiled the first 10 days of the attempted coup d'état by renegade businessman George Speight, when "some of the best reporting and analysis came from journalism students at the University of the South Pacific, on their *Pacific Journalism Online* website". On the eleventh day of the crisis, the website was closed down. The previous night, Speight's supporters had trashed the studio and offices of Fiji Television, following criticism of Speight during a current affairs show transcribed by one of my students and picked up by newswires.[28] But Revington also narrated how my students outwitted censorship by having their stories published on a special website created by the Australian Centre for Independent Journalism (ACIJ) in Sydney. He wrote:

> David Robie has been an impassioned chronicler of Pacific currents for decades, an interest developed while working as an editor for Agence France-Presse news agency in Paris during the early 1970s. After returning to the Pacific in 1977, he began covering Pacific affairs as a freelancer. He witnessed the bloody struggles for independence of the 1980s, and the attempts of independent Pacific nations to chart a nuclear-free course. He reported on the violence between France and Kanak activists in New Caledonia and the massacre of Kanak activists at Hienghène in 1984 that almost provoked a civil war. He was harassed by French secret service agents and arrested at gunpoint by the military in New Caledonia, and was on board the *Rainbow Warrior* when it evacuated irradiated Rongelap Islanders from their atoll, leaving the ship three days before it was sunk in Auckland by French secret service agents. He was in Fiji when Fiji Labour Party Prime Minister Dr Timoci Bavadra was elected in 1987, and covered the subsequent coups.[29]

A Papua New Guinean press cartoon farewelling the author on his way to Fiji in 1998 after five years running the journalism programme at the University of Papua New Guinea.

BILISO/*THE NATIONAL*

Revington also referred to my book *Blood on their Banner*, published in 1989, which is "a detailed analysis of the struggle of indigenous people around the Pacific against the remnants of colonialism. The epilogue is just as applicable today in Fiji."[30]

The present book introduces some of the key inspirational ideas and the people who have influenced my journalism, publication and media education directions—from my trans-continental journey "out of Africa" into Paris-based global news agency journalism and then the Pacific. They involve colonial legacy conflicts, environmental and indigenous struggles, "forgotten wars, elusive peace", "Moruroa, mon amour", and conclude with changing paradigms and contemporary challenges such as conflict-sensitive journalism and inclusive journalism education.

Notes

1 David Robie (1995). Touching the heart of the Pacific. In D. Robie (ed.), *Nius Bilong Pasifik: Mass Media in the Pacific*. Port Moresby: University of PNG Press, pp. 5–15.
2 Sections of this chapter were originally presented in a professorial address in journalism at Auckland University of Technology on 16 October 2012.

3   *The Huffington Post* launches Italian site with Berlusconi interview (2012, September 25). *The Drum*. Retrieved on 7 August 2013, from www.thedrum. com/news/2012/09/25/huffington-post-launches-italian-site-berlusconi-interview

4   Rachel Donadio (2012, October 26). Berlusconi is found guilty of tax fraud. *The New York Times*. Retrieved on 27 October 2012, from www.nytimes. com/2012/10/27/world/europe/berlusconi-convicted-and-sentenced-in-tax-fraud.html

5   Is Silvio Berlusconi the victim of political judges? (2013, August 9). *DNA News*. Retrieved on 7 August 2013, from www.dnaindia.com/world/1872004/report-is-silvio-berlusconi-the-victim-of-political-judges

6   Silvio Berlusconi expelled from Italian parliament over tax fraud (2013, November 28). NDTV News. Retrieved on 7 January 2014, from www.ndtv. com/article/world/silvio-berlusconi-expelled-from-italian-parliament-over-tax-fraud-451797

7   David McKnight (2012). *Rupert Murdoch: An Investigation of Political Power*. Sydney: Allen & Unwin, p. 2.

8   Defiant Murdoch stays at the helm despite investors' gripes (2012, October 22). *New Zealand Herald*, p. B6.

9   McKnight (2012), p. 3.

10 Wendy Bacon (2013). This is why we need truly democratic media. *New Matilda*. Retrieved on 15 September 2013, from www.newmatilda.com/2013/09/06/why-we-need-truly-democratic-media

11 McKnight (2012), p. 1.

12 Johan Lidberg, Chris Nash and David Robie (2012, October). Rebuilding Public Trust. *Pacific Journalism Review*, *18*(2), 223 pp. Auckland: Pacific Media Centre, AUT University.

13 The Leveson Report. Available at: www.levesoninquiry.org.uk/about/the-report/

14 Ian Burrell (2012, October 8). As Lord Leveson prepares to give his verdict, it's gone strangely quiet. *The Independent*. Retrieved on 9 October 2012, from www.independent.co.uk/news/media/opinion/ian-burrell-as-lord-leveson-prepares-to-give-his-verdict-its-gone-strangely-quiet-8201376.html

15 Murdoch's scandal (2012, March 27). *PBS Frontline: Inside the phone-hacking scandal that rocked a government and shook a media giant* [Video excerpt]. Retrieved on 12 September 2012, from www.pbs.org/wgbh/pages/frontline/ murdochs-scandal/Programme transcript: http://www.pbs.org/wgbh/pages/ frontline/media/murdochs-scandal/transcript-17/

16 Steve Hewlett (2014, January 5). The Rupert Murdoch era is as good as over. *The Guardian*. Retrieved on 6 January 2014, from www.theguardian.com/media/ media-blog/2014/jan/05/rupert-murdoch-era-over?CMP=ema_546

17 Johan Lidberg and David Robie (2012). Trust and transparency [Editorial]. "Rebuilding public trust" edition. *Pacific Journalism Review*, *18*(2): 6–12. Retrieved on 10 October 2012, from www.pjreview.info/articles/editorial-trust-and-transparency-776

18 David Robie (2001). Coup coup land: The press and the putsch in Fiji. *Asia Pacific Media Educator*, No. 10: 148–162. Retrieved on 7 January 2014, from http://ro.uow.edu.au/apme/vol1/iss10/16/

19 Journalists welcome *Fiji Times* sale but question future editorial policy (2010, September 16). Pacific Media Watch, No. 7029. Retrieved on 7 August 2013, from http://www.pmc.aut.ac.nz/pacific-media-watch/2010-09-16/fiji-journalists-welcome-fiji-times-sale-question-future-editorial-po

20 Motibhai buys the *Fiji Times* (2010, September 16). Motibhai Group website. Retrieved on 7 January 2014, from www.motibhai.com/News/Website-Training. aspx

21 Fiji's top businessman jailed (2011, April 14). Fairfax *Stuff*. Retrieved on 7 January 2014, from www.stuff.co.nz/business/world/4887600/Fijis-top-businessman-jailed

22 Vijendra Kumar (2010, September 27). Fiji: The best of the *Times*. *Pacific Scoop*. Retrieved on 7 January 2014, from http://pacific.scoop.co.nz/2010/09/fiji-the-best-of-the-times/

23 David Robie (2001). Frontline reporters: A students' internet coup. *Pacific Journalism Review*, *7*(1): 47–56. Retrieved on 20 September 2012, from www.kauri.aut.ac.nz:8080/dspace/bitstream/123456789/44/1/Pacific%20Journalism%20Review%20_&_1_47-56_Frontline%20Reporter.pdf

24 *Fri Pres: Media freedom in the South Pacific* (1996). Television documentary by David Robie and two University of Papua New Guinea students, Stevenson Liu and Priscilla Raepom, 25 min. [Video excerpt]. Retrieved on 1 October 2012, from www.youtube.com/watch?v=wSWbNSJCz54

25 Murray Horton (1992, August–September). David Robie: One of a kind. *New Zealand Monthly Review*, pp. 16–19.

26 David McLoughlin (2005, March 12). The South Pacific round. *The Dominion Post*, p. B4. Retrieved on 6 January 2014, from http://www.academia.edu/1140072/The_South_Pacific_round_Profile_

27 Mark Revington (2000, August 5). Guns and money. *New Zealand Listener*, pp. 10–11; and also in Brij V. Lal and Michael Pretes (eds) (2001). *Coup: Reflections on the Political Crisis in Fiji*. Canberra, ACT: Australian National University Press.

28 Alison Ofatalu (2000). Controversial *Close-Up*. [Transcript of the Fiji Television programme on 28 May 2000]. *Pacific Journalism Review*, *7*(1): 39–45. Retrieved on 14 February 2013, from www.pjreview.info/articles/controversial-close-672

29 Revington (2000, August 5), p. 11.

30 David Robie (1989). *Blood on their Banner: Nationalist Struggles in the South Pacific*. London: Zed Books; Sydney: Pluto Press.

PART 1

Out of Africa

Trekking freelance from Cape Town to Paris: travelling in Nigeria, 1972.   DAVID ROBIE

2

Media, mayhem
and human rights

My mother used to stay away from politics because my father
went to prison. But we can't not be involved.
By not taking a position, you take a position.

Z film director Costa-Gavras

AS A FOUR-year-old, there was no early hint of my interest in journalism, even though it runs in the family, at least in the mid-nineteenth century, but perhaps there was some slight evidence of my French connection in an early snapshot—taken of me wearing a black beret. But there was no baguette in sight in Ngaio, Wellington, at the time. In any case, my late father, David (Jim) Robie, who migrated to New Zealand with his family from Huddersfield, England, when he was aged almost seven and lived until the age of 92, said he didn't think there was any special reason for the headgear. However, post-war Monty-style berets were popular at the time.

I wasn't really fully aware of the significance while I was growing up, but apart from my father, who always brought home fortnightly bundles of fascinating public library books on topics ranging from flamenco guitar music to Robert Ruark's *Africa*, and my Aunt Ruby Dick, who was an intriguing and engaging librarian in Petone, I had a critically important person among my whakapapa. My great-great-grandfather, James Robie, was the editor and later owner of Scotland's *Caledonian Mercury* in Edinburgh in the 1860s. He was something of a media stirrer and pamphleteer who campaigned for the Free Kirk Radicals, a splinter group from the Presbyterians.[1]

James Robie and his wife, Letitia, were awarded a financial testimonial in October 1865 for his newspaper's "honest and persevering and able advocacy of such important subjects as Constitutional Government, the Amity of Nations, the Rights of Christian Churches, Anti-Slavery, Free Trade, Just Taxation, Parliamentary, Municipal and Social Reform and every other question bearing upon the great principles of civil and religious

James Robie, editor of Edinburgh's *Caledonian Mercury*, photographed in Dublin in 1870.
NATIONAL LIBRARY OF SCOTLAND

liberty". James was also presented by "a number of the leading citizens of New York" in March 1864 with a set of six volumes of *The Rebellion Record*, an elegant crimson Moroccan hide-bound history and diary of the American Civil War. Queen Victoria and John Stuart Mill, author of *On Liberty*, were also among 40 people presented with a set of the limited editions. According to the *Mercury* report announcing the gesture about "the great struggle": "This is an era in American literature, and the first time in the history of any literature that a work by one nation has been sent to another for its political edification and instruction."[2]

In yet another honour, James Robie was awarded a silver snuff box for his newspaper's campaign for a "successful vindication of the rights of lockers" in opposition to two "arbitrary orders" by Her Majesty's Customs in March 1858. Robie had taken charge of the *Caledonian Mercury* two years earlier as editor in 1856.

As historian W. J. Couper wrote in *The Edinburgh Periodical Press*, "When Robie became editor, the paper was generally regarded as moribund ... [His] vigorous work, however, did much to resuscitate its fortunes, and he gradually brought it to paying point."[3] On 7 January 1861, the *Mercury* celebrated its bicentenary, but this was rather hollow as this paper had not been publishing for an unbroken run to be able to claim, as it did on the masthead, that it was established in 1661 and thus the "oldest newspaper in

The Pacific statue of Joan of Arc in full body armour besides St Joseph's Cathedral in Nouméa, the capital of New Caledonia. The cathedral was built with convict labour between 1887 and 1897.   DAVID ROBIE

the world". The masthead also proclaimed: "In politics, independent … In religion, unsectarian."

In spite of the newspaper's crusading reputation and with editor James Robie sinking his entire testimonial into buying the newspaper and trying to save it in the face of growing competition from *The Scotsman*, the *Mercury* eventually closed.[4] But not before a notorious pamphlet and newspaper controversy when James Robie accused the Radicals of Edinburgh of having "entrapped" him into "accepting the proprietorship by unfulfilled promises of support".[5]

Curiously, this "ink in the veins" family history did not really seem to have any significant influence on me until I actually embarked on my journalism career (after a short-lived foray into forestry and starting a science degree) at *The Dominion* in 1964, possibly because there was little family discussion about James and the *Caledonian Mercury* while I was growing up.

There were other influences for me as well, such as drawing inspiration from the life of Joan of Arc—portrayed above by her statue outside St Joseph's Cathedral in Nouméa, New Caledonia. Although I did not see this "brown" statue until the 1980s, I found the Antipodean version far more inspiring as an iconic symbol of a struggle for justice than the 1874 national monument to St Jeanne in the Place des Pyramides, Paris, near

New Zealand Scouts in piupiu greeted by Prince Constantine at Marathon Bay, 1963. The author is pictured on the left. This grainy picture is reproduced from the official World Jamboree camp book.

where she was wounded in battle while trying to free Paris from English control. Ironically, beside the golden pedestal in Paris is where the right-wing National Front holds an annual rally on May Day. I prefer to see the progressive side of the Maid of Orleans' symbolism, such as the Cross of Lorraine being used for the Free French in the struggle against foreign occupation and repression. In a Pacific context, this represents freedom and justice for the colonised.

Another early influence worth mentioning was when I was chosen in 1963 as a Queen's Scout for a New Zealand contingent at the 11th World Jamboree at Marathon Bay in Greece. This was the site of the famous battleground in 490 BC when a hopelessly outnumbered Athenian force defeated a huge Persian invasion army by a cunning strategy. The jamboree was billed as the second battle of Marathon—a peaceful version, of course—and photos show our marae-style campsite and participants practising tikanga Māori. The jamboree was clouded by tragedy when the entire contingent from the Philippines—20 Scouts and four Scout leaders—perished before they even got there. Their aircraft crashed into the Indian Ocean while approaching Mumbai Airport. Crown Prince Constantine, the Chief Scout of Greece, treated the jamboree seriously and was present for the entire 11 days—four years later he was overthrown by the colonels in a bloodless coup.

Colonel Georgios Papadopoulos led a military overthrow of the government on 21 April 1967. The repressive junta lasted until 1974, but the colonels never produced evidence to support their claim that they were acting to prevent a "communist-inspired" coup. The 1969 Costa-Gavras political thriller *Z* about the junta in Greece, which I saw in Melbourne for the first time, was another inspiration. It tells the story of a young examining judge and courageous photojournalist who investigate the assassination of a leftist politician. Although fictionalised, it is largely based on the murder of democratic politician Grigoris Lambrakis in 1963—the year that I was at the jamboree. The film's title is drawn from the Greek word *Zει*—"He lives".[6] The thriller is one of the most politically insightful films ever made, exposing government hypocrisy and cover-up leading into the putsch.

My Greek and French connections evolved from this jamboree period. In 2011, a re-enactment of the original Battle of Marathon to protect Athens was staged in the bay. I was 17 at the time of the 1963 Marathon jamboree, and I journeyed after the camp to Paris where I vowed to return later and live.

'Something dark and bloody'

After working for *The Dominion, New Zealand Herald* and the Melbourne *Herald*, in 1969 I was appointed chief subeditor of a crusading newspaper in Melbourne, the *Sunday Observer*, owned by Gordon Barton, a millionaire transport mogul who owned IPEC and was convenor of the Australia Party. I became editor the following year.

The *Sunday Observer* was the first newspaper with a reasonably large circulation (more than 100,000) to campaign vigorously against Australian involvement in the Vietnam War. One of the challenges I had at the time while chief subeditor was to publish a selection of photographs of the My Lai massacre in 1968 taken by combat photographer Ronald L. Haeberle. Between 340 and 500 unarmed civilians were murdered in the hamlets of My Lai and My Khe of Son My village on 16 March that year by US Army soldiers of Charlie Company, 1st Battalion, 20th Infantry Regiment.[7]

Most of the victims were elderly people, women and children. Twenty-two soldiers were charged over the atrocities, but only one, Second Lieutenant William Calley, was actually convicted. He was jailed for life for the murder of 22 civilians but only served a three-year house arrest term.

Investigative journalist Seymour Hersh broke the story with revelations that Lieutenant Calley was being prosecuted for a war crime. My *Sunday Observer* newspaper published the Haeberle photographs on 14 December 1969—the same week as *Life* magazine in New York. We later made the photographs available to the Federal Parliament in a bid to encourage opposition to the war.

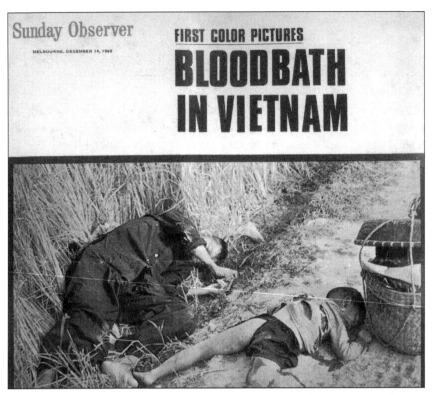

The My Lai massacre report featuring Ronald L. Haeberle's photographs in the Melbourne *Sunday Observer*, 14 December 1969.

At the time when we published the pictures, the Pentagon was still claiming the killings were an "act of war". But our report said:

> The pictures in this newspaper by Ronald Haeberle, an Army photographer who covered the massacre, and reports in the past three weeks confirm a story of indisputable horror—the deliberate slaughter of old men, women, children and babies.
>
> Eyewitness reports indicate that the American troops encountered little—if any—hostile fire, found virtually no enemy soldiers in the village and suffered only one casualty—a self-inflicted wound. The people of My Lai were simply gunned down.[8]

During my time with the *Sunday Observer*, I personally met and worked with Wilfred Burchett, an Australian who was one of the most courageous

Wilfred Burchett in Auckland with activist academic Dr Robert Mann in 1972.

JOHN MILLER

journalists I have ever encountered, but who was loathed by many of his countrymen who regarded him as public enemy number one because they believed he was a traitor who had covered the Korean and Vietnam wars from the "other side".[9]

At the time, Burchett was barred from entering his own country by a vindictive government in Canberra because he had lost his Australian passport, allegedly stolen by the CIA. He was the *Sunday Observer*'s South-East Asian correspondent and we chartered a plane to fly him into Brisbane from the New Caledonian capital of Nouméa's Tontouta airport while he was travelling with an outsized Vietnamese *carte de passage*. Once he was safely on Australian soil he was then able to regain his passport.[10]

Wilfred Burchett was pictured later while visiting Auckland by Ngāpuhi photographer John Miller, who has chronicled social justice issues in images for more than four decades. Burchett's international reputation

as a journalist and war correspondent—as outlined in *Rebel Journalism*
and many of his other books—was built upon one of the great reportage
scoops of the 20th century.[11] After the second atomic bomb was dropped
in Nagasaki in Japan in August 1945 and the Japanese had announced their
surrender, the American forces issued accreditation to several hundred
correspondents to report on the signing of the surrender documents.

All the accredited journalists dutifully made their way to the USS
Missouri, but Burchett "slipped the leash" and on the morning of 2
September 1945 boarded a train for Hiroshima.[12] Burchett travelled for
more than 600 kilometres, carrying rations for just seven meals—food was
almost impossible to obtain at the time in Japan—a black umbrella and a
typewriter.

What Wilfred Burchett saw was the total devastation of Hiroshima: a
city of some 100,000 people had simply been pulverised. Wilfred's front-
page lead in the 5 September 1945 edition of the London *Daily Express*
declared: "THE ATOMIC PLAGUE: 'I write this as a warning to the world'"
and was subtitled: "DOCTORS FALL AS THEY WORK. Poison gas fear: All
wear masks." Burchett wrote:

> In Hiroshima, 30 days after the first atomic bomb destroyed the city
> and shook the world, people are still dying, mysteriously and horribly—
> people who were uninjured by the cataclysm—from, an unknown
> something which I can only describe as "atomic plague".[13]

As I recalled in 2009, "almost four decades later, in his final book,
Shadows of Hiroshima, [Burchett] returned to this nuclear nightmare and
reflected on this racist experiment against an already defeated enemy and
a history of cover-ups over the 'atomic plague'".[14] Within the first two to
four months of the bombing, up to 166,000 people died in Hiroshima, with
about half that number dying in the first day. A further 80,000-plus died
in Nagasaki.

And this was never considered a war crime.

Probably the most outstanding newspaper that I ever worked for was
the *Rand Daily Mail*, South Africa's largest English-language newspaper,
published in Johannesburg. I was chief subeditor (1970–72) during that
newspaper's fight against apartheid, and later night editor. I was astonished
by the number of my colleagues who had been jailed for reporting "banned"
people or refusing to divulge sources. I worked under great editors such as
Raymond Louw, Allister Sparks and Benjamin Pogrund, and I learnt a lot
about human rights and crusading journalism.

For much of its 83-year history, the *Mail* blazed a trail for independence and a free press. The last editor was Rex Gibson, and his book *Final Deadline* has been dubbed "a tale of corporate manipulation, mismanagement and hypocrisy".[15] In the end, a proud newspaper died in 1985 but nobody could really explain why. In a speech marking the twentieth anniversary of the paper's closure, Raymond Louw said: "The closure caused huge damage [throughout South Africa]; it seared the country's news gathering and distribution system, from which the industry has still not recovered."[16]

Among many brave people who were my colleagues on the *Mail* was a "banned" photographer, Peter Magubane, whom I was forced to meet in secret in Soweto. Years later, the New York-published book *Magubane's South Africa* documented those ugly years of repression.[17] The then US Ambassador to the United Nations, Andrew Young, wrote in the foreword: "Who would ever believe that a man's quest for excellence as a photojournalist would bring him 586 days of solitary confinement in prison, six months or more in jail, physical brutality and five years 'banning'?"[18] Under South Africa's apartheid laws at the time, the regime could arbitrarily ban people, movements and publications. This meant that if they were banned under the *Riotous Assemblies Act 1929* or later the *Suppression of Communism Act 1950*, it was illegal for news media to quote or publish what they said. There was no appeal against a banning order.[19]

Magubane's notes about the book cover picture taken at a football match said: "A policeman with a dog is a fearful thing. One of those dogs will rip you open. ... The whip is made of hippo hide."[20]

Less than a decade later, I was back in New Zealand reporting the "shame" 1981 anti-apartheid Springbok rugby tour protests as a stringer for the London *Sunday Times* and other publications. During these protests, I was in the middle of the "lion's den" at Rugby Park, Hamilton, in the second match of the tour on July 25, which was cancelled after more than 350 demonstrators invaded the pitch. Recalled a protester: "Ripping down the fence took about 10 seconds – it was very fast. ... We ran under the goalposts into the middle. I remember the priests struggling with a bloody big cross."[21]

From South Africa, I embarked in 1973 on what was supposed to be a 12,780-kilometre overland journey from Cape Town to Cairo in a VW Kombi. It ended up being a year-long 20,000-kilometre journey in two stages from Cape Town to Paris, filing freelance stories on the way for independent news services such as London-based Gemini.[22] One of my memorable assignments was reporting on and driving along the Trans-African Highway from Mombasa to Lagos.

The author (far left) with photographer Kapil Arn (fourth from left) and Reverend George Armstrong (second on left of the group of anti-apartheid protesters with linked arms) on the field at Rugby Park, Hamilton, during the 1981 Springbok tour.   REAL PICTURES

The big problem was that most of this road didn't actually exist. This road-to-nowhere tale became a cover story for *African Development* magazine, one of the top current affairs publications of the time.[23]

> This Trans-African safari across 25 countries began in South Africa after six months of spare time planning and fitting out of the vehicle ... Among our stores we had enough jerrycans to carry 230 litres of petrol and 45 litres of water, two spare wheels and three extra tyres, a special high-lift jack for hoisting the van out of holes, an aluminium ladder, a medical kit, spades, sand mats, a range of spare parts, three months' supply of canned and dehydrated food—and the lower jawbone of an elephant![24]

In between the two stages, I was features editor of the *Daily Nation* in Kenya, the newspaper that I mentioned at the start of the previous chapter, edited by George Githii. This paper was owned by the Aga Khan and was founded as the newspaper of independence. It contested the British colonial *East African Standard* and it ended up owning that paper too. My ultimate boss

The Trans-African "road to nowhere" highway in the Ituri rainforest in 1972.   DAVID ROBIE

was Prince Karim Aga Khan IV, the Imamat of the Nizari Ismaili community, a Shia Muslim sect. The Aga Khan founded the Aga Khan Development Network (AKDN), a vast private company seeking to raise living standards and boost education across many Asian and African countries.

Finally, I ended up in Paris in 1975, driving the Kombi pictured above, after traversing the jungles of central Africa, zigzagging over the Sahara Desert and crossing Algeria. To give the sky-blue van a human touch it was painted with a dynamic African route map and "christened Tuhoe, after the iwi of the Urewera country, but many people mistook the signwriting to read 'Taboo'".[25] These were still euphoric times for the fledgling nation of Algeria, having just won its independence from France a decade earlier after a devastating eight-year war. The 1966 docudrama by Gillo Pontecorvo, *The Battle of Algiers*, is a classic film on urban guerrilla warfare based in the city's casbah.[26]

I parked the Kombi outside the American Express Building in the heart of Paris after camping in the Bois de Boulogne, sold it for cash, and got a job on Agence France-Presse (AFP) news agency where I worked for the next three years after surviving my three-day French-language trial.

"THE JACKAL—MASTER SPY" article in the South African *Sunday Express*, 13 July 1978.

While working as a foreign correspondent and news editor for AFP, I covered such events as the black African walkout in protest against New Zealand over its sporting ties with South Africa at the 1976 Olympic Games in Montreal, Canada. I also reported on stories like the hunt for "Carlos the Jackal", then one of the global masterminds of terror, such as the highlighted article below for the South African *Sunday Express*.

Ironically, this was also where I started to develop an interest in Pacific affairs, through French nuclear testing and controversial policies in French Polynesia, New Caledonia and Wallis and Futuna—and also Vanuatu, which was still to become independent at that stage. Until then, my interests had been focused on Africa.

Just across the Place de la Bourse from AFP is the headquarters of the Reporters Sans Frontières (RSF) global media freedom group. I have been a researcher and analyst for RSF on Pacific media freedom issues for more than two decades. And the Pacific Media Watch research project, which I founded with investigative journalist Peter Cronau of the ABC *Four Corners* programme in 1996, recruits postgraduate students as interns and contributing editors. The project has close ties with RSF.

I travelled back to New Zealand from France in 1979 to join the *Auckland Star*, also a crusading newspaper, and became foreign editor. My South Pacific journalism began as freelance sojourns from the *Star* while on holiday, but I eventually set up my own independent Pacific news agency.

Ignored struggles in the Pacific

Often conflicts or struggles in one part of the Asia-Pacific region are hardly known about, or barely understood, in another. Feudalism, militarism, corruption and personality cults isolate people from national—and regional—decision-making. Political independence has not necessarily rid the Pacific of the problems it faces, and, in many cases, Pacific political leaders themselves are part of the problem.

The Nuclear Free and Independent Pacific (NFIP) movement was spawned as a "voice for the people" with an initial conference "for a Nuclear-Free Pacific" in Suva, Fiji, in 1975, when delegates declared: "New Caledonia is dominated by the imperialist and colonialist government of France ... we must fight for determination of all people."[27] Headquarters were set up in Fiji and the People's Charter for NFIP was adopted at the 1983 regional conference in Port Vila, Vanuatu: "We, the people of the Pacific have been victimised too long by foreign powers," stated the charter, and it declared strong opposition to nuclear weapons and arsenals in the region. The title of this book is drawn from an NFIP placard carried by a six-year-old ni-Vanuatu schoolgirl at the 1983 NFIP rally in Port Vila's Independence Park and shown on the cover of this book. She pleaded: "Please don't spoil my beautiful face."

While the New Zealand media has long strongly highlighted the country's role championing a nuclear-free Pacific, it has been less generous about the efforts of Pacific Island leaders and countries. People like the inspirational late Walter Lini, then Prime Minister of Vanuatu, for example. His small country was the first to declare itself nuclear-free and ban visits by nuclear-armed warships. Lini wrote the foreword to my *Rainbow Warrior* book, *Eyes of Fire*,[28] and he appeared in the Alister Barry film *Niuklia Fri Pasifik*.[29] With the title taken from the Vanuatu pidgin language Bislama, the 47-minute documentary tells the inside story of the birth and growth of the NFIP movement from the first Suva conference in 1975 until the political negotiations that a decade later brought about the flawed Rarotonga Treaty, "banning" nuclear tests in the region.[30]

The 1977 book *Moruroa, Mon Amour*, Marie-Thérèse and Bengt Danielsson's damning indictment of French nuclear colonisation,[31] was republished in 1986 as *Poisoned Reign*.[32] French stubbornness over nuclear

David Robie in a *barong* at the Malacañang presidential palace in Manila, Philippines.

ALEX BALYUT

testing and demands for independence in Tahiti were then at a peak. It seemed unlikely that in fewer than two decades, nuclear testing would be finally abandoned in the South Pacific—and Tahiti's leading nuclear-free and pro-independence politician, Oscar Temaru, would emerge as the territory's new president. He ushered in a refreshing and inspirational "new order" with a commitment to pan-Pacific relations. By the time Temaru came to power and nuclear testing had ended, France had detonated 193 of its 210 nuclear bombs in the South Pacific, 46 of them dumping more than nine megatons of explosive energy into the atmosphere.

My reporting was wide-ranging in the Asia-Pacific region, traversing from an investigation into a controversial New Zealand forestry aid project on indigenous Lumad ancestral land in Bukidnon province[33] on the southern Philippines island of Mindanao—which involved issues similar to justice over Māori land rights—to the shadowy rebel military clique in the fragile democracy of the Philippines known as "The Ramboys", who were determined to oust President Cory Aquino in a coup,[34] to the Bougainville Civil War, which I covered for the first two years and wrote a cover story about for *Pacific Islands Monthly*.[35] Not widely known was the role of a New

Zealand consultancy, which was accused of whitewashing Bougainville Copper Limited's pollution of the Jaba River near Panguna Mine and thus triggering off the insurrection.[36]

In Timor-Leste, the Santa Cruz massacre on 12 November 1991 in the East Timor capital of Dili was the turning point in the global campaign for independence from Indonesia. At least 270 East Timorese were gunned down by about 200 Indonesian soldiers in the Santa Cruz cemetery, including New Zealander Kamal Bamadhaj.[37] Foreign journalists were on the ground to bear witness. US journalists Amy Goodman and Allan Nairn reported it and cameraman Max Stahl filmed it.[38] This is why the issue quickly became a global *cause célèbre*, eventually leading to the restoration of independence. An article that I wrote about this was censored by a major New Zealand daily after it had been laid out on an op-ed page, due to political pressure at the time.

In the Philippines in 1988—two years after dictator Ferdinand Marcos had been ousted by People Power—I joined the International Peace Brigade as an independent journalist to bear witness at the protests at the US Clark Air Base at Olongapo and the US Naval and Air Base at Subic Bay. With me were journalists along with peace campaigners Maire Leadbeater, Janine McCready and Owen Wilkes, and several other New Zealanders.

During the Peace Brigade, I met Del Abcede from Camarines Norte; she was one of the Peace Brigade marshals and also our group guide. Our group went to Mindanao for our countryside exposure to see human rights abuses in the region at first hand and also to visit New Zealand's Bukidnon forestry project on indigenous land funded by the New Zealand government but below the public radar.

Not only did Del help, translate and guide me on this assignment, but today she is also my wife, mentor and inspiration. In New Zealand, Del works as a leader of the Philippine Migrant Centre, producing a newsletter with a focus on women, and she is a key campaigner for the Asia-Pacific Human Rights Coalition (APHRC) and the New Zealand chapter of Women's International League for Peace and Freedom (WILPF). Del is also designer for *Pacific Journalism Review* and other publications and organiser for Project Lingap Kapwa, which has adopted a poor coastal village in her hometown of Vinzons. The project sends clothes, educational goods and other support items to the local school.

In April 1985, I joined Greenpeace's original flagship *Rainbow Warrior* in Hawai'i as a journalist to travel to the Marshall Islands on a humanitarian voyage to relocate Rongelap Islanders to a new home atoll because of the horrendous legacy of the US nuclear tests in the Pacific. With a huge

Del Abcede (in a bandana and holding a megaphone) with fellow health union campaigners in the Philippines, including her younger sister Arcelie (next to her).

ALLIANCE OF HEALTH WORKERS

hydrogen test in March 1954 codenamed Castle Bravo, 64 Rongelap people were contaminated, as were another 18 Rongelapese on nearby Ailingnae Atoll, where they were making copra and catching fish. The death of Lekoj Anjain at the age of 18 was the first radiation-linked death.

During the *Rainbow Warrior* evacuation from Rongelap in May 1985, four voyages were made to move the entire community—almost 400 people—to Mejato on the Star Wars atoll of Kwajalein. The United States did attempt to make amends for the tests. It provided some $150 million as part of the so-called Compact of Free Association to establish a nuclear claims tribunal.

After I was on board the *Rainbow Warrior* for almost 11 weeks, it was bombed by French secret agents in Operation Satanic in Auckland's Waitemata Harbour on 10 July 1985 to prevent the Greenpeace ship carrying on to Moruroa Atoll to lead a flotilla protesting against nuclear testing. "Blunderwatergate", as it was known, was a public relations disaster for the French in the Pacific. In contrast to the so-called "War on Terror" of today and the Coalition of the Willing, the British, Australian and US governments were meekly silent about the French state terrorist outrage.

My account of these events was published in my 1986 book *Eyes of Fire*, republished as a memorial edition two decades after the bombing in 2005.[39]

My old cabin was adjacent to Fernando Pereira who tragically lost his life in the bombing. He had scrambled to safety on Marsden Wharf after the first bomb exploded, but climbed back on board to rescue his cameras. He drowned after the second bomb detonated 10 minutes later.

My only personal memento (apart from photographs) from the bombed ship was my old British passport—not my New Zealand one. (Used in travelling in Africa where there was no New Zealand diplomatic representation.) When I left the *Warrior* after we arrived in Auckland three days before the bombing, I had forgotten to collect it from captain Peter Willcox's locked up safe on the bridge. It sank with the ship and Navy divers recovered it.

Even in "death", the *Rainbow Warrior* unleashed powerful emotions and creativity. Schoolchildren painted pictures of the stricken ship, donations poured in in the hope of patching her up, fundraising concerts were organised and exhibitions put on show. *Rainbow Warrior II* (originally the deep-sea fishing boat *Ross Kashmir*) replaced her namesake on the fourth anniversary of the bombing on 10 July 1989. In 2011, a state-of-the-art hybrid sailing-motor ship *Rainbow Warrior III* built in Germany became the Greenpeace flagship, billed as being one of the "greenest" vessels afloat.

Les Évènements in Kanaky/New Caledonia

In the 1980s, the French-ruled overseas territory of New Caledonia was on the brink of civil war. This was because indigenous Kanak people were asserting their rights as the colonised people after more than a century of rule from Paris. Barricades were set up through much of the territory and many Kanak people rose up in civil disobedience against French control. I reported many cover stories for international magazines, news services and special reports for newspapers during this era, trying to provide a balance to the plethora of right-wing media that portrayed New Caledonia as having been "thrown into a nightmare" of anarchy.[40]

Kanak independence leader Éloï Machoro, a former schoolteacher, inspired the barricades and protests against the French elections. He chopped open a ballot box in Canala and burned the voting papers in a symbolic gesture against French rule in November 1984. I was there that day to capture the events on film. He and a lieutenant, Marcel Nonaro, were eventually assassinated by French CIGN police snipers on 12 January 1985 at a farmhouse siege at Dogny, near the western village of La Foa. The official version claimed it was an "accident".[41]

New Caledonia is still listed by the UN Special Committee on Decolonisation—or the Committee of 24—as it is known. This would have been the committee that would have overseen independence for Timor-Leste, but the UN Security Council took over the process beginning with Resolution 1236 in May 1999, welcoming the Secretary-General's brokering of the May 5 agreement. Those negotiations were conducted under the mandate of a 15-year-old General Assembly resolution. The decolonisation process is enshrined in the Noumea Accord, signed in 1998 between pro-independence Kanak parties and the pro-French rule parties. It provides guidelines for a gradual transfer of power from Paris to local authorities, a power-sharing government, and an eventual referendum on self-determination between 2014 and 2018. French Polynesia was also added to the UN decolonisation list during 2013.

In Fiji during May 1987, Lieutenant-Colonel Sitiveni Rabuka launched his country's contemporary "coup culture" by staging a putsch against the elected government of Fiji Labour Party Prime Minister Dr Timoci Bavadra. Rabuka had been paranoid about the "leftist" Bavadra government and its nuclear-free rhetoric in a Cold War environment. The defeated Alliance government had tried to rally support against its rivals with the communist bogey over Labour's non-aligned and nuclear-free stance. Allegations of CIA involvement were widely cited in an ABC *Four Corners* programme featured in Brij Lal's 2010 book *In The Eye of Storm*.[42] But the primary reason for both Rabuka's coups was an attempt to reassert "indigenous paramountcy". I covered both the election of Bavadra and the coups for regional media, including the *New Zealand Times*, the national *Times On Sunday* in Australia, and *New Outlook* magazine among others. One of the special series of articles that I wrote analysed the so-called Taukei Movement and some of the key people who had engineered and supported the coups.[43]

These dramatic events and changes in the Pacific were recorded in my 1992 book *Tu Galala: Social Change in the Pacific*, ironically part-funded by a grant from New Zealand's *Rainbow Warrior* compensation fund. As I wrote at the time, the Pacific was in upheaval—and still is—with "environmental catastrophe, conflicts over development, communal unrest, growing militarisation, the impact of poverty, colonialism, neo-colonialism and liberation struggles".[44] Many of the contributors to *Tu Galala* were activists, campaigners and leaders writing about their struggles.

In one sense, this new book is a continuation of where I left off two decades ago with *Tu Galala*. But unlike many accounts of the challenges of the Pacific—from the viewpoint of bureaucrats representing power elites or disinterested academics—this is an ongoing narration with other "voices" of the Pacific: they are frequently the activists, campaigners and writers who have been in the vanguard of social and political change in the Pacific. The advocates for human rights and for the less privileged.

Notes

1   Sections of this chapter were originally presented in a professorial address in journalism at Auckland University of Technology on 16 October 2012.
2   Presentation to the editor of the *Caledonian Mercury* (1864, March 20). Quotation reprinted from the *New York Evening Post*.
3   W. J. Couper (1908). *The Edinburgh Periodical Press*, Vol. 1. Stirling, p. 56.
4   Couper (1908), p. 61.
5   James Robie (1867). *The Representative Radicals of Edinburgh*. Edinburgh: W. P. Nimmo.
6   Maya Jaggi (2009, April 4). French resistance: Costa Gravas. *The Guardian*. Retrieved on 9 August 2013, from www.theguardian.com/film/2009/apr/04/ costa-gavras
7   "Something dark and bloody" (1969, December 14). *Sunday Observer* photographic portfolio of the My Lai massacre by Ronald L. Haeberle. Retrieved on 1 October 2012, from www.asiapac.org.fj/cafepacific/resources/aspac/viet.html
8   "Something dark and bloody" (1969, December 14). *Sunday Observer*.
9   David Robie (2009). Public enemy number one's global journalism [Review]. *Pacific Journalism Review*, 15(2): 220–223.
10 He's home: Cheers, boos for Burchett (1970, March 1). *Sunday Observer*, p. 1.
11 George Burchett and Nick Shimmin (2007). *Rebel Journalism: The Writings of Wilfred Burchett*. Melbourne: Cambridge University Press.
12 Burchett and Shimmin (2007). *Rebel Journalism*.
13 Ibid., pp. 2–5.
14 Robie (2009). Public enemy number one's global journalism [Review].
15 Neville Gibson (2007). *Final deadline: The last days of the Rand Daily Mail*. Cape Town: David Philip Books.
16 Raymond Louw (2005). *The Rand Daily Mail*: convenient scapegoat. Helen Suzman Foundation. *Focus*: Issue 39. Retrieved on 30 September 2012, from www.hsf.org.za/resource-centre/focus/issues-31-40/issue-39-third-quarter-2005/ the-rand-daily-mail-convenient-scapegoat
17 Peter Magubane (1978). *Magubane's South Africa*. London: Secker & Warburg.
18 Ibid., p. vii.
19 Alistair Boddy-Evans (n.d.). About African History: Banning. Retrieved on 10 October 2012, from http://africanhistory.about.com/od/glossaryb/g/def_ banned.htm
20 Magubane (1978), *Magubane's South Africa*, p. 52.
21 Hamilton [Springbok rugby union tour] game cancelled. (1981, July 25). [Video]. Retrieved on 7 January 2014, from www.nzhistory.net.nz/media/video/game-cancelled-in-hamilton
22 Richard Bourne (1995). *News on a Knife Edge: Gemini journalism and a global agenda*. London: John Libbey.

23 David Robie (1974, December 28). The hard way across Africa: Jungle, desert and mountain hazards met on safari. *The Dominion*, p. 11.

24 Ibid.

25 Ibid.

26 Gillo Pontecorvo (1966). *La battaglia di Algeri* [Feature film]. Rizzoli Pictures.

27 Miriam Dorney (1984). *Politics of New Caledonia*. Sydney, NSW: Sydney University Press, p. 117. Cited by John Connell (1987). *New Caledonia or Kanaky? The political history of a French colony*. Canberra, ACT: Research School of Pacific Studies, Australian National University, p. 283.

28 David Robie (1986). *Eyes of Fire: The Last Voyage of the Rainbow Warrior*. Auckland: Linden Books.

29 Alister Barry (1988). *Niuklia Fri Pasifik (A Nuclear Free Pacific)* [Documentary film]. Wellington: Vanguard Films.

30 David Robie (1989, May 27). Giving peace a chance [*Niuklia Fri Pasifik* documentary film profile]. *New Zealand Listener*, p. 31.

31 Bengt and Marie-Thérèse Danielsson (1977). *Moruroa, Mon Amour*. Melbourne: Penguin.

32 Bengt and Marie-Thérèse Danielsson (1986). *Poisoned Reign: French Nuclear Colonialism in the Pacific*. Ringwood, Vic.: Penguin Books.

33 David Robie (1989, April 22). Cloud over Bukidnon Forest. *New Zealand Listener*, pp. 22–23, 35.

34 David Robie (1990, May 20). The Ramboys. *Sunday* magazine, pp. 38–42.

35 David Robie (1989, November). Mine of Tears: Bougainville one year later. *Pacific Islands Monthly*, pp. 10–18.

36 David Robie (1989, December 10). Bougainville: New Zealand's part in a guerilla war. *Sunday* magazine, pp. 20–25.

37 David Robie (1992, March/April). Terror in Timor. *New Zealand Monthly Review*, pp. 14–18.

38 Max Stahl (1991, November 12). Santa Cruz cemetery massacre [Rushes]. Journeyman Pictures. Retrieved on 7 January 2014, from www.youtube.com/watch?v=7HkktBcIDzg

39 David Robie (2005). *Eyes of Fire: The Last Voyage of the Rainbow Warrior* [20th anniversary memorial edition]. Auckland: Asia Pacific Network.

40 Connell (1987). *New Caledonia or Kanaky?*, p. 333.

41 David Robie (1989). *Blood on their Banner: Nationalist Struggles in the South Pacific*. London: Zed Books; Sydney: Pluto Press, p. 121.

42 Brij Lal (2010). *In The Eye of the Storm: Jai Ram Reddy and the Politics of Postcolonial Fiji*. Canberra: Australian National University Press.

43 David Robie (2013). The talanoa and the tribal paradigm: reflections on cross-cultural reporting in the Pacific. *Australian Journalism Review*, 35(1), pp. 43–57.

44 David Robie (1992). *Tu Galala: Social Change in the Pacific*. Wellington: Bridget Williams Books, p. 9.

3

The hard way across Africa, 1974

It still has a long way to go but the Trans-African Highway will certainly be no white elephant. It will give trade and contact between East and West Africa a tremendous shot in the arm.

David Robie in *African Development*

WHEN word reached the London-based *African Development* magazine in 1973 that I was about to embark on an overland journey across the continent, one of the editors, Martin Johnson, was quick to get in touch with me:[1] "I suppose you will be following the Trans-African Highway as closely as possible," he wrote. "This should lend itself to a very good article discussing the practical problems, the nature of the terrain and what roads already exist. Also whether any countries have actually started building their sections of the road. If you did a piece of 1200 words, together with some exciting photographs, we would be glad to use it in the next possible issue."[2]

As it turned out, the 6260-kilometre journey from the Kenyan port of Mombasa on the shores of the Indian Ocean to the hectic Nigerian capital Lagos on the Atlantic became a cover story for *African Development* with more like 3000 words and "exciting" photographs that included a spectacular bogging down of 20 heavily laden trucks in the mud of the rainforests on the route to Buta in northern Zaire. I wrote at the time:

> The road is considered a hell run by Zairean drivers. It is only 320 kilometres from Kisangani to Buta but they prefer to drive a roundabout 1285 kilometres through Isiro than to tackle the Tele road ... Yet trucks continually get bogged elsewhere. Midway between Mambasa and Nia-Nia, I encountered a truck which had been trapped in a one-metre-deep mudhole for 14 hours. Rescuers struggled to free it but on each attempt it was sucked deeper into the putrid mire so that the tray was level with the track.
>
> On one side, 12 trucks were held up waiting to get through and on the other side there were eight. There was no way around because the jungle grew right to the edge of the road. A road gang eventually arrived, towed

Trucks bogged down on the Trans-African Highway in what was then northern Zaire and is now the Democratic Republic of the Congo, 1974.   DAVID ROBIE/*GEMINI NEWS*

out the truck and filled in the giant hole—but not before 30 trucks had piled up waiting to get through. An everyday hazard of Zairean roads.[3]

When I made this journey, bold promises were made by then UN Economic Commission for Africa (UNECA) executive secretary Dr Robert Gardiner that "with determination and readiness, the first inaugural trip to Lagos will be made in 1976"—three years later. But the final sections of the route through the Congo Basin are yet to be completed. A UNECA report recently noted that civil wars and road conditions had made portions of the route impassable: "Although the highway carries much traffic on its paved sections in Nigeria, Cameroon, Uganda and Kenya, at present it is not a practical route between west and east since the central section across the Democratic Repubic of the Congo consists of tracks impassable after the frequent heavy rain. Rainforest and the need for frequent river crossings present huge problems to road engineers."[4]

My travels spawned a series of articles in international media, such as "AFRICA'S HIGHWAY TAKES SHAPE—BUREAUCRATS, MUD AND ALL" in *African Development,* "THIS IS THE ROAD TO PROGRESS" in the *Times of Zambia,* "HIGHWAY ROBBERY" in *To The Point* news magazine, and the following one in New Zealand's *The Dominion.*

THE HARD WAY ACROSS AFRICA

The Dominion, 28 December 1974

THE TATTERED reward notice plastered on the caked wall of a Saharan police post was enough to make us uneasy. In four languages it offered the equivalent of NZ$4000 to anyone giving information leading to the discovery of four Italians who had been missing for almost six months.[5]

The Italians—three men and a woman—had been driving a four-wheel-drive vehicle across the desert and suddenly they vanished. Their route was across the relatively well used Hoggar track—our path too.

This poster stared ominously at us from every oasis checkpoint throughout the desert. And it didn't cheer us to learn after we had been tackling the Sahara Desert for a few days that their bodies had been found, only 32 kilometres from a village.

Cases like this are relatively common in the Sahara. At the time we drove through, a group of British overlanders went missing. A few weeks earlier a French party had been found dead.

[More recently, according to the *International New York Times* in October 2013, the decomposing bodies of 87 migrants from Niger were discovered in the Sahara just a few kilometres from a water well after their two trucks broke down in the desert about 50 kilometres from Arlit, near the Aïr Mountains.][6]

Yet the Sahara's vast lunar-like wilderness of sand dunes and sun-cracked rock and mountains isn't as dangerous as it seems.

On the Hoggar Range in the heart of the desert, between Niger and Algeria, the longest stretch without petrol is 896 kilometres. The longest gap without water is 480 kilometres. And there are 320 kilometres without anything at all—not even a huddle of nomads' tents.

During the cooler months from October to February there is enough traffic, including several New Zealanders, to guarantee at least one passing vehicle a day. And on the great oceans of sand there are markers every kilometre to show the way (except when they are buried by sandstorms).

There is a strict Sahara code, which prohibits travellers from leaving an oasis without checking in with police, but this doesn't always work as it should.

For us, the toughest problem wasn't buffeting our way across corrugations the size of railway tracks, nor was it digging our way out of sand. Our headache was trying to nurse along a protesting 1970 [then two-year-old] Kombi. The van began to falter in the desert.

After an already arduous journey across Africa from Cape Town, the starter motor packed up, second and third gears jumped out, the clutch slipped and oil spurted out of the engine by the canful at times. Even the reinforced roof rack collapsed.

Sunrise in the Sahara Desert, somewhere rather uncertain, in Algeria, 1974.   DAVID ROBIE

Then in a sandstorm, the battery split open and spattered acid over the engine. We had to be towed by an Algerian gendarmerie wagon 32 kilometres to a nearby oasis. I was forced to hitch about 800 kilometres to the nearest town to get another battery before we could carry on.

This Trans-African safari across 25 countries began in South Africa after six months of spare time planning and fitting out of the vehicle ... Among our stores we had enough jerrycans to carry 230 litres of petrol and 45 litres of water, two spare wheels and three extra tyres, a special high-lift jack for hoisting the van out of holes, an aluminium ladder, a medical kit, spades, sand mats, a range of spare parts, three months' supply of canned and dehydrated food—and the lower jawbone of an elephant!

To give the van a human touch we christened it Tuhoe, after the iwi of the Urewera as a symbol of resistance. But most people mistook the signwriting to read "Taboo".

All traces of apartheid South Africa and other "imperialist" countries, such as Israel, had to be removed to avoid offending officials in independent African countries.

This meant slashing "Made in Israel" tags off tyres and peeling South African labels from canned food. The vehicle was registered in Swaziland, a neighbouring African kingdom, which few people had apparently heard of, customs documents were issued in Germany and international driving permits came from New Zealand.

Yet no amount of preparation could have prepared us properly for dealing with some of the problems of African travel such as hassling with ignorant and awkward border officials, warding off perpetual crowds of curious onlookers, keeping tabs on thieves (the van was broken into four times in Kenya alone) and changing money on the black market (in countries such as Zaire, it is virtually impossible to do business with banks in remote townships—if they can be found).

The expedition began in Cape Town and, after crossing the Namib and Kalahari Deserts, our first main hurdle was to cross the rugged central mountains of the landlocked kingdom of Lesotho.

We followed a precarious ledge being carved out of steep hillsides in the "roof of Africa" by bulldozers. Apparently it had never before been crossed by a two-wheel-drive vehicle (perhaps nobody else was silly enough to try). The trail wound over the snow-clad Black Mountain Pass (16 metres) and down the hairpin bends of Sani Pass back into South Africa.

A Basuto shepherd stopped us near the summit. He wanted a lift. When we agreed, his chubby wife suddenly appeared from out of a hut and came racing across the snow in bare feet. She clambered into the van and pulled on a pair of striped rugby socks.

Crossing from Botswana into Zambia on the Freedom Ferry (named this because of the many political refugees from apartheid South Africa who had used it as a pipeline to safety) was a delicate operation.

The Zambezi River marks a gulf between two Africas. On one side the white minority regimes of the south hold sway and on the opposite bank are the black independent republics.

Things are touchy and one wrong move could mean a cell for a while. Or even being shot at.

In our case we were merely held up for three hours because the Zambian official was insistent that the border signature wasn't the same as the one on my passport.

Corruption is the obstacle in Zaire [now the Democratic Republic of the Congo], the former Belgian Congo. On our second night in Lubumbashi, the capital of the abortive breakaway republic of Katanga, I turned into a one-way street by accident.

Immediately, I drove into another street but it was too late. Three gendarmes brandishing automatic rifles cornered us.

They were not interested in any explanation of the motoring error. This mistake was an excuse to confiscate something. And they were irate when the first bag they opened contained only knitting. We settled, reluctantly, on a payment of about two zaire (about $3) and left in a hurry.

The Trans African Highway will ease trade and other contacts between East and West Africa when completed in 1976. But the amount of work to be done on the road in the different countries through which it passes varies greatly, as DAVID ROBIE found when he travelled in his Kombi the 30,000 miles through 20 countries from Mombasa to Lagos.

AFRICA'S HIGHWAY TAKES SHAPE—
BUREAUCRATS, MUD AND ALL

AFRICA'S prestige road, the Trans African Highway from the Kenyan port of Mombasa on the shores of the Indian Ocean to the hectic Nigerian capital Lagos on the Atlantic, is taking shape mile by mile.

The 4,000-mile route through Kenya, Uganda, Zaire, Central African Republic, Cameroon and Nigeria will be completed within four years, according to experts at the highway's co-ordinating conference in Mombasa last year. Dr. Robert Gardiner, executive secretary of the UN Economic Commission for Africa, is even more opti-

tem of roads in the north-east region. However, the roads have been severely neglected in the last decade and some are now the worst on the whole Trans African route.

For nine months of the year heavy rain turns roads in the Zaire basin into treacherous slush. For the other three months the tracks dry out a little but many sections remain difficult if not impassable for vehicles without four-wheel-drive (even Land-Rovers often find them too much).

I crossed Zaire during December one

eventually arrived, towed out the truck and filled in the giant hole – but not before 30 trucks had piled up waiting to get through. The drivers take these episodes in their stride. An everyday hazard of Zairian roads.

Bridges in Zaire are also neglected. When planks rot they are not replaced and many bridges have gaping holes; north of Kisangani there are makeshift bridges of split logs. Four ferries are on the route north of Kisangani, too. Across the Aruwimi river at Banalia there is a modern 30-tonner at Banalia there is a 30-

The opening page of the *African Development* article on the Trans-African Highway, 1974.

DAVID ROBIE

Puritanical Malawi had its moments too. There I was detained for wearing shorts, which are essential in the African sun. The police ushered me into a cell where I was forced to change into long trousers.

Tanzania has a cumbersome civil service with red tape to end all red tape. In the capital of Dar es Salaam I got a clearance from the President's Office to visit a model *ujamaa* (self-help) village in the remote western part of the country to prepare an article on the socialist experiment.

When we arrived we were held at gunpoint by police who became agitated when they discovered we had been to South Africa. The area commissioner refused to let me visit the village (perhaps I was a spy, after all?) in spite of my official permission.

Ethiopia had the worst roads on our whole journey but only in a limited area. A nightmarish track of 165 kilometres between southern Ethiopia and the Kenyan border had us struggling over waterfalls and along stream beds.

And then there was the threat of *shifta*, or bandits or outlaws from the Horn of Africa. Ethiopians in remote areas are armed to the teeth, usually with home-made rifles.

Uganda had just opened its borders again to travellers when we went through at a time when dictator Idi Amin was still in power. Yet beards were still regarded as a "mercenary" characteristic, liable to get one arrested. We managed to slip through the country twice without difficulty except when one soldier tried to "get fresh" on the pretext of searching for "guns".

Our second visit to Zaire was a nervous one. In Nairobi the Zairian ambassador told me I was persona non grata, apparently for articles I had written while reporting from Lubumbashi, the country's second-largest city and hub of the copper mining industry in the south-east on an earlier visit. The visa applications for the three others travelling with me at the time were also turned down because, the ambassador said, they had been "contaminated" by me.

Yet Zaire is the only readily accessible route from East Africa to Nigeria so I had to acquire a new occupation and borrow another nationality—quite legitimate, of course—to manage a way into the country.

We had only just crossed the frontier when two soldiers armed with sub-machine guns flagged us down. We were tense. Were we on "the list" and would they discover my ruse?

But no, they just hopped on board the van and forced us to drive a few kilometres down the road, where they got off. They just wanted to freeload a ride to their village.

For nine months of the year, heavy rain turns roads in the Zaire [Congo] River basin into treacherous slush. For the three months it dries out a little but much of the tracks remain difficult, if not impassable for vehicles without four-wheel-drive.

We crossed Zaire in one of the "drier" months. But in the worst stretch there were more than 80 kilometres of up to a metre-deep mudholes and scoured-out ridges.

It took almost three days to struggle through this—nine hours to go merely one kilometre. It was hard going and we grew to hate mud, especially the putrid stench.

We picked up an African soldier and a labourer (and his bicycle, which we tied onto the roof) for extra pushing power.

They were handy for recruiting whole villages to help out in trouble spots—for payment of 10 makuta (about 20 cents) a head, bars of soap, bags of sugar and old sandals or trousers. They, in turn, scored free transport to their village.

Yet even with up to 20 local men pushing, rebuilding the track with tree trunks felled from the forest and a high-lift hoist, it took three hours of solid work getting through each of the worst holes.

Bridges were also frightening in Zaire. Planks had rotted away, leaving yawning gaps. And north of the one-time rebel stronghold of Kisangani there were makeshift bridges of split logs. Too bad if a car wheel slipped off a tree trunk.

In some parts of the jungle, trees had tumbled onto the track, forcing overlanders to push their own way through the forest.

Deep in the Ituri rainforest catchment area were groups of naked pygmies. Usually timid, they rushed forward eagerly when we stopped to trade bags of salt for hunting bows and poison-tipped arrows. However, producing our first-aid kit and treating festering sores and gummed-up eyes, we were popular in the forest.

Further north, in the Sahel belt of Nigeria, we hit the ancient red-clay city states of the Hausa people, such as Kano and Sokoto.

Then came the Sahara Desert. Even the Tuareg, the proud overlords of this desert, have been humbled by it.

These blue-cloaked men on camels with swords slung on their hips sometimes appeared as if from nowhere through a shimmering heat haze. They used to tax travellers or swoop on isolated villages in a plundering *razzia*—but now they just want water.

They have suffered badly in the Sahelian drought and thousands of them have forsaken the desert to live in wretched refugee camps on the edge of oasis towns, waiting for world aid handouts.

In the heat of the day mirages were common in the sandy plains of the Sahara and it was difficult to judge distances. For day after day we felt like we were driving into eternity .

Beyond the Sahara was Arab North Africa. Any misgivings we had about the second-class status of traditional Muslim women outside secular big cities faded. In spite of the veils of the Casbah, there were few problems.

We found Algerians to be the most hospitable of people of all the countries we had visited. One group welcomed us to a colonial French farm converted into a people's cooperative on the outskirts of Algiers. We were treated to *couscous*, Magreb delicacies and seemingly endless local wine.

Finally, we wound up our year-long expedition by crossing the lower Atlas Mountains and Morocco and then on to France, our goal. Now we had to get used to city life again, crowds, traffic jams and smog—a far cry from the crisp air and emptiness of the Sahara.

₵

THIS arduous overland trek across Africa was an awakening to global development realities, issues and poverty. After arriving in Paris in 1975 when completing the journey, I worked as an editor and foreign correspondent for the French news agency Agence France-Presse at the headquarters in Place de La Bourse for three years and began to take a particular interest in French foreign policy, especially as it played out in the South Pacific, the environment and development communication. So my growing focus on the Pacific was a back-door affair, sparked by colonialism and *la bombe*.

Notes

1   David Robie (1974, February). Africa's highway takes shape—bureaucrats, mud and all. *African Development Magazine*, pp. 11–13.
2   Martin Johnson (1973, May). Personal correspondence with the author.
3   David Robie (1974, February). Africa's highway takes shape, p. 11.
4   African Development Bank/United Nations Economic Commission for Africa (UNECA). (2003, August 14). Review of the Implementation Status of the Trans African Highways and the Missing Links: Volume 2: Description of Corridors.
5   David Robie (1974, December 28). The hard way across Africa. *The Dominion*, p. 11.
6   Adam Nossiter (2013, November 1). Scores of migrants die in Niger's northern desert. *International New York Times*, p. 8.

4

From Paris to the Pacific, 1979

The experience of Hiroshima, Nagasaki and Bikini is enough.
Nuclear tests have got to stop, and there is only one solution:
We must have our independence.
Tahitian socialist leader Jacky Drollet (Ia Mana Te Nunaa)

WORKING in Paris for Agence France-Presse news agency in the 1970s was a tremendously stimulating period. Hardly since existentialism flourished in the smoke-filled cellars of Saint-Germain-des-Prés on the Left Bank in the 1950s had a provocative philosophy taken root. The spontaneous student protests, national strikes and rioting of 1968 had gripped Paris while I had been working for the Melbourne *Herald*. The upheaval crippled and almost ousted the Gaullist government. The rise of the Socialists and President François Mitterrand to power in France was paralleled by the emergence of a small post-Sartre elite that was opposed to all ideologies. Loosely known as the "New Thinkers", they were the scourge of both the Giscardian and Gaullist conservatives and the Marxists and socialists of all shades.[1]

Their model was Socrates, the questioning Athenian philosopher and critic of the state. In the vanguard of this movement were young philosophers such as former leftist militant André Glucksmann and one-time Castro disciple Bernard-Henri Lévy, now an editor-publisher. Glucksmann said he was encouraged by the growth of dissidents around the world—anti-nuclear protesters, pirate radio operators and minorities demanding self-determination.

The socialist daily *Le Matin* branded them "naïve". And *Le Nouvel Observateur* dismissed them as "disc jockeys of ideas". But they certainly had a profound impact on contemporary French and global philosophy, an influence that was gathering momentum.

At AFP I was covering a variety of topics ranging from African affairs to international sport, including leading the English-language team covering the 1976 Olympic Games when African nations staged their boycott in protest over New Zealand's rugby union ties with apartheid South Africa. But in the years before Mitterrand came to office as the longest-serving

French President, I was becoming increasingly interested in France's neocolonial and nuclear policies in the South Pacific. This included Greenpeace skipper David McTaggart's piracy lawsuit against the French Navy when he won damages in 1974 over the ramming of his yacht *Vega* and for assault in a protest at Moruroa Atoll.

By the time I arrived back in New Zealand after more than a decade away, France had triggered 55 nuclear explosions in the Pacific over that period, including a record nine during 1979. French Polynesia, reluctant host to the test programme, had become even unhappier about its imposed role since two accidents in July 1979. After earlier filing reports from Paris about nuclear testing, I decided to investigate on the ground in Polynesia for the *New Zealand Listener* magazine.

WHAT REALLY HAPPENED AT MORUROA?

New Zealand Listener, 16 February 1980

MORUROA, a horseshoe-shaped coral outcrop on the south-east fringe of French Polynesia and home of *la bombe*, is at the centre of a new wave of hostility that has outstripped anything since the international campaign five years ago that drove France's nuclear testing underground.[2]

The current acrimony is because of two accidents on Moruroa in July 1979, the first on July 6 which killed two men and injured four, and the second on July 25, which injured two.[3] Accusations of radiation leaks, contamination and negligence, and high-level inquiries have simmered since.[4]

Now, the locally-elected Territorial Assembly's investigating select committee has stoked the fires with a report which is clearly not satisfied with France's explanations, or present civilian safeguards.

Among several demands, the report calls for the setting up of a nuclear radiation emergency service and clinic in Tahiti. It calls for the establishment of a local research unit of France's independent Central Service for Protection Against Ionising Radiation (SCPRI—*Service central de protection contre les rayonnements ionisants*) to monitor the tests.

It also demands a report from a mission of five scientists sent by France to investigate the accidents (the experts merely gave a press conference in the capital Pape'ete) and asks for several confidential documents, such as a security dossier from the Atomic Energy Commission (CEA—*Commissariat à l'énergie atomique*) on the first accident of July 6 when an explosion caused the deaths of two men.

Anti-nuclear campaigners in French Polynesia are not satisfied with the Assembly's actions—"the recommendations just don't go far enough," says Erick Monod, general secretary of Ia Ora Te Natura (Nature's Way) movement.

The biggest anti-nuclear testing rally in Pape`ete, capital of French Polynesia, 1974. Pictured in left centre (behind right shoulder of man in a light-coloured shirt) is *L'Express* news magazine publisher and Radical Party founder Jean-Jacques Servan-Schreiber and in the front (sitting in wheelchair) is iconic Tahitian nationalist Senator Pouvanaa a Oopa.

BENGT DANIELSSON COLLECTION

He expected the committee to seek the setting up of an independent laboratory to monitor the health and environmental hazards created by the tests, with the freedom to call in international experts such as those from New Zealand's National Radiation Laboratory.

Monod, 36, and other campaigners look to New Zealand to lend more support to their cause as in the early 1970s. "After all, it's your future at stake as well," he says.

Monod, who is also press secretary to Government Council Vice-President Francis Sanford—effectively Premier of French Polynesia—believes New Zealand has become a sort of "Anglo-Saxon enclave." He says it must shake itself free and show more responsibility in the South Pacific.

What actually happened at Moruroa in July? There is still some considerable confusion and doubt.[5]

The news broke in Tahiti when one of the local daily newspapers, *La Depêche*, reported an accident on Moruroa six days earlier, on July 6. But it wasn't until July 24 that the CEA admitted there had been a non-nuclear "industrial accident" with the loss of two lives and two men injured, one seriously.

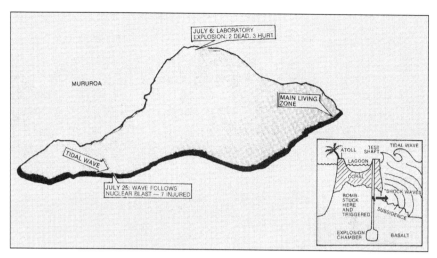

The test site at Moruroa Atoll showing the events on 6 and 25 July 1979.

ASIA-PACIFIC NETWORK

New Zealand didn't come into the picture until August 6 when Greenpeace released the text of a communiqué from the National Seismological Observatory which said it had monitored a nuclear blast on July 25 measuring 6.3 on the Richter scale.

Greenpeace said a tidal wave the same day had injured workers on the atoll. The movement sent a letter of protest to French President Valéry Giscard d'Estaing.

Two days later, the pro-socialist Paris daily *Le Matin* splashed a front-page story detailing what it claimed to be two nuclear accidents. The story is believed to be the result of an investigation by two journalists following complaints to the socialist trade union confederation (CFDT—*Confédération française démocratique du travail*) by the families of two men who died in the first accident. The families were barred from seeing the men's bodies, which were sealed in lead-lined coffins.

Le Matin said in its August 8 report that the July 6 accident was in an underground laboratory bunker code-named Meknes after an experiment with plutonium, a deadly radioactive substance.

The bunker was flushed out with a film of acetone, a solvent capable of absorbing plutonium or other radioactive particles, after the experiment and then ventilated.

Normally the laboratory would have been sealed off, but, said the newspaper, for economic reasons it had been decided to use it again.

A six-man decontamination squad was sent into the bunker, and when an electric drill was switched on, an explosion killed one man instantly, another was

An underground nuclear testing platform at Moruroa Atoll. The test site was dismantled following France's last nuclear test, detonated on 27 January 1996, but the atoll is still guarded by the French forces.

BENGT DANIELSSON COLLECTION

crushed by a hurtling door and four others were badly burnt.[6] *Le Matin* said the heat reached 1500 to 1800 degrees Celsius.

The crushed man was flown to Percy Military Hospital at Clamart, near Paris, where he later died. He was taken there with a corpse and four other victims in a secret operation because it was close to the arrival of President Giscard d'Estaing on a state visit to Polynesia.

On July 25, said *Le Matin*, a nuclear device was lowered 800 metres down a blasting shaft—where it got stuck only halfway down.

The authorities, said the newspaper, took a gamble and triggered it.

Two hours later, particularly violent shock waves, not sufficiently absorbed by the atoll because of the shallow detonation, unleashed a tidal wave which injured two men on the base.

The CEA admitted the accidents had happened but denied any nuclear link, or that the tidal wave had been caused by the blast. It said such phenomena were "natural" in the area.

The *Le Matin* account and a subsequent report in the Paris evening newspaper *France-Soir* were reprinted prominently in the Pape'ete press, which is often forced to get its information on Moruroa second-hand because of military secrecy.

Tahitian anti-nuclear demonstrators in Pape`ete, 1980. DAVID ROBIE

Ia Ora Te Natura immediately began to pressure the Territorial Assembly.

Eventually, on August 17, the Assembly—dominated by the autonomist parties Here Aia of John Teariki and Ea Api of Francis Sanford—unanimously adopted a resolution saying: "We are unable to accept the sacrifice of human lives in the conducting of uncontrollable [nuclear] tests." The Assembly demanded suspension of all tests pending:

An immediate commission of inquiry which would take statements from Polynesian workers about the July accidents; and

Immediate arrival of a team of impartial civil experts in radiation, with the team to be free to visit the atoll and make its own medical and technical studies. (Also, a permanent laboratory directed by professional and independent researchers, should be set up.)

France eventually agreed to send a mission to "reassure the people" and to allow the six-member Assembly select committee to visit Moruroa as its concession to the first demand. But nothing was done to meet the conditions of the second request.

Late in September, the French experts—led by chief commissioner Jean Teillac of the CEA, the agency defending itself—visited Moruroa. One other member

Tahiti a "golden prison" and hostage to the nuclear tests, says Eric Monod.   David Robie

of the mission was also a senior CEA man, a third was professor Pierre Pellerin, director of the radiation agency SCPRI, and the rest were academics. They were accompanied by two CEA officials.

The mission was joined by the assemblymen on September 24 for two days on part of the atoll well away from where the accidents happened.

When the assemblymen tabled their report they complained that they were unable to question Tahitian workers privately.

On their return to Papeʻete, the French mission held a press conference—without the Assembly select committee present—and explained the accidents.

In essence, the mission confirmed *Le Matin*'s reports without any admission of radiation leakage or danger.

The ecological and anti-nuclear movements have denounced the experts' findings as totally inadequate and a "whitewash".

In my view, the mission was a sham: *Why wasn't the Assembly select committee allowed to take to Moruroa three men they needed as advisers and who know the atoll intimately? Would they have known too much? Could their advice to the assemblymen have been embarrassing for the mission?*

According to information given to me by Polynesian workers at Moruroa, the area where the July 6 accident happened was contaminated by radiation until September 3.

Yet Teillac, at the press conference, said: "Most of the radioactive material had been removed when the accident occurred." Some pollution was still present in the locker rooms and a "very small quantity" settled in the area.

"We thoroughly checked all people within a 300 metre radius of the accident," he said. "We can say for sure that none of them has been contaminated, or has any health problem.

"When the explosion occurred, 72 people were in the area—including 28 Polynesians."

The Assembly select committee was denied access to the health dossiers on the men, or even their names.

Why were the badly burnt victims of the July 6 accident flown halfway around the world to France rather than taken to the Jean Prince Hospital in Pape'ete, which reputedly had been the most advanced clinic for burn cases in the Pacific region (especially set up for the Moruroa programme)?

One theory is that the CEP/CEA authorities didn't want embarrassing publicity just before President Giscard's state visit. And was there also a problem of serious contamination?

France underwrites the territory's gross national product by almost 70 percent.

To officials of Ia Ora Te Natura, the subsidised economy is in reality "hush money"—a mammoth form of bribery to keep opposition from Polynesia's elected leaders to the tests as muted as possible. Monod described Polynesia today as a "golden prison."

But Sanford and his colleagues believe they are buying time to establish new industries—such as fishing, canning and aquaculture—that will enable Tahiti to become self-sufficient.

Recent reports that France is considering dumping radioactive waste from its industry reprocessing spent nuclear fuel in French Polynesian waters have also stirred anxiety.

According to one unconfirmed report, the territory has already been used over several years as a dumping ground for contaminated material from the Moruroa tests. The dump is believed to be in a deep ocean rift about 80 kilometres north of Maria Atoll, or Nororotu, a tiny islet in the Tubuai group west of Moruroa.

So as far as French Polynesian environmentalists are concerned, one of the most deadly aspects of it all is official secrecy.

❡

WITHIN a year of this article being published, I set up my own Auckland-based independent Pacific news agency, which I ran for the next decade, reporting for media such as *Gemini News Service, GreenLeft, National Business Review, New Zealand Listener, New Zealand Times, Islands Business, Pacific Islands Monthly*, Radio Australia, *The Australian, The Times on Sunday*, and the short-lived *Sunday* magazine. A particular focus was on environmental issues, indigenous struggles, sustainable development and militarism in the Pacific.

For more than a year, I was also editor of the American Express franchise magazine *Insight* for members with a brief to turn this into a general-interest magazine in the era of *Metro*. This dramatic change was too successful; the publishing company lost the contract when AMEX backed off current affairs when my last cover story featured a controversial Tony Simpson exposé article examining the business personalities and companies that run New Zealand behind the scenes. The censored article, an advance extract from Simpson's book *A Vision Betrayed: The Decline of Democracy in New Zealand*, was published in *New Outlook* magazine instead.[7]

Notes

1   David Robie (1983, July–August). The new thinkers. *Insight* magazine, pp. 41–42.
2   David Robie (1980, February 16). What really happened at Moruroa? *New Zealand Listener*, pp. 30-33.
3   Bengt and Marie-Thérèse Danielsson (1986). *Poisoned Reign: French Nuclear Colonialism in the Pacific*. Ringwood, Vic.: Penguin Books.
4   Ludwig De Braekeleer (2006, November 13). A history of French nuclear tests in the Pacific: Part 2: 1974–1992: Underground testing. *OhmyNews*. Available at http://english.ohmynews.com/articleview/article_view.asp?at_code=371465
5   According to Danielsson and Danielsson (1986), "the fact that the CEP took over the islands illegally with neither lease nor land deed probably explains one stupid error that has been perpetuated ever since: they misspelled the name of the atoll as 'Mururoa', whereas the true name, familiar to all local people, is and always has been Moruroa", p. 73.
6   Danielsson and Danielsson (1986), p. 265.
7   Tony Simpson (1984, July/August). Who runs the country anyway? [An advance extract from his 1984 book *A Vision Betrayed: The Decline of Democracy in New Zealand* (Hodder & Stoughton)]. *New Outlook* magazine, pp. 12-16; Censored. (1984, July/August) *New Outlook* magazine, p. 13.

PART 2

Colonial legacy conflicts

Kanak protesters confront French riot police in Nouméa, 1985.   David Robie

5

Kanaky: Blood on their banner, 1984

With the present French colonial electoral system and past immigration
policies, Melanesians are a minority in their homeland. We cannot
accept that logic. Now we're putting a halt to it.

Assassinated Kanak leader Jean-Marie Tjibaou

"TOPSY-TURVY in Alice in Wonderland fashion", was how Robin Dunning described the publication of my 1989 book *Blood on their Banner*,[1] not first in New Zealand, but in Europe—in fact in two editions, the first in Swedish and then in English—before making its way to these shores.[2] A book "concerning matters vital to New Zealand and our neighbours [appeared] first, not from a local publisher, but in a Swedish translation from one of Sweden's largest publishers—and launched at the mid-1989 Göthenburg Book Fair".[3]

I found it rather puzzling at the time as there was a big publishing gap for a book examining the region as a whole and putting events such as the Fiji coups, the Vanuatu crisis and the Kanak struggle for independence into a meaningful perspective and context, but the would-be New Zealand publishers suddenly turned around after I had completed the manuscript and said they wanted a third cut out. Just as unbelievable, they wanted the section on the illegally occupied Indonesian colonies of East Timor and West Papua to be removed. It would have been virtual censorship. While Indonesia claimed both territories were integral provinces of the republic—after annexation by invasion—the Timorese, at least, said there was no legitimate Indonesian involvement in their country.

But as the overseas publishers, reputable London-based Zed Books, saw no reason to tamper, I refused to make cuts and handed the complete publication to them. This, though, was just one step in a convoluted process getting *Blood on their Banner* into the public domain; the Swedish version was the first out, in a Wiken hard-cover edition from Bra Böcker and translated by Margareta Eklöf. Shortly after, a more up-to-date English edition came out from Zed Books and this in itself was something of an international affair.

OCH VÄRLDEN BLUNDAR...

David Robie

WIKEN

A masked Kanak militant near Thio, New Caledonia, 1985, on the cover of the Swedish and Filipino editions of David Robie's 1989 book *Blood on their Banner*. This evocative cover photo was dropped by the English-language publishers Zed in favour of palm trees on a beach that were eventually later swapped for a flag picture—but not actually the Kanak banner of the book title.   DAVID ROBIE

It was then published in Australia in association with Pluto Press and later in the Philippines by Malaya Books, but the original book was designed and packaged in Auckland, New Zealand, and the actual printing was done in England. At the time, I regarded the New Zealand blocking moves as an attempt to gag the East Timor and West Papua content, and perhaps even some of the content on Kanaky. But there were also other perspectives. *Listener* "Bookmarks" columnist Robin Dudding wrote:

> It is also clear that any cuts suggested by the original New Zealand publisher had a lot to do with harsh economic facts—that is, keeping the unit production costs low enough to allow for what may have been

huge New Zealand sales. Moreover, despite the lack of New Zealand-based books on politics in the South Pacific, it would be fair to hazard a guess that while a journalist's "devastating exposé of the political forces which have shaken the region" might suit a distant radical publisher, it might not be quite right for here.[4]

When the Pacific was still in the grip of Cold War geopolitics, France claimed that it wished to retain its South Pacific presence for similar reasons to the United States—a concern about communism and the old Soviet Union, the desire for stability and the maintenance of the "balance of power". But there were other, more sinister, factors behind the publicly stated reasons. French colonialism in both New Caledonia and Tahiti in the 19th century was largely motivated by the wish to prevent the South Pacific becoming a "British lake".[5]

New Caledonia became the most critical factor in this political equation. When Vanuatu became independent from Britain and France in 1980, France's then State Secretary for Overseas Territories, Paul Dijoud, pledged that "battle must be done to keep New Caledonia French".[6] The closest Pacific island neighbour to Australia and New Zealand, New Caledonia was at that time the last "domino" before French Polynesia where the vital nuclear tests for the *force de frappe* (nuclear strike force) were carried out.

It is in this context that the 1984 Kanak revolt against French rule took place, which eventually cost 32 lives—most of them Melanesian, with the Hienghène massacre the most devastating early clash, and culminating in the assassinations of independence leaders Jean-Marie Tjibaou and Yéiwene Yéiwene on 4 May 1989. Within eight weeks of the start of the rebellion, militant Kanak leader Éloï Machoro, who had bloodlessly captured the mining town of Thio, was dead—shot by French police marksmen. From then on nationalist tensions in New Caledonia rapidly became convulsions, spreading throughout the South Pacific.[7]

BLOOD ON THEIR BANNER
New Zealand Listener, 27 October 1984

LEADERS of New Caledonia's independence movement say that time is running out. Their blood has already been spilt and they fear more bloodshed lies ahead.[8]

A new flag flutters defiantly from makeshift flagpoles in a handful of villages in New Caledonia. It is blue, red, and green-striped—symbolising the sky, blood and earth. A golden orb represents the rising sun.

Kanak villagers guard a barricade near Bourail, New Caledonia, 1985. The Kanak flag bears a red band representing the blood sacrificed in their struggle.

DAVID ROBIE/LONDON *SUNDAY TIMES*

This premature banner of independence was first hoisted in Lifou Island during an official ceremony recently marking the 44th anniversary of General de Gaulle's call for a Free France.

Mayor Edward Wapae, of the ruling Independence Front, recalled that de Gaulle's speech in 1940 showed a determination to "liberate France soil from the Nazi occupiers and to reconquer French independence, the principles of which had made her the home of the rights of man and liberties".

In the next breath, Wapae said that the children and the grandchildren of the Kanaks (the largest single ethnic group in New Caledonia), who had fought for France then, were fed up with vain promises. He made a "last chance" plea for France to honour "her declarations condemning colonisation and defending the right of each people to decide their own future".

The flags are just one manifestation of a growing mood of impatience and disillusionment among Kanaks demanding independence in the French-ruled South Pacific territory—New Zealand's closest major Pacific Island neighbour. Another is the talk in villages of the "sacrifices" made by peasants during the Algerian war of independence.

South Pacific Forum leaders, meeting in Tuvalu during August, again caution against putting too much pressure on France while urging that Paris speed up the colonisation process.

Yet for the Kanaks, and neighbouring Vanuatu, this take-it-easy attitude is rather bewildering. "The Forum sees things the same way as the French socialists and *our* position—their Pacific brother—isn't seriously considered," complains Jean-Marie Tjibaou, who as Vice-President of the Government Council holds the territory's highest elected post. He has been particularly disillusioned with Australia and New Zealand, at least until Prime Minister David Lange's sudden "reconnaissance mission" to Nouméa in early October.

Vanuatu's Prime Minister, Father Walter Lini, also disappointed at the Forum's lukewarm support, plans to press the New Caledonian case at the United Nations and try to get it reinstated on the UN Decolonisation Committee's list. He blames the Forum if violence erupts in the territory and fears "foreign opportunists may exploit the instability".

The Independence Front, now renamed the Kanak Socialist National Liberation Front (FLNKS), recently decided to boycott and obstruct fresh elections due in the territory next month[9] in protest against a new statute of autonomy. Instead, the FLNKS has called its own parliamentary elections for November 11, planning to form a provisional government by December, and renamed the country Kanaky.

Although the statute calls for a referendum on independence in 1989, the Forum believes this should be advanced to 1986—while the FLNKS wants independence next year [1985].

Lini criticises the view, often expressed by Australia and New Zealand, that Paris has been doing all it could and should be given time to decolonise. "The history of French decolonisation frequently has not been peaceful … and no other South Pacific nation, apart from Vanuatu, has suffered it."

Vanuatu's ruling Vanua'aku Pati has made a resolution that opens the door for the FLNKS to form a government-in-exile in Port Vila. But Vanuatu's government ministers are reluctant to discuss this and it is believed they would prefer a "people's government to be with the people" in New Caledonia.

In Tuvalu, Lange won support for establishing a five-nation Forum ministerial delegation—including New Zealand and Vanuatu—to visit Nouméa for talks with French authorities and the *indépendantistes*. After briefly flying to Nouméa and Port Vila at the end of his hectic trip, he stressed it was clear all New Caledonian political groups apart from the right-wingers wanted independence. He hoped to bring the factions together before the elections but his peaceful initiative may already be too late.

Why are the *indépendantistes* taking this more militant stance when they are at present in the driver's seat as the senior coalition partner in the government? "With the present colonial electoral system and past immigration policies, Melanesians are a minority in their homeland," explains Vice-President Tjibaou, a 48-year-old sociologist. "We *cannot* accept that logic. Now we're putting a halt to it.

French Pacific Regiment troops on ceremonial parade outside New Caledonia's Territorial Assembly. DAVID ROBIE

"We need a statute that will accept *our* logic—the logic of Kanak sovereignty."

The bitter reality for New Caledonians, both brown and white, is that the French government has pushed through an autonomy statute that *nobody* wants. The Territorial Assembly in Noumea unanimously rejected the bill earlier this year. Justin Guillemard, leader of the extreme right-wing Caledonian Front, describes the law as an "administrative monstrosity" and "racist" in favour of Melanesians.

President Francois Mitterrand's government, so keen to foster a strong middle ground, now seems further away than ever from any consensus among New Caledonians. And the *Caldoche* (settlers) are alarmed at the FLNKS's determination to seek foreign help.

Wealthy businessman Jacques Lafleur, a deputy in the French National Assembly and leader of the Republican Congress Party which held local power until two years ago, denounced as "provocative" a visit by Tjibaou to Port Moresby in August when he lobbied an Asian-Pacific leaders' regional summit. Lafleur also condemned a recent visit to Libya by two other Independence Front leaders.

The 51-year-old Lafleur is a fifth-generation *Caldoche* and a great admirer of former Prime Minister Sir Robert Muldoon—"the only South Pacific leader who understands us".

With an air of cynicism, he says: "Maybe there could be independence in 20 years or so, but it depends on what sort ... I would never be a Kanak citizen. We

Jacques Lafleur: New Zealand's Sir Robert Muldoon "the only South Pacific leader who understands us".   DAVID ROBIE

are French people and the Kanaks are French too ... One bad move and there will be blood in the streets."

But for the Kanaks, blood has already been flowing in the streets and they fear more being spilt. French authorities have been quietly building up the strength of military forces in the territory to maintain order, if necessary. It is believed more than 4000 paramilitary and regular troops are now garrisoned there.

One MP, Yann-Célene Uregei, has a photograph in his office of his face battered and bleeding from the blows of a policeman's truncheon at a protest rally during a previous French government's rule. Two years ago a group of extremist white thugs burst into the Territorial Assembly chamber and attacked pro-independence MPs. They received light sentences. There have also been sporadic riots.

On the night of 19 September 1981, French-born Pierre Declercq, 43, secretary-general of the Union Calédonienne and a leading strategist of the Independence Front, was shot with a riot gun through the study window on his Mt Dore home. It was the first assassination of a South Pacific political leader. Now, three years later, nobody has yet been put in the dock for the murder.

During August more than 600 people marched on the Noumea courthouse demanding that a trial be held over the killing of "white martyr" Declercq. Similar protest rallies were held in Poindimie, Pouebo, Voh and on Lifou Island in the Loyalty group.

Kanak with a "white martyr" T-shirt honouring an assassinated early FLNKS leader, Pierre Declercq.   DAVID ROBIE

A young motorcycle mechanic, Dominic Canon, was arrested and charged four days after the murder. Another man, Vanuatu-born barman Martin Barthelemy, was arrested a year later. But both suspects have been freed on bail.

Marguitte Declercq accuses justice officials and gendarmes of obstructing inquiries into her husband's killing; League of Human Rights secretary-general Jean-Jacques Bourdinat has called the judicial delay scandalous.

When I spoke to the cherubic-faced Canon, now 22, in his workshop on the outskirts of Nouméa just after his release on $5000 bail from the notorious Camp Est prison, he insisted: "I'm innocent. They put me in jail for nothing."

New Caledonia's problems stem from its complex racial mix. Kanaks number only 60,000 out of a population of 140,000. About 50,000 Europeans form the next largest group, and the rest are a *potpourri* of Vietnamese, Indonesians, Tahitians and Wallisians.

New Caledonia was annexed by France in 1853, mainly for use as a penal colony. In three decades after 1860 more than 40,000 prisoners—including leaders of the 1871 Paris commune insurrection and other political exiles—were deported to the colony.

For almost a century the Kanaks were deprived of political and civil rights. But after they finally won the vote in 1951, they began to wrest a limited share of their own country's development—which was later fuelled by a nickel boom.

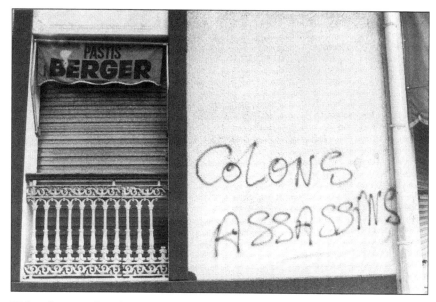

"Colonial assassins" graffiti denouncing French colonial rule in the Place des Cocotiers, Nouméa, 1984.   DAVID ROBIE

According to Vice-President Tjibaou, the New Caledonian territorial government has less power now than during the controversial *loi cadre* years between 1956 and 1959, when the territory was almost self-governing. Later conservative French governments favoured policies which meant New Caledonia was governed as an integral part of France until the Mitterrand administration embarked on reforms in 1981—after the assassination of Declercq.

The *indépendantistes* argue that the current French reforms, far from being progressive, have in fact only been restoring some of the progress made in the 1950s. And they fear that if the Socialists lose office in the French general election due in 1986 they will be faced with another stalemate. Hence their urgency for independence next year [1985].

They claim President Mitterrand betrayed a commitment to independence made before being elected, and again at a roundtable conference at Nainville-les-Roches, France, last year.

The controversial statute will increase the Territorial Assembly from 36 seats to 42 (slightly favouring the *indépendantistes*); create a unique style of upper house comprising custom chiefs and representatives of elected town councils; introduce six regional (Kanaks prefer the word *pays*, or cultural community) administrations; and establish a special commission to prepare the way for a referendum on self-determination in 1989.

FLNKS leaders meeting at their Nouméa headquarters. Standing: Yéiwene Yéiwene (assassinated by a Kanak dissident in 1989), to his right, Jean-Marie Tjibaou (also assassinated in 1989), and, to his left with his face turned away, Éloï Machoro (assassinated by French military sharpshooters, 1986). DAVID ROBIE

"We haven't any choice but to oppose the application of the statute," says Tjibaou. "We must impose an 'active' boycott, because if we accept these elections under the statute of autonomy, we accept the colonial logic behind them."

Tjibaou believes the election result would be insignificant and unrepresentative of the territory. Many FLNKS leaders consider that the French government couldn't allow an unrepresentative local government, so they would annul the elections and be forced into making quicker concessions for electoral reforms.

French officials concede there could be a case for a qualified franchise, such as Fiji's nine-year residential clause, but consider the FLNKS demand that voters should be only Kanaks or people with at least one parent born in New Caledonia to be "unconstitutional". Fearful of eventual independence, white *Caldoche* are applying in droves for immigration permits to Australia. Wealthy New Caledonians are also buying land in New Zealand's South Island, California, Hawai'i, Queensland and the French Riviera.

Most Kanaks support the Independence Front, a coalition of five parties until the Kanak Socialist Liberation, led by charismatic Nidoishe Naisseline, split away recently over the election boycott decision. Naisseline, a Sorbonne-educated grand chief, says Kanaks "shouldn't try to copy nationalist movements in Africa and Indo-China".

The majority of Europeans back Lafleur's Republican Congress Party which used to advocate continued integration with France. Now it is outflanked on the right by the Caledonian Front while the centrist Caledonian New Society Federation (FNSC), also mainly European, has been supporting the Independence Forum for the last two years.

New Caledonian politics is highly complex, and feelings are potentially explosive.

While the rest of the South Pacific—apart from Vanuatu, which was forced to cope with an abortive secession—peacefully gained independence, New Caledonia seems fated to break that pattern. Little wonder the *indépendantistes* have included symbolic blood on their banner.

¶

OVER the next seven years, I closely reported the ongoing conflict in Kanaky for *Islands Business* and other media. Multimillionaire mining and property mogul Jacques Lafleur, one of the richest men in France and the biggest thorn for Kanak independence even though he eventually reluctantly signed two critical accords paving the way for a possible referendum, died in 2010 aged 78.[10] He dominated New Caledonian politics for more than three decades, including 29 as a member of the French National Assembly. Described as a "giant in New Caledonia's political scene" by one of his successors as territorial president, Philippe Gomes, Lafleur outlined his version of history in an autobiography, *L'Assiégé* (*The Besieged*) in 2000.[11] His political star began to wane after his anti-independence coalition split in 2004. He was defeated in the French National Assembly elections two years later and then he retired from politics in 2010. Along with Jean-Marie Tjibaou, Lafleur signed the 1988 Matignon Accord and then the Nouméa Accord in 1998, and he honoured a pledge to Tjibaou to open the way for a Kanak stake in the nickel mining industry. Lafleur agreed to sell his controlling stake in Societe Miniere du Sud Pacifique (SMSP) to the Kanak-dominated Northern Province government in 1990. Several years later, he was furious when environmentalist and New Caledonian coral reef defender Bruno Van Peteghem won a court judgment against Lafleur, with a ruling that an apartment complex in Nouméa's Moselle Bay constructed by one of his companies was illegal. Lafleur branded Van Peteghem as an opportunistic campaigner and a "*petit saligaud*", or "little scum".[12] The developers were ordered to remove the apartment block, but eight years later it was still there.

New Caledonian nickel is shipped to many Asian countries where it is processed to manufacture steel, electronics and consumer goods. The nickel industry has made many Caldoche wealthy, with minerals accounting for 90 percent of the territory's export revenue. Criticism of the industry is highly unpopular with the establishment. Nevertheless, Peterghem's passionate campaign to have the coral reef declared a UNESCO World Heritage site led to him being awarded the Goldman Environmental Prize in 2001.

My reporting of New Caledonia led to a protracted and acrimonious dispute with Fiji's *Islands Business* publisher Robert Keith-Reid when the magazine started attacking me in 1989 for my alleged "leftist" support of Kanak activists and an article I wrote about the "muzzling of the Pacific press".[13] The controversy was extensively reported in the *New Zealand Journalist*[14] and led to an unprecedented editorial by the *Pacific Islands Monthly* condemning its rival for using the "pages and editorial resources of an established publication ... in a personal vendetta" against me.[15] The late John Richardson, editor of *IB* for most of my eight-year tenure as a chief correspondent there, also weighed in, saying: "David's articles reflect a journalist who is neither anti-right nor pro-left. He is, however, pro-Pacific ... [reporting] injustice heaped on South Pacific people while remaining dispassionate."[16] *Pacific Islands Monthly* pledged to preserve its balanced perspective of regional forces by continuing to publish my articles. However, while I did continue writing for *PIM*—founded in 1931, the oldest and best regional Pacific news magazine—it was relocated by News Limited from Sydney to Suva in 1990 and milked by *The Fiji Times* group until it was eventually closed a decade later.

Notes

1 David Robie (1989). *Blood on their Banner: Nationalist Struggles in the South Pacific.* London: Zed Books; Sydney: Pluto Press; also editions in Sweden (Wiken Books, 1989, translated) and the Philippines (Malaya Books, 1990).
2 Robin Dudding (1989, May 20). Bookmarks: Out of the Pacific, *New Zealand Listener*.
3 David Robie (1989). *Och Världen Blundar ... Kampen för frihet i Stilla Havet [And the World Closed its Eyes—Campaign for a free South Pacific].* [Swedish trans. Margareta Eklöf]. Hoganas, Sweden: Wiken Books.
4 Dudding (1989).
5 David Robie (1989). Introduction. In *Blood on their Banner*, p. 17.
6 Cited in Robie (1989), ibid., p. 17.
7 Ibid., p. 18.
8 David Robie (1984, October 27). Blood on their Banner. *New Zealand Listener*, pp. 14–15.

9   November 1984.
10 New Caledonia's Jacques Lafleur dies aged 78 (2010, December 5). Radio New Zealand International. Retrieved on 7 January 2014, from www.radionz.co.nz/international/pacific-news/194123/new-caledonia%27s-jacques-lafleur-dies-aged-78
11 Jacques Lafleur (2000). *L'Assiégé: une histoire partagée avec Nouvelle-Calédonie.* Paris: Plon.
12 Paul Tolmé (2002, June 1). Little scum takes on big mining. *National Wildlife.* Retrieved on 7 January 2014, from www.nwf.org/News-and-Magazines/National-Wildlife/News-and-Views/Archives/2002/Little-Scum-Takes-On-Big-Mining.aspx
13 David Robie (1988, November-December). The muzzling of the Pacific press. *New Zealand Monthly Review*, no. 314, pp. 20-22.
14 Harry Stoner (1989, April). Robie target of vendetta. *New Zealand Journalist*, p. 8.
15 The art of balance: a press perspective (1989, March). [Editorial] *Pacific Islands Monthly*, p. 7.
16 Ibid.

6

The massacre of Hienghène, 1984

France is putting into place the legal tool which will allow,
with impunity, the killing of Kanaks—the perpetration of genocide
against the Kanak people.

Pro-independence newspaper *Bwenando*

A BOYCOTT of the New Caledonian territorial elections in November 1984 precipitated fast-moving, violent events in the Pacific territory. Two weeks later, on the evening of December 5, the slaughter of 10 unarmed Kanak militants by a group of settlers in an ambush almost provoked civil war. An eventual acquittal by a Nouméa court for the self-confessed killers was condemned as a miscarriage of justice in the South Pacific. It was a further stain on France's colonial record.

The reporting of the massacre and the court proceedings were an indictment of the territory's only daily newspaper, the anti-independence *Les Nouvelles Calédoniennes*, which framed the killers as a "clan of métis" (mixed race) defending a peaceful and pluri-ethnic "true Caledonia" against Kanak rebellion. As Alaine Chanter argued in an analysis about the portrayal of violence in the media 14 years later, *Les Nouvelles* contributed to a climate of racism that accepted "Kanaks returning in their trucks [to their village community] could be ambushed and mowed down with bullets".[1]

Seventeen men were in the unarmed party returning from an election meeting that night. The bush track they were travelling along in two pickup trucks was blocked by a felled coconut tree. Most of them were shot repeatedly as they tried to escape; some managed to swim across the nearby Hienghène River. As well as the 10 men killed—almost the entire male population of the village of Tiendanite—four were wounded.

The men were gunned down outside the house of settler Maurice Mitride who became a suspect. He was arrested and charged with murder and jailed pending trial five days later. The other six settlers involved— Raoul Lapetite and four of his sons, Jess, José, Jacques and Jean-Claude, along with an adopted Melanesian son, Robert Sineimène—surrendered to an investigating judge. After being flown to Nouméa, all six were also charged with murder and jailed on remand.

Almost two years later, the charges against all seven accused were dismissed on the grounds of "self-defence" and they were freed from jail. However, the state prosecutors appealed. Two days after being released from Nouméa's Camp Est prison, the seven accused were portrayed by *Les Nouvelles Calédoniennes* in a celebratory front-page picture with their arms linked as if they were sporting buddies. The image was captioned "FREE … but it isn't finished".[2]

The court ruling was overturned with a 10-day trial eventually taking place from 19 October 1987. After hearing all the damning evidence, the jury deliberated for two hours (including meal time) and returned a not guilty verdict on self-defence grounds.[3] According to Chanter, the Kanak political opponents were portrayed by *Les Nouvelles* as "a form of animal sub-species deserving of eradication".[4] *Bwenando*, the pro-independence publication, commented that the acquittal demonstrated that the "Kanak hunt was now open".[5]

> France is putting into place the legal tool which will allow, with impunity, the killing of Kanaks—the perpetration of genocide against the Kanak people. The Kanak hunt is therefore open, but this hunt is not even regulated [the chasing of deer at night with spotlights is prohibited].[6]

According to Chanter, *Bwenando* was referring to the use of hunting spotlights by the assassins to light up the fleeing Kanaks—an allegation they denied. Although I never reported at the trial, I was in New Caledonia at the time of the massacre and travelled to Hienghène and attended the heart-breaking funeral at Tiendanite, the village of Kanak leader Jean-Marie Tjibaou and his murdered brothers. The following account was based on the survivors' stories and transcripts of sworn testimony in the Pierre Declercq Committee Report[7] and originally reported as extracts in my *Islands Business* stories and then as a chapter in my book *Blood on their Banner*.[8]

THE MASSACRE OF HIENGHÈNE

Blood on their Banner, 1989

MOONLIGHT filtered through the coconut palms and bamboo thickets on the track skirting the Hienghène River. Night had just fallen. Two battered pickup trucks bumped along the rutted earth surface; 17 Kanaks squeezed into the vehicles joked and laughed as the trucks lurched along.

Islands Business cover story on the Hienghène massacre by the author in January 1985.
Inset: Jean-Marie Tjibaou.   DAVID ROBIE

A two-hour meeting of the local *comité de lutte* (struggle committee) at the Hienghène Cultural Centre had ended on a happy note. It had been called that afternoon, Wednesday, 5 December 1984, to explain why the FLNKS had decided to lift the barricades and abandon its campaign of destabilisation, a decision announced the day before in Nouméa. About 50 people attended the meeting. At 7.30pm the local militants left and headed for home. Fourteen piled into the two pickups; three others hitched a ride along the 14-kilometre track to Tiendanite, home village of the Kanak provincial government leader Jean-Marie Tjibaou. One of Tjibaou's three brothers, Louis, chief of the Tiendanite *tribu*, drove a Mitsubishi. Behind, travelling almost bumper to bumper because his headlights were smashed, was a younger brother, Vianney, at the wheel of a Chevrolet.

At Wan'yaat, eight kilometres up the valley, the track is hemmed in between a cliff and the river. Beside the track are a barbed-wire fence and cleared pasture leading to the river 20 metres away. When the Mitsubishi reached a house belonging to Maurice Mitride, a 50-year-old settler of mixed race, it stopped abruptly. A felled coconut palm blocked the way.

"Road block ... road block," shouted 17-year-old Joseph Wathea in the back of the truck. Louis Tjibaou, who hadn't seen the tree until five metres away, backed off and bumped into the Chevrolet.

An explosion ripped open the right-hand side of the Mitsubishi as two sticks of dynamite slung from a wire made contact. Spotlights lit up the track and a deadly crossfire from rifles and shotguns opened up from Mitride's house and from the other side of the track.

"Everybody out," yelled Vianney Tjibaou, dragging himself through the barbed-wire fence and fleeing towards Tiendanite. Some of the other men also managed to jump out of the trucks and run for cover by the river. Vianney, 38 at the time, and one of the two survivors of the ambush who were unhurt, recalls:

> I saw flames coming out of the gun barrels when the shooting started from Mitride's house and from the river. I opened the car door [and shouted to everybody to get out] and then I jumped. I … ran towards the river. Then I followed it upstream and felt a burn on my shoulder. While I was running [they kept firing] but never hit me.
>
> After a while, I came to a bend where there was a fence and saw another two or three people firing. I stopped about 200 metres from the ambush site to watch and listen, hiding in the coffee bushes.[9]

Louis Tjibaou sat frozen in the Mitsubishi. Beside him, Pascal Couhia ducked under the steering wheel to dodge the shots. As soon as Couhia slid through the door, he was hit by two bullets in the thigh. He crawled along a ditch and hid under a stand of dead bamboo which had fallen into the river, staying there until the doctor arrived after the ambush. Wathea, also wounded, joined him under the bamboo.

Vianney recognised Maurice Mitride, another settler, Henri Garnier, his wife, Rose, and other ambushers among the shadows. He saw Garnier walk towards the body of Louis, who had scrambled past the coconut tree before being shot.

"You bastards, we've got you," Garnier snarled. Vianney saw Garnier shoot Louis point blank in the head.[10] Slipping away, Vianney ran to a causeway where the Tiendanite track left the river. A horse was tethered there and he rode to the village to warn the women and children of the *tribu*. They hid in the bush.

Mickael Maepas was wounded and dragged himself into the river. He floated in the river until about 10am next morning, when he was found still alive. (He died a day later, after giving evidence.)

In the back of the Chevrolet, Lucien Couhia, Pascal Mandjia and Tarcisse Tjibaou lay unable to move—shots had shattered their spines. They lay silently in agony until Tarcisse, unable to bear the pain any more, cried out. Some of the killers returned with spotlights and opened fire from close up.

Lucien Couhia was wounded in the right forearm and chest. He stopped breathing. Mandjia pretended to be dead. Tjibaou was dead. (His body was later incinerated in the truck.) After the killers went off to the river to hunt the wounded, Couhia dragged himself off the truck , escaped to a Kanak family further along the track and was taken to the Hienghène dispensary.

Bernard Maepas, aged 27, in the back of the Chevrolet, had been one of the first to run for his life. He recalls:

> At first it was the people in front of [Mitride's] house doing the shooting, so we ran to the left of the cars. We didn't see the guys below, in the pasture, because they had not begun to shoot. But as we passed the barbed-wire fence, they started too. Some were even sitting down and they shot at us point blank.
>
> I was wounded then and got shot in the lower abdomen. At that time, those who were up at the house began to walk down the drive and let the dogs loose. They had flashlights. I hid in the river bank. I was unable to swim but managed to hide under some plants. There were wounded men lying in the grass near me. When the dogs, who followed the scent of blood, found them, the people followed and shot at the men on the ground.
>
> They finished off the wounded, took their bodies and dragged them into the water. All the time they insulted us. I heard one of the killers shout, "There's Auguste [Wathea]," and the others screamed, "kill him, kill him."[11]

Maepas kept hearing shots for about 20 minutes. Then silence. When the dogs barked, the ambushers would find another wounded man and finish him off. By the time the assassins thought everybody was dead, they began to talk loudly. Maepas thought there were 15 of them.

Joseph Pei was down the river too. He had been shot twice in the foot. They could not swim across because the killers were on the river bank, lighting up the water with their spotlights. Maepas recalls:

> I saw one man swim. He was obviously hurt and couldn't swim very well. The killers came with their lights and saw him. Two or three of them started to fire on him. The man was struggling for life in the water. And they shot at him until he no longer moved.[12]

As the attackers blasted away at the wounded, 14-year-old Jerry Lapetite went to the bank and shone his spotlight over the river. The water was red with blood. He called over his companions, shouting, "Hot shit, look at all that blood!"

When the killers moved away, Bernard Maepas crawled out from under some patchouli plants. "I was walking on bodies. They had not yet thrown the bodies into the river," he recalls. "I felt I was going mad. Among the bodies was Louis Tjibaou. When they found him the next day, he was [riddled] with at least 30 bullets and [shotgun pellets]." Twenty-year-old Jean-Luc Vayadimoin also escaped, with superficial wounds.

> I came upon Êloi Maepas, who was moaning. I was about to carry him when I saw the spotlights go on [again] and lay down. I took a good look at the people. On the other side the shooting continued—shot after shot … They talked loudly among themselves, Henri Garnier said, "I'm gonna kill those lousy Kanaks."
>
> I got up and ran, but didn't make it as far as the canna lilies because the searchlights turned on again and shots came in my direction. I heard a bullet whistle past. I dived into the water and they continued to light up the river. I recognised the voice of Jacky Charles who asked, "Where is he? Who are you shooting at?"[13]

They shot at the bodies in the river. Vayadimoin heard the bullets hit the swirling water. He stayed hidden in pampas grass for a long time, flat on his belly.

"There's someone in this car," shouted Jesse Lapetite.

"Kill him, kill him," replied Henri Garnier. Roger Tein screamed, "Shoot … shoot." Vayadimoin heard three shots. First one, then two together.

Six men died that night.[14] And a further four died in the next two days from their wounds. Seven survived, four of them gravely wounded; a fifth suffered superficial wounds. The survivors spent the night by the river or crawled and ran to a nearby village. Mickael Maepas was airlifted by helicopter next day to hospital in Nouméa, when the gendarmes and the reinforcements arrived. Five bodies were found within a 50-metre radius of the vehicles; another, that of Tarcisse Tjibaou, was found in the fire-gutted shell of the Chevrolet.

Although alerted within an hour of the start of the massacre, the local gendarmes at Hienghène did not arrive at Wan`yaat until almost midday on 6 December—16 hours after the slaughter. By Saturday four more victims had died in hospital from their wounds.

When I arrived at Wan`yaat two days later for the traditional burial ceremony at Tiendanite, the only obvious evidence of the massacre were the bullet-scarred and charred pickup trucks. Police recovered 200 cartridge cases which had been fired in the half-hour of terror.

To the outrage of the *Caldoches*, the French army flew the 10 coffins by Puma helicopter to Hienghène Valley where they were transported by military truck to Tiendanite. Heavily armed *gendarmes mobiles*, with armoured personnel carriers and machine-gun-festooned trucks, guarded the track through the valley and the ambush site.

About 600 Kanaks came to the village to bury the dead—but not Tjibaou himself. Tjibaou, mayor of Hienghène, was believed to be in danger and was closely guarded by armed FLNKS militants. After several hours of wailing and custom rites, and a tribute to their martyrdom by Kanaky's Interior Minister Yéiwene Yéiwene, the victims were buried in a line with their casket draped in the blood-red, blue and green bands and golden orb of the Kanaky flag, and frangipani and hibiscus blooms. Déwé Gorodé wrote a poem dedicated to the victims.

> *The river weeps*
> *Tears of blood*
> *The mountain groans*
> *Echoes of mourning*
> *The trade winds breathe*
> *Soothing words*
> *The forest covers*
> *The gaping wound ...*[15]

Senator Dick Ukeiwe, president of the territorial government, flew back from Paris and was welcomed by a mainly European rally of about 6000 people protesting against independence. Though they gave a minute's silence for the tragedy victims, their message was clear: most New Caledonians wanted to remain French, while the FLNKS were "terrorists and rebels" and should be outlawed. The Kanak Socialist Liberation occupied the Territorial Assembly chamber in a symbolic protest against the "insensitivity" of Ukeiwe's rally in the wake of the killings.

For Edgar Pisani, a former Gaullist cabinet minister with a reputation for giving Third World countries a fairer deal, the events were a baptism of fire. He arrived in Noumea just two days before the massacre and a few hours after a local French journalist, Frank Depierre, of the right-wing daily *Les Nouvelles Calédoniennes*, and a UTA Airlines staffer had been shot and wounded at a barricade at Saint Louis, near the hospital.

Identified by survivors and other witnesses on the night of the ambush, the killers escaped along a forest track to the west coast European township of Voh after burning down Jean-Marie Tjibaou's house near the Hienghène River. They were helped by other settlers to elude police. After five days, on 10 December 1984, Maurice Mitride gave himself up, saying he "couldn't live with his conscience".[16] The following day, bull-necked, stockily built Raoul Lapetite, aged 58, four of his five sons, Jacques, Jean-Claude, Jose and Jesse, and Robert Sineimene, aged 24, were also arrested, near Voh. Lapetite's fifth son, Jerry, was caught in a Noumea disco but later released as a minor. At least another eight, mostly white attackers—including a woman—identified as having taken part were never charged.

A French military helicopter lands near Tiendanite village, December 1984.   DAVID ROBIE

Several of Mitride's ancestors came from Réunion, a French possession in the Indian Ocean. He is slight and dark-skinned with short kinky hair. Raoul Lapetite's father was French but his mother was a Kanak. He is also dark-skinned; his sons could easily be mistaken for Kanaks. Sineimene's mother is a Kanak from Lifou; his father Javanese. Yet all seven fervently consider themselves European. Like other *Caldoches*, they defended the capitalist notion of land ownership. Once Kanak clans began to suggest to Mitride and Lapetite that their land should be shared again with traditional, indigenous owners, battle lines were drawn.

The "no case" scandal

The sordid judicial aftermath of the massacre of Hienghène is certain to go down as one of the greater stains on French colonial history in the South Pacific. Almost two years after the massacre, the self-confessed killers were set free by examining magistrate Francois Semur who ruled *non-lieu*—no case to answer. They had been charged with the murder of 10 Kanaks and attempted murder of seven others.

Citing a rarely used highway robbery law dating back in Napoleonic times, magistrate Semur said the accused had acted in "self-defence". He referred to the exceptional circumstances at the end of 1984—the three-week period of unrest and barricades which gripped New Caledonia after the Kanak boycott of the elections on November 18. Yet in the Hienghène and Tiendanite valleys there was

French policeman guards the bush track to Tiendanite, December 1984.　　Dᴀᴠɪᴅ Rᴏʙɪᴇ

little violence and less trouble than anywhere. Semur ignored this; his decision reflected the settler version of events.

The magistrate neglected to mention the fact that at the time of the ambush the Kanaks who died had been unarmed and were returning from the meeting at which it had been decided to resort to peaceful negotiations with the French authorities.[17] Semur did not explain why he shunned the testimony of more than 20 witnesses which showed the attack was an unprovoked slaughter of unarmed Kanaks. Nor did he question or charge other settlers named by the survivors—at least two of them regarded as gendarmes as "seriously implicated". Semur rejected a request by lawyer Gustave Tehio, a barrister representing the families of the victims, to carry out a reconstruction of the ambush. Some lawyers claimed the magistrate was acting under pressure from the French government to drop the case.

A young French military doctor, Gustave Savourey, stationed at Hienghène, made an ambulance trip on the night of the ambush. He rescued two wounded survivors and also picked up Rose Garnier, who was alleged to have been one of the attackers. The settlers later claimed that the house belonging to her and her husband Henri had been in an attack by the Kanak villagers. However, the doctor reported that the house was intact when he passed by. But his testimony was hushed up and he was posted back to France.

Semur appears to have ignored or suppressed almost all evidence indicating a careful orchestrated and premeditated massacre. "After 21 months of investigation," he said, "I am convinced there is no case for holding these men on murder charges."

Released from Camp Est prison before dawn on 1 October 1986, the killers were taken to a secret hideout in Nouméa. Photographs of them were splashed across the front page of *Les Nouvelles Calédoniennes*, and they appeared on a state television defending the massacre: *Les Nouvelles* greeted their release in triumph as if they were popular war heroes.

France's Association of Magistrates denounced the ruling as a "mockery of justice". It added in a statement: "On the evidence, this provocative ruling is purely political and we fear the consequences for public order in New Caledonia."

"This is a monumental judicial gaffe," said New Zealand author James McNeish. "It is going to have serious consequences in France and is bound to cause an international *cause célèbre*." McNeish, visiting Noumea at the time of the *non-lieu*, covered the event for British and New Zealand newspapers. He reported for the *New Zealand Listener*:

> In a 153-page judgment of almost unbelievable colonial bias, [magistrate Semur] described the Tiendanite Kanaks as having a "bad character". He spoke of a state of "insurrection" and "war" in the valley; of settlers "abandoned" by the then socialist authorities of Noumea; of the "mere certainty" of an impending Kanak "attack"; of almost daily burning and pillaging by Kanaks; of settlers held hostage by a state of siege, terror and menace.
>
> Far from menacing the settlers, however, the Hienghène Kanaks appear to have helped them—in one case offering shelter to a settler woman whose house it was revealed ... had been burned by the settlers themselves in provocation on the eve of the ambush.[18]

The Pierre Declercq Committee, a human rights group set up in 1981 to investigate the still unsolved assassination of the French-born leader, denounced the *non-lieu* order as an open invitation for white settlers to kill Kanaks with impunity. New Caledonia's local chapter of the International League of Human Rights said the "scandalous" move deprived Kanaks of the right to justice. The Declercq committee also attacked the ruling on these points: the examining magistrate only gave credence to European witnesses of the massacre (lawyers representing the victims later organised their own reconstruction); the accused had not faced the survivors in a courtroom; no action was taken against other witnesses implicated by witnesses; and the order was not based on judicial grounds, but as a political measure against the FLNKS.[19] The committee also cited other cases where there had been a denial of justice involving Kanaks or the independence movement.

Two men charged over Declercq's assassination were freed without ever facing trial and no further arrests were made. Kanak Security Minister Éloi Machoro and his lieutenant, Marcel Nonaro, were shot dead by police sharpshooters and nobody was charged over the killings.

A week after the Hienghène killers were freed, the league and the Declercq committee called a press conference in Noumea and made public the testimony of the witnesses for the first time. Their evidence was handed to the world human rights groups like Amnesty International and the League of Human Rights. In Paris, four leading French lawyers went on television to denounce a miscarriage of justice, political "manipulation" and appealed to President Mitterrand to intervene. Countering this, a new right-wing settler group calling itself the Patriotic Action Committee (CAP) sent an open letter to Mitterrand and Prime Minister Jacques Chirac urging them to uphold magistrate Semur's ruling.

Ironically, the scandal over the release of the killers broke while Jean-Marie Tjibaou was at the United Nations lobbying to help the South Pacific Forum's case for New Caledonian independence. At the time of the killings, Tjibaou, grieving over the loss of two brothers, declared:

> Since the beginning of the colonial times it has always been Kanaks who die. During our present campaign 10 have died on our side with two seriously wounded in hospital—and one white has died. My father's mother was killed by soldiers' bullets and colonisation is still trying to destroy the Kanak people.
>
> This speech [Hienghène] with rifles is the same as existed in the United States, in Australia. And it's in Tasmania—where there are no more blacks— that it worked best.[20]

Tjibaou's moderate stance came under severe pressure as a result of the *non-lieu*. Then the fragile truce collapsed at the eastern mining town of Thio. A pro-independence stronghold and symbol of resistance under the grip of Machoro before his death, the township was chosen by the anti-independence National Front RPCR for a provocative rally in November 1986 which ended in a shoot-out. (*Caldoche* extremists set fire to a pro-independence bakery on 16 November 1986; shooting broke out with one 14-year-old white boy dying and 12 people wounded.) Four days later, cars belonging to barrister Tehio and his brother-in-law, Claude Le Ray, an FLNKS official, were firebombed in an attempt to frighten them into abandoning the case.

The attack coincided with the surprise appeal tribunal ruling on 20 November that the seven Hienghène killers had to stand trial. A three-judge tribunal ruled the slaughter was premeditated and the freed settlers must be put in the dock.[21]

Nouméa's infamous Camp Nou prison on the Île Nou, January 2012. The old walls of the *ancien* jail for political prisoners transported to the colony are enclosed within the new penitentiary surrounds.   DAVID ROBIE

But the accused remained at liberty until the trial, almost a year later. "It's a matter of too little, too late," complained Jean-Pierre Deteix, a spokesman for the League of Human Rights. "All those implicated should stand trial."

When the trial began on 19 October 1987 it was not in Noumea's Palais de la Justice because the main wing of the law courts had been destroyed in a bomb attack two years earlier by settlers in an attempt to get the accused freed. Instead, the Assize Court heard the case amid tight security in a hilltop cultural centre overlooking the port and the French High Commission.

Three leading French civil rights lawyers and Tehio represented the survivors and the families of the victims. They included Francois Roux, who defended Tahitian independence leaders Pouvanaa a Oopa and Charlie Ching, and French League of Human Rights vice-president Michael Tubiana. "Public feeling among settlers in this mainly European city is so strong for the accused," said Deteix, "it is hard to see how an unbiased jury can be chosen."

Calling for sentences of nine and seven years for the accused, public prosecutor Henri Lucazeau described the killings as ritual executions—"a psychosis and collective intoxication for [murder]". The ambush, he said was planned and premeditated: "All the dead were found face down on the ground or in the river and they were riddled with bullets and lead shot."

In court, the accused denied having told the examining magistrate that they had deployed themselves in "combat formation". Or that they had confessed to hunting down their victims with dogs and searchlights. They claimed, instead, to have stood and shot without moving. One said, "We shot at shadows. I couldn't tell the difference between the cows and the people."[22]

Not surprisingly, 10 days later the jury of nine (all white except one part-Indonesian woman) acquitted the killers. After considering the evidence for two hours, including time out for dinner, the jurors returned a verdict of "legitimate self-defence". The not guilty ruling was greeted by applause, cries of Vive la France! and singing of *La Marseillaise* from settlers who packed the courtroom. In a cruel contrast, scores of the several hundred Kanaks gathered outside the building wept.

"Kanaks can now be gunned down like pigs," said Tjibaou. "There will be no justice in New Caledonia before independence." The FLNKS branded the acquittal the most "infamous, abject and unbearable affront possible against Kanaks," which threatened to lead to a "situation of extreme violence". It added the verdict had "inflicted the most extreme humiliation upon the Kanak people" and "opens the door to barbarism".

ABOUT 1000 Kanaks marched peacefully through Nouméa and staged a peaceful sit-in protest outside the gates of the High Commission after the widely condemned verdicts. Lawyers for the victims' families prepared appeals to the World Court and the European Court of Justice.

But who were the real winners and who the losers? The seven killers may have won the legal battle, but their "war" was irredeemably lost. They and their families could no longer go home, their subsistence farming lifestyle ruined. They were condemned to live in a drab high-rise apartment block outside Nouméa where they existed on a meagre pension and handouts from the right-wing National Front.

Ten graves in Tiendanite's cemetery today remind the villagers of the night a massacre cut down most of their menfolk—and their denial of justice. At Wan`yaat, on Mitride's former farm, the ambushed trucks are mounted in concrete as a memorial to their sacrifice. Among the billowing strips of traditional cloth—or traditional *bois tabou*—tied to the rusting vehicles is a simple, marble slab inscribed with the epitaph:

> *Give your blood. Give your life. For the beloved land.*
> *Your brothers. Your widows. Your young children weep.*
> *In a supreme gesture, you were offered in a holocaust*

And cried liberty.
You have gone. Keep in your memory
That the conquest of Kanaky
Is written in letters of blood forever.

Notes

1   Alaine Chanter (1998). A better way forward: research on media and violence in the Pacific. *Asia Pacific Media Educator*, 4: 8–23.

2   *Les Nouvelles Caledoniènnes*, 2 October 1986.

3   Chanter (1998), p. 16.

4   Ibid., p. 17.

5   *Bwenando*, November 1987.

6   Ibid.

7   Attempt To Reconstruct the Crime (1986). Pierre Declercq Committee, 8 October.

8   David Robie (1989). The massacre of Hienghène. *Blood on their Banner: Nationalist Struggles in the South Pacific*. London: Zed Books; Sydney: Pluto Press, pp. 105–15.

9   The Declecq Committee Report.

10 Ibid.

11 Ibid.

12 Ibid.

13 Ibid.

14 The 10 victims were Antoine Couhia, Michel Couhia, Simileon Couhia, Éloi Maepas, Mickael Maepas, Pascal Mandjia, Louis Tjibaou, Alphonse Wathea and Auguste Wathea.

15 *La rivière pleure* is a poem dedicated to the victims of the Hienghène massacre; from a collection of revolutionary poetry by Kanak activist and later cabinet minister Déwé Gorode, *Sous les cendres des conques* (1985). Nouméa: Edipop.

16 David Robie (1985, January). Slaughter in the moonlight. *Islands Business*, p. 12.

17 The accused claimed the first shot was fired from the Chevrolet pickup. But the only gun recovered from the trucks was found charred in the Mitsubishi, wedged behind the driver's seat, with one bullet in the chamber. It had not been fired. No trace of a gun was found in the Chevrolet.

18 James McNeish (1986, November 15). The road to Tiendanite. *New Zealand Listener.*

19 David Robie (1986, November). Mockery of justice, *Islands Business*, p. 37.

20 Robie (1986). Slaughter in the moonlight, p. 12.

21 David Robie (1986). Aftermath of Hienghène *Islands Business*, p. 31.

22 David Robie (1987, October 19). Massacre accused in dock, *The Dominion.*

7

Rise of the Flosse dynasty in Tahiti, 1986

For several weeks, a torrent of lies, defamation and insults have been heaped on the voters by the opposition. But you cannot build a country on hatred.

Flosse party newspaper *Te Tahoeraa*

ONE political cartoon depicted Tahitian President Gaston Flosse as a vampire. A potted "species" note in an opposition party newspaper, *Te Teo o Tamuitahiraa*, described him as *Flossilus vampirus* and added that he easily mistook the party colour, orange, for gold.[1] Another cartoon displayed him as a giant crab scuttling off with a pile of money. Yet another portrayed the president as Bokaflossa I, after deposed Central African emperor-for-life Bokassa—with the party slogan "always more for myself". A fourth caricature showed him as a traditional Tahitian high chief with slaves offering him the French airline UTA and the fuel tanker *Petrocean* on a plate.

That was more than a quarter of a century ago, in 1986, when Gaston Flosse was already starting to dominate Tahitian politics. But although he has been President of French Polynesia five times and was the incumbent, while also being a senator in the French National Assembly, when this book was being written, the epithets are perhaps even more appropriate today. On 21 June 2006, he was convicted of corruption and given a three-month suspended sentence.[2] In February 2013, he was given a further four-year suspended sentence for corruption and his hold on the presidency looks rather tenuous.[3]

At the time of the political cartoons cited here, I was reporting a cover story for *Islands Business* magazine on French Polynesia and I noted that rarely in any previous Tahitian election had a personality become such a target for cartoonists and satirists. Flosse largely ignored the critical barbs, as he has done ever since, determined to make his reply through the ballot box. But then he could afford to. Most of the local mass media supported him and his opponents were forced to attack through small-circulation party newspapers—and the coconut wireless. However, occasionally the criticism stung and he retaliated.

An editorial in Flosse's Tahoeraa Huiraatira party paper *Te Tahoeraa* recalled the words of Archbishop Michel Coppenrath, head of the Catholic Church in Tahiti, at the beginning of the election campaign: "Say and do what you wish, carry out your campaign work, but respect the inhabitants of our country and don't oppose them. Peace above all."

But the editorial failed to deflate the scathing satire. Some of the attacks were witty rather than wretched. One satirical commentary in *Te Reo* about a meeting between Gaullist envoy Bernard Pons and Flosse portrayed the relationship like this:

> "Gaston, are you Gaullist?"
> "Yes, long live De Gaulle."
> "Fine Gaston, but do you truly know what Gaullism is?"
> "... Not very well. Can you just fill me in a little?"
> "A true Gaullist must hold the interests of the state above all and the public interest must take precedence over private interest ... The chief who represents his country must have a dignified attitude, noble, heroic if it is needed, and when required must sacrifice himself completely for the nation ... He must have a higher goal of leading his people and show an example ... Gaston, do you really want to be a Gaullist?"
> "No, actually, I would rather not. I'm more Flossiste than Gaullist. *Vive* myself. *Vive* Flosse!"[4]

FLOSSE'S IRON GRIP

Islands Business, April 1986

SOME brand him the Pacific's "Papa Doc"; others regard him as the man with a vision which will turn Tahiti into the economic and cultural showpiece of the region.

For two decades Gaston Flosse has been the mayor of the affluent Pape'ete suburb of Pirae. Ten years ago [1976], he was the Speaker of the Tahitian Territorial Assembly. But the real start of his phenomenal rise to power was four years ago when his neo-Gaullist party, Tahoeraa Huiraatira, wrested control from the jaded Front Uni coalition of Francis Sanford. Since then, the 54-year-old businessman has consolidated his power in such a devastating way that his opponents are bitterly talking of "another Haiti", a dictatorship or one-party rule.

A younger Gaston Flosse during the 1986 election campaign. He went on to dominate Tahitian politics for more than two decades.   DAVID ROBIE

In 1985 he assumed the title of President of French Polynesia with the authority of a prime minister under a statute reform, which granted the territory considerable self-government powers. And barely three days after his crushing defeat of the fragmented Tahitian opposition parties at the polls in March 1986, he was named by incoming French Prime Minister Jacques Chirac to the newly created post of State Secretary for Pacific Affairs.[5] It was a triumph for his platform of internal autonomy for Tahiti and a greater say in French Pacific policy by Islanders. Already he is being touted as the powerbroker of the region.

Delighted, Flosse praised Chirac for keeping his pledge. "I've aready told him," he added, "that I would only accept the job providing he gave me the means necessary to apply the policies of France in the Pacific."

But, warned his opponents, the move increased his powers to an unhealthy degree. He would, for example, hold senior ranking to the French High Commissioner in Pape`ete. "Chirac has just given Flosse a baby's rattle to play with for a while—he'll have no real power in the Pacific," snapped Jacques Drollet, leader of the pro-independence party Ia Mana Te Nunaa. "And, in any case, the Chirac government won't last a year."

Personality attacks against Flosse have been the most savage ever seen in an election campaign. Although his policies have meant a giant economic leap forward, his critics claim only supporters of the party have cashed in. Even when Flosse turned the tables on his opponents on polling day, 16 March 1986, by becoming the first Tahitian leader in 30 years to win an outright majority in an election, the nasty barbs continued.

Tahoeraa Huiraatira, which won power through a coalition in 1982, retained office with 21 seats, a majority of one in an expanded 41-seat Territorial Assembly. (The number later rose to 22 when an Electoral Office ruling gave Tahoeraa another seat.) The vote also gave the *indépendantistes* a surprise success.[6]

But, alleged Flosse's opponents, Tahoeraa achieved its win by "buying" votes with favours and gifts of building materials for Islanders on many of the 120 small outlying island and atolls in Polynesia. The opponents also claimed that an electoral reform had gerrymandered the remote islands, which cover an area of the Pacific almost as large as Australia, to Tahoeraa's advantage.

"It is an outrage that Tahoeraa should win a majority in the Assembly with a minority of the votes," said Quito Braun-Ortega, one of the leaders of opposition coalition Amuitahiraa No Polinesia. "We cannot accept this result. On the Windward Islands of Tahiti and Moorea, where two-thirds of French Polynesia's 160,000 population live, Tahoeraa won just over a third of the vote. Yet this was still enough to gain nine seats out of the 22 at stake. Overall, Tahoeraa won 40 percent of the 74,000 votes cast. (A record 105,000 voters were registered.)

By the end of the week, Ortega's accusations had become increasingly bitter. He declared the "real majority" would resist Flosse's government and said the electoral law was "unjust and scandalous". Pape`ete mayor Jean Juventin, leader of another key opposition party, Here Ai`a, added: "A real fight is starting." The seven opposition parties held a series of meetings to consider a strategy for seeking an annulment of the results, particularly in the Tuamotus, where Tahoeraa won four crucial seats.

Ortega accused Tahoeraa of using state funds and the territorial institutions for the benefit of the electoral campaign. There was also talk of occupying the Territorial Assembly building in protest so that the new Parliament could not convene on March 27.

With Flosse and Vice-President Alexandre Leontieff away in Paris to meet Chirac, Tahiti's Minister of Internal Affairs, Patrick Peaucellier, called a media conference in which he accused Amuitahiraa of using "seditious language" in challenging the election results. Defending the electoral law, he said: "Tahiti isn't a banana republic where *coup d'etats* can take place any old time."

It was a grave situation when the opposition could talk about taking to the streets. Peaucellier said the opposition lacked political maturity. He warned the government would not tolerate any attempted occupation of the Territorial

Assembly, as happened in 1976 when Front Uni assemblymen were agitating against Paris for reforms.

However, the socialist Ia Mana Te Nunaa also formally accused Tahoeraa of electoral corruption and demanded a territorial commission of inquiry. "With only 40 percent of the vote, Tahoeraa has obtained its victory by corruption—and I weigh my words carefully," said Drollet. His proposed commission would have three government members with three from the opposition and would be given three months to investigate the election campaign.

"If it doesn't have anything to hide," added Drollet, "Tahoeraa should be happy to have the inquiry. If it opposes it then our suspicions are confirmed. But I maintain there has been massive corruption."

Criticism on a similar theme has persisted over the last few months. One Paris newspaper, *Liberation*, published a full-page article in January citing the alleged corruption. Flosse responded by filing a defamation suit against the paper. An issue of the party paper, *Te Tahoeraa*, also denied the allegations in a report headed: "Monsieur 10 percent doesn't exist." It also quoted Drollet telling Agence France-Presse: "None of the accusations against Flosse to this day have been substantiated. Nobody has been able to prove anything."[7]

The electoral allegations have centred on two government agencies, the $10 million Islands Aid Fund (FEI) set up in 1984 to help develop the outer islands, and the Territorial Reconstruction Agency (ATR), established after hurricane devastation in 1983. ATR has built more than 1000 houses for the homeless.

However, the opposition claims that some houses or building materials have benefitted party supporters while many Tahitian homeless remain without a place. *Fei* is also the Tuamotu word for the special kind of red banana used as the party symbol for Tahoeraa. So in the minds of many Islanders, development work done by the FEI was immediately associated with personal assistance from Flosse's party.

The opposition claimed the government abused its powers by using both FEI and ATR to further its electoral prospects. Ortega also accused the French administration of being at least "ambivalent" over the election and having contributed to the alleged fraud.

Flosse rejected the allegations, saying: "They're absolutely false." He denounced the local newspapers and television station for "encouraging" the attacks. He also pointed out the electoral law had been in use for several years. "You know very well there hasn't been any fraud," he told *La Dépêche*. "The best proof is at Pirae, where a magistrate was present and in charge of scrutineering. The same at Pape'ete, at Faa'a … in all the big centres a magistrate was present. It's the Opposition which was carrying out a fraud."

But the electoral figures, as cited by Ortega, were hard to ignore. "Nobody had time to seriously study the implications of the new electoral law," said Ortega. "But what it means is that a voter from the remote Austral or Tuamotu islands is equal to three voters from Tahiti. What sort of democracy is this?" In effect, it took about 2400 votes to win a seat on Tahiti and only about 800 votes on outer islands.

The opposition won 63 percent of the votes in the Windward Islands (Tahiti and Moorea) against Tahoeraa's 37 percent; more than 54 percent on the Leeward Islands, against Flosse's less than 46 percent; more than 54 percent in the Tuamotus (against 45.5 percent) and more than 57 percent in the Australs (against nearly 43 percent). It was only in the Marquesas where Tahoeraa actually won a majority of votes (more than 66 percent against 34 percent for the opposition).

In the most "scandalous" case, Tahoeraa won four out of five seats in the Tuamotus with 45 percent of the vote. The other seat was won by Tapuro Napo, the one-man-band party of Napoleon Spitz, who later announced he would support Tahoeraa. The Tuamotus were the islands that benefitted most from FEI's development assistance.

"We cannot confer power on a minority which has so clearly been rejected by most Tahitians," said Ortega. "Or the Tahitian people are in danger of revolting like in the Philippines. We hope the state will have the wisdom to realise this." But there seemed to be little hope of a "grand coalition" of opposition parties as Ortega had hoped—the differences were too great. "This idea is a *moe moea*—a big dream," scoffed Drollet.

"There isn't much difference between Amuitahiraa and Tahoeraa—it's just a struggle between money and money." The opposition looked likely to settle into three factions with the Assembly line-up as follows:

Government:	seats
Tahoeraa Huiraatira	22
Tapuro Napo	1

Opposition:	
Amuitahiraa No Polinesia	6
Here Ai'a Taatira	4
Ia Mana Te Nunaa	3
Tavini Huiraatira	2
A'a No Maohinui	1
Ora Api O Tahaa	1
Tamarii Tuhaapae	1

Amuitahiraa and Here Ai`a, the party once led by the late exiled nationalist leader Pouvanaa a Oopa and then John Teariki before his death in 1983, were expected to form two major opposition blocs. Ia Mana and Tavini Huiraatira's

A Tahoeraa Huiraatira supporter having a sleep outside a Pape'ete polling booth in 1986.
DAVID ROBIE

Oscar Temaru, the rising star of Faa`a, were likely to form a pro-independence bloc with the possible support of Maohini, elder statesman Francis Sanford's one-time party now led by Senator Daniel Millaud. Tutuha Salmon (Tahoeraa) and Jean Juventin lost their deputy seats in the French National Assembly. They both went to Tahoeraa, the first time a Tahitian party had won the "double".

Gaston Flosse and Alexandre Leontieff, the President's technocrat right-hand man, were to fill them. However, Flosse's post in the French cabinet meant he would have to surrender his deputy's seat, which went to his son-in-law, Edouard Fritch, the 34-year-old Mines and Energy Minister.

The well-oiled Tahoeraa Huiraatira political machine, backed by local and multinational business interests, steamrollered its way through the election campaign in a way not seen elsewhere in South Pacific elections. Estimates of the election bill, including campaign costs, ranged between a massive $1 million and $5 million. Using American-style razzamatazz, Tahoeraa imported 17,000 orange-coloured T-shirts from Korea for the party faithful, staged village extravaganzas with pop singers, balloons and bands, and even built a temporary stadium with seating for 7000 people on Pape`ete's harbour-front Quai de Commerce for a one-night rally. Quite a sight for the cruise ship *Liberty* when it docked alongside the quay.

As a final election eve carrot, Flosse pledged to build cheap housing to provide adequate homes for all poor Polynesians. But this was a sore point with some

Francis Sanford, the *metua* (father) whose retirement from politics at the end of 1985 helped pave the way for the Gaston Flosse era: "I fear for the future of Tahiti."   DAVID ROBIE

political leaders who were already asking embarrassing questions about why many Tahitians remained homeless after the big hurricanes of 1983 had left more than 5000 people without housing.

Even the daily newspapers, *La Dépêche* and *Les Nouvelles*, were partisan during the campaign in support of Flosse. An independent newspaper, *Le Nouveau Journal de Polynesie*, was due to be launched at the beginning of March, but the Flosse government reportedly blocked delivery of the printing press until after the elections.

Tahiti has by far the highest living standards—for some—of any South Pacific nation or territory. It has more than 40,000 cars, 20,000 television sets and the most comprehensive social welfare system. The Tahitian budget totals $200 million a year and cabinet ministers are far more highly paid than in the independent Pacific nations, about $120,000 a year. In addition, France pumps in more than $500 million a year to cover a major part of the civil service sector and the nuclear Pacific Experiments Centre (CEP).

During the campaign, Ortega offered a political platform based on "integrity … competence" and declared Tahiti would remain a part of the French republic for at least five years. He was a hard-driving lieutenant for Emile Vernaudon, the "sheriff" mayor of Mahina who helped Flosse to power in 1982 and then split.

Gaston Flosse warned Tahitians against the "political amateurism" and irresponsibility of his opponents. "All they do is nit-pick about our ideas and our programme," he sneered. "They hurl invective and hate at us, abuse us and defame us ... all without proof." And the party's 200-page manifesto was a document of progress, which the opposition couldn't match.

Outside the polling booths of Faa`a, the airport township on the outskirts of Pape`ete, a former Tahitian head of government nodded sadly to me. "I fear for the future of Tahiti," said Francis Sanford, the *metua* (father) whose retirement from politics at the end of 1985 helped precipitate the elections more than a year early. "Big money is now ruling Tahiti and there are serious social troubles ahead."

Millaud, the man who took over the leadership of Sanford's party, said his objective was to put an end to scandal and return morality to public life. "It's the Paris town hall which has been running things here," he said (Chirac is mayor of Paris).

The historic success of Flosse winning a majority didn't detract from the remarkable gains made by the parties seeking independence and an end to nuclear tests. Their share of the vote doubled to 20 percent.

Oscar Manutahi Temaru, the charismatic mayor of Faa'a, led his party Tavini Huiraatira No Porinesia to win two seats. Campaigning on the slogans INDEPENDENCE TOMORROW and GOD IS OUR LEADER with the Christian cross as his party symbol, Temaru drew large crowds to his rallies. He is regarded as potentially the most powerful force to emerge in Tahitian politics since Pouvanaa.

"France is going to be forced to listen to us and respond now that we are in Parliament," he warned. Temaru has embarrassed French authorities in the past three years with pro-independence and anti-nuclear rallies. Earlier in March, a New Zealand peace campaigner, Annie Maignot, and a West German member of the European Parliament, Dorothy Piermont, were expelled for addressing a Faa`a rally at the invitation of Temaru. He also has close links with the Kanak Socialist National Liberation Front (FLNKS) in New Caledonia.

Ia Mana, which made its Assembly debut in the 1982 elections, retained three seats but lost votes to Temaru. "We've only just begun our fight," said Temaru. "Many Tahitians are beginning to hear our message. They had forgotten our independence and our freedom, which has been buried under the corrugated iron and plywood of colonialism."

♪

Pro-independence and regionalist leader Oscar Temaru, committed to a "pan-Pacific" future for Tahiti.   DAVID ROBIE

Bitter power struggle

OSCAR Temaru was as good as his pledge. His pro-independence Tavini Huiraatira (People's Servant Party) and later the Union for Democracy rapidly gained traction with the people of Tahiti and finally ousted the two-decade-old Flosse regime in the May 2004 parliamentary elections. Since then he has faced a bitter struggle with Flosse for power in a fragile political system with both leaders being elected president five times.

I recall the first time I interviewed Temaru in his lively maire of the airport township of Faa`a in 1986, the second-largest in Tahiti with around 23,000 inhabitants, when he was already taking on the part-time mayoral position to seriously improve the lot of poor Tahitians. The son of a Tahitian father and Cook Islands Māori mother, Temaru is committed to a "pan-Pacific" future for Tahiti, not necessarily French. Even to get to see him hadn't been easy. Ready to chat as he is—and his public day starts at six—Tahitians line up by the score, hoping to get a chance to share their problems with the *metua* (father):

His office is simply furnished. On the wall behind him is a picture of Jesus Christ and the new flag of Kanaky. On another wall are posters demanding independence for Guadeloupe, a French territory in the Caribbean, and an end to nuclear testing by President Mitterrand. Opposite him is a declaration by Australian Labor MPs appealing for a halt to the Moruroa nuclear tests.

As I sat waiting, a news item from Nouméa flashed across the television screen: A police raid on the post office had uncovered a network of French phone taps on leading local politicians, both for and against independence.

"That's nothing," snapped one of Temaru's aides. "The French have been bugging us all along."[8]

For Gaston Flosse, the future remains uncertain. Although he has also been a French senator since 1998, the incumbent President of French Polynesia currently risks possible prison time at the age of 81, stiff fines and ineligibility for public office. France 24 journalist Joseph Bamat reported after Flosse's most recent presidential election:

> In January [2013], judges said he took 1.2 million euros in bribes for government contracts between 1993 and 2005. In February, in a separate embezzlement case, he was found guilty for his role in a vast fake jobs scam.
>
> His lawyers filed appeals in both cases, in a move that allowed him to participate in the [May] elections.
>
> Besides politics, Flosse has made a career in dodging justice. The pending charges, which if upheld could send him to prison for five years and have him pay more than 200,000 euros in fines, are only the tip of a mountain of allegations dating back to 2001.
>
> Reacting to Monday's election results, French MP René Dosière, a Socialist, said the results were an embarrassment to France, labelling Flosse "the most corrupt man of the Republic."[9]

The JPK affair

Flosse has also been implicated in accusations over the disappearance of Tahiti journalist Jean-Pascal Couraud, known as "JPK",[10] who was editor-in-chief of *Les Nouvelles* newspaper and investigating corruption allegations against the Flosse administration when he vanished at the age of 37 on 15 December 1997, leaving his wife and two children in despair. Media freedom advocates and other investigators have focused on the likelihood that he was murdered. In June 2013, a Pape`ete investigating judge indicted two members of the local militia Polynesian Intervention Unit (GIP) for the "abduction, sequestration and murder" of Couraud.[11] But a defence lawyer for the two accused Tahitians, Tutu Manate and Tino Mara, called for the charges to be dropped.[12] The pair were charged with kidnapping and murder nine years after JPK's family first filed a complaint with police. The assassination claim was initially made by former spy Vetea Guilloux in 2004. He backed off after being arrested and imprisoned for slander against Flosse, but then he repeated his allegations in 2012 and media reports indicated new evidence had come to light. A French television crew made a damning documentary about the affair, *Troubled Waters in the Pacific*, broadcast on the eve of the 2005 Tahitian elections. JPK was described as an idealist and a "ferocious opponent of Flosse" with a "thirst for justice".[13] Flosse branded the film by journalists Pierre Eurelle and Damien Vercamere as a smear campaign. Flosse was also condemned in a new book in 2013, which portrayed him as a highly ambitious political manipulator "seeking to become king".[14] Supporters of JPK created a Facebook page in the journalist's honour and to highlight updates.[15]

In February 2014, Flosse was charged with abuse of public funds. The case invovles the Pape`ete satellite town of Pirae "paying for the water supply to the Erima neighbourhood", an exclusive community where Flosse and other ex-politicians reside. Flosse denies doing anything illegal, saying the water supply was linked to the French nuclear weapons programme.[16]

Notes

1   David Robie (1986, April). Caricature of a leader. *Islands Business*, p. 14.
2   Former French Polynesian president Flosse gets suspended jail sentence for corruption. (2006, June 21). Radio NZ International. Retrieved on 23 August 2013, from www.rnzi.com/pages/news.php?op=read&id=24909
3   Charles Richardson (2013, May 9). Gaston Flosse back as president for French Polynesia, but tenure dubious. *Pacific Scoop*. Retrieved on 23 August 2013, from http://pacific.scoop.co.nz/2013/05/gaston-flosse-back-as-president-for-polynesia-but-tenure-dubious/
4   Robie (1986, April). Caricature of a leader, p. 14.
5   David Robie (1986, April). Flosse's iron grip [Cover story]. *Islands Business*, pp. 10–20.
6   David Robie (1986, April). Third flag of Faa'a. *Islands Business*, pp. 16–20.
7   Robie (1986, April). Flosse's iron grip, p. 11.
8   Robie (1986, April). Third flag of Faa'a, p. 16–20.
9   Joseph Bamat (2013, May 9). Tahiti's scandal-plagued "Old Lion" bounces back. France 24. Retrieved on 24 August 2013, from www.france24.com/en/20130509-french-polynesia-gaston-flosse-president-wins-election-

corruption-embezzlement

10 Jean-Pascal Couraud used his initials as an alias to sign his vitriolic articles against Gaston Flosse and this became his nickname.

11 Jean-Paul Marthoz (2013, July 11). JPK's disappearance becomes murder case in Tahiti, Committee to Protect Journalists. Retrieved on 24 August 2013, from http://cpj.org/blog/2013/07/journalist-jpk-disappearance-murder-tahiti.php

12 Tahiti defence dismissive of JPK murder charge (2013, June 27). Radio NZ International. Retrieved on 7 January 2014, from www.radionz.co.nz/international/pacific-news/213263/tahiti-defence-dismissive-of-jpk-murder-charge

13 *Troubled Waters in the Pacific* (2005). [Documentary]. English subtitled version available on YouTube. Part 1: www.youtube.com/watch?v=rHWmPNRVMcE; Part 2: www.youtube.com/watch?v=MG3fLj6H1CQ

14 Gerard Davet and Fabrice Lhomme (2013). *L'homme qui voulut être roi*. Paris: Stock.

15 Jean-Pascal Couraud (2014). [Facebook social media page]: www.facebook.com/pages/Jean-Pascal-Couraud/129063783826628

16 President of French Polynesia charged with abuse of public funds (2014, February 21). Radio New Zealand International.

8

French recipe for trouble in Kanaky, 1987

France is using the same tactics in Algeria and Vietnam against us. It is a provocation all the time. They hope our people will react in a violent manner so they can justify the presence of their troops.

Assassinated Kanak leader Jean-Marie Tjibaou

WHEN French Overseas Territories Minister Bernard Pons visited New Caledonia (Kanaky) in February 1987, he was feted by most of the *Caldoche* settlers who were opposed to independence. The message he brought was just what they wanted to hear.

But in the bitterly polarised climate that gripped the colony at the time, Pons was snubbed by the Kanaks seeking independence. They regarded him as a foe who could not be negotiated with. In fact, it was a bilateral snub. As Pons put it: "We have decided almost by mutual agreement that we have nothing more to say to each other."[1]

Even before the Pons plan for the referendum was presented to the National Assembly on February 18, the broad outline was already apparent; the July ballot would ensure French control and the territory's new regions would be gerrymandered to the disadvantage of Kanaks. The plan was due to be debated in the National Assembly in April 1987.

Three days before Pons arrived in New Caledonia, a congress of the Kanak Socialist National Liberation Front (FLNKS) was held at the northern village of Arama. Although it established guidelines for FLNKS strategy to be adopted towards Paris, it refrained from announcing the expected boycott of the referendum. Instead, the FLNKS directed energy into exposing the Pons plan as a farce and seeking United Nations and Pacific Islands Forum help in achieving a referendum formula that would be more favourable to independence. The Kanak leadership also wanted Paris to name a new negotiator if any serious dialogue was to be possible.

Kanak leaders claimed that France was seeking revenge for the December vote by the United Nations General Assembly to relist New Caledonia with the Decolonisation Committee by strangling the regional economic and political structure set up by the previous Socialist French government.[2]

The French military were also being accused of using a strategy of "nomad-isation" based on techniques used to try to crush insurgents in the Algerian War of Independence in an attempt to provoke pro-independence Kanak villages into violent reaction so that Paris could undermine FLNKS credibility by portraying it as a "terrorist" movement.

"Kanaky looks like an occupied country," said FLNKS leader Jean-Marie Tjibaou who was also president of the Northern Region local government. "The troops everywhere is just like France at the end of the Second World War. The present French government has virtually declared war on us."

Prime Minister Jacques Chirac's government also directed its pique against the Pacific Islands Forum, singling out Australia and Vanuatu for punitive action. Aid to Vanuatu was slashed while ministerial visits between Canberra and Paris were suspended. The most bewildering of French acts towards Australia was the expulsion of Consul-General John Dauth from Nouméa in January 1987. Allegations were made that he had disbursed sums of money in New Caledonia in "inappropriate" ways and that he had gone too far with supporting the FLNKS.[3]

Describing the expulsion as "capricious" and "totally unjustified", Australian Foreign Minister Bill Hayden rejected the allegations. He cited discretionary fund payments, including $4500 to the Kanak Cultural Centre of the north-eastern town of Hienghène, and "circumspect and quite limited" contacts with FLNKS leaders, which were in line with Australian policy.

Curiously, New Zealand was spared the repercussions from the UN vote. Although a planned visit of Tahitian President Gaston Flosse, who was also French Secretary of State for Pacific Affairs, to Australia was cancelled, he had still been due to visit New Zealand to try to improve French relations with Wellington in the wake of the *Rainbow Warrior* bombing. But Prime Minister David Lange scrapped the visit after Flosse resigned from his position as president.

It was in this context that I arrived in New Caledonia in February 1987, one of my many trips as a journalist visiting the territory. This time I had planned to do a series of articles, including exposing the "nomadisation" policy. Portraits of the incumbent President (François Mitterrand at the time) usually adorn most French town halls and public offices, even in New Caledonia and Nouméa. But in three out of four regional government offices in New Caledonia, controlled by the FLNKS, Mitterrand was nowhere to be seen. Instead, photographs of Éloï Machoro, the martyred Kanak schoolteacher and FLNKS Security Minister shot by French sharpshooters on 12 January 1985, were proudly displayed.

Éloï Machoro, an iconic figure of the 1984 insurrection, with the axe that he used to chop open a ballot box.   DAVID ROBIE

Machoro was one of the charismatic and iconic figures of the 1984 insurrection against French rule. His portraits are a reminder to Kanaks that his sacrifice was not in vain. But to the *Caldoche* settlers, he represented the "evil" that would end French rule in the South Pacific territory. He had to be stopped and it was a great relief to them when he was assassinated in the siege of a farmhouse near La Foa.[4]

While reporting on these events and the military "nomadisation" policy, I became an unwelcome journalist and faced harassment by authorities for two weeks. I was even detained at gunpoint by the French military near the village of Canala, on the first of two occasions in 1987 when I was arrested by the gendarmerie and military. I wrote about this experience in a two-page article in *Islands Business* magazine, which was also published on the front page of the *New Zealand Times* and the *Times on Sunday* in Australia. The affair was narrated in my 1989 book *Blood on their Banner*:

> It began like something out of a B-grade police comedy. As the French say in New Caledonia, "*c'est le cinema*". But the funny side quickly turned sour.
>
> At first, the French authorities gave me a two-hour grilling at Tontouta international airport. A police "welcome squad" awaited me

"'A subversive in Kanaky'", an article about David Robie's first arrest by the French military in February 1987. Published in the February edition of *Islands Business*, pp. 22–23.

at the arrival lounge when I flew in to cover political developments in the South Pacific [territory] leading up to this year's referendum on independence and the military "nomadisation" of Kanak villages in the *brousse* [bush].

Then I was tailed constantly and kept under surveillance by security police in Noumea. Later, I was actually arrested by soldiers armed with automatic rifles, submachineguns and bayonets near the eastern township of Canala and interrogated incommunicado for four hours ... The deputy commander of [Canala gendarmerie] ... accused me of taking unauthorised photographs of military installations, loosely using the world "espionage" ... Although calm, at one point [during the interrogation] I snapped, "Is this a democracy?"

The officer replied, "No, this is France ..."

"*Non ... non, ici c'est Kanaky!* [This is Kanaky]," interrupted Edmond Kawa [an FLNKS official with me]. The gendarme gave him a warning.[5]

I was given no official answers about why I was detained like this and handed by the military to the local gendarmerie, especially as I had informed the French High Commission in Nouméa before arriving and had requested interviews with officials and high-ranking officers. But it seems that there was still a lot of sensitivity about my book *Eyes of Fire* on the *Rainbow Warrior* bombing by French secret agents published the year before.[6] Here is one of my articles about "nomadisation".

"NOMADISATION": OCCUPATION OR PROTECTION?

Islands Business, March 1987

SNOWY-HAIRED Maurice Lenormand burst into the room, angry. Brandishing a tattered old copy of the *Revue Militaire d'Information*, the former deputy of New Caledonia, one of the first *Caldoche* to advocate independence, thrust it in front of his colleagues.[7]

Lenormand told the members of the Kanak Socialist National Liberation Front (FLNKS) political bureau that he had discovered in the January 1957 issue of the magazine an article explaining the "nomadisation" military strategy used for repression in the Algerian War of Independence.[8]

It noted how "nomad" mobile units, led by elite troops in action against the Algerian "rebels", countered the "Marxist-Leninist doctrine of revolutionary war" and prepared "pacification". Once established in controlling strategic points, the soldiers divided and "mastered" the local population. The article said:

> This control could be achieved in different ways. The most efficient was to set up a network of small active posts so the garrisons are able to get to know the local population. But it isn't always possible to use this system: it's a serious mistake, in effect, to establish posts too weak, which can quickly become encircled and threatened.
>
> It is better that the quality of the troops enables "nomadisation", which has the advantage of keeping the rebels guessing about the activity of our detachments or setting up big camps far too strong to attack ... Experience proves that the only way to control the population is to live close by all the time.[9]

Lenormand found this article in May 1986. The previous month, the French military had embarked on a new strategy in New Caledonia involving setting up small mobile camps. Ten months later, the east coast and northern tip of the main island, Grand Terre, appear to be under the yolk of an army of occupation. More than 20 "nomad" camps of elite troops have been established in strategic villages known to have strong pro-independence support.

France has about 6000 troops, gendarmes and riot police in the territory—one for every 24 civilians in a population of 145,000. The military claim only about 1100 "nomad" soldiers are on the east coast but during a week-long tour of villages in the area, I estimated considerably more. The 8th Marine Infantry Paratrooper Regiment was among the first units deployed in the mobile camps. Less than a year previously, the regiment intervened against Libyan-backed rebels in Chad. A year before that it was in Beirut.

In 1987, France had about 6000 troops, gendarmes and riot police in New Caledonia—one for every 24 civilians in a population then of 145,000.   DAVID ROBIE

Both the black-beret 3rd Marine Infantry Regiment and the red-beret 6th Marine Infantry Paratrooper Regiment are currently providing nomad patrols. And off-duty soldiers usually outnumber the tourists on the beaches of Nouméa.

"It's just like Algeria all over again—France never learns from its colonial history," said Jean-Jacques Bourdinat, 51, a Sydney-educated fourth-generation *Caldoche*. A human rights campaigner and supporter of the FLNKS. He had just heard of the occupation of the remote Belep Islands by paratroopers during January 1987 in the latest military operation.

"This is crazy. We are the powder keg of the Pacific and the military carry on as if they are already at war. They are determined to crush us; if not by intimidation, then by provocation."

But General Michel Franceschi, commander-in-chief of French forces in New Caledonia, rejected comparisons with Algeria. He said the military had restored law and order and earned respect from Kanaks by providing them with aid and protecting them from attack from heavily armed, white anti-independence vigilantes.

"We would have had a problem with revolution here," he said. "The context here has been a little explosive. What we are doing is a matter of security. If we hadn't acted, I believe there would have been violence in the tribal areas. We are reassuring the people. It's an old military principle—nothing new."

A French "nomadisation" military camp at Negropo, near Canala, on the east coast of Grand Terre. Shortly after this photograph was taken, the author was arrested at gunpoint in 1987.

DAVID ROBIE

Franceschi, 56, a two-star general, took command in New Caledonia three months before the rebellion by Kanaks following the 18 November 1984 election boycott. At that time, the military took no direct role in law and order apart from guarding key communications and strategic installations, and providing transport for squads of *gardes mobiles* (paramilitary police).

In fact, under the French system the military usually can only act against an external enemy. The task of maintaining law and order is up to the gendarmes and *gardes mobiles* but the distinction is becoming blurred in New Caledonia.

A change of policy began less than a month after Prime Minister Jacques Chirac's conservative government replaced the Socialists in March 1986. As nomad camps were set up in the *brousse* (bush), fewer paramilitary police were needed.

The FLNKS claims the strategy to "win the hearts and minds" of the people is a disguise for intimidating Kanak villagers and gathering intelligence on local independence leaders and any fresh Kanak campaign tactics.

"Not at all," said Franceschi. "The army is not political. Political problems are the government's problems. We are not there to say to the Kanaks, 'You must vote in the referendum.' It is merely a matter of security. Our soldiers perform useful tasks locally, like carrying out road works and providing transport. Another job of the military in the region is to do humanitarian tasks like the hurricane relief work provided by our soldiers in Wallis and Futuna and the Cook Islands."

A Kanak youth searching a vehicle for weapons at a pro-independence road block in 1984 before the French "nomadisation" campaign took effect.   DAVID ROBIE

Franceschi claimed there had been few incidents of tension between soldiers and Kanaks, a view that isn't shared by villagers I talked to or the FLNKS leadership. Among recent incidents:

- On 6 September 1986, 17-year-old Jean-Christophe Poupeyron was shot and wounded by a lieutenant in the village of Nakety on the east coast. An inquiry was hushed up and the soldier posted back to France without facing any disciplinary action.
- Kanaks in several villages on the west coast have accused soldiers of having entered and searched houses on the pretext of hunting for Kanaks dodging the military draft, or of looking for stolen firearms.
- Troops in the Houailou area have been involved in harassment raids. On 8 January 1987, a company of 60 *gardes mobile* raided and occupied the agricultural college of Do-neva, which belongs to the pro-independence Evangelical Church. Teacher Ismet Kurtovitch was arrested and held for 48 hours before being released.
- On 16 January 1987, 104 paratroopers and other soldiers, and 20 *gardes mobile*, occupied the Belep islands off the north-western tip of Grand Terre to "nomadise" the area. The islands are one of the most peaceful parts of New Caledonia with a population of 900, mainly women and children. Faced with bitter protests by Kanak leaders, the soldiers were withdrawn a week later.

Military authorities are reluctant to talk to foreign journalists about the operations in the bush. However, four months ago a small group of journalists was given a briefing and taken on tour. Kanak leaders accuse the military of staging a public relations "whitewash" because the journalists were shepherded away from troubled villages. According to one account in the *International Herald Tribune*, paratroopers were now pruning coffee trees, hauling road metal and "studying" the 13,000 Kanaks in the 75 *tribus* (tribal villages) under their jurisdiction.[10]

"When we first arrived, they said we would rape the women, kill the men and bring AIDS to the country," the newspaper quoted one paratrooper as saying.[11] "They described us as the killers of Indochina." The paper added that the men were brought in to Goyetta, near the east coast nickel plant of Poro, for a "totally novel mission for the regiment".

Said a colonel: "There was little left here when we arrived. No butchers, no food, spare parts or repair facilities. Now the tension has eased. Our presence has reassured both sides and people come to us for help on all sorts of problems."

But almost all Kanaks that I spoke to were anxious about the presence of troops. A sculptor from Canala, called Alphonse, bitterly attacked the soldiers:[12] "Sending them here is an excuse to hound us and oppress us. They claim they are helping us. But actually they are spying on us; gathering information ready for the day they want to waste us," he said.

"They are mapping our bush tracks, searching for guns so we will be defenceless, smashing their way into homes at night and chasing our young women."

Instead of making contact with villagers, said Alphonse, the soldiers remained aloof and were often racist. He said the troops were on only a three-month tour of duty and were rotated between nomad camps frequently so that they had little time to form friendships with villagers. "They do this so that when the time comes for them to move against us, it will be easy," he said. "And they will know how to track down our leaders in any resistance."

Several villages have protested or filed petitions against the presence of soldiers—in vain. One protest letter signed by several villagers from Ponerihouen said: "The important activities of the troops include preparing maps of our tracks, showing a pornographic film (in a church in the presence of women, children and elderly people) and spying on us."

One of the biggest sources of tension between the military and the people of Canala was the Poupeyron affair. Accounts of what happened differ sharply between the official military version and the villagers. According to the military, Poupeyron was shot when a group of youths who had been drinking heavily stoned two soldiers in a Jeep on the road into Nakety village, near Canala. The lieutenant fired into the air and wounded Poupeyron accidentally because he was standing on the rise of a hill.

French Pacific Regiment troops preparing for parade in the streets of Nouméa in 1987.

DAVID ROBIE

Villagers reject this story. Eyewitnesses told me the group of youths had cynically offered the soldiers a beer as they drove into the village to speak to the chief to arrange a football match. As the jeep left, Poupeyron gave a rude gesture to the soldiers with his forearm. The lieutenant swung around in his seat, aimed his pistol, shot Poupeyron in the stomach and then drove off.

The eyewitnesses point out there was no hill, as the military claimed, and there were no stones on the road. The conflict in the military account was pointed out to the investigators but the inquiry was dropped.

"They claim they are here to help us and respect our traditions—but the soldiers just do what they like," said Joseph Bouarate, deputy mayor of Hienghène. "It is an arrogant colonialism." (His grandfather, a great chief, was exiled for seven years for defying French authority.)

A nomad post is situated about 30 kilometres up a rugged mountain track in the valley of Hienghène River. According to the military, the soldiers are there to help build an all-weather road from Hienghène River to the mining township of Kaala-Gomen to improve communications between the east and west coasts. However, the FLNKS claims the real purpose of the road is for faster deployment of troops and *gardes mobiles* on the east coast against Kanaks.

"France is using the same tactics in Algeria and Vietnam against us," said FLNKS leader Jean-Marie Tjibaou. "It is a provocation all the time. They hope our people will react in a violent manner so they can justify the presence of their troops."

French Pacific Regiment troops on parade in the streets of Nouméa in 1987.   DAVID ROBIE

A Kanak girl watches French Pacific troops on parade in a Nouméa street in 1987.

DAVID ROBIE

"But," added Tjibaou, who lost two brothers in the Hienghène River massacre by settlers in December 1984, "we will not rise to their bait."

¶

The bloody aftermath on Ouvéa

IN SPITE of Tjibaou's peacemaking and optimism, "*Les Évènements*" rapidly reached a bloody climax in 1988 during the April–May presidential elections when the FLNKS planned another territory-wide boycott. This protest led to a hostage-taking crisis known as the siege of Ouvéa that led to the massacre of 19 Kanak militants. Six months after the presidential elections, the Matignon Accords between France and the FLNKS were signed on 6 November 1988 with a referendum on independence proposed for 1998. However, two of the key leaders who signed this agreement, Jean-Marie Tjibaou and Yéiwene Yéiwene, were assassinated at an event marking the cave siege on 4 May 1989. A subsequent agreement, the Nouméa Accord, was signed between the FLNKS and the French president on 5 May 1998 providing for a process of self-government over a two-decade period. The Jean-Marie Tjibaou Cultural Centre memorial was also established. A vote on independence is scheduled between 2014 and 2019 and some progress has been made with reforms. The Kanak flag now flies officially alongside the *Tricolore* on official buildings—a nation of two flags.

When the headlines hit France in April 1988 about the critical turning point in "*les Évènements*" down under in New Caledonia, maverick French filmmaker Mathieu Kassovitz was just 18. He remembers the gritty images of the Gossanna cave siege on television. Indigenous Kanaks were reported to have massacred a quartet of gendarmes with machetes and shotguns and taken 27 others hostage (three others were captured later). There were also false reports of alleged decapitations and rape on Ouvéa in the remote Loyalty Islands. But in 1999, Kassovitz's father handed him the League of Human Rights report on the cave siege and he read the chilling real story for the first time.[13]

A French military force of some 300 had been deployed in a retaliatory "invasion" of the island (pop. about 2700 at the time) and the report detailed atrocities and summary executions that had left 19 Kanak hostage-takers dead in a dawn assault on 5 May 1988. Kassovitz (*La Haîne* and *Café au Lait*) noted then how a dedicated and reflective negotiator, Captain Philippe Legorjus of the elite police counter-terrorism unit CIGN, was a central character in the disturbing report. "I knew then there was the material for

The two flags of Kanaky/New Caledonia—the colonial Tricolore and the Kanak flag of independence—flutter above the French High Commission in Nouméa in 2012.

DAVID ROBIE

a wonderful movie and the script was virtually written," Kassovitz recalled in a *Femail* interview. "The dramatic structure was in the report of those 10 days."[14]

On his first trip to Ouvéa to explore the possibility of making the movie, it seemed many obstacles could block getting such a project off the ground. "Ten years had passed but people were still withdrawn into their grief. The subject was *tabu*. There had been no closure," he says. "There was a lot of religious and political in-fighting within the Kanak community."

A decade on and 25 film scripts later, against all the odds and being forced to make the film on the French Polynesian island of Anaa (pop. 300) in the Tuamotus instead of Ouvéa, a courageous 136-minute testimony to the Kanak struggle and search for justice has been finally achieved. The film was released in France in November 2011 with the title *L'Ordre et la Morale*—a play on words from the title of the Legorjus autobiography, *La Morale et l'Action*, and on a statement by the hated Minister of Overseas Territories Bernard Pons, who said rather cynically: "Sometimes some deaths are necessary to uphold order and morality."

In July 2012, the gripping docudrama was screened for the first time at the New Zealand International Film Festival (and also the Melbourne Film Festival)—under the English-language title *Rebellion*, which loses the nuances of the French name. But the film was never shown in New Caledonia on general release in the largest cinema chain. The Pacific territory's French cinema operator refused to screen it. Smaller, independent cinemas played the film to packed audiences, both Kanak and French.

The film succeeded with the inspirational and credible performances of both director Kassovitz as the frustrated but professional lead character Legorjus—who tried hard to seek a peaceful solution to the hostage crisis—and the Kanak pro-independence militant leader Alphonse Dianou, played superbly by his cousin Iabe Lapacas, aged only six at the time of the tragedy.

Negotiator Legorjus—who was ultimately also taken captive—and Dianou ironically formed a trusting bond of fraternity and understanding and the French officer was released in a bid to broker a deal. But tension built up as the film covered the 10 days of negotiations until the expediency of the power struggle between right-wing Prime Minister Jacques Chirac and Socialist President François Mitterrand in Paris over the imminent outcome of the presidential elections took over. Mitterrand called for negotiations—but in reality ordered the full catastrophic assault on the cave to free the hostages just three days before the crucial runoff ballot. He won the election.

Legorjus felt betrayed by the military (who cynically used a helicopter carrying "journalists" as a ruse to approach the cave) and politicians and subsequently resigned from the elite force after the assault. Dianou felt betrayed and was horrendously allowed to die from his wounds from the cave firefight. Other Kanak prisoners were simply killed in cold blood. And the Kanak community felt betrayed by both Legorjus and the pro-independence FLNKS. This sense of betrayal ultimately led to the assassination of charismatic FLNKS leader Jean-Marie Tjibaou and his deputy Yéiwene Yéiwene a year later in a ceremony marking the anniversary of the martyrs.

Pastor Djubelly Wea, whose character featured in the film giving Legorjus a Kanak history lesson while manacled to a coconut tree, was the assassin. He never forgave the FLNKS leadership for failing to negotiate on their behalf and a sense of betrayal by the *indépendantistes*. Wea in turn was gunned down by Tjibaou's bodyguard. Having reported on the Kanak independence struggle for several years, watching *Rebellion* was an emotional rollercoaster for me. In fact, I shared a hotel room in Manila at a Peace Brigade conference with Wea just five months before the double assassination.

Gossanna cave was *tabu*—and the film portrayed traditional "custom" and beliefs evocatively. In Kanak tradition, a promise made face to face is never broken. I don't believe the militants ever intended to harm their captives—they were simply negotiating leverage after things went wrong in the Fayaoué hostage-taking. In fact, as portrayed in the film, the hostages were about to be freed anyway.

At the time, I wrote a narrative about the tragedy in my book *Blood on their Banner*—the "blood" being that symbolised on the Kanak flag as shed by the martyrs of more than a century of French rule.[15]

Notes

1   David Robie (1987, March). Pons' recipe for trouble [Cover story]. *Islands Business*, pp. 25–31.

2   David Robie (1987, March). End of the regions? *Islands Business*, pp. 26–27.

3   Robie (1987, March). Pons' recipe for trouble, p. 26.

4   David Robie (1989). Martyrdom of Machoro. In *Blood on their Banner: Nationalist Struggles in the South Pacific*. London: Zed Books; Sydney: Pluto Press, pp. 116–126.

5   David Robie (1987, February). "A subversive in Kanaky". *Islands Business*, pp. 22–23.

6   David Robie (1986). *Eyes of Fire: The Last Voyage of the Rainbow Warrior*. Auckland: Linden Books.

7   *Revue Militaire d 'Information* (1957, January). Available at: http://www.worldcat.org/title/revue-militaire-dinformation/oclc/46876186

8   David Robie (1987, March). Occupation or protection? *Islands Business*, pp. 28–29.

9   Ibid., p. 29.

10 Ibid.

11 W. S. McCallum (1994). French South Pacific policy under Mitterrand (1981–1993). Unpublished doctoral thesis. Christchurch: University of Canterbury.

12 Alphonse is not the sculptor's real name; his name was changed to protect his identity.

13 David Robie (2012, October). Gossanna cave siege tragic tale of betrayal. *Pacific Journalism Review*, 18(2): 212–216.

14 *Femail* (2012). *Rebellion* interview. Available on femail.com.au

15 Robie (1989). The siege of Ouvéa. In *Blood on their Banner*, pp. 270–280.

9

Fiji: Countdown to a coup, 1987

Let us not yield ... let us not tarnish the image of tolerance and goodwill
for which Fiji is renowned. Where is the justice and reason in trying to
destabilise and remove a government as soon as it has been elected?
Fiji's first commoner Prime Minister Dr Timoci Uluivuda Bavadra

IT WAS Fiji's Black Thursday, 14 May 1987. Right-wing trade unionist Taniela
Veitata was making his maiden speech for the Alliance Party, in opposition
in Fiji for the first time since independence in 1970.

"Peace is quite distinct from the political philosophy of Mao Zedong
when he said that political power comes out of the barrel of a gun," said
Veitata with an eagle eye on the public gallery and the entrances to the
parliamentary chamber.

"In Fiji, there is no gun ..."

This was the cue. This was the phrase coup leader Lieutenant-Colonel
Sitiveni Rabuka and Veitata had agreed would be the signal for 10 elite New
Zealand-trained Fijian soldiers to burst into Parliament at 10am and kidnap
the Fiji Labour Party-led Coalition government of the newly installed Prime
Minister, Dr Timoci Bavadra.[1] And the late former Prime Minister, Ratu Sir
Kamisese Mara, evidently knew an hour before the coup when it was going
to happen; he confirmed this by telling *Islands Business* publisher Robert
Keith-Reid, the first journalist to speak to him after the coup, that he had
been told "around 9am" about the takeover by Colonel Rabuka.

The Governor-General, Ratu Sir Penaia Ganilau, was also believed to
have known of the imminent coup. When Militoni Leweniqila, a dissident
Alliance MP who had been elected Speaker, telephoned Ratu Ganilau to
brief him about the coup, the Governor-General was said to have reacted
with an apparent lack of surprise. And when Colonel Rabuka arrived
shortly after at Government House his first words to Ratu Ganilau were:
"Well, sir, I've done it!"

A tribal-based group of conspirators orchestrated the coup—first of
four in Fiji over little more than two decades. The conspirators represented
an eastern chiefly clique from the Tovata confederation which believed its

Special report in *New Zealand Outlook* magazine, June 1987: "No photos": An angry Fijian soldier points to photographer Matthew McKee outside the *Fiji Times* office.

MATTHEW MCKEE/*NEW ZEALAND OUTLOOK*

right to rule had been challenged by the outcome of the April 11 election, which brought Dr Bavadra and his Indo-Fijian supported Coalition to power after 17 years of an Alliance monopoly on power. The leaders of the eastern tribal establishment did not accept this state of affairs and wanted to reassert their political control.

There was a conflict between the traditional rulers and the new, better-educated, more modern group of indigenous Fijians who were prepared to change their traditional vote and usher in a government which not only sought a more equitable distribution of wealth and social justice, but which bridged an ethnic divide between Fijians and Indo-Fijians.

Just a month before this first coup in Fiji, I had been one of only two New Zealand journalists in Suva reporting on the dramatic victory of the Labour Party-led Coalition. I was also in Fiji for the 2000 George Speight coup, then as a journalism educator and as chief editor leading a group of students covering the putsch. When the 14 May 1987 coup happened, most journalists covering the crisis focused on an exaggerated racial divide instead of the fundamental changes that had happened in Fiji to lead to the election upset—and then the military takeover. My reports, such as this one, the first of a series for *New Zealand Outlook*, focused on the changing paradigms of political struggle and background to the coups.

"SIT DOWN EVERYBODY. THIS IS A TAKEOVER!"

New Zealand Outlook, June 1987

SAKEASI BUTADROKA fingers his trademark blood-red bow tie and laughs: "This represents the blood of Christ that flowed from the cross on Calvary." He says it also represents the danger facing indigenous Fijians and the sacrifices they are prepared to make.[2]

A Methodist lay preacher and poultry farmer who exudes charm and good humour in spite of the firmness of his beliefs, "Buta" was the man responsible for the brief downfall of Ratu Sir Kamisese Mara's Alliance government in the first of two general elections in 1977. Unashamedly campaigning along racial lines, he also had a hand in the final ousting of Ratu Mara after 17 years in power in April 1987; his Fijian Nationalist Party ironically gained enough ethnic Fijian votes to help the new multiracial Coalition government win office.

Butadroka's controversial political career appeared to have ended after a heavy defeat in 1982, but he did not waver in his struggle to change the Fijian Constitution and give ethnic Fijians exclusive rights to lead the country. He advocated "thinning out" the Indo-Fijian population by encouraging migration. "The nationalist ideal will live on—it will never wither like a flower," he remarked, prophetically, during the election campaign. "Those who say we are finished are nothing but fools."

Following the defeat of Mara, however, a group of hard-line Alliance Party leaders, Butadroka's opponents, also adopted a nationalist policy—a policy which in May led to the biggest protest rallies ever seen in Fiji, with barricades and firebomb attacks against prominent Indo-Fijians, and finally to a right-wing military coup.

Does Butadroka regret lighting the racial fuse? No. At least, not even until Lieutenant-Colonel Sitiveni "Steve" Rabuka—also a Methodist lay preacher—deposed the Coalition government and imposed martial law.

"Why do you think I've been campaigning all these years?" he asked before the coup. "I've had one objective: to get rid of the Mara government so that Fijians would realise they are in danger. Now the fight has begun, I am happy."

But standing outside Parliament Buildings, stunned, after the May 14 takeover, he said: "No, no ... the bastards cannot do it like this. They'll destroy democracy forever. This is a tyranny. Blame Ratu Mara for this. Where is the Judas?" Police hustled him away.

Butadroka, who was jailed under the *Public Order Act* for "incitement" in 1977, has always advocated constitutional changes through democratic means. The Taukei (indigenous) Movement used to claim that Butadroka was anti-Indian while it was pro-Fijian but the movement's recent actions have been more extremist than Butadroka's nationalists ever were.[3]

The Taukei Movement plot theory "who's who" in the military, *Times on Sunday*, 12 July 1987.

The end came for the Labour Party-led Coalition on the morning of Thursday, May 14, when 10 soldiers wearing masks and balaclavas, and armed with pistols, burst into the parliamentary chamber. Sitting in the public gallery, Colonel Rabuka rose, moved toward Prime Minister Dr Timoci Bavadra, and ordered: "Sit down everybody. This is a takeover!"

The soldiers then abducted Dr Bavadra and 26 of his MPs at gunpoint, herding them into military trucks to take them into detention. Heads of the military and police forces were deposed, the Constitution suspended and Colonel Rabuka formed a provisional council of ministers. The Coalition had only survived a month in office.

More than a racial struggle, the Taukei attempts at destabilising the Coalition government and then the coup were part of a three-stage strategy for the Alliance Party to seize back power at all costs. The speed with which the coup came after the protests had lost steam has prevented prosecution cases expected against several former Alliance ministers for alleged corruption and misappropriation of public funds.

"The Coalition government was perceived to be dangerous by the Alliance and had to be overthrown," says University of the South Pacific historian Dr Robbie Robertson (later the author of two books on Fiji coups), "because it was a challenge to the existing power structure and was crossing racial barriers."[4]

Fiji's original coup leader Lieutenant-Colonel Sitiveni Rabuka, third-ranked in the Fiji
Military Forces in May 1987: "Sit down everybody. This is a takeover!"
                    MATTHEW MCKEE/*PACIFIC JOURNALISM REVIEW*

Dr Timoci Uluivuda Bavadra, in a white shirt, tie and *sulu*, had been relaxed in
spite of the constitutional storm blowing around him—until he was put under
house arrest. "Doc", as the 52-year-old former civil servant is known to friends
and party stalwarts, had slipped into the role of Prime Minister with ease and was
approaching his task with the air of a physician with a kindly bedside manner.

Some now say *too* kindly. He was under pressure from several of his cabinet
colleagues to take a hard line against the dissidents. But Bavadra regarded reports
of the extent of the opposition to his government as exaggerated. Still, the day after
firebombings in Lautoka, he began to take harsher action. A daylong emergency
meeting reviewed security.

Prosecutions for corruption against other previous Alliance ministers were
expected to follow.

Shortly before the coup, Bavadra's cabinet heard a report from the police
Special Branch about the presence of two CIA agents in Fiji. Cabinet opinion was
divided on whether the two agents should be expelled.

Sources close to the Prime Minister said Rabuka had been seen playing golf
with the two men and Ratu Mara the Sunday before the coup, only a week after
US Ambassador to the United Nations General Vernon Walters, a former director
of the CIA, visited Suva. Walters has been described by *New Statesman* magazine
as "having been involved in overthrowing more governments than any other
official serving the US government".[5] The diplomat had talks with Foreign Minister
Krishna Datt and would have reported to Washington on his assessment of the
minister and the government's non-alignment policies.

Where it all began in May 1987: Fiji's old Parliament Buildings, now the Supreme Court in Suva. In the foreground is a statue honouring Ratu Sir Lala Sukuna, Fiji's most revered chief, scholar, soldier and statesman.　　　　　　　　　　　　　　　DAVID ROBIE

Bavadra, the sources said, also summoned the US ambassador to his office and complained US aid funds had been used to help fund the Taukei Movement. The Australian-owned Emperor Gold Mines company was also accused of providing buses to help transport Fijian protesters to anti-government rallies.

Bavadra earnestly had defended his government, saying it was "unthinkable" that he would consider sacrificing the welfare of ethnic Fijians. He was saddened that dissidents suggested he would allow the government to put the welfare of Fijians at risk.

We have been elected on a platform of improving the lives of all Fijians, not just one race, and not just a ruling elite," he said. "Lack of housing, poverty and poor wages should not be blamed on racial grounds."

His government gained power on promises to improve social welfare, education, health and housing, and to eliminate corruption. But the way to do this, he argued, was through fairer distribution of the country's wealth and better use of government resources. Bavadra allocated the sensitive public service, Fijian affairs and home affairs portfolios to himself. Another Fijian, Mosese Volavola, became Lands Minister.

Dr Timoci Bavadra's supporters of all races join the media throng to welcome his release from detention by the Fiji military five days after the coup on 19 May 1987.

MATTHEW MCKEE

Bavadra also pointed out that his government was elected by a five percent swing among ethnic Fijians away from the Alliance—mainly educated Fijians, particularly women, and young, underprivileged urban indigenous Fijians. Two nationalist candidates were declared bankrupt when counting began, but the Nationalist Party's high polling split the Fijian vote in four crucial Suva electorates to boost the Coalition victory.

"Fiji needs this government to develop our maturity as a nation," says Health and Social Welfare Minister Dr Satendra Nandan, 48, a poet and former literature lecturer at the University of the South Pacific. "It is vital for our peaceful future to show that a real multiracial government can run Fiji; we cannot keep brushing racial issues under the carpet."

Nandan, who had been tipped as likely Foreign Minister (Fiji Labour Party secretary-general Krishna Datt got the job instead), is fiercely critical of how the Alliance exploited racial fears during the campaign. "It tried racism, but we have broken the Alliance's back on this issue," he says. "It also tried scaremongering over land. When it failed to shoot holes in our domestic policies, it switched to foreign affairs—and it thinks the Fijian people are gullible."

The *Fiji Sun* bitterly attacked the emotive smears used by the protesters, blaming them for worsening race relations. Rival *Fiji Times*, while conceding the

Constitution was open for improvement, said it would "not be by brute force, threats or other illegal means". [Both of Fiji's daily newspapers at the time were foreign-owned—the *Sun* by a New Zealand-Hong Kong owned company, and the *Times* by Rupert Murdoch's Herald and Weekly Times Ltd.] Although several high chiefs condemned the protests, Ratu Mara's failure to do so drew severe criticism and heightened suspicions about direct Alliance involvement, in spite of the party denying it.

When Ratu Mara surfaced as Foreign Minister in the military regime's provisional government, it was widely believed that he was among the Alliance leaders who instigated the coup. Denials by Mara and Rabuka were unconvincing; the colonel needed the backing of the Alliance to stage the coup.

During at least one media conference, Colonel Rabuka was clearly being "coached" by the military regime's Development Minister Peter Stinson and Information Minister Dr Ahmed Ali, both previous Alliance ministers worried about the Coalition's pledge to open the financial books.

Both of Mara's former deputy prime ministers, Ratu David Toganivalu—regarded as the "Mr Clean" of the previous Alliance administration—and Mosese Qionibaravi, would have nothing to do with the military regime.

Among the Taukei leaders, beside Apisai Tora is a right-wing trade unionist widely described as a "political chameleon", Taniela "Big Dan" Veitata. A former member of the Fijian Nationalist Party, Veitata is regarded by many as a particularly virulent racist.

"A new form of colonialism has been imposed on us, not from the outside, but from within our own country by those who arrived here with no rights and were given full rights by us—the Taukei," says Tora. But while Tora claimed Bavadra was a "puppet and prisoner" of the Indo-Fijians, allegations were being made that Tora himself was a front for covert interference by the United States. When the new government took office, documents were found which purportedly linked Tora with American backing.[6]

The "puppet" allegations against Bavadra were based on his quick elevation of lawyer Jai Ram Reddy to the Senate and appointment as Attorney-General and Justice Minister. Reddy was an astute former Opposition Leader, but he resigned from Parliament three years earlier after a series of bitter clashes over what he considered the dictatorial style of Speaker Tomasi Vakatora. However, Reddy was the National Federation Party's architect of the merger with the Fiji Labour Party and it was widely expected he would be rewarded with a cabinet post.

Like Butadroka and Rabuka, Tora wants the Constitution amended so that only Fijians are elected to Parliament and to replace the Senate with an upper house based on the powerful, traditional and privileged Great Council of Chiefs, rather

A Fiji soldier keeps watch on an urban crowd in Suva after the May 1987 coup.
MATTHEW MCKEE

like Britain's House of Lords. As Butadroka puts it: "We should follow Gandhi and
Nehru in India: they told the British to get out of Parliament but have a free reign
in business."

The so-called Indian legacy began on 14 May 1879 when 489 Indians arrived as
indentured labour to work in the British colonial-run sugarcane plantations. Just
five years earlier, through a Deed of Cession—rather like New Zealand's Treaty
of Waitangi—signed by 13 high chiefs, the 320 islands which make up Fiji had
become a British colony. One condition of the deed was that while property fairly
acquired by European settlers could be retained by them, Fijian rights to the rest of
the fertile land should be protected.

These two events more than a century ago are at the heart of the present
dispute. Descendants of those 489 Indians, joined by others over the following
37 years at a rate of about 2000 a year, now outnumber the indigenous Fijians
both within the 715,000 population and in Parliament. Forty-eight percent of the
people are now Indo-Fijian, 46 percent indigenous Fijian and the rest "general", or
Europeans, Chinese and part-European. Nineteen of the Coalition's 28 MPs are
Indo-Fijian. [Indigenous Fijians regained an almost 60 percent majority by 2007
after the country's four coups.][7]

In theory, Ratu Mara's Alliance was a coalition of three parties: the Fijian Alliance, the Indian Alliance and the General Electors Association. After the Suva protests, however, two senior Indian Alliance officials quit and called on other Indians to abandon the party.

Party general secretary Naresh Prasad said the protests had ruined the Alliance's commitment to multiracialism and tolerance: "I get the feeling the Fijians actually hate my guts, yet they smile to keep my support."

Britain's departing colonial masters created a system of government which ensured each of the three founding ethnic groups would be represented and any party or coalition forming the government would have substantial support from at least two of the three communities. Adapted from a Westminster-style democracy, the result is probably the world's most complex—and misunderstood—electoral system. Each Fijian elector is represented by four members – two from that voter's ethnic background and two which must *not* be from that community.

Parliament's 52 seats are divided into two main sub-categories and then into three sub-categories, making a total of six classes of seats—25 national and 27 communal. Voters from all ethnic groups elect the national MPs while only specific ethnic communities elect communal MPs. The seats are broken down as:

Fijian national	10
Indian national	10
General national	5
Fijian communal	12
Indian communal	12
General communal	3

To make the situation even more complicated, the six classes of seats overlap geographically.

Land distribution is fundamental to politics in Fiji. Under the 1970 Constitution, indigenous Fijians are guaranteed ownership of almost 83 percent of the land. Such Fijian land is inalienable and is owned collectively by the *mataqali* (clan). About 80 percent of the remaining freehold land is owned by Europeans, while the 350,000 Indians have freehold rights over only about 1.7 percent.

Nearly 120,000 hectares of Fijian land is leased, 75 percent of it to Indians—who naturally would prefer to own it. The Coalition government promised during the election campaign to open up more land for productive use, to "lease crown land to all citizens".

But the government was also careful to stress that it recognised Fijian land ownership rights, and said no change would be considered "without the full consultation and approval of the Great Council of Chiefs. The Coalition is committed to uphold, protect and safeguard the ownership rights of people over their land and private assets as guaranteed under the Constitution and other laws of Fiji."

The Alliance's election campaign capitalised on Fijian fears over their lands and tried to portray the Coalition as "communist" with a secret strategy designed to strip the people of their land and hand it to the Indo-Fijians. Even if the allegations were without foundation, they struck a responsive chord with some Fijians.

"It is neo-colonialism by Indians," said "Big Dan" Veitata. "Unless we stop it now, we will be no better off than the Kanaks in New Caledonia, the Australian Aborigines and the New Zealand Māori."

There were many prosperous *Gujeratis* (ethnic Gujerati-speakers who frequently gain prominence as merchants in overseas disapora), but Fijian business is still dominated by mainly Australian, New Zealand and local European ownership. And many of the poorest people in Fiji are Indian squatters or jobless.

However, the Indian community dominates the sugar-growing industry, which is the mainstay of the Fijian economy. Nearly all the crop produced by Indians is grown on land leased from native landlords on the basis of limited tenure.

Ideally, the Indian community would like to have increased land rights, or, failing that, a greater security of tenure on leased land. Fijians, however, determinedly stick to the traditional system of land distribution, the basis of their hold on power.

In the late 1950s, there were barely 130 children of Fijian-Indian marriages. Since then the segregation of the races practised by the colonial administration through legal decrees has largely disappeared. Mixed marriages are now more common and mixed-race children more numerous than a generation ago. Figures are difficult to establish because children in Fijian-Indian marriages and relationships are not regarded as a separate category.

The colonial administration segregated living areas for the different racial groups. For example, in Suva, Vatuwaqa, Samabula and Signal Station were reserved for Indians while areas like Toorak, the Domain and Tamavua Heights were for white settlement. Draiba was for Indian civil servants. This was coupled with a policy that non-indigenous races were barred from living in Fijian villages.

"The British practised a form of dictatorship from 1875 to 1963," says Professor Vijay Naidu, a University of the South Pacific sociologist. "From 1904, whites had representation in the legislature and Indians were represented by nomination in 1916 and by election in 1929. The governor and the official members could veto any resolutions of the elected representatives. Indigenous Fijians voted for the first time in 1963. This was not all, 'democracy' as practised in Fiji meant that Europeans, though numerically a minority, had parity with the other ethnic categories."

Dr Timoci Bavadra with his media adviser Richard Naidu, then an award-winning Fiji
journalist and later a prominent media and constututional lawyer.   MATTHEW MCKEE

According to Dr Naidu, the friction between Fijian and Indo-Fijian is highly
exaggerated. "For black labour in Fiji, the owners and managers of transnational
corporations, who are largely white, constitute the main antagonists." He also
says that the general electors (voters who are neither Fijian nor Indo-Fijian) have
traditionally been the most racial in their voting patterns, something hardly
remarked on by foreign or even local journalists.

However, in spite of his comments (or perhaps because of them), Dr Naidu
found himself on the military regime's "hit list" of about 300 people regarded as
founders or sympathisers of the Labour Party. He went into hiding when police
arrested two people wrongly identified as him.

"Fijians opposing the Coalition are led by those who have lost their privileges by
being ousted—it is political rather than racial," says Dr Tupeni Baba, a flamboyant
university lecturer who became Education Minister. "The Alliance wanted a less
open government than ours, judging from its failed attempts to prosecute people
who delved into its actions and from the way it shielded itself from the media. It
suffers a fortress complex."

¶

NOTORIOUS for political instability, Fiji became branded by some journalists as "coup coup land" after the third coup in May 2000, a putsch not actually precipitated by the military, although renegade elite Counter-Revolutionary Warfare Unit soldiers took a key role. The frontman for the coup was failed businessman George Speight, a charismatic opportunist, who took the elected government of Mahendra Chaudhry prisoner for 56 days and held the nation to ransom. He was eventually persuaded to give up his adventure and is now serving a life sentence in prison for treason.

But in spite of the political upheavals, Fiji is not a "failed" state, argue professors Jon Fraenkel, Stewart Firth and Brij Lal in their 2009 book exploring the enigmas of the country's "coup culture", *The 2006 Military Takeover of Fiji*. Citing the UN Human Development Index, they declared Fiji deserved to be ranked with countries such as Iran, Paraguay and Tunisia, not with poor Pacific neighbours such as Solomon Islands, Vanuatu and Papua New Guinea.

> Most children go to school; at least half the population is urban; the literacy rate is high; the health system is passable; and government administration is efficient by Pacific Island standards. Fiji has a diversified export sector based on sugar, gold and niche products such as Fiji Water. Tourism and remittances supplement foreign exchange earnings; and keep the current account roughly in balance.[8]

Almost 25 years after carrying out the first coup in Fiji, Rabuka astonished many by making a public apology for his actions.[9] He took a fullpage advertisement in *The Fiji Times* on New Year's Day in 2012 to make the apology,[10] explaining later to Radio Australia's *Pacific Beat* programme that his apology was part of the move to democracy with elections due in 2014: "I'm hoping that people will be responsible about the use of their freedom."[11] "Too little, too late", retorted the Auckland-based Coalition for Democracy in Fiji's Nikhil Naidu.[12] Calling for Rabuka to "tell the whole coup story" and name all the plotters, *Indian Weekender* chief subeditor Arvind Kumar asked in a column did the apology mean trying to "right the wrongs he did in 1987".[13]

"As a young journalist at the *Fiji Sun*, I was subjected to service in the newsroom as young 'trigger-happy' soldiers stood behind us with the guns pointed at our heads ... Does Rabuka feel that his apology will stop other aspiring Rabukas and Bainimaramas carrying out coups in the future? Was Bainimarama inspired by Rabuka's coups?"[14]

Although two ghost-written books have provided Rabuka's own per-spectives on the coups, *Rabuka: No Other Way* and *Rabuka of Fiji*, much remains to be revealed.[15] But certainly he is conciliatory and optimistic with the planned 2014 elections. And he appears committed to try to "repair" the damage of the coup culture he started.

Former Bavadra-era cabinet minister Dr Satendra Nandan, now a professor of literature at the Australian National University and visiting professor at the Fiji National University, has praised the regime's 2013 Constitution as a breakthrough for the people of Fiji and the Pacific region. But the process was highly controversial as the draft Constitution drawn up by the Constitutional Commission, led by international legal authority Professor Yash Ghai after extensive public consultation, was rejected in favour of a regime-initiated version.[16] In an article analysing the implications of the Constitution in *Pacific Scoop* for the 2014 post-coup election, Nandan wrote:

> All Fiji citizens are now called Fijians for the first time in a Fiji Constitution, irrespective of their origin, colour, creed, gender or religious beliefs.
>
> Fiji has fewer than a million people, more than half of them will be eligible to vote, the voting age has been reduced to 18 years from 21. There is no compulsory voting but the young have the potential to influence the outcome of an election.
>
> The Constitution provides for the development of a "genuine democracy" in multi-ethnic Fiji—in the past so damagingly beset by communal constituencies, racial categorisation, colonial hierarchies, feudal patriarchy, discrimination and dispossession of many kinds, coupled with inventions of traditions and institutions to rule rather than to serve.
>
> All that has gone out the window into the waves of the Pacific, floating like the debris from a pirate shipwreck. Fiji will be a better and fairer society for all that. And this Constitution provides several windows of opportunity for the future.[17]

But others, including the Citizens' Constitutional Forum (CCF), have been far more critical in their assessment. The CCF rebuked the regime for its "lack of integrity" in the review process. Executive director Reverend Akuila Yabaki said that by the regime placing the military directly under the presidential commander-in-chief, instead of the prime minister and defence minister's responsibility, put it "above the law". He added: "This document cannot be considered a Constitution by the people of Fiji following the discarding of the people's constitution … It is a government Constitution."[18]

Notes

1 David Robie (1987, July 12). Why the Fijian plot theory is gaining ground. Sydney *Times on Sunday*, p. 12.

2 David Robie (1987, June). "Sit Down Everybody. This is a Takeover!" Fiji: Countdown to a Coup. *New Zealand Outlook*, pp. 22–29.

3 See Robie (1987, July 12), "The Fijian plot theory", for more detail on the Taukei Movement.

4 Robert Robertson and Akosita Tamanisau (1988). *Fiji: Shattered Coups*. Sydney: Pluto Press; Robert Robertson and William Sutherland (2002). *Government by the Gun: The Unfinished Business of Fiji's 2000 Coup*. Sydney: Pluto Press.

5 Glenn Alcalay (2010, February 22). The not-so-pacific Pacific. *Cultural Survival*. Retrieved on 29 August 2013, from www.culturalsurvival.org/publications/cultural-survival-quarterly/fiji/not-so-pacific-pacific

6 See Wikipedia profile on Apisai Tora. Available at http://en.wikipedia.org/wiki/Apisai_Tora

7 The outflow of Indo-Fijians from the country after four coups changed this population balance dramatically with indigenous Fijians becoming a majority again. According to the 2007 Fiji National Census, of the total population of 837,271, 475,739 (56.8 percent) were indigenous Fijian, 313,798 of Indo-Fijian descent (37.5 percent) and "others" totalled 47,734 (5.7 percent).

8 Jon Fraenkel, Stewart Firth and Brij V. Lal (2009). *The 2006 Military Takeover in Fiji: A Coup to End All Coups?* Canberra: ANU Press, p. 4.

9 Sitiveni Rabuka had earlier given an apology in a traditional ceremony to the former president, the Tui Vuda, Ratu Josefa Iloilo, for ousting the elected Bavadra government in Viseisei village on 14 April 2010. See Vuda accepts Rabuka apology (2010, April 16). *Fiji Times Online*. Retrieved on 7 January 2014, from www.fijitimes.com/story.aspx?id=144524

10 Timoci Vula (2012, January 3). Repentive Rabuka, *Fiji Times Online*. Retrieved on 7 January 2014, from www.fijitimes.com/story.aspx?id=189876

11 Rabuka sorry for leading Fiji military coups (2012, January 3). Radio Australia. Retrieved on 7 January 2014.

12 Rabuka apology "too little, too late" (2012, January 24). *Indian Weekender*. Retrieved on 7 January 2014, from www.indianweekender.co.nz/Pages/ArticleDetails/14/2814/Fiji/Rabuka-apology-too-little-too-late

13 Arvind Kumar (2012, February 12). Rabuka needs to tell whole coup story and expose the plotters, *Pacific Scoop*. Retrieved on 7 January 2014, from http://pacific.scoop.co.nz/2012/02/rabuka-needs-to-tell-whole-coup-story-and-expose-the-plotters/

14 Ibid.

15 Eddie Dean and Stan Ritova (1988). *Rabuka: No Other Way: His own story of the Fijian coup*. Sydney: Doubleday; John Sharpham (2000). *Rabuka of Fiji: The*

authorised biography of Major-General Sitiveni Rabuka. Rockhampton, Qld: Central Queensland University Press.

16 New constitution for Fiji (2013, August 27). Development Policy Centre. Retrieved on 7 January 2014, from http://devpolicy.org/in-brief/new-constitution-for-fiji-20130827-1/

17 Satendra Nandan (2013, August 27). Fiji Constitution offers better and fairer society for all—a window of opportunity. *Pacific Scoop*. Retrieved on 27 August 2013, from http://pacific.scoop.co.nz/2013/08/fiji-constitution-offers-better-and-fairer-society-for-all-a-window-of-opportunity/

18 Fiji citizen group says new constitution is not representative (2013, August 22). Radio NZ International. Retrieved on 16 September 2013, from www.rnzi.com/pages/news.php?op=read&id=78525

10

The Chinese connection in Tonga, 1991

*New Zealand and Australian aid is aimed at capacity building and
grassroots development projects like classrooms, clean water supplies
and health clinics. Chinese aid so far has been on showcase projects,
including public buildings like the Fa'onelua Conference Centre.*
Publisher, broadcaster and social commentator Kalafi Moala

FOR CHINESE migrants in Tonga, Black Thursday on 16 November
2006 tarnished a South Pacific dream. Some of the 600 Chinese living
in Nuku`alofa became a target that day when unprecedented rioting
and arson were unleashed on the Tongan capital. The 16/11 events
when some 80 percent of the downtown business heart of Nuku`alofa
was torched, looted and razed are still recalled with anguish by many
Tongans today.

The resentment against some Chinese businesses and small shops,
many built up from scratch through sheer hard work and dedication over
the past two decades, had its roots in a Tongan passport scandal in the
late 1980s and early 1990s. Although anti-Chinese rioting in the Pacific
had also happened in Honiara, Port Moresby and Pape`ete, the Tongan
connection was rather different. Hundreds of foreigners had successfully
applied—and obtained—Tongan passports. The scheme was particularly
popular with Hong Kong Chinese who feared what would happen to the
British colony when the territory reverted to mainland Chinese rule in
1997. It was widely expected, but wrongly, that rule from Beijing would be
highly authoritarian with curbs on many freedoms, including the media
and travel.

Although then Immigration Minister, the noble `Akau`ola, pledged
in Parliament at the time that the majority of Chinese holding Tongan
passports would not travel to Tonga or live there, many still did go to the
"Friendly Islands".[1] But as Tongan newspaper publisher and broadcaster
Kalafi Moala noted in his book *Tonga: In Search of the Friendly Islands*
about contemporary national identity dilemmas, many other Chinese also
sought residency in Tonga even without the controversial passports-for-

sale.[2] They were looking to escape "oppression" and to start a new life in the kingdom. Moala offered personal insights into Chinese settlers and how they had adapted to Tongan custom and lifestyle as many took over most of the capital's small general stores, *falekoloa*. He based this on a series of interviews he did in April 2007.

In spite of the targeting of Chinese stores during the riots, there were also "demonstrations of courage and compassion" as Tongan youths protected some Chinese stores in their neighbourhood. "As Nuku`alofa burned," recalls Moala, "Chinese people everywhere in Tongatapu started to panic."[3] More than 150 people whose homes or shops were "destroyed by the mobs" took refuge in the Chinese Embassy in Nuku`alofa. Moala describes the destruction:

> A pattern started emerging throughout Nuku`alofa during the riots. The rioters would send a scouting vehicle to the Chinese stores, and then by mobile phone contact the trucks, which carried the looters and arsonists. The stores that were attached to homes were better protected, particularly in the Kolomotu`a area, but a store located unattached in the Hihifo Road was looted and burned. Several trucks would arrive, the attackers then throwing an iron bar with hooks tied to the door. The trucks would then pull the doors open, allowing the looters in. When they were finished, they threw firebombs into the store and left. On one occasion, however, people from the neighbourhood ran to the store and fought off the looters, who then fled in their trucks.[4]

During Moala's research, he concluded he was shocked by the attitude displayed by many Tongans towards the Chinese: "Even before 16/11, some of their stores have been robbed many times over, even at gunpoint. The have been mugged on our streets. They have been sworn at and told 'to go back to China'." In reality, believes Moala, the Chinese have been wrongly accused as being a threat to Tonga's economy and social wellbeing. In fact, they are more integrated in Tongan life and the *Fua Kavenga* (social obligation) system than most other *palagi*.[5]

In 1991, while reporting the Pacific region, I wrote several articles on the Tongan passport affair, including this one in the *Auckland Star* as details emerged about some of the identities of those who benefited from the passport sales.[6] As pro-democracy campaigner `Akilisi Pohiva told me at the time of a controversial court case over the passports issue, the challenge had triggered a "domino" fear in the kingdom—cabinet ministers didn't know what would fall next along the road to reform:[7]

People are increasingly aware that the government is trying to make easy money, to gamble, to use the country. People are now more aware that a privileged few in high places in government are using unlawful tactics and strategies for their personal benefit. They are milking the system for themselves.[8]

TONGA'S PASSPORT SCAM

Auckland Star, 1 April 1991

TONGA's hasty legal juggling act to grant citizenship to more than 400 foreigners—including Imelda Marcos, wife of the late Philippines dictator Ferdinand Marcos—has failed to quell unrest over the passport scandal.

Commoner MP and pro-democracy campaigner `Akilisi Pohiva told packed meetings of Tongans in Auckland that he would carry on his fight to expose government lawbreaking in the passport scandal that has stunned the South Pacific kingdom.

Pohiva has agreed to the dismissal of his court case challenging the passports. But he has also won a remarkable victory by forcing the kingdom's government to admit the illegality of the passports and to plan to change the Constitution.

"Nothing will stop me ... I'll go on challenging the government," Pohiva said, revealing that he was planning his next step.

"It is unconstitutional for the government to hide the money involved in the passport case," he said.

"In seven years there has been no audited accounting to Parliament for the passport scandal."

Pohiva claimed Police Minister `Akau`ola should have resigned, and "probably Finance Minister Cecil Cocker as well".

`Akau'ola has accepted responsibility for the illegal sale of passports and naturalisation certificates.

Weeping
Weeping and praying, more than 2500 protesters—led by the Catholic bishop, Patelisio Finau, Pohiva and other commoner MPs—marched to the royal palace in an unprecedented demonstration a week after legal proceedings ended.

They presented two petitions to King Tafau`ahau IV through his private secretary. The King was urged to cancel citizenship to the 426 foreigners and sack the Police Minister, `Akau`ola, who has accepted responsibility for the illegal sales of naturalisation certificates and passports.

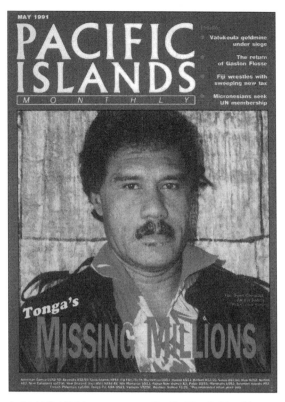

Tonga's "Quiet Crusader" ˋAkilisi Pohiva cover story, *Pacific Islands Monthly*, May 1991.

DAVID ROBIE

ˋAkauˋola had earlier told an emergency session of the Legislative Assembly: "I take the blame ... it is my fault. We acknowledge that things have been done illegally and we need to correct them."

He admitted that his department has now been reported by the government-run newspaper, *Tonga Chronicle*, to have said the kingdom could not afford the expense of cancelling the passports.

He said changing foreign exchange rates for the Tongan paˋanga, plus possible lawsuits by passport holders, meant that paying out refunds and declaring the documents null and void would be too heavy a burden for the country.

He also said none of the foreigners were living in Tonga and most were unlikely to do so.

Impeach
About the demand for the ousting of the Police Minister, the King said it was up to Parliament to amend legislation and to impeach ministers.

Most of the foreigners involved are Asian. They include 189 mainland-born Chinese, 152 Hong Kong Chinese, nine Macau Chinese, nine Thais, nine Burmese, eight Singaporeans, four Filipinos and two Indonesians.

One of the ethnic Chinese is Sam Wong, a Filipino-born businessman who plans to build a multimillion-dollar business complex in the capital, Nuku'alofa.

Former Hong Kong Stock Exchange chief Ronald Li, who is serving a four-year jail term for corruption, and textile magnate Chen Din-hwa and Diamond Importers' Association chairman Maximilian Ma Yung-kit are also reportedly listed among the passport holders. The combined assets of Chen and Ma are estimated to be more than NZ$1 billion. (Both later told Hong Kong's *Sunday Morning Post* that they had returned passports because they were "useless" as they needed visas wherever they went.)[9]

Then exiled Imelda Marcos is the best-known foreigner to get a Tongan passport and the Philippines government has announced it would reject any passport application from her.

Reports have said she is about to file an application at the Philippines Consulate in New York.

Marcos, 61, fled into exile with her deposed husband when the people power revolt in the Philippines installed Corazon Aquino's government in February 1986. Ferdinand Marcos died in Hawai`i in 1989. [Imelda Marcos was pardoned and returned to the Philippines in 1991. She was elected as a congresswoman in Leyte in 1995 for three years and again in Ilcos Norte in 2010.][10]

Besides Imelda Marcos, her daughter Aimee and son Ferdinand Martin, other nationalities gaining Tongan passports include Americans, Libyans, South Africans and a Palestinian businessman, Toufic Barakeh, with five of his relatives.

Tonga has been operating the illegal passports scheme since 1984. Under the scheme, two kinds of Tongan passport have been for sale to foreigners: the Tonga Protected Person Passport and the Tongan Passport (issued to those who became naturalised).

The "protected person" passport was created in 1983 as primarily a travel document for non-Tongans who had difficulties travelling beyond their own national boundaries. It sold for US$10,000 each.

However, as this document did not give the holder automatic right of residence in Tonga and a visa was needed, a growing number of countries—including New Zealand—did not recognise it.

Further legislation was introduced in 1984 to deal with this problem. The King was given power to grant naturalisation to any foreigner of "good character on humanitarian grounds".

The naturalisation fee was US$20,000, but additional fees could take it up to more than US$35,000.

Commoner MPs and their lawyers exposed the scheme and challenged it as unconstitutional.

Repeal

In 1988, `Akau`ola admitted that the 1984 legislation was unconstitutional because it violated Clause 29 of the Constitution which requires residence of at least five years before naturalisation. The 1984 law was then repealed by the 1988 *Nationality Act*.

It is uncertain how many foreigners have been naturalised or how much money has been made from the scam, as these figures have not been revealed in Parliament—but it is believed that considerably more than the 426 people named in the *Government Gazette* may have acquired passports.

Tonga's Consul in Hong Kong, George Chen, who succeeded his father, Tom Chen, in 1989, told *Matangi Tonga* how the scheme works. Opened in 1981, the consulate was said by Attorney-General Tevita Tupou to have issued all but three of the purported naturalisations.

The Chens and South Pacific Sea Land Air Limited secured a 30-year lease on the volcanic island of Fonualei, in the northern Vava`u group. Through this "leasehold operation", foreign nationals could buy Tongan passports. By 1990, about 900 of the 20-year leases on Tongan land had been sold to foreigners.

According to Chen, a passport applicant needed to qualify first under the leasehold scheme before applying for protected person status or naturalisation as a Tongan.

Chen reportedly said that his consulate had issued about 900 protected person passports and 80 certificates of naturalisation. He added that about US$5 million had been received and this had been invested in the Tonga Trust Fund account with the Bank of America, San Francisco.

Emergency

Late in 1989, Pohiva and his legal counsel, Auckland barrister Dr Rodney Harrison and solicitor Nalesoni Tupou, filed a controversial lawsuit against the kingdom and the Police Minister, claiming the passports should be declared invalid because the sales were unconstitutional and illegal.

Tupou says he is being harassed and "punished" by Tongan authorities who in March 1991 barred him from entering his homeland without a special permit. He claims the moves against him are part of a plan to "cut off legal assistance and advice" to Pohiva.

After lengthy proceedings and arguments for more than a year, the case was finally about to go before the Supreme Court. Chief Justice Geoffrey Martin had been due on February 22 to set a date for an opening hearing.

However, four days earlier the government suddenly called an emergency session of Parliament in an attempt to legalise its passport practices over the previous six years.

Parliament was bitterly divided between the cabinet and the nobles who supported the passport legislation and seven of the commoner MPs who argued it would be damaging for Tonga to amend the Constitution to legalise a mistake.

Pohiva and his colleagues also argued that Parliament should allow the court to pass its final ruling before any further legislation was adopted.

Attorney-General Tevita Tupou insisted that the government was mainly concerned with the fate of 426 foreigners who had bought their passports in "good faith". He also warned of the consequences for the kingdom if the passports were not made legal.

"In addition to the inevitable return of all the money paid for these naturalisations and passports (plus accrued interest)," he said, "the country is exposed to very substantial claims for damages, which could be catastrophic if, for example, earlier nationalities have been relinquished ... or annulled."

Pohiva declared that the government was passing laws that would legalise what had been done illegally.

"This is totally unacceptable in any civilised society," he said.

Pohiva eventually stormed out of Parliament after distributing a letter saying the government was withholding important information from the debate.

Tongatapu's two other people's representatives, Laki Nui and Viliami Fukofuka, also later walked out after failing to pass amendments trying to block the legislative changes, which were adopted by a decisive 15–4 vote.

Mockery

"It is just unbelievable to amend the Constitution like that, they are making a mockery of the Constitution," Fukofuka said. "This is the beginning of the end."

When the passports case was dismissed by the Supreme Court on March 1, Chief Justice Martin awarded Pohiva NZ\$23,500 in court costs.

Pohiva told the court his legal advice was that now the Constitution had been changed it was no longer possible to press proceedings. However, he added that "the position I have taken on behalf of the people ... has been vindicated by the statements of the Attorney-General to Parliament acknowledging that what was done by the defendants was unconstitutional.

"With the passage of the amending legislation," he added, "I believe that the issue has ceased to be one appropriately to be determined by the courts. But the case does not end. It marks a new page in our history."

ʠ

Tongan passport exposure case lawyer Nalesoni Tupou: "harassed and punished".

DAVID ROBIE

IN SPITE of the ongoing controversy over Black Thursday and the aftermath of the passports scandal, publisher and broadcaster Kalafi Moala believes the Tongan relationship with China is beneficial and will continue to grow. After his 2002 book *Island Kingdom Strikes Back*,[11] in which he chronicled the saga of his *Taimi `o Tonga* newspaper's long and inspiring struggle to survive in the face of the repression by the establishment, Moala later wrote about issues of identity, culture and social justice in his evolving kingdom. His reflective 2009 book *Tonga: In Search of the Friendly Islands* included a critique of the political events leading to the devastation in downtown Nuku'alofa of 2006 and also a defence of ongoing Chinese aid in the Pacific.

> Foreign observers of China have often been faulty in predicting accurately what China will do or become. The relationship between our two countries, China and Tonga, is not a short term one but is here to stay, even after the events of 16/11. From a Tongan perspective, it is part of the "Look East" policy that the late King Taufa`ahau Tupou IV initiated and [was] carried on by his successor, King George Tupou V. The late king urged Tongan students to learn to speak Chinese; he also urged Tongan business people to learn from the Chinese how to do business.[12]

Moala argues that the bilateral relationships Tonga, and other Pacific nations, have with other nations and cultures should not be defined by "the colour of their skin, their race, or by which political bloc they are part of" in the world.[13] The key issue should be whether the relationship is beneficial to Tonga. Australia and New Zealand should not have a monopoly on these relationships.

Notes

1 Kalafi Moala (2009). *Tonga: In Search of the Friendly Islands.* Kealakekua, Hawai'i: Pasifika Foundation Press; Auckland: Pacific Media Centre, p. 53.
2 Ibid.
3 Ibid., p. 56.
4 Ibid.
5 Ibid., p. 58.
6 David Robie (1991, April 1). Tonga's passport scam: Tonga has admitted its passport-for-cash scheme is illegal, but unrest continues. *Auckland Star,* pp. 14–15.
7 David Robie (1991, May). The quiet crusader. *Pacific Islands Monthly,* pp. 14–17.
8 Ibid., p. 17.
9 Danny Gittings (1991, May). Tonga's missing millions. *Pacific Islands Monthly,* pp. 10–14.
10 Exiled Imelda Marcos was acquitted in a US federal court in 1990 on racketeering and fraud charges. She returned to the Philippines and contested the 1992 presidential election and was beaten into fifth place by President Corazon Aquino. Three years later she was elected in a landslide vote to represent Leyte in Congress. She was still a member of Congress in 2014 (representing Ilocos Norte at the age of 84).
11 Kalafi Moala (2002). *Island Kingdom Strikes Back: The Story of an Independent Island Newspaper—Taimi 'o Tonga.* Auckland: Pacmedia Publishers.
12 Kalafi Moala (2009). *Tonga: In Search of the Friendly Islands,* p. 71.
13 Ibid., p. 72.

11

Human rights abuses in the Pacific, 1992

This is how the [Rabuka] regime always deals with any public criticism or opposition. It claims that indigenous culture and tradition are under threat ... or the chiefs are being insulted ... or their land is being taken away.

Fiji academic Dr Anirudh Singh

UNTIL the mid-1980s, international human rights organisations gave Pacific Islands states a relatively clean bill of health. Apart, that is, from colonised East Timor and West Papua, which figured regularly in the annual Amnesty International Reports through documentation of Indonesian violations. Now human rights violations have become a growing concern in the region, especially over gender and domestic violence, leading researchers to monitor it more rigorously, and this is an issue Pacific political leaders have been reluctant to face.[1]

Former Papua New Guinean Justice Minister Bernard Narokobi, for example, branded Amnesty International a "criminal, illegal and immoral organisation" in an extraordinary outburst in August 1990 after it had made public a damning report about violations on Bougainville Island.[2] Narokobi had been once an outspoken champion of human rights.

The Amnesty International Report for 1990 and 1991 detailed violations in Fiji, Kanaky/New Caledonia,[3] Timor-Leste and West Papua as well as Bougainville.[4] The partial lifting of the 10-month economic (including medical) and communications blockade of Bougainville in January 1991 enabled journalists and researchers to investigate allegations that up to 3000 Islanders had died through lack of medicines or treatment. Papua New Guinea withdrew troops and riot police in March 1990 after it failed to quell a rebellion that left more than 150 people dead and devastated the copper-producing island's economy. Port Moresby imposed a blockade two months later—a policy alleged by some to be "bordering on genocide". Already there had been mounting evidence of extrajudicial killings,

The late Yann-Célene Uregei, a Kanak independence leader of the United Kanak Liberation Front (FULK), was brutally beaten in human rights violations in New Caledonia. He was Minister of Foreign Affairs in the 1984 provisional government of the Republic of Kanaky and was the target of hostility after taking a group of 17 youths to Libya for "training".

DAVID ROBIE

torture and beatings by the military, and the Bougainville Revolutionary Army (BRA) had also carried out assassinations and ill-treatment of its opponents.

According to an Amnesty International document made public in November 1990, at least 19 people had been killed in extrajudicial executions, or after being tortured in police and military custody. More than 50 people were reported as ill-treated or tortured by members of the security forces.[5] Forms of ill-treatment included beatings at road blocks, death threats, sexual abuse and the deliberate torture of detainees. The victims were suspected members or sympathisers of the BRA and included political leaders, journalists, medical professionals, government workers and ordinary villagers.

Most of the violations were said to have happened within the legal framework of Papua New Guinea's state of emergency, which gave security forces sweeping powers of arrest, detention and seizure. Amnesty also received other reports of alleged extrajudicial executions and other ill-treatment that it was not able to immediately confirm.

But it was allegations about the involvement of Australian military aid in what became dubbed the St Valentine's Day massacre that provoked most controversy. On 14 February 1990, United Church pastor Raumo Benito and five of his congregation were savagely beaten by PNG Defence Force personnel and then shot dead. An eyewitness to the macabre killings escaped, but the bodies were never recovered. Amnesty International reported that one of the four former Royal Australian Air Force Iroquois helicopters handed to Papua New Guinea as aid during the Bougainville rebellion was used to dump the bodies in the Pacific Ocean. The pilot was an Australian, although New Zealand pilots were also hired to fly the helicopters. The case was among several alleged human rights violations investigated by Australia's Joint Parliamentary Foreign Affairs and Defence Inquiry, which visited Papua New Guinea in February 1991.[6]

Amnesty described the institutional, legal and constitutional provisions for protecting human rights in Papua New Guinea as "vulnerable" when confronted with a serious political crisis. It blamed the breakdown of safeguards on two major factors: First, judicial and quasi-judicial institutions that were responsible for enforcing constitutionally guaranteed rights failed to operate in practice.

> Second, the government and Parliament failed to act decisively when confronted with serious allegations of human rights abuse. As a consequence, few, if any, of the alleged perpetrators have been brought to justice and the vast majority of victims have been left without redress.[7]

While the situation in Papua New Guinea, particularly during the Bougainville War, was arguably the worst in the South Pacific, more recent reports, such as by Amnesty International, have focused mostly on the "shocking and unacceptable levels of violence against women" in many Pacific nations.[8] In May 2013, the Pacific held centre stage at an inaugural Human Rights Conference organised by Amnesty International Aotearoa that discussed a "mosaic of human rights challenges", including "appalling" prison conditions, unreasonable use of force, torture by security forces, "corrosion" of the rule of law as well as violence against women.[9]

Civil and human rights have been fragile in Fiji since the four coups in 1987 (twice by Rabuka), 2000 (attempted by Speight and although it ultimately failed, his political agenda was adopted), and in 2006 (Bainimarama). The case of the kidnapping and torture of an academic by five soldiers during October 1990 was a blatant example of human rights violations with the apparent tacit support, if not actual instigation, of some authorities.

Fiji academic Dr Anirudh Singh, his right arm still in a splint, had medical treatment in New Zealand after being abducted and tortured by soldiers in retaliation for a protest burning of the discriminatory 1990 Constitution.   DAVID ROBIE

Political fallout from the case continued after the academic, Dr Anirudh Singh, then a 40-year-old senior lecturer in physics at the University of the South Pacific, visited Australia and New Zealand for medical treatment in November–December 1990. When the lecturer publicly spoke out against the torture, Fiji Information Minister Ratu Inoke Kubuabola—now Foreign Minister in the Bainimarama regime—issued a press statement that implied threats against Singh.[10] Kubuabola said that by making statements about a pending case in Fiji during his trip abroad, Singh had "openly flouted" due process of the law to "discredit the Fiji government and judiciary".

At a human rights public meeting in Auckland addressed by Dr Singh, his right arm still bound in a splint as a result of the torture, two Māori activists purporting to be from the separatist Te Ahi Kaa (Keepers of the Fire) movement disrupted the gathering to read out the minister's statement.[11] Two members of the Taukei Movement also threatened Dr Singh with further physical ill-treatment.

But Dr Singh refused to be intimidated by the threats and flew back to Fiji in early January 1991 to face charges of sedition and unlawful assembly. Six other Indo-Fijians were also charged—economics lecturer Dr Ganeshwar Chand (now vice-chancellor of the Fiji National University), education lecturer Dr Sudesh Raj Mishra, physics lecturer Dr Surendra Prasad, lecturer Trilochna Reddy, physician Dr Ram Krishna Reddy and former schoolteacher Ram Sumeshwar Yadav. The charges followed a peaceful protest at a prayer meeting during which a copy of the racially discriminatory republican Constitution was symbolically burned. Three *Daily Post* journalists were also charged for "maliciously fabricating" a report about further protests against the Constitution.

"THEY PUT A NOOSE AROUND MY NECK"

Auckland Star, 17 December 1990

SOFT-SPOKEN and unassuming, Dr Anirudh Singh plays down his role in Fiji as a human rights activist. Recalling the events of the past two months that led to his abduction and torture, the Indo-Fijian academic seems remarkably surprised at the international publicity he has unleashed.[12]

He is anxious to put things in perspective: "Ask me who am I? What am I? Nobody has really asked me these things.

"I'm really a scientist. I wasn't so interested in politics at all before this happened."

It troubles him. Besides the brutal physical attack on him by soldiers, the scars left from the torture and the smear attempts by the "regime's propagandists", Dr Singh wants to set the record straight.

He isn't from Britain, as some newspapers have said. He proudly says he is a Fiji citizen. Now a University of the South Pacific lecturer, he was in Britain for just over three years, completing his doctorate in physics.

And he would like to return to Leicester University to complete his research into the atomic structure of solids using a new technology, which involves the use of a particle accelerator.

But, Dr Singh, visiting New Zealand to address a public meeting in Auckland about his ordeal and other human rights abuses in Fiji, must wait until at least after January in 1991 when he and six colleagues face charges of sedition and unlawful assembly.

Defence lawyers believe "political interference" is involved in the case and filed an application for a High Court trial.

Dr Singh's lawyer, Miles Johnson, a former Fiji Law Society president and an outspoken critic of the new Constitution, regards the case as a test of the legality of the interim government.

"We're putting the case fairly and squarely that an accused cannot be guilty of sedition if the government itself is not legitimate," he said.

The military-backed government was installed after two coups in 1987.

Three journalists also face charges of "maliciously fabricating" a report about further protests against the Constitution.

Their newspaper, the *Daily Post*, reported a plan by University of the South Pacific-based protest groups to burn further copies of the Constitution.

This is believed to be the first time any prosecutions have been brought under the vaguely worded Section 15(a) of Fiji's *Public Order Act 1976*, which declares: "Any person who ... fabricates or knowingly spreads abroad or publishes, whether by writing or by word of mouth, or otherwise, any false news or false report tending to create or foster public alarm, public anxiety or disaffection or to result in the detriment of the public ... shall be guilty of an offence."

The three *Post* journalists—publisher Taniela Bolea, chief subeditor Robert Wendt and reporter Subash Verma—face a maximum penalty of one year in jail or $1000 fine if found guilty.

Media sources in Suva say the arrests could be part of a campaign by the interim government to close down the indigenous Fijian-owned newspaper because its outspokenness has become an "irritant" to the regime.

A report from the human rights group Amnesty International warned the accused activists and journalists would be considered "prisoners of conscience" if they are found guilty and jailed.[13]

"We are certainly keen to protect human rights on our doorstep," said Amnesty's New Zealand executive director, Colin Chiles.

Amnesty considers the so-called "Constitution 10" have been charged over the non-violent exercise of their constitutionally guaranteed rights to freedom of expression, assembly and association.

Interviewed by phone in Canberra, Dr Singh said he had no regrets about the symbolic burning of the new republican Fiji Constitution at a protest rally on October 18 during the Hindu Festival of Diwali.

"It won't even burn," one of about 200 protesters shouted at the time, amid cries of "*Azadi!*" ("Freedom!"). The burning incident sparked off the brutal kidnapping.

"It was a spontaneous event, but we're not apologising for it," said Dr Singh. "We have a right to freely express our views against the racial discrimination of the Constitution."

He rejects a *Daily Post* editorial that declared after the burning, such a "provocative" act would always attract reaction from extremists.

"It wouldn't have been provocative at all if it hadn't been used by the propagandists and mischief-makers of the regime to stir up trouble," he said.

"This is how the regime always deals with any public criticism or opposition. It claims indigenous culture and tradition are under threat ...or the chiefs are being insulted ... or their land is being taken away.

"The mischief-makers provoke hostile and racist feelings."[14]

After the burning of the Constitution, regime officials called the incident "despicable and treasonous" and ordered police to investigate.

Reports said the Public Prosecutions director described the burning as a seditious act intended to "raise discontent or disaffection among the inhabitants of Fiji". The demonstration itself was said to be illegal.

Four days after the burning, Dr Singh, chairperson of the Group Against Racial Discrimination (GARD), was among several academics and students briefly detained by police for questioning.

On October 24, five soldiers in plain clothes abducted Dr Singh in daylight near his Suva home in Flagstaff as he walked to work.

They bundled him into a car with the number plate D8654, which was later said to have been traced to an officer in the Fiji Military Forces.

The abductors drove Dr Singh to the Colo-i-Suva rainforest area on the outskirts of the capital where they held him prisoner for 11 hours.

He alleged he was tortured by three of them while being interrogated about his political activities.

According to an Amnesty International report, Dr Singh said his captors covered his head with a hood, looped a rope around his neck, which they tied to his feet, and bound both his hands and feet.

Then the kidnappers beat him on his face, chest and arms. Later, when the hood had been removed from his head, Dr Singh's hair was roughly cut and some of it was burned with lighted cigarettes.

While his hands were still bound, they were held against the base of a tree and beaten repeatedly with a steel pipe by his captors as they questioned him about the identities and addresses of other protesters.

Finally freed at 8pm that night, Dr Singh staggered to safety. He was taken to Suva's Colonial War Memorial Hospital where he was treated for broken bones in his hands and multiple wounds and bruises on other parts of his body.

Dr Singh has also received further treatment in Australia and is still unable to make a fist with his hands.

Amnesty International twice wrote to the interim Prime Minister, Ratu Sir Kamisese Mara, on October 24 and 29 expressing concern about the kidnapping and torture of Dr Singh.

However, the regime replied there was "no evidence to suggest the involvement of police or military personnel".

In its second response, on October 30, the regime confirmed a police investigation had been launched immediately after the abduction. But it made no mention of the arrest of five soldiers—a captain and four corporals—in the same day .

The soldiers, including Captain Sotia Ponijiase, who had reportedly received Special Air Service elite training in Britain and New Zealand, pleaded guilty to abduction and grievous bodily harm charges. On November 22, they were given one-year suspended jail sentences and fined $170 each.

Adi Kuini Bavadra, then leader of the Fiji Labour Party-led Coalition, accused the Fiji military's shadowy Counter-Revolutionary Warfare Unit of having organised the abduction.

Condemning the abduction and torture, the *Daily Post* also protested over the arrest of its journalists involved in the affair.

The newspaper said the arrests seriously challenged the freedom of the press: "The worrying thought that emerges here is if the police action is a possible start of suppression of this freedom ... while the *Post* men were in custody, the real culprits (burners of the Constitution and Dr Singh's bashers) were still at large. Someone appears to be barking up the wrong tree."

Dr Singh is under no illusions. He believes he was driven to the Constitution protest because freedom of speech has been stifled under the regime and the news media operates under conditions of strict self-censorship.

"The *Daily Post* has been the bravest of the media and the consequences are upon it now," he said. "We have been totally frustrated by our lack of freedom of expression."

Since the Constitution burning and abduction, the regime has clamped down even harder.

"After I was tortured, the military visited the newspaper offices and seized pictures that showed me with my injuries. The staff were told, in effect, to behave or else!"

Dr Singh condemns the atmosphere of racial hatred and animosity encouraged by the regime. He now believes he is a marked man for daring to speak out.

"The worst thing about it is that things have got so worked up I might be attacked in the street by ordinary people who recognise my picture in the paper."

An excerpt from how Dr Singh described his torture to *The Fiji Times*:

I saw two men walking towards me. They looked suspicious but I didn't pay much attention.

The suddenly one of them hit me ... and then the other. I fell down. [A car arrived.]

I struggled and tried to make as much noise as possible, but they managed to drag me into the car. They covered my eyes with some sort of padding and they pulled a balaclava over my head.

The balaclava was tied around my neck. I found it difficult to breathe normally and had to use my mouth ...

One of my abductors tied my hands together, the other my feet while another put a noose around my neck.

They then punched and questioned me repeatedly, asking the where-abouts of certain people. [He was beaten in three spells before one man went away.]

The two others then went to sleep … They woke up about 6pm and started hitting me on my eyes and face.

They then laid my hands against a root of a tree and smashed my hands repeatedly with a steel pipe. They also chopped off my hair and burned strands with cigarettes.[15]

HUMAN rights violations in the Asia-Pacific region and a climate of impunity are most serious in Indonesia, especially the Melanesian region of West Papua, and the Philippines. In Indonesia, a controversial award-winning film about the massacres during the anti-communist purges in 1965-6 provided a context for the ongoing alleged atrocities in West Papua by Indonesian soldiers.[16] In *The Act of Killing*, the documentary highlights the virtually taboo topic of the "horrific slaughter [which] claimed hundreds of thousands of alleged and committed communists (possibly a million tortured and executed souls) and led to the jailing of another million".[17] The film interviews "some proud death squad alumni", such as right-wing Pancasila Youth paramilitary leader Anwar Congo—who not only boast about their past crimes, but reenact their assassination techniques on the screen. In the Philippines, according to a USAID report in May 2013, there has been a "resurgence" of political killings, assassinations of journalists and other forms of human rights violations in the country over the past seven years.[18] In fact, this has been continuous ever since the Marcos dictatorship. "Varying estimates, depending on the source, put the number of people killed for their political beliefs anywhere from more than one hundred to almost a thousand during this period," the report noted:

Compounding the problem is the general sense of impunity for the perpetrators. To date, very few violators have been convicted of extra-legal killings or enforced disappearances of political activists. While the best deterrent to human rights violations is the fair and full enforcement of the law, the state's capacity to prosecute and convict violators is hampered by a range of factors that include: overloaded judges and prosecutors with little or no training in handling human rights cases, weak investigations, lack of evidence, and the lack or unwillingness of witnesses to come forward.[19]

Authorities under all the presidents since the Marcos dictatorship ended in 1986 have rolled over corruption and pacifying techniques for dissidents among the population, and have capitalised on the "language of terror". Here is a guide to the euphemisms used:

- **Salvaging**: A grisly contribution of the Philippine military to the English language, referring to the summary execution of thousands of Filipinos by military and vigilante groups. Under the Marcos regime they were supposedly being "saved from communism".

- **Sparrows**: Sparrow squads are groups of rebels who assassinate soldiers, military informers, policemen and public officials accused of "crimes against the people".

- **Vigilantes**: Ill-disguised anti-communist death squads, usually criminal groups armed and trained by the military. Sometimes they are bizarre fundamentalist sects with distorted views on Christianity, or like Tadtad, are ritual killers.

- **Zoning**: This involves cordoning off an area, such as a village, or several city blocks, for intensive house-to-house searches for suspected "subversives". Not only do the troops fail to have search warrants, but they frequently plunder livestock, possessions or valuables belonging to the peasants or workers.

- **Hamletting**: A military strategy reminiscent of Vietnam in the 1950s and early 1960s, which peaked in the post-Marcos years. During 1987, for example, more than 18,000 families were forced to move from their homes to military-controlled hamlets in efforts to isolate rebels.

The so-called "Asia pivot" strategy by Washington towards the region to counterbalance China by strengthening political, security and economic ties with countries such as Indonesia and the Philippines is likely to mean a diminished US commitment to addressing human rights violations, corruption and undemocratic behaviour by partner nations. The security focus is in the context of "anti-terrorism". According to

Indonesian troops show off a "trophy" West Papuan victim in an atrocity comparable with the violations in Timor-Leste before independence was restored in 2002.   APHRC

analyst Ed McWilliams, "the Obama administration's expansion of ties to regional military forces in Indonesia, and also in Vietnam, the Philippines and Burma (Myanmar) have proceeded notwithstanding well-founded concerns that these security 'partners' have well-documented histories of human rights violations, corruption and undemocratic behaviour".[20] A number of the prospective security partners also have records of repression against minorities, such as the Vietnamese government's "ethnic cleansing" of indigenous Montagnards.[21] Indonesia's worst human rights record is in West Papua, the troubled western half of New Guinea island forcibly annexed in the 1960s and endorsed by the sham "Act of No Choice" in 1969.

In 2005, Victoria University of Wellington legal academic Petra Butler argued for a regional human rights framework such as a charter for the Pacific region, pointing out that Asia was the only other region in the world lacking such a charter.[22] She also stressed that 15 years had elapsed without progress since the 1989 Law Association for Asia and the Pacific (LAWASIA) Charter had been proposed. The main objection had been identified as a fear by Pacific states that their cultural identity might be in jeopardy. But the situation had changed in the Pacific, Butler noted:

> The establishment of the Fiji Human Rights Commission in 1997, the unrest in the Solomon Islands and the subsequent peace and reconciliation movement, and also the ever-increasing judgments referring to human rights by the courts of the Pacific are only some examples to show that political buy-in for a Pacific Human Rights Charter might be easier to achieve than 15 years ago.[23]

Pacific human rights problems identified by Butler included:

- the self-determination of peoples;

- the rights of indigenous peoples;

- the rights of cultural minorities—often immigrants from elsewhere in the region; and

- the status of women.

In 2009, the International Committee of the Red Cross published a booklet on Pacific conflict, human rights and humanitarian law entitled *Under the Protection of the Palm*. It retold anecdotal "tales of humanity" in the middle of traditional wars in the Pacific.[24] It also highlighted parallels with contemporary humanitarian law principles, including the protection of women and children. Based on research by a group of law students from the University of the South Pacific, the booklet focused largely on traditional warfare between Pacific nations or tribes. But it overlooked conflict caused or intensified by occupying military forces such as in Bougainville or West Papua. While tribal warfare was seen as a "male activity" in Papua New Guinea's Highlands, for example, "women were viewed as the inspiration for wars":

> If a woman was raped, abducted, eloped or committed adultery with men of other political units, this called for redress through hostilities.[25]

In May 2013, former Fiji Human Rights Commissioner Graham Leung and currently a senior trainer for the Secretariat of the Pacific Community Regional Rights Resource Team (RRRT) human rights programme delivered a keynote address at an Amnesty International conference in

Auckland. Leung described violence against women as "surely … one of the most serious human rights violations" in the Pacific.[26] Characterising the state of human rights in the region, he said:

> For decades it was fashionable to believe that the Pacific was indeed that—Pacific; tales of the South Seas by countless sailors, fortune hunters and colonialists, and later tourists seeking to bask in the warm tropical sunshine conjuring up notions of an idyllic region people by "friendly smiling natives". While in many respects this romanticised version of the Pacific has elements of veracity, it has disguised some ugly realities about the region we call home. I think today we know better.

Reeling off a series of challenges, including torture and "human rights violations of many kinds on a daily basis", Leung also talked about law and democracy problems and political instability in Nauru, Solomon Islands and Vanuatu caused by politicians "crossing the floor".

"In my own country, Fiji, a military-backed regime now enters its seventh year of rule by decree," he said. "There is increasing evidence that subtle corrosion of the rule of law and judicial independence is occurring in some countries … Corruption is a major concern." In a report about the controversial 2013 Fiji Constitution, Amnesty International said that contrary to claims by the Fiji regime, "the new Constitution actually weakens human rights protection in the country".[27]

But it was the issue of violence against women that Graham Leung mostly addressed: "In some Pacific countries … two out of every three women are affected by violence across the Pacific. Every day many Pacific women live in fear of violence."

> A 2008 WHO survey found that 23 percent of women in Kiribati reported abuse during pregnancy, while 68 percent of women aged 15–49 experienced violence from an intimate partner. In Papua New Guinea, 67 percent of women are beaten by their husbands—100 percent in the Highlands—with gang rape and pay-back rape common.

By the end of 2013, the major human rights issue was Tony Abbott government's "shameful" so-called Pacific solution to the asylum seeker issue by blocking their entry to Australia by shipping them to detention centres on Manus Island in Papua New Guinea and Nauru. Amnesty International called for an urgent independent investigation by Australian authorities into the death of an asylum seeker, 23-year-old Reza Berati from

Iran, and 70 others who were injured in a "distressing" riot at Manus Island camp in February 2014.[28] About 1200 asylum seekers were detained there indefinitely in "deliberately harsh and humiliating" conditions. An SBS *Dateline* programme on February 25 alleged that the Australian government was maintaining a "charade" by pretending to process the claims of asylum seekers when in fact the camp was designed to be nothing more than a deterrent. The camp was guarded by Australian taxpayer funded security contractor G4S. Migration agent Liz Thompson said: "The process … cannot continue after an asylum seeker has been brutally murdered in the care of the people who were supposed to be looking after him."

In March 2014, Vanuatu Prime Minister Moana Carcasses Kalosil made an impassioned speech at the United Nations Human Rights Council in Switzerland in support of the West Papuan people and self-determination, accusing the international community of "neglect" over the issue. Likening the West Papuan struggle to the Vanuatu's own story of seeking independence from the Anglo-French condominium of the New Hebrides, widely branded as "pandemonium" because of the dual colonial systems in 1980, Carcasses said: "We fought for our independence because it is our God-given right to be free." He told the council:

> Since the controversial Act of Free Choice in 1969, the Melanesian People of West Papua have been subject to ongoing human rights violations committed by the Indonesian security services. The world has witnessed the litany of tortures, murders, exploitation, rapes, military raids, arbitrary arrests and dividing of civil society through intelligence operations.
>
> The Indonesian National Commission on Human Rights (KOMNAS HAM) concluded that these acts constitute crimes against humanity under Indonesian Law No. 26/2000.
>
> In this climate of fear and repression of political dissent, and blatant negligence by the international community including the UN and the powerful developed countries since 1969, we find this forgotten race still dare to dream for equality and justice. Yet the democratic nations have kept silent.[29]

Three days after the fiery UN speech, a Fiji musician, *vude* king Seru Serevi, released a song entitled "Rise Morning Star" inspired by the exiled group Black Brothers and in honour of those who have been jailed for raising the pro-independence flag banned by Indonesia.

Notes

1 David Robie (1993). Human rights abuses in the Pacific. In Kevin Clements (ed.), *Peace and Security in the Asia Pacific Region*. Tokyo: United Nations University Press; Palmerston North: Dunmore Press, pp. 124–41.

2 David Robie (1990, September 4). Amnesty accusations draw fire. *The Dominion*.

3 John Connell (1987). The fight for Kanaky. In *New Caledonia or Kanaky? The political history of a French colony*. Canberra, ACT: Research School of Pacific Studies, Australian National University, pp. 318–72.

4 *Amnesty International Report 1990* (1990). London: Amnesty International Publications.

5 *PNG: Human Rights Violations on Bougainville, 1989–90* (1990, November). London: Amnesty International Report, p. 1.

6 Robie (1993). Human rights abuses in the Pacific.

7 *PNG: Human Rights Violations on Bougainville, 1989–90*. Amnesty International.

8 Amnesty International Human Rights Conference (2013, May 4). Papers presented at the conference. Retrieved on 20 September 2013, from www.amnesty.org.nz/humanrightsconference2013

9 Graham Leung (2013). A perspective on "human wrongs" in the Pacific: The perennial challenge of addressing violence against women. Unpublished keynote address at the Amnesty International Aotearoa annual conference, 4 May 2013.

10 Fiji Ministry of Information (1990, December 17). Press statement.

11 Maori interrupt academic (1990, December 27). *The Press*. [Public meeting addressed by Dr Anirudh Singh, Auckland, 18 December 1990.]

12 David Robie (1990, December 17). "They put a noose around my neck". *Auckland Star*, p. A9.

13 Fiji civil rights activists and journalists arrested (1990, November). London: Amnesty International Report.

14 Dr Anirudh Singh (1990, December 12). Telephone interview with the author, Canberra.

15 *The Fiji Times* (1990, October 25).

16 Joshua Oppenheimer (2012). *The Act of Killing* [Documentary]. See http://theactofkilling.com

17 Asawin Suebsaeng (2014, January 10). Inside The Act of Killing's guerrilla film distribution campaign in Indonesia. *Pacific Media Centre Online*. Retrieved on 10 January 2014, from www.pmc.aut.ac.nz/articles/inside-act-killing-s-guerrilla-film-distribution-campaign-indonesia

18 USAID (2013, May 30). Strengthening human rights in the Philippines project. Retrieved on 20 September 2013, from http://philippines.usaid.gov/programs/democracy-governance/strengthening-human-rights-philippines

19 Ibid.

20 Ed McWilliams (2013). Implications of the "Asia Pivot" for US policy in Indonesia. *Scoop*. Retrieved on 21 September 2013, from www.scoop.co.nz/stories/WO1309/S00207/west-papua-report-september-2013.htm

21 Ibid.

22 Petra Butler (2005). A human rights charter for the Pacific. *Human Rights Research Journal*, 3 [Online edition], p. 2. Retrieved on 20 September 2013, from www.victoria.ac.nz/law/centres/nzcpl/publications/human-rights-research-journal/publications/vol-3/Butler.pdf

23 Ibid., p. 3.

24 International Committee of the Red Cross (2009). *Under the Protection of the Palm: Wars of Dignity in the Pacific.* Suva, Fiji.

25 Ibid., p. 9

26 Leung (2013). A perspective on "human wrongs" in the Pacific, p. 1.

27 Fiji: New constitution fails to protect fundamental human rights (2013, September 4). Amnesty International [Media release]. Retrieved on 20 September 2013, from www.amnesty.org/en/news/fiji-new-constitution-fails-protect-fundamental-human-rights-2013-09-04

28 Australia must investigate fatal incident on Manus Island (2014, February 18). Amnesty International. www.amnesty.org

29 Vanuatu PM blasts Indonesian human rights violations in West Papua (2014, March 6). Pacific Media Centre Online. Retrieved on 9 March 2014, from http://www.pmc.aut.ac.nz/articles/vanuatu-pm-blasts-indonesian-human-rights-violations-west-papua

12

The jailing of the 'Tongan three', 1996

*The solutions to Tonga's problems are going to involve more than just a
system reform. Reforming into a democracy does not solve problems of
poverty, crime and social justice.*
Taimi `o Tonga publisher, broadcaster and social critic Kalafi Moala

WHILE Papua New Guinea, the country with the largest news media in
the region, was preoccupied with threats to its own press freedom in
the mid-1990s, several remarkable events affecting media freedom were
taking place around the rest of the South Pacific: a cartoon published in
the *Cook Islands News* on 28 September 1995 was belatedly cited by the
Parliamentary Privileges Committee for contempt; a Tongan journalist,
*Taimi `o Tonga* acting editor Filokalafi `Akau`ola, was given an 18-month
suspended prison sentence in February 1996 over the publication of a letter
criticising then Police Minister Clive Edwards; the Vanuatu government
tried to suppress news about a post-electoral prime ministerial seesaw; and
in Fiji the government ordered an urgent comprehensive review of laws
regulating mass media. The Fiji review was expected to include advice to
the government on whether it should impose a limit on foreign ownership
of news organisations—and if so, at what level of shareholding.[1]

But the single most disturbing media affair was the jailing in Tonga
during September 1996 of `Akau`ola, his editor, Kalafi Moala, and outspoken commoner MP and publisher `Akilisi Pohiva for alleged contempt
of Parliament. After a wave of international condemnation, the Supreme
Court finally ruled that the detention was unconstitutional and in violation
of the Assembly's standing orders. The accused men were set free after
serving 26 days of their 30-day sentence.

In a letter to Pacific Media Watch, *Pacific Journalism Review* and the
Australian Centre for Independent Journalism (ACIJ) thanking them for
their role in helping win the dissident advocates their freedom, Moala wrote:

> We were not aware of what was going on until we were released. In jail
> we were not allowed radio or any other reading material other than a

Bible, so we were out of touch for 26 days. The prison wardens would now and then pass on bits and pieces of information, but they were mostly local news.

The three of us were very moved when we came out of jail to find that your organisation as well as others from around the world were protesting [against] our jailing. The signed petition you put together was something else![2]

Moala had launched Tonga's first independent newspaper, *Taimi ʻo Tonga*, in 1989 with the objective of "bringing alternative perspectives and voices into the Pacific Island kingdom's public sphere".[3] His efforts ultimately contributed to greater freedom and progress towards political and democratic reform. His 2002 book, *Island Kingdom Strikes Back*, gave a vivid and inspiring account of his newspaper team's struggle for a more open society and his family's sacrifices for the cause.[4] He was awarded the inaugural Pacific Media Freedom Award that year by the Auckland-based Pacific Islands Media Association (PIMA) and won the award again in 2003. But, curiously, the Suva-based main regional Pacific Islands News Association (PINA) never similarly honoured Moala. In *Island Kingdom*, Moala cited a Pacific Media Watch dispatch headlined "PROTESTS MOUNT OVER TONGAN JOURNALIST JAILING", in which I wrote: "International media organisations and Pacific islands groups joined in a chorus of protest over ... [the] jailing of two Tongan journalists and a pro-democracy Member of Parliament." The dispatch under my name and my Pacific Media Watch colleague Peter Cronau, said in part:

We protest over the campaign of media harassment and suppression of freedom of expression by the Tongan government which has led to the detention of journalists and politicians for the third time in less than a year.[5]

But the struggle wasn't over when the "Tongan three" were finally set free. Barely were they out of their cells when the following month, November 1996, ʻAkauʻola was again harassed. He was detained for questioning along with Pohiva, and another pro-democracy MP, Teisina Fuko. But this time ʻAkauʻola was released after half an hour while police prepared sedition charges against the MPs over an article calling for democracy in the kingdom. My article for *Pacific Journalism Review* assessed the kingdom's pressure on the media.[6]

THE CONTEMPT CASE OF THE "TONGAN THREE"

Pacific Journalism Review, November 1996

GAGS, threats, defamation cases with the threat of bankruptcy and vilification are nothing new to Samuela `Akilisi Pohiva. The pro-democracy movement leader who has been a broadcaster and publishes a best-selling "muckraking" newsletter has faced everything he thought the establishment in the kingdom of Tonga could throw at him.

But the imprisonment of commoner MP Pohiva and two journalists for 30 days in September 1996 for alleged contempt of Parliament shocked media and human rights circles in the Pacific and internationally. Pohiva, arguably the best-known whistle-blower in the region, has waged a decade-long campaign for open government and he exposed the notorious Tongan passports-for-sale scandal in his newsletter *Koe Kele`a*.

Many media commentators see the jailings in Tonga as the most serious threat to media freedom in the South Pacific since the Fiji coups in 1987, and Fiji Prime Minister Sitiveni Rabuka, who led both coups, sees the harsh move as a lesson for journalists. Other critics, including a spokesperson for the Commonwealth Journalists Association, regard the issue as one of a need for greater professionalism.

Feuding between some media organisations over the support campaign backing the jailed three—Pohiva, *Taimi `o Tonga* editor `Eakalafi Moala and subeditor Filokalafi `Akau`ola—also added a curious twist to the affair. Although Australian news media largely ignored the jailings, in spite of a parallel situation with five journalists having faced jail sentences or fines in recent contempt of court cases, several organisations treated the issue seriously—including a daily "Tongan jailings update" on the Online Journalist website (http://acij.uts.edu.au).

One of the jailed men, `Akau`ola, had been detained for 24 hours in February 1996 after his newspaper published a letter criticising Police Minister Clive Edwards. An Auckland-based Agence France-Presse correspondent, Michael Field, who has closely reported Tongan affairs, was barred from entering the kingdom for the Pacific Islands News Association (PINA) convention in August because of alleged critical writing.

The three men walked free on October 14 after serving just three weeks of their sentence when the Tongan Supreme Court ruled they had been detained illegally in violation of the Constitution.

New Zealand civil rights lawyer Barry Wilson, acting for the Commonwealth Press Union, said from Nuku`alofa that their release was encouraging for emerging democratic freedoms in the kingdom: "The court found that the three

Taimi `o Tonga publisher Kalafi Moala being interviewed at the Auckland launch of his 2009 book *Tonga: In Search of the Friendly Islands.*   DEL ABCEDE/PMC

had not been covered by the normal safeguards for a trial provided under the Constitution. Therefore [the court] came to the conclusion that they were being illegally detained."

Wilson successfully filed a writ of habeas corpus on October 11 after two earlier attempts had failed. Wilson said: "I'm also not happy with the jail conditions under which the men are being held." He added they were being treated differently as political prisoners. Amnesty International declared the three men as political prisoners and international media freedom groups and human rights movements mounted several appeals for their release.

A petition organised jointly by the Australian Centre for Independent Journalism (ACIJ) and Pacific Media Watch, and signed by more than 170 academics, journalists, media commentators and students—including teachers from Saint Joseph's International School in Port Moresby—was faxed to King Taufa'ahau Tupou IV seeking his intervention to free the men.

Pohiva had been jailed for contempt of Parliament on 20 September 1996 after having leaked an impeachment notice against Justice Minister Tevita Tupou. Moala and `Akau`ola were jailed for publishing the leaked document in a front-page story in the *Taimi `o Tonga.*

The Supreme Court found that the constitutional provisions such as clause 10 for trials and sentencing under law, and clause 11 providing for indictments, defence procedures and the right to call witnesses, were breached. It also ruled that the three men had not been correctly found guilty by the Legislative Assembly of the offence they were accused of under clause 70 of the Constitution. The Tongan government defended its parliamentary action, saying the journalists broke the law and should be accountable.

The "Tongan three" furore erupted after the *Taimi ʻo Tonga* published a Tongan-language story on September 4 under the headline "PARLIAMENT IMPEACHES MINISTER FOR JUSTICE" about an untabled impeachment notice alleging abuse of office against Justice Minister Tevita Tupou.

As the Tongan government has tried in the past to silence Pohiva and journalists who have tried to shed light on the maladministration of cabinet and Parliament, it moved quickly to stifle dissent over the jailings by suspending the Legislative Assembly on October 4 until the middle of [1997].

King Taufaʻauhau Tupou IV used his powers as absolute monarch to close the House after it had voted to impeach Justice Minister Tupou. Tonga's 30-member Legislative Assembly is dominated by 21 unelected representatives of the Kingdom's noble families (cabinet ministers are appointed by the King) plus nine elected people's representatives.

Shocked Tongans interpreted the closing of Parliament as a way for the monarch to "buy time for the nobles to regroup as the House faces growing democratic demands. The decision to close the Legislative Assembly, which normally sits until mid-November, was announced in a radio broadcast but the palace would not comment further.

According to *New Zealand Herald* Pacific affairs reporter John Manukia, himself Tongan, leaders from the Tongan community did not wish to be identified because they feared they might be looked upon as questioning the King's authority.

Kalafi Moala challenged Parliament over the "historical trial", claiming the three had been given a prejudiced hearing. In an article in the *Taimi ʻo Tonga* headlined "WE DIDN'T GET A FAIR TRIAL", Moala defended his paper's action in publishing an untabled motion seeking the impeachment of Justice Minister Tevita Tupou for allegedly going to the Atlanta Olympics and being paid full parliamentary allowances.[7] Pohiva also defended his role in a commentary in the same edition of *Taimi ʻo Tonga*.[8]

"We firmly believe we didn't do anything wrong," wrote Moala. "What we published was factual and truthful. It is true that the people's representatives had already signed a petition calling for the impeachment of the Justice Minister because he travelled to the Olympics even though his request for leave was refused."

Moala said it was also true that the motion had been registered and placed in the Deputy Speaker's files so had already been in the parliamentary process. "This newspaper only reported that the petition had been submitted, the allegations of the petition, and who were the MPs who had signed it."

Amnesty International declared the three prisoners of conscience—a term the organisation uses to describe people who are in any form of detention because of their political, religious or other conscientiously held beliefs—provided that they have not used or advocated violence. In a letter on September 23 to the King, Amnesty International urged the Tongan head of state to exercise his powers to lift the detention orders "immediately and unconditionally".

Amnesty said it believed the three men had been imprisoned as a result of their peaceful exercise of the right to freedom of expression, guaranteed by Article 19 of the Universal Declaration of Human Rights and protected by Article 19 of the International Covenant on Civil and Political Rights.

The organisation noted that Clause 7 of the Tongan Constitution of 1875 states: "It shall be lawful for all people to speak and write and print their own opinions and no law shall ever be enacted to restrict this liberty. There shall be freedom of speech and of the press forever but nothing in this clause shall be held to outweigh the law of slander or the laws for the protection of the King and the royal family."

But the Tongan government reacted bitterly over the flood of international criticism about the jailings, claiming that the men had set themselves up to be "martyrs" and accusing press freedom and other organisations of waging a campaign of "media terrorism" against the kingdom.

Acting Chief Secretary `Eseta Fusitu`a said the government had received a series of "incorrect, unjust, biased and malicious" press condemnation following the jailings and called on protesting media organisations to publish the "facts". In a "background" statement defending government actions faxed to several media organisations on September 26, including Pacific Media Watch, *Pacific Journalism Review* and the Australian Centre for Independent Journalism (ACIJ), Fusitu`a claimed the issue was not one of "freedom of the press, nor the right of the public to be informed about matters of public interest". She said the issues were "the right of the House and the Minister for Justice to be reported truthfully, and the right of the people to correct information" in a newspaper.

> Both of these are fundamental human rights, and are the elementary demands of the principles of natural justice. Both rights, however, were violated by Moala, `Akau`ola and Pohiva, and are still being violated by many overseas organisations and media services.
>
> Despite this most regrettable reality, of media terrorism against Tonga, we are still hopeful that reputable media services will one day ask for the facts, and will one day publish them.

Fusitu`a acknowledged Agence France-Presse news agency, Radio Australia and Radio New Zealand International for contacting the government to seek information, but condemned a "blacklist" of protesting media organisations. Fusitu'a criticised the World Press Freedom Committee (USA), Australian Centre for Independent Journalism (Sydney, Australia), *Pacific Journalism Review* (Papua New Guinea), National Press Club (PNG), Pacific Star Pty Limited (publishers of *The National*, PNG), International Press Institute (France), Word Publishing Company Limited (PNG), New Zealand Journalists Training Organisation, New Zealand Engineering, Printing and Manufacturing Union, Amnesty International (UK), the *New Zealand Herald* and "many other" print and radio media.

"The history of the media provides very meagre evidence of voluntary corrections of misinformation. To do so is bad for the actual authors of the misinformation, for the reputation of the media organisation, and, of course, for their sales," Fusitu`a said. However, a spokesperson for *Pacific Media Watch* said the Tongan government had failed to recognise the difference between the role of "news gathering" media organisations and those "protesting" over the jailing.

Among other reactions, the International Federation of Journalists, the world's largest organisation of journalists, representing more than 400,000 journalists in 95 countries, expressed "dismay" and appealed for their release. "This act of punishment is a clear violation of freedom of expression and opinion," said senior vice-president Christopher Warren in a letter to the King. "Given the widespread anxiety of human rights organisations and journalist colleagues in the Asia-Pacific region, I hope you will intervene to release unconditionally those journalists [who] have been jailed. The IFJ also asks you to intervene to guarantee the rights of journalists in Tonga, who belong to our member organisation, the Pacific Journalists' Association."

Warren said the IFJ was concerned that this attempt to punish and intimidate journalists and to impose systems of media control "are an offence to democracy and undermine the capacity of people to participate openly in society".

In other reaction, *The National* newspaper of Papua New Guinea and the *Fiji Times* published harshly critical editorials on the Tongan government. *The National* described the kingdom as an "archaic monarchy" and said it needed change: " 'Libelling the Legislative Assembly' is a weak excuse. Upsetting the King would be more to the point." Gagging the three men with jail terms would "keep the country in the dark ages", warned *The National*. "That era belonged in the 15th and 16th centuries. Today even the famous British monarchy is agonising over its role and trying to change its ancient ways to fit into modern times."

The Fiji Times said: "It has driven home the fact that freedom of expression is very much under threat in the Pacific and could very well become a reality in Fiji. The authorities say 'negative' reports show a lack of respect for them and any such criticism is immediately labelled 'culturally insensitive'—the façade they hide behind to prevent scrutiny of their actions." *The Times* praised the courage of Moala, `Akau'ola and Pohiva.

However, Fiji Prime Minister Sitiveni Rabuka said his country had "no business" interfering with the Tongan government's media policy and regarded it as a warning to local journalists. While media freedom of expression in Fiji is guaranteed by the Constitution, according to the coup leader, the media has a role to protect that freedom by ensuring at all times that it reports "accurate and fairly".

A rift between several Tongan journalists and the major regional media organisation, Pacific Islands News Association (PINA), which primarily represents the publishers and owners, and its newly created Pacific Freedom of Information Network, burst into the open. Following a deputation to the King by PINA's administrator Nina Ratulele to seek the jailed men's release, a move widely welcomed in the region, PINA executive director Tavake Fusimalohi angrily resigned. Fusimalohi, general manager of Radio Tonga and a longtime PINA stalwart but personally opposed to Pohiva, was quoted by Radio Australia as saying he had resigned over "personal attacks" against him and the local PINA affiliate, Tonga News Association, by PINA president Monica Miller of American Samoa.

Fusimalohi said she had accused them of remaining silent over the jailing of their Tongan colleagues. But Miller appealed to journalists in the region not to lose sight of the main reason why the three men were jailed—the *Taimi `o Tonga* had published information which the people of Tonga had a right to know.

The jailings were the latest confrontation between Pohiva and the Tongan establishment which is opposed to open and accountable government. During 1993, Pohiva faced five lawsuits—three libel cases involving damages totalling 180,000 pa`anga, and two gagging actions seeking to prevent him publishing information considered confidential in his newsletter *Ko `e Kele`a*, and also in an attempt to force him to reveal his sources.

"If these actions succeed it will silence the news media—it will effectively shut down a free press in Tonga," said Auckland lawyer Nalesoni Tupou, who had himself become exiled from his homeland because of his legal work on behalf of Pohiva.

Although Pohiva lost defamation cases totalling more than 60,000 pa`anga in damages, he remained defiant. But he believed the Tongan establishment was trying to destroy him by making him bankrupt.

AFTER the November 2006 riots in Nuku`alofa, Kalafi Moala became more critical of some elements of the Tongan pro-democracy movement, including Pohiva. In his 2009 book *In Search of the Friendly Islands* analysing the changes in Tonga and the challenges for the future, and written after his return to Tonga and a reassessment of the kingdom's realities, Moala wrote that while Pohiva would go down in history as the man who had headed a "reform movement that had shaped Tongan socio-politics for two decades", he was now surrounding himself with people "whose ambitions and ways lack integrity".[9]

In the first 15 years of the movement, people of character and wisdom surrounded Pohiva. I can think of the late Dr Sione `Amanaki Havea, the late Bishop Patyelisio Finau, Professor Futa Helu, `Uhila Liava`a, Laki Niu, Dr Uili Fukofuka, Dr Feleti Sevele and many others. But since 2004, the people who had stood in the frontlines with Pohiva had either died or disassociated themselves from him. Others quickly moved in to take their place. They were people who used to be supporters of the royal family and government but had been embittered for one reason or another. Some of them were enemies of Pohiva previously. Notable among them are turncoats such as Clive Edwards, a former Minister of Police; young broadcaster Sangster Saulala; Semesi Tapueluelu, former Prison Superintendent; businessman `Uliti Uata and his son, Tu`i, and others.[10]

Moala admitted that a major issue that had troubled him was an apparent "lack of understanding and commitment to non-violent activism" by some pro-democracy supporters. In fact, Moala blames some of the pro-democracy leaders of carrying part of the responsibility for unleashing the Nuku`alofa riots.

Eight people died in the riots and police arrested some 571 people, including several pro-democracy leaders being charged with sedition, according to *Matangi Tonga*.[11] A two-year state of emergency was declared while Australian, New Zealand and Tongan police launched Operation Kaliloa, an investigation into the riots. But in spite of this tragic setback, King Saiosi Tupou V, Taufa`ahau's eldest son, in mid-2008 embarked on far-reaching political reforms that involved relinquishing much of the King's power and his day-to-day involvement in running government affairs and ushering in the historic first "democratic" elections in November 2010. He pledged to also sell his substantial business interests, a promise he was not able to keep completely by the time he died from leukaemia on 15 March 2012 in Hong Kong. While Saiosi's younger brother became King Tupou VI, his conservatism raised questions about commitment to the reforms.

In his book *In Search of the Friendly Islands*, Moala cited a message from Martin Luther King from a Birmingham, Alabama, jail: "I have consistently preached that non-violence demands that the means we use must be as pure as the ends we seek.".[12]

Moala noted that in the early days of the reform movement, "freedom of the press was one of its primary aims".[13] But in more recent times, the movement appeared to have taken an opposing tack and used notions of a free press and freedom of speech to "launch vicious propaganda campaigns seeking to destroy rather than build".[14] In the latest of a series of crippling lawsuits in 2013, more to do with professionalism and knowledge of media law than to do with press freedom, the Magistrate's Court in Nuku`alofa ordered *Koe Kele`a*,[15] its editor and publisher to pay more than 62,000 Tongan pa'anga in damages for defaming Prime Minister Lord Tui`vakano and six cabinet ministers.[16] Solomone Palu was also ordered to pay a further T$62,000 for allegations over a payment of T$24 million to Tongasat.[17]

In September 2009, Pohiva and four co-accused were acquitted on charges of seditious conspiracy.[18] Subsequently, in December 2013, Pohiva was presented with the Defender of Democracy Award by Parliamentarians For Global Action for "pushing for democracy" for more than three decades.[19]

Notes

1 David Robie (1996). Editorial. "News media under fire" edition. *Pacific Journalism Review*, 3(2): 5–9.
2 Kalafi Moala (1996, October 22). Letter to Pacific Media Watch, *Pacific Journalism Review* and the Australian Centre for Independent Journalism (ACIJ). Cited by *Pacific Journalism Review*, 3(2): 8, 12.
3 David Robie (2009). Back cover legend. In Kalafi Moala (2009). *Tonga: In Search of the Friendly Islands*. Kealakekua, Hawai`i: Pasifika Foundation Press; Auckland: Pacific Media Centre.
4 Kalafi Moala (2002). *Island Kingdom Strikes Back: The Story of an Independent Island Newspaper—Taimi `o Tonga*. Auckland: Pacmedia Publishers.
5 Ibid., p. 243.
6 David Robie (1996). The contempt case of the "Tongan three". *Pacific Journalism Review*, 3(2): 10–19.
7 Kalafi Moala (1996, September 25). Editorial. "We didn't get a fair trial". *Taimi `o Tonga*. Republished by *Pacific Journalism Review*, 3(2): 13–14. Translated from the Tongan by Lopeti Senituli.
8 Samuela `Akilisi Pohiva (1996, September 25). Commentary: From Samuela `Akilisi Pohiva. *Taimi `o Tonga*. Republished by *Pacific Journalism Review*, 3(2): 17–18. Translated from the Tongan by Lopeti Senituli.
9 Kalafi Moala (2009). *Tonga: In Search of the Friendly Islands*. Kealakekua, Hawai`i: Pasifika Foundation Press; Auckland: Pacific Media Centre, p. 40.
10 Ibid.

11 Rioting crowd leaves trail of wreckage in Nuku`alofa (2006, November 20). *Matangi Tonga*.

12 Moala (2009), p. 40.

13 Ibid, p. 41.

14 Ibid.

15 *Koe Kele'a* website: www.kelea.fakatau.com

16 Court rules that *Kele`a* newspaper defamed PM and cabinet ministers (2013, June 14). *Islands Business*. Retrieved on 7 January 2014, from www.islandsbusiness.com/news/tonga/1507/court-rules-that-kelea-newspaper-defamed-pm-and-ca/

17 The law is paralysed when dealing with the leaders (2012, October 29). *Koe Kele`a*.

18 Tongan MPs acquitted over 2006 riots. (2009, September 17). Radio Australia.

19. Tonga's Pohiva says Defender of Democracy Award important. (2013, December 17). Radio New Zealand International.

PART 3

Indigenous struggles

Indigenous Igorot family in the Cordillera, Philippines, 1990.   DAVID ROBIE

13

First Nation rights in Canada, 1989

They're afraid for the world to see how they have violated the rights of First Nations here in this country. It is astounding that a government that advocates the protection of human rights in South Africa and peace in Central America could be dead against opening its own conduct to the light of day.

Chief Georges Erasmus

"I'M A LITTLE nervous," admitted Dennis Laboucan as he fidgeted in the cab of his battered pickup truck. "We've never done anything like this before." The 24-year-old Lubicon Cree Indian was psyching himself up for the barricades and a looming confrontation with the Royal Canadian Mounted Police troops over land rights.[1]

Declaring themselves a sovereign "nation" on traditional hunting and trapping lands in the middle of one of the richest oil and mineral tracts in northern Alberta province in 1989, the band, or tribe, didn't have to wait long for its high noon. A few days later police helicopters swooped on the blockaded roads leading to their Little Buffalo village near Lake Lubicon. The barriers were torn down and 27 people were arrested. This had a parallel with New Zealand's Ngāti Whātua's occupation of ancestral land on Auckland's Bastion Point when the police and army forcibly removed 218 protesters in 1978 after a peaceful occupation for 507 days.[2]

In the Stein River Valley of southern British Columbia "wilderness only" campaigners joined forces with indigenous Indians in a struggle to keep out the loggers. British Columbia Forest Products Limited, a subsidiary of New Zealand's Fletcher Challenge Canada Limited, was embroiled in the confrontation over aboriginal land and the New Zealand company also had a fight on its hands with plans to log an area on the west coast of Vancouver Island.[3]

Elsewhere in British Columbia, other Indian bands were battling to defend their traditional rights over large slices of forest land. As Dee Brown had observed in *Bury My Heart at Wounded Knee* about the Indian struggle for survival across the border in the United States, "the white men ... who talked so much of peace but rarely seemed to practise it ..."[4]

BATTLE
FOR THE LUBICON

Canada recently passed an act enshrining multiculturalism. The national upheaval over the issue and Indian rights has parallels with the Treaty of Waitangi debate and is embroiling at least one New Zealand company.

by David Robie

Canada passed an act enshrining multiculturalism in 1988. The national upheaval over the issue and indigenous Indian rights in the 1970s and 1980s had parallels with the Cree totems in Vancouver. The Lubicon Cree in Canada's Alberta province are still struggling for their survival against the encroachments of oil and gas exploitation.   DAVID ROBIE

Indians in the south of Vancouver Island vowed to risk jail and fines in a fight to prevent federal government-backed commercial fishing in their traditional waters. Tom Sampson, chairman of the First Nations of South Island Tribal Council, warned that the Canadian government would face confrontation and lawsuits if it didn't negotiate with the indigenous people over fishing rights in the Saanich Inlet.

"We won't allow anybody to come here and fish," said a Tsawout tribal elder. "If a boat comes in, our boats will hound them. We won't allow them to drop nets in our waters."

Treaty of Waitangi debate in New Zealand has embroiled at least one New Zealand major company in Canada. Although Prime Minister Pierre Trudeau had declared back in 1971 that Canada would adopt a multicultural policy and the country was innovative in this respect, it took a further 17 years before the Canadian *Multiculturalism Act* was passed to ensure the rights of every Canadian are protected equally, including the indigenous First Nation peoples. The law recognised Canada's multicultural heritage, aboriginal rights, use of other languages other than the official English and French, and minority cultural rights. In mid-1989, I visited Vancouver on a book promotion visit for my *Blood on their Banner* and undertook a reporting assignment on the new law in action for the *New Zealand Listener*.

BATTLE FOR THE LUBICON

New Zealand Listener, 11 February 1989

AFTER 50 years of waiting, nine years of court battles and a week-long barricade revolt, the Lubicon Cree Indians have finally reached a land-claim agreement with the Alberta and federal governments in what is being hailed as a highly symbolic victory for aboriginal rights in Canada.[5]

Forgotten by government negotiators when treaties were drawn up with other Indian nations in Alberta last century, the 457-strong band has won a reserve of 205 square kilometres, which includes mineral rights, and surface rights on a further 40 square kilometres.

Chief Bernard Ominayak, the 23-year-old Lubicon leader, is full of praise for his negotiating counterpart, Alberta Premier Don Getty: "This man has great courage for taking the bull by the horns and doing what he has done." However, barely had Ominayak and the uncharacteristically emotional Getty joined hands in a victory salute when the Lubicon Indians faced another rebuff at the hands of federal officials.

Although Indian bands are traditionally entitled to define their "nationals", known as status Indians, officials in November 1988 rejected almost half the tribespeople as being members of the small band. Ottawa also refused to consider the band's demand for as much as $100 million in compensation.

Among land rights and sovereignty disputes that frequently have parallels with Māori efforts to redress historical grievances, the case of the Lubicon Indian has become a landmark for the whole of Canada.[6] The issue was an embarrassment for Prime Minister Brian Mulroney as the country faced the November general election in which his conservative government was re-elected with a reduced majority.

"How Canada and Alberta deal with the Lubicon is a reflection of our society as a whole. Is it to be a society of justice and injustice?" asks Nancy Kariel, of the Toronto-based Quaker Committee on Native Concerns. "Many Canadians have already chosen to demand justice for the Lubicon people. Their proposals for a prompt and equitable settlement are undeniably legitimate and long overdue."

The Lubicon victory now means thousands of indigenous Indians and Metis (people of mixed Indian and European heritage) who have been similarly denied recognition and land rights, will redouble their struggles.

The land claimed by the Lubicon is in the so-called Peace River "arch", containing one-third of Alberta's remaining petroleum resources. Although the Lubicon first applied for land in 1933, Ottawa has sat on their request for decades, forcing them into a long, frustrating fight .

In 1970, the Alberta government decided to open up the traditional Lubicon territory to exploit its rich oil and timber resources. About 370 oil wells were sunk; trapping lines were bulldozed to service the wells; and wildlife that the Lubicon depended on for their livelihood was driven away . By 1982, $1.2 million in oil and gas was being extracted daily from the claimed traditional lands—and it is far higher now.

Until the breakthrough in October, the Alberta government had fought to maintain control over mineral rights while the Lubicon insisted the benefits of the resources should go to them. Traditionally, these resources have been ceded to aboriginal peoples along with the surface land rights .

As their drawn-out struggle has raged with the provincial and federal authorities, the Lubicon people have become demoralised and troubled by social crises: "The incidence of stillbirths, miscarriages and premature births have increased to the extent that there are now few normal full-term births," says Kariel. "Alcohol and suicide rates are problems for the first time. This results in extreme stress for all members of the community."

Hardships have been severe. Two years earlier only 19 moose—the Lubicon's chief source of meat—were culled, compared with 200 a year less than a decade previously.

A survey has revealed the average band member is now 10 kilograms underweight. There is no running water or sewerage in the community and a tuberculosis epidemic is striking one out of three.

Although severe, the conditions are understood to parallel many of the social problems on several other Indian reservations. So it wasn't altogether surprising that National Chief Georges Erasmus had this to say after his landslide re-election by the Assembly of First Nations in Edmonton during May 1988:

Canada, we have something to say to you—a warning: You're playing with fire. Many of us are starting to believe the people assembled here may be the last generation to sit down peacefully to negotiate. Canada, deal with this generation or there may be violence from the next generation.

The mainstream press in Canada immediately seized on the statement and treated it sensationally in a similar way to how many Māori leaders have been reported in debate over the Treaty of Waitangi.

It was probably coincidental, concedes Maurice Nahanee, editor of *Kahtou*, Vancouver's First Nations newspaper which covered the assembly, but the next day more than 200 RCMP troopers converged on the Kahnawake community of Mohawks near Montreal. Armed with rifles and protected by bullet-proof vests, the police arrested 17 Indians living in the village on charges of selling contraband cigarettes.

Police chiefs said they seized almost $500,000 worth of cigarettes, which they claimed were bought duty-free by Canadian Indians across the border in the United States. The Indians retaliated by setting up a barricade on a highway passing through their nation.

The potentially explosive confrontation ended when federal government officials guaranteed there would be no further raids until the matter of cigarette sales had been cleared up. (A registered status Indian does not pay income tax and can buy consumer goods on any Indian reserve exempt of any tax by any level of Canadian government.)

Nahanee believes the police action was a typical example of the victimisation frequently encountered on reservations. Ironically funded by federal grants, his newspaper was founded in 1985 and is one of several reporting on indigenous issues. Several weeks after the Mohawks raid, Premier Getty ordered an inquiry into police behaviour towards the 7000 "blood" Indians on Canada's biggest reserve at Stand Off, near the southern town of Lethbridge. (The reserve village's name is said to have come from a clash between police and whisky traders in the 19th century.)

The inquiry was called after the gangland-style killing of an Indian and allegations that three other Indians from the reservation had been murdered. Two whites were charged with the latest killing and Indian leaders called for the probe to become part of a national investigation into the treatment of indigenous people by the Canadian legal system.

In October, a Manitoba commission of inquiry into native justice was told by the Assembly of First Nations that it had received a flood of complaints from Indians claiming to have been victimised by the legal system. High-profile cases of Indians who have suffered under the law—such as Donald Marshall, a Micmac jailed for 11 years over a murder he reportedly never committed—have been widely publicised.

Such cases are not unique, claims Chief Gordon Peters: "These particular cases are not isolated incidents, but serve as examples of the relationship that exists between the Canadian justice system and the original inhabitants of the land."

In spite of the recent passage through the Canadian Parliament of the *Multiculturalism Act*—the first of its kind in the world—representatives from several First Nations have condemned the federal government's attitude towards indig-

A Canadian protest in support of the Lubicon Cree in 2010.   AMNESTY INTERNATIONAL

enous people and its opposition to a planned United Nations Human Rights study on treaties between indigenous people and nation states.

"Canada has been lobbying actively and aggressively for many months to scuttle proposed United Nations study," says Chief Erasmus, "because they're afraid for the world to see how they have violated the rights of First Nations here in this country. It is astounding that a government that advocates the protection of human rights in South Africa and peace in Central America could be dead against opening its own conduct to the light of day. It must be because they have something to hide."

Indian sovereignty was affirmed by the royal proclamation of 1763 by King George III, which recognised the nation-to-nation relationship between the Indian people and the British Crown. That recognition was reinforced by other agreements, and finally by the *Canada Constitution Act 1982.*

Erasmus says his people's ancestors agreed to share their lands and resources with the settlers, and had made "international agreements" with their governments through the treaty-making process. However, once the balance of power had shifted, provincial governments felt no obligation to keep their part of the treaties.

"Today, Canada refuses even to discuss these obligations with us, and government officials dare us to go to court. Only federal and provincial governments

Melina Laboucan-Massimo, a local Lubicon Cree human and environmental rights activist, looks at a sample of the black, foul-smelling sludge that comes out of this spill site.

with their tax revenues can afford long battles in their courts," says Erasmus. "First Nations cannot. There are no viable domestic remedies in Canada to resolve treaty issues or the dispossession of lands and resources that has taken place in the past. We have been forced to turn to the United Nations."

Indian Affairs Minister Bill McKnight has been accused of acting against indigenous rights and is under growing pressure to resign. "Despite his rhetoric, McKnight is neither willing nor capable of acting in the interests of the First Nations," says Erasmus. But the minister denies this allegation.

Erasmus warns there will be no surrender of sovereignty and the Indian people will no longer tolerate the situation where the federal government refuses to sit down to negotiate the settlement of Indian claims in British Columbia. Also, where tribes do have treaties they have not been fully honoured by the government, which further angers the Indian people.

"We say," says Erasmus, "if you don't deal with this generation of leaders you will not like the violence of the next generation."

"Many years ago," says editor Nahanee, "a group of Yankees refused to pay taxes to the British government; we are talking pre-American Revolution when the United Sates was formed and cut its apron strings from the mother country. I think the new Kamloops Amendment (empowering tribal councils to impose taxes on their own 'designated lands') is something revolutionary .

"Like the Americans, we should not have to pay taxes if we are not to receive the benefit of paying taxes—no taxation without preservation.

"We have paid dearly for our peaceful co-existence with the intruders to this land of ours. It's about time they started paying the price for living with us.

CHIEF Bernard Ominayak, who was 23 when I wrote this article for the *New Zealand Listener*, and his people are still struggling to defend their lands, environmental, social and cultural rights almost a quarter-century later. Ominayak was unanimously retained in the Lubicon Lake Nation election earlier in 2013 in spite of determined efforts by federal and Alberta provincial authorities to undermine his leadership.[7] In his book, *Last Stand of the Lubicon Cree*, John Goddard wrote:

> Faced with the destruction of their way of life, Ominayak and the band have gone to court. They are seeking environmental control over their land, hoping to limit oil development to a level where hunting and trapping might continue … The Lubicon Cree, the province maintains, are "squatters on Alberta Crown land". Either they recognise provincial jurisdiction, give up their land claim and buy property in the hamlet, or they will be forced to leave.[8]

In June 2013, the Lubicon Lake Nation filed a second historic $700 million lawsuit against the Canadian federal and Alberta governments accusing them of theft of their natural resources by granting illegal licences to oil and gas development companies and for "interference in First Nation governance".[9] On their own website, the Lubicon Cree people document the oil development destruction wreaked on their lands and declare:

> The Lubicon Lake Nation citizens alone have the right to determine who their government is. However, the government of Canada has, since 19 July 2012, refused to acknowledge the rightful government of the Lubicon Lake Nation, asserting that they did not know and could not adjudicate who was the rightful government.[10]

Notes
1   David Robie (1989, February 11). Battle for the Lubicon. *New Zealand Listener*, pp. 24–29.
2   In 1991, the New Zealand government formally apologised and returned the land with NZ$3 million in compensation to the Māori iwi, Ngāti Whātua. See www.

nzhistory.net.nz/eviction-of-protestors-from-bastion-point A documentary, *Bastion Point - The Untold Story*, is online at: www.nzhistory.net.nz/eviction-of-protestors-from-bastion-point

3   David Robie (1989, February 11). Fletcher challenged. *New Zealand Listener*, pp. 28–29.

4   Dee Brown (1971). *Bury My Heart at Wounded Knee: An Indian History of the American West*. London: Picador.

5   Robie (1989, February 11). Battle for the Lubicon.

6   Ward Churchill (1998). *A Little Matter of Genocide: Holocaust and Denial in the Americas, 1492 to the Present*. San Francisco: City Light Books; Brown (1971). *Bury My Heart At Wounded Knee*.

7   Garrett Tomlinson (2013, June 4). Lubicon Lake holds 2013 general election: Longtime chief Bernard Ominayak retains title. Lubicon Lake Nation website. Retrieved on 27 August 2013, from www.lubiconlakenation.ca/index.php/breaking-news/archived-releases-letters-and-info/417-lubicon-lake-nation-general-election-press-release-june-4-2013

8   John Goddard (1991). *Last Stand of the Lubicon Cree*. Vancouver: Douglas & Macintyre.

9   Garrett Tomlinson (2013, June 10). Lubicon Lake Nation files aggressive 700 million dollar lawsuit against Canada—highlights theft of natural resources and illegal interference in First Nation governance. Lubicon Lake Nation website. Retrieved on 27 August 2013, from www.lubiconlakenation.ca/index.php/breaking-news/most-recent-news-release/418-lubicon-lake-nation-lawsuit-press-release-june-10-2013

10 Lubicon Lake Nation www.lubiconlakenation.ca

14

A cloud over Bukidnon forest, 1989

*If a major project isn't based on sound development principles of
partnership with the local community then it is likely to be a disaster—
just another chapter in the Third World rip-off story.*
Development aid advocate Rupert Watson

THE MOOD in the chapel on the outskirts of Malaybalay, capital of Bukidnon
province in the southern Philippines island of Mindanao was sombre. Six
datu (chiefs) and several delegates of the indigenous tribal Lumad people of
the region were airing their concerns about a controversial New Zealand-
backed $5.7-million forestry aid project for the Philippines.[1] Ironically, less
than 100 metres away, in a derelict building nestling amid a plantation of
Benguet pines on land earmarked for the project, were living about 80
so-called "squatters" who in a sense symbolised the problem at the root
of the scheme. Squatters would be the term used by some New Zealand
officials and their technical advisers. But it was hardly appropriate for the
indigenous people, and reflected the insensitivity of officials to many of the
social and economic problems in the province.

The homeless people belonged to the Bukidnon Free Farmers and
Agricultural Labourers' Organisation, or Buffalo, as it was generally known.
Their story was one of injustice, victimisation and harassment, only too
common in the Philippines.

Since 1987, about 200 peasants had occupied a 3000-hectare tract
of idle farmland and a 5000-hectare forest reserve belonging to Central
Mindanao University but which they had traditionally tilled. Evicted by the
university in March 1988, two farmer leaders were shot by members of the
private "paratrooper" security agency employed on the campus.

Buffalo was formed to campaign for the free distribution of the
university's idle lands to the traditional tillers. When the farmers were
finally forced off the land by Filipino troops and their homes bulldozed in
October 1988, they set up a protest camp outside the offices of provincial
governor Ernesto Tabios.

Embarrassed by the protest and the deaths of malnourished and ill children, the governor gave the Buffalo people temporary quarters in the building in Malaybalay forest included in the Bukidnon New Zealand-backed forestry aid project. The scheme was endorsed by an exchange of notes between the Philippine and New Zealand governments in February 1989 a week before I wrote a concluding op-ed article in a four-part series about the aid project for *The Dominion*.[2]

The issue of ancestral land, titles and right to live was crucial to the Lumads' case. Lumads are among indigenous people known as "Tribal Filipinos", of which there are some 4.5 million out of a total Philippines population of 96 million living in remote areas of Luzon, Mindanao and some islands of the Visayas. According to the TABAK tribal advocacy organisation, they comprise a diverse collection of more than 40 ethnolinguistic groups, each with a distinct language and culture.[3] Historically, they were least influenced by three centuries of Spanish rule and Christianity and they were able to preserve their indigenous culture, communal lifestyle and tribal customs. But this changed from the start of American rule in the Philippines from 1898 until the Japanese invasion in the Second World War. Tunay na Alyansa ng Bayan sa Katutbo (TABAK) noted in a report about "development aggression", indigenous rights and ancestral domain:

> Ever since the start of American colonial rule, the forces of market economy and central government have slowly, but steadily, caught up with them. Lowlanders, backed by state legislation, seized communal lands and eroded local self-sufficiency in the process ... Since they occupy areas rich with natural resources, Tribal Filipinos are besieged by a growing number of foreign and local corporations engaged in mining, logging, plantations and other export industries.[4]

The Bukidnon project evolved out of a visit to the Philippines in May 1986 by New Zealand Prime Minister David Lange, who was the first head of government to arrive in the country after "people power" had ousted the Marcos regime. Having heard disquieting stories about the aid project, I travelled to Bukidnon to see for myself. Also in the group were Maire Leadbeater of the Philippine Solidarity Network; Janine McGruddy of Peace Movement Aotearoa; and concerned local people, including representatives of the indigenous tribal Lumad people. Leadbeater recalled later:

> The truth about the forestry project and its probable impact on the lives of local people ensured that this "exposure" was also disturbing ... Sadly,

this is an area that needs forestry development, and the New Zealand concept of tree-farming, although not well understood, has appeal. The area allocated for initial development, Malaybalay Forest, already has scattered pines and evidence of much man-made damage. But the "RPNZ" project, as it is known locally, has fatal flaws.[5]

Among the flaws was the militarisation of the area and alleged human rights violations. The Lumads continued to protest over the "inadequate and rushed" project and petitioned the Philippines government, condemning what they described as a lack of adequate consultation. Seeing the violations at first hand, I wrote a series of articles that led to a Television New Zealand current affairs report, further media coverage, questions in Parliament and finally a review of the project that recommended changes.

CLOUD OVER BUKIDNON FOREST

New Zealand Listener, 22 April 1989

ABOUT 200,000 indigenous Higaonon tribespeople are scattered among the mountain ranges bordering Agusan Norte, Agusan Sur and Bukidnon, three of the most militarised provinces of the Philippines.[6] Historians say the Higaonon once lived in the fertile lowlands on the southern island of Mindanao but were driven into the mountains by settlers. Intrusions by transnational and Philippine logging corporations in the late 1960s forced them into higher and more remote areas.

Stubborn resistance has become part of the tradition of the Higaonon, one of three tribes of Lumads (the generic term for all non-Moslem indigenous peoples on Mindanao) living in a rugged and strategic region developed for a controversial New Zealand forestry aid project. This tradition has produced several rebel chieftains like Datu Mangkalasi, who resisted loggers invading ancestral lands until he was assassinated in 1972.

Another is Hucad Mandahinog, alias "Kumander Jabbar", a New People's Army guerrilla commander operating in north-central Mindanao, who has an 80,000-peso ($NZ6250) price on his head.

Now some of the Lumads, split by offers of instant wealth by Philippine government officials or by being co-opted by the Presidential Assistance for National Minorities (PANAMIN) agency, are being steadily drawn into a counter-insurgency role not unlike that of the Montagnards of the Central Highlands in Vietnam, which the United States Special Forces trained and deployed against the Viet Cong.

"A low-key, often vicious, Green Beret style type of warfare is being waged by the Armed Forces against the gritty Higaonon," says Romi Gatuslao, a leading

"Squatters" on their ancestral tribal land in 1989. Conrado Dumindin (second from right rear) and other Lumads in Bukidnon Forest, Mindanao, Philippines.   DAVID ROBIE

Mindanao journalist who has been reporting on the 20-year-old insurgency. "At times, the military could combine this with conventional means like multi-pronged infantry attacks, shelling, or—worse—air strikes on *barrios* (villages) which the tribals swore terrified them at first."

It is in this context that New Zealand's biggest aid scheme in the Philippines, the Bukidnon Industrial Tree Plantation Project, finally got under way in December 1988 after adverse reports about opposition from some Lumads. Philippine Foreign Affairs Secretary Raul Manglapuz and the New Zealand Ambassador, Alison Stokes, ended three years of delicate negotiations when they exchanged notes in Manila during February 1989. Project manager William Ellis, a Rotorua-based forestry consultant, set up headquarters in the Bukidnon provincial capital of Malaybalay and began preparations for a hardwood species nursery.

Expected eventually to cost $25 to $30 million, the project will initially cost New Zealand $1 million a year for five years while the Philippines will put up $2.7 million for the five-year period. The Philippine government share will be funded by the Asian Development Bank.

The reafforestation scheme [is planned to] develop a 14,000-hectare area in the strategic north-eastern hill country of Bukidnon, near Mt Tago. The three-stage plan, developed over 18 years, will eventually involve three parcels of land. After initial development of the 3680-hectare Malaybalay Forest, which already has an existing but scattered and fire-depleted pine plantation of 2400 hectares, the

A Bukidnon mother living on the land intended for forestry in 1989 feared for her future.

DAVID ROBIE

project will be extended to the Kibalabag (5500 hectares) and Siloo forests (4800 hectares). Kibalabag is reportedly the subject of ancestral Higaonon land claims and other areas are claimed by the three main Lumad tribes in the province— Higaonon, Bukidnon and Manobo.

Already the project, the result of a visit to Manila by Prime Minister David Lange in March 1986, just weeks after the so-called snap revolution ousted President Ferdinand Marcos from power, has become a severe test of the New Zealand government's aid strategy. Labour's policy when it was elected in 1984 pledged that "aid will be directed specifically to carefully monitored projects that will enhance development among poor and rural dwellers in recipient countries".

In spite of the insistence by New Zealand aid officials that the project has a degree of local involvement and representation which is a "significant advance" in the style of management of aid projects, many local Lumad leaders have identified several flaws. Among their fears is that the project might inevitably be drawn into the military's "low-intensity conflict", a concern shared by a Māori consultant engaged by the Foreign Affairs Ministry to investigate the project's implications for the indigenous peoples. Yet this concern has apparently been ignored by New Zealand officials.

Manuka Henare, executive director of the Catholic Commission for Justice, Peace and Development, warned in his report to the government after the visit to Mindanao last May: "The New Zealand government should not be seen to be party to the militarisation of the Bukidnon forestry project. Whenever possible , assurances should be sought from the Philippine government that it will not be part of the project's development."

Yet the New Zealand government's own "appraisal" report on the project, drawn up in July 1987 by Rotorua consultants Murray North and the Ministry of Forestry, dismissed the political and military implications for the project in less than one-third of a page. And in terms described by Filipino critics as "rather naïve".

The 1975 *Revised Forestry Code* drawn up under the Marcos dictatorship and not repealed by President Corazon Aquino's government, specifically calls for the deployment of military units in areas where tree plantations are to be established. The apparent rationale for this militarisation is to counter the growing insurgency in rural areas.

Since late 1981, large areas of Mindanao have been affected by military counter-insurgency strategy, also reminiscent of Vietnam, known as "hamletting". Under this strategy, peasant or Lumad families are forced to move from their farms or homes into fortified hamlets in an attempt by the military to isolate and engage the insurgents.

"Evidence suggests that sections of the military continue to insist on their involvement in many of the forestry schemes, ostensibly to maintain greater security," says Henare. "In many cases there has been active growing resistance by the people to such forestry schemes."

According to church-backed Task Force Detainees Agency's statistics on Mindanao from January until mid-November 1988, there were 322 political arrests; 47 "salvagings" (murders—*see "Human rights abuses in the Pacific, 1992" on page 135*); 51 killed and 40 wounded in 21 massacres; 140 torture victims; and 47 forced evacuations. Not included in these figures have been a series of unsolved killings by the military and right-wing vigilantes in the Bukidnon *barangay* (village) of Kapalaran, about 40 kilometres south of Malaybalay, and a forced exodus of at least 320 families in the region.

Another portion of the New Zealand government's 1987 report which has upset Lumad leaders, declared: "[The Lumads] are willing to forgo their claims to the land in exchange for tangible benefits. The *datus* are a pragmatic lot and would consider the offer if they are consulted."

Although New Zealand officials dismiss this statement as unimportant and misleading, it has nevertheless caused great anxiety and concern about the project among the tribespeople. According to organiser Yul Caringas of Kahulpungan sa Lumadnong Kalingkawasan (KLK, Organisation of Tribal People's Liberation), the Lumad people have not been treated seriously because they are looked upon as being nomadic: "We're labelled as uncivilised or squatters because we hop from one place to another; we're regarded as economically unstable."

Caringas says the New Zealand project violates the Lumad concept of *Bunkatol ha bulawan*, an expression difficult to translate into English, but which is often described as a "jar of virtues".

"At first we were happy it was a reafforestation project," he says. "But when we investigated it further we realised the project wasn't going to benefit our communities—it was an economic business venture. It will turn our farmer brothers into hired labourers on their own land." An estimated 3000 Lumads out of a total population in the forest area of 14,000 people could be affected.

Although KLK reportedly raised no specific objections at a recent meeting of the project management committee in Malaybalay, its officials have expressed their concerns to Henare, to myself during a recent visit, and to a deputation of the International Peace Brigade, including Philippine Solidarity Network Aotearoa campaigner Maire Leadbeater and Peace Movement Aotearoa campaigns co-ordinator Janine McGruddy.

Dismissed by some New Zealand officials as "political activists", KLK have nevertheless been identified by Henare as the legitimate voice of the Lumads. He believes that the project can be genuinely successful only if it has the support and co-operation of the KLK. Some of the Lumad concerns appear to be influenced by the exploitation their people have experienced at the hands of transnational and Philippine logging corporations.

"Critical studies of the industrial tree plantation programmes instituted by the Philippine government since the 1970s show evidence of major problems despite the fine intentions," says Henare. "The studies indicate that the farmers of Mindanao affected by these programmes are confused about them, especially the security of their occupancy and use of the land.

"Two aspects of these tree-planting programmes are particularly worrisome to small settler farmers: the involvement of large corporations in the planting and marketing of these commercial tree species; and the intensification of militarisation in the area targeted for these tree programmes."

In December 1988, the bishops of the Philippine Episcopal Commission on Tribal Filipinos (ECTF) protested to President Aquino and the government over the Department of Environment and Natural Resources' (DENR) "immoral and unjust" contract reafforestation programme. "We laud the effort to be noble in intent for it seeks to prevent a bleak and catastrophic future for the Filipinos," the ECTF said. "Yet we are greatly concerned because we believe ... that the programme could ultimately dispossess tribal Filipinos and upland people of their land.

"It is a programme that will probably lead to bloodshed. It is a programme that opens possibilities for graft and corruption. Even from an ecological [standpoint], we believe that the programme will not work."

Lumad leaders find it difficult to see the New Zealand project in isolation from their own government's reafforestation programme, especially when it is the DENR which is the agency working with the New Zealand government. However, counsellor Warren Searell at the New Zealand Embassy in Manila believes the "differences and misunderstandings" will be ironed out now that the project is under way.

Aid officials stress the strong association between New Zealand and the Philippines in forestry, particularly through the ASEAN regional model established in Tarlac province in 1980. Lessons learned on that project and applied to Bukidnon are regarded as a logical next step for New Zealand development aid.

Forestry consultant Warren Ellis, who has wide experience in developing countries, including Malaysia, Papua New Guinea and the Solomon Islands, believes the project is vital for the future of the Philippines: "Indiscriminate and excessive exploitation over the last few decades has eliminated, or significantly degraded, most of the country's virgin forests. The Bukidnon project could make a vital contribution to the future of this country."

Ellis cites last year's Asian Development Bank forestry sector report, which indicates that not more than seven million hectares of the forest in the Philippines could be adequately stocked. Of this area, virgin production forests amount to only 1.2 million hectares. Satellite scans suggest the situation is even worse and forest destruction continues at an alarming rate, possibly in excess of 100,000 hectares a year.

Although the New Zealand government regards it as primarily the responsibility of the Philippine authorities to ensure the local community is informed and consulted about the project, the embassy in Manila took the initiative in 1988 by funding information programmes. Last July, Ambassador Alison Stokes answered open questions on a radio broadcast in Malaybalay.

Yet although several *datus* circulated a draft petition in January demanding more time to consider the project, the Philippine and New Zealand governments pushed through the agreement. Among Lumad leaders that I met who were critical of the project was *barrio* captain Conrado Dumindin, who says: "None of the tribal people actually affected have been consulted."

Ellis insists the project will benefit the local people, including the Lumads. "It is recognised that the project's success hinges on people's acceptance," he says. "This means we need to convince the people of their benefits."

Plans as part of this scenario include cash cropping of the land as it is being developed, "stewardship" for families currently living in the project area, development of related agriculture, a worker share in the return from growing trees and "selected social programmes".

An estimated $1.3 million a year from the sale of coffee would go to the local people, as well as the provision of 66,000 tonnes of firewood a year and "cash returns or family food" produced from the 1000 hectares cleared each year. Permanent employment would be provided for an estimated 465 people, with further work for 3700 people in associated operations.

The Council for International Development (CID), an umbrella group on non-governmental aid organisations, is investigating the issues raised by the Bukidnon project.

"There is debate in the NGO community about whether support can modify the overall impact of a big aid project," says Rupert Watson, a spokesperson for CID. "Possible projects of this type could be in health, education and small-scale business. However, there is a very strong view that such moves would be mere window dressing.

"If a major project isn't based on sound development principles of partnership with the local community then it is likely to be a disaster—just another chapter in the Third World rip-off story."

❡

IN JANUARY 2012, Bukidnon Vice-Governor Jose Ma. R. Zubiri Jr branded the reforestation efforts of the privatised Bukidnon Forests Incorporated—previously the New Zealand-backed Bukidnon Industrial Tree Plantation Project (BIPP)—as a failure.[7] He called for the incorporation to stop operating before its 25-year industrial forest management agreement is due to end in 2016.

Instead, said Zubiri, the 38,000-hectare project area should be given to the indigenous Lumad people who had applied for a Certificate of Ancestral Domain over it. General manager Reynaldo Abordo of the partially state-owned incorporation admitted that only 7000 hectares had been reforested, but denied the project was a failure. The project never gained the consent of the Lumads in the area when the project began in 1989 with New Zealand funding. New Zealand officials claimed only 10 percent of the land involved indigenous ancestral domain. According to a damning Mindanao Interfaith People's Conference research report on the project in 1997 which recommended closure:

> Access to some traditional worship areas for the Lumads has been severely affected by the BIPP/BFI project. Most of the traditional landmarks—stones, trees, rivers—have either been removed, pulled

out/transported or destroyed because the BIPP/BFI has no use for them in the project.

Numerous laws supposedly protect and recognise indigenous peoples' ancestral claims in the Philippines, but these have been so defined as to make many feel that the laws themselves are treacherous … [I]t is of great concern that the New Zealand government's approach to the matter in relation to this project has been to minimise and gloss over something which is clearly a complex, widely felt issue of fundamental importance for the Lumad people of Bukidnon.[8]

New Zealand's involvement, eventually costing taxpayers almost $10 million, ended in 1998 when the project was terminated as a foreign-assisted project of the Department of Environment and Natural Resources. The area was heavily militarised because of this project.

Notes

1 David Robie (1989, February 17). Row over Bukidnon forestry project. *The Dominion*, p. 11. The final part of a four-part series on the Philippines under Aquino.
2 Ibid.
3 TABAK (1990). *Struggle against Development Aggression: Tribal Filipinos & Ancestral Domain*. Quezon City, Philippines: Tunay na Alyyansa ng Bayan Alay sa Katutubo.
4 Ibid., p. xvii.
5 Maire Leadbeater (1989, March). Tribal people object to New Zealand forestry aid project. *Peacelink*, #69, pp. 8–10.
6 David Robie (1989, April 22). Cloud over Bukidnon Forest. *New Zealand Listener*, pp. 22–23, 35.
7 Philippines: Zubiri says Bukidnon reforestation effort a failure (2012, January 10). *Minda News*. Retrieved on 17 September 2013, from www.forestcarbonasia. org/in-the-media/philippines-zubiri-says-bukidnon-reforestation-effort-a-failure-wants-it-stopped/
8 Bukidnon—Report slams New Zealand's biggest aid project in the Philippines (1997, October). *Kasama*, 11(4). Solidarity Philippines Australia Network.

15

Cell lines and commodities— the Hagahai 'biopiracy' affair, 1995

The globalisation of international capital and markets has brought with it a push to copyright and patent everything under the sun—including indigenous peoples' traditional knowledge and science, and even their human cells.

Pacific News Bulletin editorial

GOROKA, Papua New Guinea (AP): He's out there somewhere in the wild gorges of the Yuat River, hunting pig, harvesting yam, a young tribesman whose heart belongs to the jungle—but whose blood belongs to the United States government.

Or so says Patent No. 5,397,696.

The story of the Hagahai tribesman, of how the US patented the blood cells of one of the Earth's most primitive citizens, could only be a tale from the bio-engineering Nineties, a time when the prehistoric can still come face to face with the futuristic, and the technology of tomorrow often outwits the society of today.[1]

From the time the first European vessels reached the shores of continents long inhabited by indigenous people, European colonists adopted a *terra nullius* world view. Only recently has the world begun to concede the inaccuracy of and the racism behind this view. There is an almost desperate attempt by the descendants of colonisers to consign the *terra nullius* perspective to history, but recent developments in the area of human genetic research, engineering and human gene patents brings back haunting and painful memories to indigenous peoples of a legacy of European colonial domination.[2]

On 14 March 1995, the United States government issued a patent on the human cell line, or culture, of a foreigner—an indigenous man from a remote rainforest area of Papua New Guinea. While global moves had been under way to protect the knowledge and resources of indigenous people, the US National Institutes of Health (NIH) were issued patent No.

5,397,696 by the Patent and Trademark Office (PTO), the first time that an indigenous person's cells had been patented.[3]

The act, described by some critics as ushering in a "new and outrageous" era of intellectual property, unleashed a major controversy embracing ethics, the law and the media over human genetic material. The Hagahai man was one of a group of 24 people whose cell lines were sampled in 1989, and in a similar case two Solomon islanders were sampled in 1990.

The Hagahai, a tribe numbering fewer than 300 people, live in a remote part of the Western Schrader Mountains in Madang province. In 1983, due to communal medical problems, the tribespeople initiated contact with the outside world by visiting Baptist missionaries who lived some distance away. The following year, they had their first sustained contact with outsiders when an evangelist set up camp at the nearby settlement of Yilu.[4] Accompanying a Papua New Guinean government census team the same year was an American medical anthropologist, Dr Carol Jenkins, who was affiliated with the PNG Institute of Medical Research (IMR). The team found the Hagahai to be suffering from endemic diseases with a low birth rate and high disease mortality.[5] The following year, Jenkins began a decade-long research programme funded by the US National Geographic Society.

Following the discovery of the Hagahai patent six months after it was registered, the Canadian-based non-governmental organisation Rural Advancement Foundation International (RAFI) distributed an international media release on 4 October 1995, claiming the Hagahai man had "ceased to own his genetic material".[6]

Pat Mooney, executive director of RAFI, was quoted as saying: "This patent is another major step down the road to commodification of life. In the days of colonialism, researchers went after indigenous peoples' resources and studied their social organisations and customs. But now, in biocolonial times, they are going after the people themselves."[7]

RAFI and other NGOs argue that the World Health Organization (WHO) should establish internationally accepted medical ethics protocols covering the commercialisation or patenting of genetic material obtained from human beings.[8] No such agreed ethical code exists at present. RAFI also believes the Convention on Biological Diversity (CBD) should "come to grips with its legal obligation" to conserve and protect human diversity, and to establish binding procedures for the international exchange of human genetic resources. Finally, RAFI argues that it is concerned over the interest of the US Army and Navy researchers in HTLV-infected human cell lines from around the world with its implications for biological weapons research.

But some leading scientists with links to the research, such as Temple University anthropologist Dr Jonathan Friedlaender and law professor and ethicist Dr Henry Greely, dismissed the controversy over the Hagahai patent as a "tempest in a teapot".[9] Former director of Pacific anthropology at the National Science Foundation, Friedlaender said the campaign "reflects on the widespread distrust of the scientific technological enterprise and on the willingness of many to believe the worst of people with scientific knowledge".[10]

The issue also involved allegations of harassment against a key scientist involved, Dr Carol Jenkins, initially by at least one newspaper in Papua New Guinea, which eventually led to her seizure off an aircraft in Port Moresby by Foreign Affairs officials on her way to a conference abroad.[11] At least two scientists accused the newspaper, *The National*, of waging a vindictive campaign against the PNG Institute of Medical Research in Goroka, capital of the Eastern Highlands province. Jenkins was one of the scientists named in the patent.

Although the US government moved to register the patent in 19 other countries—including Australia and New Zealand—under the international Patent Cooperation Treaty, the controversy dogged its efforts. Finally, the US retreated in late 1996 by ambiguously offering to abandon its rights in a decision welcomed by some critics as "a step back from the aggressive patenting of life forms".[12]

LEGAL ROW OVER ATTEMPTS TO PATENT LOST TRIBE'S BLOOD

The Independent, 27 October 1995

SOUTH PACIFIC campaigners, alarmed at a "biopiracy" threat to isolated indigenous communities, are mounting a fight against blood patenting which may lead to a test case before the International Court of Justice.[13]

At stake is a legal tug-of-war over attempts in the United States to patent the blood of the recently discovered Hagahai people of a remote area in Papua New Guinea and other Melanesian tribesmen in the neighbouring Solomon Islands.

Cancer researchers in the US are interested in the Melanesian strain of a virus in the blood because, unlike, the metropolitan version, it doesn't cause leukaemia.

United States blood patent claims involving an indigenous Guaymi tribeswoman in Panama have now been dropped, leaving the two Melanesian tribes as the only test cases.

A Hagahai tribesman from Papua New Guinea: This photo was published on The Garamut blog along with the legend: "The Hagahai ... should be multi-millionaires." GARAMUT

Non-governmental organisations in the region are trying to persuade the governments of Papua New Guinea and the Solomon Islands to take a joint case before the court to The Hague.

"It's a new idea to challenge bioprospecting under international law and the Pacific governments have a good chance of pressing a test case," says Jean Christie, director of international liaison with the Canada-based Rural Advancement Foundation International (RAFI).

RAFI and Swissaid International are spearheading the campaign to help the governments prepare a case. RAFI wants the court to give a legal opinion on whether the US government and researchers have rights under US or international laws to claim patent rights on cell lines sampled from a group of 24 Hagahai people in 1989, and two Solomon Islanders in 1990.

But a PNG government scientist has hit out at "confusion" over the issue, saying the patent claim concerns a virus strain known as the Melanesian variant.

"This virus causes a form of cancer and a form of paralysis in many countries of the world," says Michael Alpers, director of the Goroka-based PNG Institute of Medical Research.

"These diseases are quite rare but are nevertheless important because they may be spread through blood transfusion—and in this respect they are like AIDs.

The "legal row" article about the Hagahai controversy in New Zealand's *Independent*, 1995.

"We've known for some time that the virus infection is common in Papua New Guinea but the disease, such as leukaemia, seem to be completely absent. After a lot of effort, the virus was isolated through collaboration with colleagues at the National Institutes of Health in the US.

"This discovery revealed that the HTLV-1 virus in Papua New Guinea is a variant of the cosmopolitan virus, which may explain why it does not cause disease here."

He says there is little chance of any commercial benefit from the discovery but it may be used to develop a test for the HTLV-1 variant virus of a vaccine against the worldwide cosmopolitan strain.

"Given that the patent application was being made in the US," Alpers says, "it was better to have the Hagahai part of it than to have taken the ethical stance not to be involved and to have allowed all the rights to reside in the US."

In 1985, the 300-strong Hagahai tribe was discovered in the isolated Western Schrader range, tucked away on the border of the Madang and Western Highlands provinces in Papua New Guinea.

Jean Christie and her colleagues argue the US patent applications amounted to "biopiracy"—profiteering from the biological inheritance of indigenous people.

Biodiversity prospecting, also known as "bioprospecting" and "biopiracy", is the exploration, extraction and screening of biological diversity and indigenous knowledge for commercially valuable genetic and biochemical resources.

Under most bioprospecting agreements, indigenous people sharing information or genetic materials effectively lose control of their resources.

"The globalisation of international capital and markets has brought with it a push to copyright and patent everything under the sun—including indigenous people's traditional knowledge and science, and even their human cells," says *Pacific News Bulletin*, a newsletter published by the Fiji-based regional Nuclear-Free and Independent Pacific movement.

"But indigenous peoples themselves have not been included in the discussions about international agreements, treaties and conventions."

A conference in Suva earlier in 1985 launched an action plan calling for a moratorium on bioprospecting in the Pacific and urging indigenous peoples to refuse to cooperate with the controversial research methods until "appropriate protection mechanisms" are in place.

The conference also sought the establishment of a treaty declaring the Pacific to be a life forms patent-free zone.

It wants Pacific governments that have not already signed GATT [General Agreement on Tariffs and Trade, which was replaced by the World Trade Organization in 1995] to refuse to do so.

Pacific News Bulletin editor Ellen Whelan says: "Current intellectual property laws favour white scientists in lab coats rather than the indigenous people who have nurtured biological diversity for centuries."

Christie says international NGOs such as the World Health Organization, United Nations Educational, Scientific and Cultural Organization, United Nations Development Programme and others should be persuaded to join the bioprospecting initiatives. She believes GATT/WTO does not guarantee protection of humans from biomedical research.

Alpers says the US government's bid to patent a virus isolated from the Hagahai people raises ethical as well as scientific and legal issues. He wants a public debate by the people and government.

Alpers defended his decision to approve the patenting moves by the US Department of Health. The virus is kept at the American Type Culture Collection in Rockville, Maryland.

One of the key researchers in the case, PNG Institute of Medical Research fellow Dr Carol Jenkins, says she understood the Hagahai were protected and that 50 percent of all royalties from any commercially viable product developed from the virus would go to them.

Having studied the tribe for a decade, Jenkins says: "Despite what exploitation may take place around the world, in this case the rights of the Hagahai have been specifically safeguarded.

♪

THE EMOTIVE term "biopiracy" describes a form of "colonial pillaging" in which Western corporations allegedly reap profits by taking out patents on indigenous plants, food, local knowledge, human tissues and drugs from developing countries and turn them into lucrative products.[14] Countries with exceptionally high levels of biological and cultural variety—such as Brazil, India, Indonesia, Mexico and Papua New Guinea—are targeted. The exploitation is also often referred to as "internal conquest", an analogy to the "external conquest" of colonialism.

In the end, the US National Institutes of Health marked Human Rights Day by announcing in December 1996 it was "disclaiming" Patent No. 5,397,696, thus relinquishing all control.[15]

"I hope this is the end of what is arguably the most offensive patent ever issued," said Alejandro Argumedo, of the Canada-based Indigenous Peoples' Biodiversity Network (IPBN). RAFI's executive director Pat Mooney also praised the decision, saying: "Three up, three down." This was a reference to the success in also halting two other US indigenous patents, the Guaymi in Panama, and in the Solomon Islands.

Notes

1 Charles J. Hanley (1996, April 20). Patent on tribesman's blood raises ethical questions. Associated Press report carried in abbreviated version on CNN News.
2 Aroha Te Pareake Mead (1996). Genetics, Sacredness and the Commodities Market. Unpublished conference paper.
3 David Robie (1997). Cell lines and commodities: The Hagahai patent affair. *Pacific Journalism Review*, 4(1): 78–91.
4 Carol L. Jenkins (1987). Medical anthropology in the Western Schrader Range, Papua New Guinea. *National Geographic Research*, 3(4): 412–430.
5 *Los Angeles Times* (1987, December 27). Disease threatens survival of remote, Stone Age folk.
6 RAFI—Rural Advancement Foundation International (1994, January/February). [*RAFI Communiqué*].
7 RAFI (1995, October 4). Indigenous person from Papua New Guinea claimed in US government patent [Media release].
8 RAFI (1996, March/April). New questions about management and exchange of human tissues at NIH: Indigenous person's cells patented. [*RAFI Communiqué*], pp. 1–12.
9 Jonathan Friedlaender (1995), as cited by Henry T. Greely in an internet communiqué distributed via the NATIVE-L e-listserver for Native Americans on October 27.
10 Gary Taubes (1995, November 17). Scientists attacked for "patenting" Pacific tribe. *Science*, Vol. 270.
11 Author's telephone interview with Dr Carol Jenkins, 5 February 1996.
12 *The National* (1996, September 27). US retreats on patent for Hagahai bloodline. From an Associated Press dispatch.

13 David Robie (1995, October 27). Legal row over attempts to patent lost tribe's blood. *The Independent*, p. 23.

14 We Make Money Not Art website (n.d.). Retrieved on 27 August 2013, from http://we-make-money-not-art.com/archives/2008/05/raised-above-the-ground-with.php#.UiByvbzHHJw

15 US government dumps the Hagahai patent (1996, December 15). [Media release on ETC Group]. Retrieved on 27 August 2013, from www.etcgroup.org/content/us-government-dumps-hagahai-patent

PART 4

Forgotten wars, elusive peace

Papua New Guinea soldier guards the road to Panguna, Bougainville, 1989.   DAVID ROBIE

16

Bougainville:
The valley of the Rambos, 1989

The original [Panguna mine] agreement overrode our customs, denied us our land rights and was too rushed. It contradicts our way of life; what comes from the land should benefit the landowners ... nobody else.

A Nasioi landowner

APART from convoys with soldiers riding shotgun and yellow ochre Bougainville Copper Limited trucks packed with security forces sporting M16s, you would hardly guess that a guerrilla war was in progress near the Bougainville provincial capital of Arawa. But once you reached the sandbagged machinegun nest in Birempa village at the foot of the rugged mountain jungles of the Crown Prince Range, the tension started to rise.

Scanning the dense vegetation for a sign of the militants of the Bougainville Republican Army (BRA)—known as Rambos in the first year of the decade-long civil war—the Papua New Guinea Defence Force soldier manning the machinegun didn't notice the irony of the T-shirt he was wearing.

Scrawled across his chest were the words MINE OF TEARS, a word play on the title of Richard West's 1972 book *River of Tears: The Rise of Rio Tinto-Zinc Mining Corporation.*[1] The book was an exposé of the mining operations by BCL's (Bougainville Copper Limited) parent company CRA Limited of Australia—a subsidiary of Britain's Conzinc Riotinto—and it had already become the "Bible" of many of the militants.

At the time I was reporting on the fledgling war for a cover story featured by *Pacific Islands Monthly* in its November 1989 edition entitled "MINE OF TEARS: BOUGAINVILLE ONE YEAR LATER".[2] No other journalists were on the ground at the time, and the only other people staying at the small hotel in the port town of Kieta were soldiers, some cradling guns on their knees while having dinner. The atmosphere was surreal and ghostly in those early days. I concluded in that *PIM* report after a week travelling around Panguna, inspecting the environmental devastation of the Jaba River valley and talking with militant landowners:

A Papua New Guinean soldier in 1989 wearing a "Mine of Tears" T-shirt usually worn by BRA supporters.   DAVID ROBIE

The problems of Bougainville cannot be divorced from the rest of the country, or even from the rest of the Pacific. At stake are the crucial issues of a conflict between Western concepts of land ownership and indigenous land values, the equity between the national government, provincial administration and the traditional landowners, and a choice between genuine sovereignty over resource development projects or dependence on foreign control.[3]

The tiny landowner guerrilla force—numbering no more than a few dozen at the time—had been holding one of the world's largest open-cut copper mines, 2000 security forces and the national government of Papua New Guinea to ransom for a year. Now its leader, former company surveyor Francis Ona, and seven of his lieutenants, had a price of $380,000 on their heads. Ona became an elusive character until he died from malaria in July 2005 with only one Western journalist succeeding in interviewing him in his jungle hideout during the war—Vanuatu-based photojournalist Ben Bohane, who specialised in Melanesian storytelling.

Leaving Birempa, the road to Panguna Mine snaked through the jungle, past river gorges and ideal ambush sites until it reached the 1011-metre summit of Karokata Pass through Pakia Gap. With names like Shoo-fly Pass and Fingerpoint Corner, the prudent traveller wouldn't stick around too long to risk becoming a potential target. It was easy to be mistaken for a mine executive or employee.

A long straight above Fingerpoint Corner had been a favourite spot for militants to attack vehicles and mineworker buses with shotguns or bows and arrows. The wild stretch up to Pakia was where the vital 35-kilometre electricity lifeline to the mine had been repeatedly sabotaged, with power pylons dynamited off their concrete footings.

Troops guarded the strategic Guava village area high on the southern rim of the "big hole" that scarred the earth at Panguna. On the northern side of the mine, the International School sports field had been commandeered by security forces as a helipad controversially for three of four Iroquois helicopters supplied by the Australian government to Papua New Guinea.

When I told mine officials I planned to visit the polluted Java and Kawerong rivers, where ghost villages and burn-out hamlets skirted the tailings-devastated valley out into the Solomon Sea, they were astonished.

"Nobody in their right mind goes there any more—it is too dangerous," said one. Officials regarded anywhere west of the huge waste ore dump where a pipeline disgorged tailings into the Kawerong River, a tributary to the Jaba, as undefended "no-man's-land".

More than 3000 villagers had been "relocated", the official euphemism for being forcibly evacuated to create free fire zones against militants. They had been moved to makeshift camps near Arawa. Anybody left was presumed to be a rebel.

A villager from Jaba—known and trusted by both the security forces and the militants but who didn't want to be named—agreed to take me on a tour of the area. But from a New Zealand perspective, the civil war had its roots in an environmental impact report rejected by the landowners as a betrayal. Yet this was a story largely untold in the New Zealand media until I wrote about this in *Sunday* magazine.

BOUGAINVILLE: NEW ZEALAND'S PART IN A GUERRILLA WAR

Sunday magazine, 10 December 1989

IT IS A bitter, stormy meeting in the chapel at the Bougainvillean township of Panguna—site of one of the world's largest open-cut copper mines. Finally Francis Ona, soon to be a rebel leader with a $380,000 price on his head, marches up to Wellington environmental consultant Martin Ward.[4]

He thrusts his face menacingly in front of Ward and points to the altar crucifix. *"Em big fella kilim i dai,"* he hisses in Tok Pisin. *"Mipela nogat likem report bilong you, mipela kilim you dai."* Ona draws his finger across his throat in case Ward misses the point.

His meaning is crystal clear even to those not fluent in pidgin. Ward and his team of consultants—most of them New Zealanders—are to provide the report that Ona and other Nasioi tribal landowners want to hear. Or else.

The New Zealand consultants are expected to come up with a damning verdict on the massive environmental damage the tribesmen claim is being done by the huge mine run by an Australian company, Bougainville Copper Limited (BCL), dominated by the British company Rio Tinto Zinc.[5]

Ona, secretary of the Panguna Landowners' Association, is sceptical about the benefits of the consultants' report and asks the meeting: "Why are we having this review? We've had the politicians, the researchers, all here. We don't need this survey to tell us the line has polluted our rivers and destroyed our environment."

He is also unhappy about the impartiality of the review team. After all, they are white, the landowners black. And, anyway, aren't they Australian?

That last accusation, particularly, stings Ward. There are no Australians on the team, which comprises two Britons, two Papua New Guinean men (including a Buka Islander from Bougainville) and four New Zealanders (including Ward).

"I realised for the first time the seriousness of the job I was getting myself into," says Ward.

Ona's threat to Ward came in November 1988 and was the first step in an escalating crisis. When the report from the New Zealand consultants does not meet his expectations, Ona, in his 30s, moves into the jungle with his guerrillas and becomes the most wanted man in Papua New Guinea.

His small band of militant landowners, the self-styled Bougainville Revolutionary Army (BRA), has waged a year-long guerrilla war against the largely Australian-owned BCL and the national government—more than 900 kilometres to the west in Port Moresby.

Bougainville Revolutionary Army leader Francis Ona (in bush hat and holding a samurai sword) and some of his men at Guava village in 1994. He became an elusive character until he died in July 2005 after proclaiming himself "King of Meekamui" a year earlier.

BEN BOHANE

The "Rambos", as they are known, have forced the Panguna mine to stay shut for the past six months—except for eight hours one day in September. They triggered the state of emergency in June and about 40 people have died so far. About 2000 soldiers—two-thirds of the country's security forces—are trying to quell the uprising.

The Rambos want 10 billion kina [about NZ$19 billion at the time] as compensation for the environmental damage, withdrawal of the military, secession from PNG and permanent closure of the mine. Prime Minister Rabbie Namaliu considers such demands non-negotiable.

Papua New Guinea celebrated its 14th anniversary of independence on September 16 while facing its most critical crossroads. The Bougainville crisis cast a pall over the celebrations and, if it remains unresolved, then national unity could slide into economic and political collapse.

The national government and foreign mining interests portray Ona as an insurgent or terrorist. But he is a folk hero among most Bougainvilleans who regard him as a sort of Robin Hood character defending their traditional rights.

The centre of the dispute is the mine—a massive 400-hectare hole in the ground that discharges tonnes and tonnes of tailings (mining residue), and which is earmarked for further expansion.

So what of the New Zealand role in all this? Ward says he was under no illusions about the volatile situation when he and his colleagues embarked on their fieldwork. His company, Applied Geology Associates Limited (AGA), was appointed as independent consultant by the PNG government in response to mounting frustration by the tribal landowners. The company's brief was to determine the "overall impact the mining operations at Panguna have had on the social and environmental aspects of the area" and "the likely future impact of continued mining operations".

However, matters came to a head for the review team near the end of their three-month study. At a meeting held by the consultants in the North Solomons provincial government offices in the capital, Arawa, a group of landowners arrive late.

They are just in time to hear the review team's public health specialist, Iain Aitken, say the people are fat because of changes in their diet, including some bad habits picked up from modern Western civilisation. The changes are a result of modernisation, Aitken says. The diseases affecting plants are from other factors.

It is not what the landowners want to hear. They are convinced that the mine has driven away the island's fruit bats, ruined banana crops and caused girls to begin menstruation much earlier than previously.

Anger surfaces when they realise that the report will not be as damning as they want. When one consultant says that it cannot be scientifically proved that the killing of fish in the Jaba River is due to pollution, one landowner sneers: "Have you drunk from it?"

Eventually Ona storms out, declaring: "The only way is for us to shut the mine." He and his supporters take to the jungle and launch a long war of attrition and sabotage against the mine. So far more than 3000 villagers have been "relocated" to camps from the embattled areas.

Anyone found in those areas is regarded as a rebel by the military. At least a dozen New Zealanders fled the violence at the end of September.

"The truth is that there is an environmental mess," admits Ward, who maintains that the report was unfairly prejudged by landowners not sufficiently aware of its full contents. "But you cannot say with scientific certainty that there is a relationship between the mine and some of the things they are blaming on the mine."

Many of the landowners regard the report as a "whitewash". The late North Solomons provincial Premier Joseph Kabui believes the report was the catalyst for the militant action after BCL executives refused to negotiate with the landowners for more than a year.

Papua New Guinea soldiers in a trench above Panguna mine on Bougainville, 1989.

BARRY MIDDLEMISS

"It was not the right sort of report," says Kabui. "It was okay as far as the legal framework was concerned. But the general feeling is that it didn't adequately address the environmental pollution.

"The people of Bougainville agree that it is necessary to take a more radical approach to avoid the catastrophe we have gone through now. This experience has opened the eyes of our politicians. We believe the report was a failure. The investigating team didn't have time to get to the bottom of questions. Three months was too short—that's what the owners wanted."

However, BCL, whose 1988 annual report has an "environmentally sound" cover depicting lush rainforest, was satisfied with the AGA verdict. "It showed there was no blame on us," says commercial general manager Ken Perry, whose office overlooks the "big hole".

"The problem is that double the size of the population is now competing for the same resources. What I said to the landowners was: 'You have asked the wrong questions. You asked the consultants to prove BCL did it. You should have asked why is it happening—that's why you're unhappy.'"

In fact, the report, completed earlier in 1989, does describe extensive environmental damage. Provincial government officials who have studied it closely, regard it as far more critical of BCL—and the national government—than the landowners realise.

"The impact on the physical environment of the mine has been extreme by any measure and most of the adverse impacts are long-lasting—in some cases permanent," the report says.

"They were permitted, even to some degree encouraged, by the Australian administration initially and then by the government of Papua New Guinea. On a national scale, they have been judged an acceptable cost for the considerable income the mine has generated. But the costs have been borne by the Nasioi people and, in particular, several hundred landowners who have lost land and lifestyle."

The vast mine is already 400 hectares in size and there are proposed pit extensions totalling 1210 hectares. Mine tailings covering 3000 hectares are devastating the Kawerong and Jaba river valleys.

There is also a 900-hectare delta of discharged tailings in Princess Augusta Bay. There are 300 hectares of waste rock dumps. These could increase to 550 hectares, if the mine's life is extended by 15 years.

According to economist Dr Roman Grynberg, a former adviser to the Papua New Guinea national government, 90 percent of the land loss at Panguna is a result of the manner in which BCL has disposed of its tailings. "BCL has opted for the environmentally sound method only when it is the least expensive solution," he says.

In its initial proposal in the 1960s, the company argued that dumping the tailings into the river would cause large-scale land loss. But later, because it was cheaper, they decided to dump the tailings in the Kawerong and Jaba rivers after all.

The Bougainville problem has hamstrung Prime Minister Namaliu's government. They have tried to reach a negotiated solution but were forced to put a controversial peace package on hold after the assassination in September of a provincial cabinet minister, John Bika. He was an advocate of statehood for Bougainville.

Opposition Leader Paias Wingti has condemned the failure of the government to find a solution but at the same time he has been reluctant to force a censure motion. He does not want to inherit the crisis.

Bougainville is geographically, ethnically and culturally part of the Solomon Islands. The island was swapped by Britain for Western Samoa in the 19th century and was absorbed into Papua New Guinea during World War One when Australia captured the German-held territories.

Those factors explain how the idea of secession has found fertile ground on the island. Just 15 days before independence in Papua New Guinea in September

1975, former seminarian Leo Hannett raised the secessionist flag of the short-lived "Republic of North Solomons".

In spite of the present revolt, big foreign investors such as Conzinc Riotinto Australia Limited (CRA)—BCL's parent company—and the American oil company Chevron are persevering with other projects. Ventures like Chevron's drilling in the northern highlands and the Hidden Valley gold mine are already well committed.

But will this confidence continue if BCL, the mainstay of the national economy, is put into mothballs for a year, as company executives threaten, or is shut down altogether? Some optimistic observers believe the hardship caused by full closure of the Panguna mine would be a blessing in disguise—forcing the country into reducing its dependence on mining and into developing its neglected agriculture sector.

Another suggestion is that a new gold mine at Porgera and increased production at the OK Tedi mine could soften the loss from Bougainville.

Apart from the environmental devastation caused by the Panguna mine and the disappearance of ancestral land belonging to tribes such as the Nasioi, a crucial factor in the upheaval is profit. The national government (which owns 19 percent of BCL) takes 58 percent of the profits from Panguna while the provincial government takes 5 percent and the landowners get a mere 1 percent in royalties and compensation.

The remaining 36 percent is shared among other shareholders—mostly foreign investors with the biggest being CRA—under an agreement worked out before Papua New Guinea's independence.

Panguna has provided 17 percent of the national government's revenue and 45 percent of its exports since 1972. Before it was closed, Panguna was pumping one million kina a day into the coffers of the national government and profits of 1.5 million kina a week to BCL.

The Catholic Church in Bougainville has traditionally been sympathetic to the landowners' demands and is perhaps the one institution trusted by the militants. It has played a vital mediation role so far.

"Even though 10 billion kina was an unimaginable figure for me when I first heard it, when one thinks of the damage that has been caused to the environment then even that much money can never put things back the way they were," says Bishop Gregory Singkai.

He trekked into the jungle in July for a four-hour talk with Ona—the last direct contact with the militant leader.

The diocesan priests appealed for the landowners to be given legislative powers to sue BCL over pollution and to close the mine through court order if the allegations were upheld against the company.

Wounds much deeper than bullets make have been inflicted on thousands of people in the North Solomons. Some of these wounds can be seen in statements of some of the militant leaders:

- "Mining is an emotional issue—our lives have been ruined by modern technology. My health has been damaged. My mind has been changed."
- "BCL is like an octopus."
- "Our people were forced to sell their land in colonial days. The agreement was only between the national government and the mine—not with the landowners."
- "Our parliamentarians are … too involved in national politics, which is full of white advisers who have come and greased us, tried to buy us off, and told us to buy shares."
- "Black men in the top offices are just window dressing." [Papua New Guineans are rare among senior mine management jobs. Only one Papua New Guinean is on the board of directors of BCL and he is not from Bougainville.]
- "The original agreement overrode our customs, denied us our land rights and was too rushed. It contradicts our way of life; what comes from the land should benefit the landowners … nobody else."

British author Richard West wrote a book called *River of Tears*,[6] which has become the Bible of the militant landowners. In it, he says: "The excavation, refining and shipping of [Panguna copper] ore to the smelters of Japan could bring great profit over the next 20 years to the shareholders of Rio Tinto-Zinc—at the cost of damage to the physical, social and spiritual well-being of Bougainville, which, until the mine came, was a peaceful and prosperous island. Moreover, there is a danger that arguments over the ownership of the mine could cause political strife, even civil war, in this part of the South Pacific."

That warning was published in 1972.

SHORTLY after my series of articles was published, in May 1990, the Port Moresby government imposed a blockade on Bougainville and Francis Ona retaliated with a unilateral declaration of independence.[7] Later, in the 1990s, I had further opportunities to report on the Bougainville conflict, or rather my student journalists did, as by then I was head of the journalism programme at the University of Papua New Guinea. With several Bougainvillean students on the programme, such as Gorethey Kenneth, now chief-of-staff at the *Post-Courier*, and Michael Miise, the student

Bougainville's contentious Panguna copper mine in 1989: Now the subject of controversial debate over whether it should be reopened.   DAVID ROBIE

newspaper *Uni Tavur* kept a lively interest in Bougainville and reported strongly on the mercenary crisis in March 1997 when military commander General Jerry Singirok defied the Sir Julius Chan government and forced him to resign over Bougainville.

Isolated from Australian and New Zealand military help in the face of mounting human rights violation allegations against PNG soldiers, Chan turned to a British-based mercenary company, Sandline International. Sandline contracted former special forces soldiers with experience in the Angola and Sierra Leone civil wars. However, the plan was exposed by Solomon Islands-based journalist Mary-Louise O'Callaghan and Singirok hatched Operation Rausim Kwik with a dramatic dawn raid to seize and arrest all the mercenaries.[8]

This was a virtual coup by the military, but Singirok had no intention of seizing power and recalled the troops to barracks once Chan was forced to resign and elections were called. The dilemmas of the period have been evocatively recreated in the 2013 film version of *Mr Pip*, the award-winning novel by Lloyd Jones about a young girl being captivated by Charles Dickens' *Great Expectations* being read at school by her inspirational expatriate teacher.[9]

In January 1998, BRA military commander Sam Kaouna split with Francis Ona and joined former provincial Premier Joseph Kabui to negotiate with Prime Minister Bill Skate in a New Zealand-brokered Lincoln Peace Agreement. Papua New Guinea withdrew its soldiers and enabled a multinational Peace Monitoring Group with Pacific soldiers to maintain law and order and support reconstruction. Since November 1999, a Bougainville Interim Provincial Government and now Autonomous Bougainville Government (ABG) has governed Bougainville with former priest John Momis as president. A referendum on independence is due to be held by 2020 and there have been highly controversial discussions about the possibility of reopening Panguna mine.[10]

Opposition has been mounting in Bougainville against reopening the mine. Critics have appealed to the ABG to consider "other industries" to generate revenue instead of mining. The Bougainville Independent Indigenous Peoples' Foundation's Bernadine Kama asked: "Can we not be left alone to live our lives in peace on our land? Many people are going where the wind blows them and they will not even consider the dire consequences of mining."[11]

According to Rio Tinto's 2012 Annual Report, a study undertaken in 2008 indicated "costs in a range of US\$2 billion to US\$4 billion would be required to reopen the mine assuming all site infrastructure is replaced". BCL reported a net loss of \$2 million for the 2011 financial year based on actual transactions.[12]

Notes

1 Richard West (1972). *River of Tears: The Rise of the Rio Tinto-Zinc Mining Corporation*. London: Earth Island Ltd.
2 David Robie (1989, November). Mine of Tears: Bougainville One Year Later [Cover story]. *Pacific Islands Monthly*, pp. 10–18; David Robie (1989, November). Caught in a crossfire. *Pacific Islands Monthly*, pp. 51–53.
3 Ibid., p. 10.
4 David Robie (1989, December 10). Bougainville: New Zealand's part in a guerilla war. *Sunday* magazine, pp. 20–25.
5 Bougainville Copper Limited was established in 1967. Its major shareholders are Rio Tinto (53.8 percent), the Papua New Guinea government (19.1 percent) and the European shareholders of Bougainville Copper (ESEC, about 4 percent). Just under a quarter of the shareholding (23 percent) is held by private investors.
6 West (1972). *River of Tears*.
7 Wayne Coles-Janess (1998). *Bougainville—Our Island, Our Fight* [Documentary]. ABC *Foreign Correspondent*.
8 Mary-Louise O'Callaghan (1999). *Enemies Within: Papua New Guinea, Australia and the Sandline Crisis: The Inside Story*. Sydney: Doubleday.

9   Andrew Adamson [Director] (2012). *Mr Pip* [Feature film]. Pre-release trailer retrieved on 10 September 2013, from www.youtube.com/watch?v=tRn3gr8Pt_o

10 Brian Thomson (2011). *Blood and Treasure* [Documentary]. SBS Dateline. Available at: www.sbs.com.au/dateline/story/watch/id/601246/n/Blood-and-Treasure

11 Bougainville against mine (2013, August 22). *PNG Post-Courier*. Retrieved on 2 September 2013, from www.postcourier.com.pg/20130822/thhome.htm

12 Rio Tinto Annual Report (2012). Footnote on Bougainville Copper Limited (BCL).

17

Philippines: The Ramboys, 1990

*Although the dictator Marcos has died in exile, his legacy lives on in
the form of political instability, ambitious cronies and, above all, a
factionalised, politicised military.*

Philippines historian Alfred W. McCoy

LITTLE changed under the Corazon Aquino presidency in the Philippines
after the Marcos dictatorship years when it was government policy to
brand community leaders and activists who became advocates for the
poor as "subversives". President Aquino drew criticism in some quarters
when she lauded the Alsa Masa, a notorious right-wing vigilante group
from Davao, largest city of the southern island of Mindanao, as a model
of counter-insurgency tactics.[1] Cinemas and television networks showed
films depicting vigilante killers—beheading was a favourite pastime of
some groups—as heroes.

The Supreme Court in July 1990 upheld the government's introduction
of arrests without warrants as "constitutional". When the court made this
controversial ruling in the so-called Umil case (named after one of eight
jailed men seeking writs of habeas corpus), it found the arbitrary arrests
were legal because the petitioners had been under suspicion.

Judge Abraham Sarmiento said the ruling had "accorded the military a
blanket authority to pick up any Juan, Pedro and Maria without a warrant
for the simple reason that subversion is supposed to be a continuing crime".[2]

Normally in the Philippines, a person could be arrested only on the basis
of a warrant issued by a judge. This was supposed to guarantee citizens a
right to liberty and security as mandated by the International Bill of Rights
and by the Bill of Rights of the Philippine Constitution.

The military wasted no time in invoking its apparent new powers to
arrest suspects and critics without charge—creating de facto martial law.
In fact, on the day the court made its ruling, soldiers arrested 13 suspected
activists in Ozamiz City.

"Now, if someone wants revenge, all he has to do is denounce a person
as a subversive to the military intelligence agents," said Father Shay Cullen,

a human rights advocate then writing a regular column for the *Philippine Daily Inquirer.* In the three decades since the fall of Marcos, thousands of people have disappeared, presumed murdered. In a United Nations investigation in 2007, it was reported that there had been a "grisly death toll" of more than 800 people during the six-year presidency of Gloria Macapagal-Arroyo alone.[3] The assassinations included journalists, judges, trade unionists and lawyers suspected of being sympathetic to "leftist causes".[4] In reality, during the many visits I made to the Philippines over this period it was clear that the most subversive elements in Filipino society were rogue military leaders. In the first four years of the Aquino presidency alone, six attempted coups were made—all by dissidents in the military.

THE RAMBOYS

Sunday magazine, 20 May 1990

IN THE Philippines the Ramboys—a shadowy clique of military officers—are again thirsting for political power. As they once targeted ex-President Ferdinand Marcos, they are now aiming their arrows at the person they helped to win power in 1986—President Corazon Aquino.[5]

They are suspected to have been behind the December 1989 bloody coup attempt that so nearly hurled Aquino out of office and it seems they will stop at nothing in their quest to try again.

Formed originally in opposition to the Marcos dictatorship, the leader, Senator Juan Ponce Enrile, a Defence Secretary under Marcos, led the military rebellion that crushed the old regime and opened the way for Aquino's election on a wave of "people power". But now, in a sinister about-turn, the Ramboys have forged an alliance with powerful ex-Marcos cronies.

Many fear the Ramboys will ultimately seize power. Alan Robson, a New Zealand academic who has been doing doctoral research in the Philippines for the Australian National University, says: "They're a bunch of psychopaths and if they seize control they will make the purges and massacres of Indonesia in 1965 look like a picnic."

Influential *Daily Globe* publisher Teodoro Locsin is just as scathing: "Now is the moment of truth … the moment for democracy in our country against the forces of would-be dictatorship. The old dictatorship is dead. It savaged and robbed the Filipino people for more than 13 years. It takes new bodily shape [through the Ramboys]. A reformist movement, [as] they describe themselves, they would reform democracy with all its virtues and vices out of existence.

A Filipino soldier on patrol in a country with decades of armed conflict.   DAVID ROBIE

"The Philippines will be a concentration camp again. No human rights, only orders from the military dictatorship—with its civilian front. The so-called cause-oriented [activists] and nationalists would be taken as 'communist tools or fronts' to concentration camps with their interrogation chambers and state-of-the art methods of torture—if not summary execution or "salvaging" [state murder] the Marcos way."

Who are the Ramboys? While the international press has often portrayed them as young idealists out to clean up corruption and to install efficient government, the reality is far more sinister. They take their name from the group they owe allegiance to—the Reform the Armed Forces of the Philippines Movement (RAM). Enrile was among their leaders.

A constant thorn in the side of President Aquino, since he helped her to power, the 66-year-old Enrile is extremely wealthy and has powerful links to the military. He is regarded as a man with an insatiable thirst for power. During a recent radio interview he apologised for having helped install Aquino in 1986, saying she isn't fit for the job.

Following the December attempted coup, which he is suspected of having helped mastermind, Enrile was arrested in February and charged with rebellion linked to murder. He turned himself over to agents of the National Bureau of Investigation, saying his arrest would pave the way for renewed tyranny in the country.

Shortly before his arrest he made a speech in the Senate in which he vowed the Aquino government would not silence him. "The regime of Corazon Aquino has marshalled all its forces in fabricating charges against me," he said, "in order to silence the voice of the Opposition in this chamber. As I leave you today, I pledge to you that no jail or prison shall stop me from trying my best to voice the grievances of the people."

Ironically, as martial law administrator for Marcos from 1972 to 1986, Enrile ordered the arrest of thousands of perceived enemies of the state.

Several newspaper columnists condemned Enrile's arrest and claimed he had been railroaded into jail. His lawyers filed a writ of habeas corpus. After a week in prison, he was freed on NZ$7500 bail in spite of the objections of government prosecutors who claimed he would be free to plot another military mutiny.

Filipino political scientist Professor Ed Garcia of the University of the Philippines says the Enrile case shows how weak the Aquino government is. "His arrest was almost bizarre. He was guilty of far more serious crimes in the past—like complicity in so many murders during martial law and electoral fraud. He once publicly admitted that he had been personally responsible for 300,000 votes for Marcos. Yet people talk as if he is a martyr."

The notorious renegade Colonel Gregorio "Gringo" Honasan is one of the leading Ramboys and is among the top suspects for the December attempted coup along with Enrile. In 1986 he was a national hero.

At the age of 37, he commanded troops that helped oust Marcos. Since then he has had a hand in just about every attempted coup, if not all. Famous for his ruthless combat bravado—which some say makes even Sylvester Stallone seem like a wimp—Honasan has a black belt in both goju karate and an ancient Filipino martial art called *arnis*.

According to one story, when Honasan was asked whether he really sliced off his enemies' ears, he replied: "Most of them were dead—well, almost dead."

On the day the fifth coup attempt started—28 August 1987—Honasan was seen leading a flying column in a midnight stab at the Malacañang Palace, the presidential residence, but missed it by taking the wrong street. Honasan clearly masterminded that attempted coup and was visible among its critical moments.

When the attempt failed, he was said to have vanished either into the sky in a mysterious helicopter, or into the back streets of Quezon City astride a Harley-

Filipino soldiers on patrol in Bacolod City, Negros.   DAVID ROBIE

Davidson motorcycle. Later, he was captured and imprisoned on a boat in Manila Bay, but managed to escape by persuading all 14 of his guards to join him.

During the December attempted coup, after victory over the rebels was proclaimed by government forces, a strange thing happened. Seven rebel officers appeared in a nearby hospital, leaned their automatic rifles against the wall, changed out of their uniforms into civilian clothing, waved at wounded rebels and vanished.

There are others behind the crisis as well. One is Brigadier-General Edgardo Abenina—who some regard as potentially more dangerous than Honasan—and another whose presence explains the tremendous amount of money available for the coup, Marcos loyalist paymaster Brigadier-General Joe Maria Zumel.

Behind Honasan, Abenina, Zumel and Enrile is possibly billionaire Eduardo "Danding" Cojuangco, according to speculation in national newspapers. He is said to be the most loyal and powerful of Marcos' crony capitalists. He left his secret exile in the United States and arrived back in the Philippines just one week before the December attempted coup. Speculation immediately centred on his timing.

The coup attempt was so well financed and planned—and the cooperation between military leaders and Marcos cronies so marked—that there is a strong suspicion that Cojuangco bankrolled the rebels. There are strong suggestions that some of the highest-ranking rebels were paid more than NZ$300,000 to join the coup attempt.

Observers believe that the Aquino government faces a precarious future. One, American political scientist Alfred W. McCoy (who wrote a series of articles in the *Daily Inquirer* exposing the Ramboys), says the events of the past few months show that the Philippines has not yet moved past the Marcos era.

"Although the dictator has died in exile," McCoy says, "his legacy lives on in the form of political instability, ambitious cronies and, above all, a factionalised, politicised military. After two decades in power, the Marcos regime became much more than just one man and his wife. By manipulating his martial law powers, Marcos transferred vast financial resources from established business groups to kin and courtiers who became known as crony capitalists."[6]

Since the December attempted coup—it lasted nine days and ended with a death toll of 113 with a further 600 wounded—Aquino has invoked emergency powers under the Constitution. Predictions of an imminent "second phase" military putsch are persistently featured in the newspapers and radio commentaries.

Aquino has drastically reshuffled her cabinet, protesters have demonstrated against the emergency powers—and United States military bases—and NZ$100,000 bounties have been placed on each of the nine coup leaders still at large. There is a NZ$500,000 reward out for Colonel Honasan while 25 other senior military officers have been indicted on charges of rebellion.

In April 1990, masked rebels raided Manila's city jail and freed a suspected Colonel Billy Bibit. He was one of about six suspects who have escaped. More than a dozen officers are still in detention.

Professor Ed Garcia believes the coup has left the military in a stronger position for intervention. "We don't even need a successful coup," he says. "The constant threat of a military coup is enough to prepare the ground for a political coup as happened with the defeat of the Sandinistas in Nicaragua. Our Achilles' heel is our troubled economy."

After 20 years of authoritarian rule, says Garcia, the Philippines has a democratic Constitution and a Bill of Rights, but it also has a highly politicised military and an economy where 70 percent of the 60 million population live below the poverty line.

"We have 11 percent unemployment and 46 percent of our foreign exchange earnings goes towards servicing our national debt. We cannot speak about political democracy without economic democracy."

Commentators like Garcia are now openly discussing the possibility, or even inevitability, of a military-civilian junta. In the United States, fears of another coup attempt have accelerated emergency plans for more than 100,000 nationals who live in the Philippines. The *San Francisco Examiner* has quoted American officials

An arrested "Ramboy", Colonel Billy Bibit, with a raised fist at a media conference in Camp
Aguinaldo before his escape from Manila's city jail In 1990.　　　　　Dᴀᴠɪᴅ Rᴏʙɪᴇ

as saying a "rapid withdrawal" operation has been rehearsed by the US forces
based in the Pacific.

The slashing of US compensation for the use of the Subic Bay naval station
and Clark air base by $96 million, at a time when the country is in dire need of
every dollar it can lay its hands on, has angered the Philippines and led to growing
tension between the Aquino government and Washington.

Garcia has no doubt that a subtle and sophisticated American destabilisation
campaign has been involved in the coup attempts. In his view, the US has wanted
a more pliant and subservient government.

Aꜰᴛᴇʀ a major international Peace Brigade series of protests against the
US military bases in the Philippines, a groundswell of opposition by the
country's political leaders led to their eventual demise. Clark Air Base at
Angeles City closed in 1991 and Subic Bay Naval Base at Olongapo, at that
time the largest overseas US military base, was shut down in 1992. It is now
the Subic Bay Freeport Zone. The last time I visited the base was in 2005,
when I fed chickens to tigers in a tourist wildlife park.

Filipino troops guard the US Clark Air Base at Angeles City from peaceful protesters. The base was closed in 1991. DAVID ROBIE

But the Philippines is an integral part of the US-led global "War on Terror" and has remained so under four presidents since Corazon Aquino—ex-general Fidel Ramos, Joseph Estrada, Gloria Macapagal-Arroyo, and Corazon's incumbent son, Benigno Aquino III. During this period, there have been persistent allegations of human rights abuses and disappearances or murders of civil rights activists, civil society advocates and journalists. According to Amnesty International's 2013 Annual Report on the Philippines, "human rights defenders and journalists [remained] at risk of unlawful killings, and thousands of cases of grave human rights violations remained unsolved".[7] Ironically, several of the alleged "Ramboys" coup plotters became leading Filipino politicians. As well as Senator Juan Ponce Enrile, who resigned as Senate President in June 2013 amid allegations over a slush fund, Colonel Gregorio "Gringo" Honasan was elected as a popular independent senator in 1995 and again in 2013. He had earlier escaped after being imprisoned as a coup leader on the *Manila Bay* warship and was pardoned by President Ramos in 1992. Colonel Billy Bibit, now dead, unsuccessfully contested the congressional elections in 1992.

Amnesty International commended the Philippines government for signing a Framework Agreement with the Moro Islamic Liberation Front in October 2012, which "laid the ground for a peaceful resolution to decades of armed conflict in Mindanao". But the agency also noted that the agreement did not "address human rights comprehensively". It also noted the enactment by Congress in October of the *Cybercrime Prevention Act*, which allows for a person to be jailed for up to 12 years for posting online comments judged libellous. Branded by opponents as the "E-Martial law" in reference to a cyberspace version of the Marcos repression, the law was suspended in November 2012 pending judicial review in the wake of a public outcry. It was confirmed as constitutional in February 2014.

The most serious human rights violation in recent years was the Maguindanao massacre, or the Ampatuan massacre, of some 58 people travelling in an electoral convoy on 23 November 2009 in Mindanao. Perceived as rivals for local elections, they were kidnapped and murdered in cold blood by state-armed militia supporting the Ampatuan warlord family that had held local political power for many years. At least 34 journalists were among the victims in what the Committee to Protect Journalists described as the "single deadliest event for journalists in history". Executive director Joel Simon of the CPJ added in a protest statement that "even as we tally the dead in this horrific massacre, our initial research indicates this is the deadliest single attack on the press ever documented by the CPJ".[8] Even before this massacre, media freedom monitoring organisations had often cited the Philippines as the most dangerous country for journalists after Iraq. Simon also condemned the apparent culture of impunity in the Philippines. When this book went to press, almost five years after the killings, none of the 197 suspected assassins had been successfully prosecuted over the murders.

In an editorial entitled "Stranglehold", the *Philippine National Inquirer* warned of the dangers of political dynasties for the future of the country, referring to Alfred McCoy's classic description of Philippine politics in the early 1990s as "an anarchy of families".[9] The newspaper declared after the 2013 midterm polls that

> while guns, goons and gold continue to play a huge part in how this country elects its leaders, a fourth element—bloodline—has the strongest grip of all on the system. The guns and goons were actually at a historic low in the past electoral exercise, according to international observers ... What the poll observers found particularly disturbing was something else: the overwhelming number of political dynasties in both the local and national levels. It's these Mafia-style family conglomerates in power that contribute to and exacerbate the main problems they saw

in the conduct of the recent polls, such as election-related violence, vote-buying and election management.[10]

The *Philippine Daily Inquirer* noted that of the country's 80 provinces, 73 were ruled by political clans.[11] Of about 178 dominant dynasties, about 100 were old feudal land-based families, and the rest, new clans that arose and gained power after the People Power Revolution and the post-Marcos years. While the *Inquirer* is undoubtedly the best newspaper in the Philippines, I clashed with its then editor-in-chief, Federico Pascual, in 1989 over an op-ed human rights article about "salvagings" published in *The Dominion*.[12] In an editorial headlined "Idiots sent to smear us",[13] he attacked me for accusing the paper of suppressing some human rights stories—one of his own senior reporters had given me a file of affadavits about such self-censored reports and I had cited these.[14] I wrote a letter to the paper for publication, challenging Pascual. It was never published. Neither was a further letter sent to the paper's ombudsman. A year later, I met Pascual by chance at the University of the Philippines when we were panellists together in a discussion about press freedom. When I spoke to Pascual and mentioned his column, the editor denied having written anything and then scurried away in embarrassment.

Notes

1   David Robie (1991, February 28). Filipino priests face rule by the gun. *The Dominion*, p. 7.

2   Ibid.

3   Marwaan Macan-Markar (2007, February 11). UN probes extra-judicial killings. Inter Press Service. Retrieved on 3 September 2013, from www.ipsnews.net/2007/02/rights-philippines-un-probes-extra-judicial-killings/

4   Cher S. Jimenez (2007, February 13). Deadly dirty work in the Philippines. Asia Times Online. Retrieved on 3 September 2013, from www.atimes.com/atimes/Southeast_Asia/IB13Ae01.html

5   David Robie (1990, May 20). The Ramboys. *Sunday* magazine, pp. 38–42.

6   See also Alfred W. McCoy (2009). *Policing America's Empire: The United States, the Philippines and the Rise of the Surveillance State*. Madison: University of Wisconsin Press.

7   Amnesty International Annual Report 2013 (2013, May). Philippines. Retrieved on 3 September 2013, from www.amnesty.org/en/region/philippines/report-2013

8   Alcuin Papa (2009, November 26). Maguindanao massacre worst-ever for journalists. *Philippine Daily Inquirer*. Retrieved on 3 September 2013, from http://newsinfo.inquirer.net/breakingnews/nation/view/20091126-238554/Maguindanao-massacre-worst-ever-for-journalists

9   Stranglehold [Editorial] (2013, May 21). *Philippine Daily Inquirer*. Retrieved on 3 September 2013, from http://opinion.inquirer.net/53087/stranglehold

10 Ibid.

11 Ibid.

12 David Robie (1989, February 15). The tragedy of human wrongs, *The Dominion*, p. 13.

13 Federico D. Pascual Jr (1989). Idiots sent to smear us [Editorial "Postscript"], *Philippine Daily Inquirer*.

14 Cited in Murray Horton (1992, August-September). David Robie: One of a Kind, *New Zealand Monthly Review*. No. 332, p. 19.

18

Forgotten victims of a silent war, 1991

Statistics don't tell the full story. Evacuees usually have to leave in a hurry. Many of them—perhaps as many as 60 percent—are terrified children or old people.
Internal refugee advocate Zenaida Delica

MARCELLO Torres was a survivor. Escaping with his life, after being shut in a cave and the entrance set ablaze by soldiers on the central Philippines island of Negros, he decided to fight back. He and his wife, Dixie, trekked 120 kilometres, along with five children and 12 other families, to confront the governor of their province. For almost a month, they camped in squalid conditions in the provincial capital of Bacolod City.[1]

First, outside the provincial government offices, to the embarrassment of Governor Daniel Lacson of Negros Occidental, then beside the bishop's residence, Domus Dei. They would have starved had the Catholic Church not helped them and volunteers of the women's group GABRIELA not given meals to the children each day.

Finally, they were given safe conduct passes back to their ghost village of Buenavista, promised compensation and pledged that militarisation of their area would be halted. A fleet of six trucks, carrying about 50 people each, ferried them "home". They were among the "internal refugees" of the Philippines—an estimated one million civilians who had fled their homes since 1986 in a desperate attempt to escape the fighting between government troops and the communist-led New People's Army (NPA).

As a casualty of a 21-year-old insurgency, they were ignored. Because the Aquino government refused then to fully recognise the displaced people, there was no official aid programme to deal with their plight. Before the 52-year-old Torres left with his family, he and his companions talked through an interpreter about their suffering. His story:

The soldiers and the CAFGU [Paramilitary Citizens Armed Forces Geographical Units] came to our village and asked us if any rebels stayed there.

I said, "We cannot pinpoint anybody because we don't know any rebels." I was beaten by the CAFGU. They clubbed me onto my knees, beat my head and then kicked me on the ground.

I pleaded, "I cannot tell you ... I don't know."[2]

The soldiers stripped the villagers of their rice supplies, cooking utensils and *bolos* (cane knives). Torres was pushed into a cave with several other men. A fire was lit in the entrance and one man suffocated from the smoke before other villagers were able to rescue them.

In another incident related by the refugees, Remedios de la Torre was shot dead by soldiers and her one-year-old baby Nene drowned in a *carabao* mudhole. Three other daughters—Linda, 17; Lora, 15; and Niza, 13—were abducted by the military and haven't been seen since.

A relative described what happened:

The three girls were walking to a nearby town when the soldiers arrived. Frightened, they ran home while their mothers came out to find out what the fuss was about.

However, she was immediately shot by the soldiers. Her husband Carlito jumped out of the house and escaped while the soldiers also fired at him. The baby was drowned and the three daughters were taken away by the soldiers.[3]

The 61st Battalion—one of nine military and paramilitary battalions on the highly militarised Negros—was accused of the atrocities in both incidents, and in many other cases. However, the only prosecution case was brought against a lieutenant charged with killing Mrs de la Torre.

When I tried to visit a resettlement camp at Payao in central Negros with several Australian and Filipino journalists, we were barred by armed goons of the CAFGU. Guarding the only track into the area, their leader told us we could enter only if we had authority from the nearby 61st Battalion headquarters.

When we arrived at the barracks, the sentry on guard duty was asleep. He hurriedly pulled on his black beret and grabbed his M-16 after we approached. Then he fetched an off-duty officer. We exchanged pleasantries for an hour and the answer came finally: "No!"

Although the officer seemed friendly enough, he wasn't prepared to risk his neck. What did they have to hide at the Payao camp?

The issue of internal refugees was highly sensitive for the Aquino government. The one million figure was an estimate made by non-

Internal refugees Marcello Torres, his wife, Dixie, five of their 10 children and a nephew with their possessions tied up in sugar sacks in Negros, Philippines, 1991.   DAVID ROBIE

governmental organisations documenting the displacement of civilians by the insurgency.

But NGO workers believed the number could be far higher. Many other refugees were said to have fled to remote villages that were difficult to reach.

It was hard for the government to acknowledge the scale of the problem; to do so would have forced it to admit serious excesses in the counter-insurgency strategy. And the rebels would also be able to press the propaganda advantage.

About 60 percent of the refugees were children, according to NGOs. Many of them, particularly in the southern island of Mindanao and in the mountainous northern Cordillera region, are tribal minorities. Indigenous at that time comprised about seven million out of the total population of 62 million.

Since these refugees did not cross any international border and remained within the Philippines, they became known as internal refugees. According to one NGO spokesperson, the refugees were defined as "individuals,

A refugee child in Bacolod City, Negros, in 2001. David Robie

families and communities displaced from their habitual residence and sources of livelihood by incidents arising from ... the armed conflict".

The Citizens Disaster Rehabilitation Centre (CDRC), a Manila-based umbrella secretariat for a network of 17 NGOs assisting refugees, blamed the crisis on the Aquino government's "total war policy".

In 1989, almost 36,000 people were displaced in the military's notorious Operation Thunderbolt on Negros. Although the strategy was officially shelved for a while, it is clear the operation was used as a trial for similar mass operations against civilians elsewhere in the country.

Militarisation on Mindanao led to far greater numbers of refugees—126,000 by the end of 1989 alone.

At the time I reported on this crisis, a major operation had been under way in the Marag Valley, in the northern province of Cagayan.

Journalists were barred from the zone and fact-finding missions were refused entry until senator Bobby Tanada personally intervened on behalf of a team that went there in February 1991.

"The military say the Marag Valley is a stronghold of the NPA," said the CDRC's executive director, Zenaida Delica. "But it seems that is how they view any place where there are people's cooperatives, people's empowerments and self-help schemes. The Marag is a beautiful area, untouched by government projects. It isn't surprising if people organise themselves and progress through their own initiative—the government isn't doing it."

After Operation Thunderbolt on Negros, 257 children died in evacuation camps. Diarrhoea, malaria, measles and respiratory illnesses were common, especially among young children. "But the damage is psychological, too," noted a report by the Philippine Center for Investigative Journalism. "Many refugees have witnessed violent killings of friends, and neighbours, even of relatives. In the camps, children suffer from recurring nightmares."

Among a series of reports that I wrote about internal refuges in the Philippines, was the following article about the important role of the Philippine Independent Church, which split away from the Catholic Church just as the protestant and reformist churches in northern Europe created their own identity separate from the Vatican.

CHURCH TAKES ON STRUGGLE THEOLOGY

The Dominion, 11 July 1990

As THE economic and social crisis deepens in the Philippines, both the Philippine Independent Church—the "daughter of a revolution"—and the Roman Catholic Church have been taking on a higher political profile.[4]

For the bishops and priests of the Philippine Independent Church this is nothing new. Their church, among one of the world's most remarkable Christian institutions, was founded on nationalist struggle—first against three centuries of Spanish colonialism and then in the Philippine–American War 1899–1902.

During the failed military coup in December 1989, thousands of Filipinos gathered at parish churches and village chapels and prayed for peace. The Catholic Church enjoys the support of the country's 61 million people and a church official recently disclosed it was considering becoming a "political force" in the future.

The revelation, by Father Fausto Gomez, director of the Social Research Center of the University of Santo Tomas, came amid growing awareness of the widening involvement of the Catholic Church in the country's political affairs following its participation in the 1986 "people power" uprising, continued support for President Corazon Aquino's democratic administration, and the alleged involvement of some church members in the latest bloody uprising.

In a country that has embraced Catholicism for more than four centuries, many citizens believe the church should play a key role in both the spiritual and political lives of the people.

The Philippine Independent Church's recently elected Supreme Bishop, Tito Pasco, who is now also chairman of the Philippine National Council of Churches, has pledged that his church will remain true to "its commitments to the continuing nationalist struggle of the Filipino people".

He added that it was a "people's movement against domination and suppression done in any form and committed by anybody, whether foreign or national".

The history of the Philippine Independent Church is characterised by the nationalist and revolutionary ideals and aspirations of the Filipino people at the time of the Philippine Revolution of 1896 against Spanish colonial rule.

Led by Isabelo de los Reyes, founder of the first labour union in the Philippines, the church was proclaimed on 3 August 1902. From that date, the priests split with the Vatican and consolidated the break with a constitution two months later.

But the founding spirit of the church was really Gregorio Aglipay Labanan, who was an active revolutionary Catholic priest during the war of independence—or the "Tagalog war"—against Spain in 1896–8. While acting as assistant priest to a Spanish friar, he founded a secret branch of the underground Katipunan movement.

After being the military vicar-general of the revolutionary army, he later became a guerrilla general in the Ilocas region, fighting against the new American colonisers. When he finally surrendered, not all his troops' firearms could be accounted for.

"Whenever any were discovered," says historian William Henry Scott, "their owners claimed that Aglipay had told them to keep them hidden and well-oiled."

Aglipay became the Independent Church's first Supreme Bishop—a position he held until his death 40 years later. Yet in spite of his exalted ecclesiastical position, Bishop Aglipay remained a dissident or friend of dissidents for most of his life.

"The Aglipay church was truly a people's church," says leading Filipino columnist Renato Constantino, "having been forged as an instrument of spiritual liberation from the Roman Catholic Church which was then an institution used by both the Spanish and American colonisers as a means of spiritual subjugation."

Support given by millions of Filipinos to the new Philippine Independent Church was the result of a struggle that began with the demands for secularisation and Filipinisation of the clergy, at first during the Spanish occupation and then under American colonial rule.

On 17 February 1872, three Filipino priests—Jose Burgos, Mariano Gomes and Jacinto Zamora—were publicly executed with the garrotte by Spanish friars on suspicion of supporting the Cavite rebellion against Spanish rule. A memorial

Supreme Bishop Tito Pasco of the Philippine Independent Church. DAVID ROBIE

to the martyrs stands today in Manila opposite the Senate building; they are also honoured by a painting in one of the Independent churches.

In the early part of the 20th century, a quarter of the Filipino population belonged to the church—a reflection of Filipino aspirations for independence.

During the American occupation, nationalism was suppressed, flying of the Filipino flag outlawed and advocacy of independence banned. Nationalist sentiments of the people were expressed through "non-political" movements—the labour union founded by de los Reyes and the Philippine Independent Church.

American authorities stripped parish churches and property taken over by the Aglipayan priests and restored them to the Roman Catholic Church. American bishops replaced Spaniards and Catholic dominance was guaranteed.

"Our people had to start again from scratch," says Bishop Pasco. "Frequently, we had mere *nipa* huts in contrast to the gothic buildings of the Roman church."

The "theology of liberation" evolved during the early years of the Aglipayan church and was later introduced to Latin American countries. Now the church's bishops and priests talk of a revival—"we hope to produce a theology of struggle", said one.

For a time, during the Marcos dictatorship, the Aglipayan church lost sight of its people's vanguard role. Some critics even condemned it as being a collaborator with the Marcos regime.

Seminarians uphold the "critical conscience" traditions in a "Christians unite" demonstration against authoritarian rule in Manila, Philippines, in 2000.   DAVID ROBIE

"We were dubbed the 'silent church' during the Marcos era," recalls Bishop Pasco. But the church still has more than four million members, compared with 40 million Catholics in the Philippines.

"Now we are trying our best to recapture the traditional role our church has played," says Bishop Pasco. "So we are discovering our historic heritage and vocation."

The church has embarked on a comprehensive nationalist programme "which is in response to the needs of the times." Five broad themes are included—faith and witness, education, social justice and community service, liturgy and music, and ecumenical relations and international affairs.

Part of the struggle is to develop a liturgy linked to the lives of the people and to compose music that reflects this," says Bishop Pasco. "We must sing our own song and drink from our own wells.

In a four-page pastoral letter marking its 87th year, the Philippine Independent Church renewed its original vows. Read out in the institution's 600 churches during 1989, the letter by the 50-member Supreme Bishops Council declared: "We shall offer and open our churches and our diocesan centres and ourselves in solidarity with the oppressed sectors who struggle for life and journey toward the fulfilment of God's will."

Anti-imperialism is clear in the pastoral letter, which cited the "political, economic and cultural structures" imposed by a foreign power as the source of the Filipino people's dehumanisation.

The pastoral letter called for nationalist industrialisation, implementation of the nuclear-free provision of the 1987 Constitution, genuine land reform, withdrawal of the draconian letter of intent to the World Bank over the country's 30 million peso national debt, and a 30 peso across-the-board wage increase for workers.

Catholic Center researcher Father Vijan Dumol, editor of a book of selected writings by Jaime Cardinal Sin, *A Cry ... A Song*, says there were moves for closer cooperation between the Catholic and Independent churches.[5]

He recalls a time when Bishop Aglipay avoided the ban on the Filipino flag by giving a sermon dressed in vestial clothes tailored from the ensign. "I realised one day the nationalist vision would be a treasure," Father Dumol says. "I made the sign of the cross.

"Our task now is how to keep ourselves on our toes. We still have to work together and be self-reliant. The aspirations of the Filipino people need to be met."

In a speech after the abortive Ramboys coup, Cardinal Sin condemned the actions of "unprincipled soldiers and officers who for money and only money spilled the blood of fellow Filipinos". The rebel leaders, he said, must be hunted down.

But he also launched into a surprising indictment of nepotism and exploitation by the Aquino administration, adding: "Where there is so much misery ... how can we dream of peace?"

§

IRONICALLY, the Philippines, one of the few countries in Asia to have signed the 1951 Refugee Convention, and in spite of its own internal refugee problem, became the second country in the world to offer temporary sanctuary to refugees. The administration agreed to become a transit country for at-risk international refugees. "The Philippines is again setting the protection benchmark in Asia ... [by] implementing a national asylum law and procedure," said Raymond Hall, Southeast Asia regional coordinator of the United Nations refugee agency UNHCR.[6]

In February 2013, the Philippines Congress passed a new law that seeks to protect the rights of the more than one million internally displaced people (IDP), or internal refugees—action taken 22 years after I first wrote about this problem.[7] The measure was seen as a milestone for the protection of internal refugees in the wake of decades-long armed conflicts and natural disasters, especially in Mindanao where an estimated 300,000 people are now reportedly displaced.

"For the first time, we'll have a specific law in the region that can make a difference in the lives of people who have fled and run for their lives due to conflict and disaster," said UNHCR's representative in the Philippines Bernard Kerblat. "The bill establishes a system to protect people and give them assistance."[8]

Allegations of human rights violations have continued to dog all the post-Marcos democratic governments. Journalists have also paid a high price for freedom of information and free speech in the Philippines (see page 309), but social media has also contributed to the downfall of a President. On 17 January 2001, loyalists in the Philippine Congress voted to block important evidence during the impeachment trial of President Joseph Estrada. However, less than two hours after the congressional vote, protesters used social media with seven million text messages to mobilise a huge demonstration in metro Manila.

"The event marked the first time that social media had helped force out a national leader," wrote Rita Safranek in an analysis of the impact of social media in global crises.[9]

Notes

1 David Robie (1991, February 27). The forgotten victims of a silent war. *The Dominion*, p. 11.
2 Ibid.
3 David Robie (1991, March 6). Forgotten victims of a silent war. *Auckland Star*, p. A7.
4 David Robie (1990, July 11). Church takes on struggle theology. *The Dominion*, p. 11.
5 Jaime L. Sin and Vijan Dumol (eds) (1989). *A Cry ... A Song: Selected Writings of Jaime Cardinal L. Sin*. Quezon City, Philippines: Vibal Publishing House.
6 Refugees in danger will find temporary sanctuary in the Philippines (2009, August 31). *UNHCR News*. Retrieved on 3 September 2013, from www.unhcr.org/4a9be1526.html
7 Philippines passes historic bill to protect internally displaced (2013, February 8). *UNHCR News*. Retrieved on 3 September 2013, from www.unhcr.org/5114dd5c9.html
8 Ibid.
9 Rita Safranek (2012, March). The Emerging Role of Social Media in Political and Regime Change. *ProQuest Discover Guides*. Retrieved on 3 September 2013, from www.csa.com/discoveryguides/social_media/review.pdf

19

Timor-Leste:
The horror of Santa Cruz, 1992

Human dignity is freedom. It is the same principle that Pacific governments upheld to defend Kuwait and peace in Cambodia yet they ignore the plight of the indigenous people on their own doorstep who seek self-determination.

Timorese human rights advocate Francisco Pang

SHORTLY after the Santa Cruz massacre on 12 November 1991, when un-provoked Indonesian troops opened fire on a peaceful demonstration in a cemetery in the Timor-Leste capital of Dili, killing at least 270 people, I wrote a detailed account of that tragic day for one of New Zealand's leading daily newspapers. It was accepted and laid out as an op-ed page article. However, the evening before publication, in early December, I was advised by the features editor the article would not run. He was embarrassed and very apologetic and said as a freelancer I would be paid a "kill" fee for not publishing—a rather obscene term in the context. Clearly there had been political pressure for the article to be quietly dropped.[1]

A New Zealander was among those who were brutally murdered by Indonesian troops on that tragic day. Yet the New Zealand media seemed reluctant to publish much about the truth. My article (an expanded five-page version) was eventually published in the *New Zealand Monthly Review*, a small-circulation national magazine.

The incident was perhaps the most extreme example of mainstream media self-censorship on the issue that I have personally experienced. But it is always apparent to me that many editors have a "blind" mindset over Indonesia and East Timor, or Timor-Leste as the independent nation is now known as, and West Papua issues. Australia has been far worse, except for the public broadcast media, than New Zealand (whose government and media, after all, take their cue from across the Tasman). The Pacific media all but ignored the Timor issue for many years. In the United States, no single network television report, including public television, was carried on East Timor between 1975 and 1991.

Timor-Leste villagers greet the unilateral declaration of independence on 28 November 1975 before Indonesian troops invaded the former Portuguese colony.   TAPOL

Perhaps the mindset was at least partially altered by John Pilger and the controversy over his *Death of a Nation* television documentary, which exposed the hypocrisy and blatant self-censorship practised by *The Australian* and several other Australian news media over the issue.[2] But in many respects, Pilger was simply reporting what many of us independent journalists in the Pacific following Indonesian neocolonialism had been saying for years. Publication of "The Timor Papers" in his 2004 book *Tell Me No Lies* outlines the "crime against humanity": "The invasion was the prelude to a genocide that saw the population of the Portuguese colony fall by 200,000, or a third: proportionally, a greater slaughter than the Holocaust."[3]

In 1994, Geoffrey Gunn's timely critique of news media responses to Indonesian colonialism was highlighted in his *A Critical Review of Western Journalism and Scholarship on East Timor*.[4] It comprehensively deconstructed the double standards and hypocrisy of Western governments—particularly Australia, given the heroic sacrifice of the East Timorese people in support of Australian commandos in the defence of Australia from Japanese fascism during World War Two; the eagerness of Australia to militarily intervene alongside the forces on the side of the "free world" in South-East Asia in the 1960s; Australia's special role in brokering the peace plan for Cambodia in 1990; and the defence of "democracy" against tyranny in the rescue of Kuwait from Saddam Hussein.

Castigating the "myopia" of the Australian and New Zealand governments and media over East Timorese self-determination in the wake of Indonesia's invasion in 1975, Gunn argued that an independent East Timor posed no other threat than being another South-East Asian state, one that has strong ties with many of the independent Pacific nations. This gradually changed after the Santa Cruz massacre and in the lead-up to independence as Timor-Leste in 2002.[5]

Although the United Nations still officially recognised Portugal as the administering power in East Timor, Australia signed the Timor Gap Treaty with Indonesia in December 1989 to gain access to oil, a move challenged by the Portuguese as illegal before the International Court of Justice. Twelve of the 14 judges said the court was unable to invalidate the treaty because Indonesia had not accepted the court's compulsory jurisdiction at the time. The other two judges supported Portugal's claim.[6]

In 1990, Western countries supported with enthusiasm the US-led Coalition forces that went to war because oil-rich Iraq invaded its neighbour, Kuwait, and declared it a province. Yet ironically most of the same countries said little when Indonesia, also oil-rich, did the same thing against East Timor in 1975—and many remained pragmatic. Perhaps a key difference was that Saddam Hussein was a pariah to the West while Suharto was a friend/client, eager to do business.[7]

TERROR IN TIMOR

New Zealand Monthly Review, March/April 1992

BARELY a week before Kamal Bamadhaj died in the Santa Cruz massacre, one of the scores of people gunned down by Indonesian security forces among the gravestones in an East Timor cemetery, he sensed an impending tragedy. The 20-year-old New Zealander confided in letters sent to friends in Sydney that a kind of "lull before the storm" had seized the Timorese capital of Dili.[8]

Tension had been high as the Timorese prepared themselves for the long-awaited visit of a Portuguese parliamentary delegation due to have started on 4 November 1991. Some Timorese saw the planned visit as the first step towards a referendum in the Indonesian-ruled colony; some hoped the Portuguese could somehow bring about immediate independence.

New Zealander Ahmed Bamadhaj, killed by Indonesian troops in the 1991 Santa Cruz massacre, portrayed in a still from Annie Goldson's documentary *Punitive Damage*.
© PUNITIVE DAMAGE

But others saw the visit as the long-awaited opportunity for an uprising against the Indonesian invaders. After being occupied by Indonesia 16 years earlier and "integrated" by the colonisers for almost as long, most Timorese seemed to Bamadhaj to have much the same aspiration—independence.

"Youths in Dili and in other towns in East Timor have been secretly painting pro-independence banners, organising demonstrations and, as many have admitted to me, preparing to die for their people if the Indonesians try to stop them," wrote Bamadhaj in his last letter.

Timorese of all ages and walks of life have been signing up to be on the list of interviewees for the Portuguese fact-finding mission. Considering that talking to foreigners about the situation in East Timor is risky, there are large numbers who have decided to take the plunge and talk to the Portuguese when they come.

The Indonesians, too, have been preparing for the visit, launching an intensive campaign of intimidation and rounding up Timorese for public lectures where they are threatened with imprisonment or death if they dare speak up.

Freshly dug mass execution sites have been discovered throughout East Timor, perhaps another method of intimidating the locals into silence. The

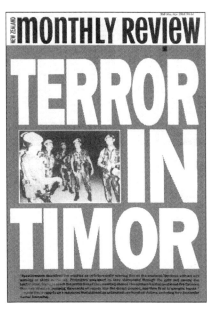

"Terror in Timor" edition of *New Zealand Monthly Review*, March/April 1992.

Timorese church has also come under heavy military surveillance for its role in helping the people prepare for the visit.[9]

However, the risks taken by the Timorese—witnessed by Bamadhaj and five foreign journalists—were in vain. The Portuguese visit promised them much hope. But a few days before the delegation was to arrive, word filtered through that the parliamentarians would not come.[10] They had been forced to abandon their visit because the Indonesians barred Jill Jolliffe, a respected Lisbon-based Australian journalist and author of *East Timor: Nationalism and Colonialism* and *Balibo*.[11]

The ill-fated demonstration on 12 November 1991 was partly in compensation for the cancelled Portuguese visit—it was planned to coincide with a visit to Dili of the United Nations Special Rapporteur on Torture, Peter Kuijmans. It was also a march to the Santa Cruz cemetery to pay tribute at the grave of Sebastião "Gomes" Rangel, a young Timorese killed on October 28 when Indonesian troops entered the parish church of Motael. Rangel and about 20 other political activists had been hiding in the church.

Amnesty International and other human rights organisations estimate more than 200,000 people in East Timor—a third of the population—have died in the fighting, or from hunger and executions, since the 1975 Indonesian invasion,

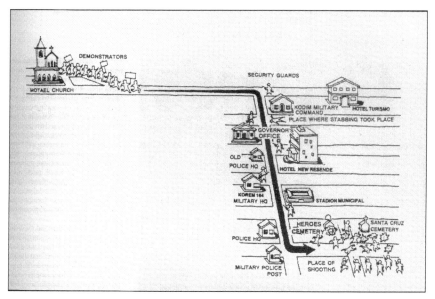

A map of the procession route from Motael Church to the Santa Cruz cemetery in Dili, Timor-Leste, on 12 November 1991 where the massacre happened.   TAPOL

a scale of genocide said to be comparable on a per capita basis with that of the Khmer Rouge slaughter in Cambodia.

According to Bob Muntz, South-East Asia officer for Community Aid Abroad, the Australian aid agency for which Bamadhaj worked as an interpreter for three days before he died, the handful of foreigners held a meeting the night before the march to decide whether to take part.

Bamadhaj had admitted earlier that he felt "exposed and frightened" after three weeks in East Timor—but he argued strongly that he and the other foreigners should be at the march.

All of them were "scared", said Muntz, but they decided to go. After all, they thought, a foreign presence might restrain the military and prevent them from attacking the crowd.

Besides Bamadhaj and Muntz, the group included a British television cameraman, Chris Wenner, who used the pseudonym "Max Stahl" to protect his Timorese helpers. His footage challenged crude Indonesian attempts to cover up the horror of the massacre.[12] Also present were American journalists Amy Goodman and Alan Nairn (both brutally beaten by Indonesian soldiers).[13]

Stahl was filming inside the cemetery when firing began, taking cover behind the tombstones. Although he managed to delete footage on a tape in his camera when he was under arrest, he later retrieved tapes of the massacre hidden under tombstones.

About 3000 protesters took part in the rally, which was fairly uneventful until they reached the cemetery. They were mostly students and young people protesting against the Indonesian occupation; many were women and children.

The procession stopped along a road hemmed in by high walls when military trucks drove up. Soldiers, perhaps about 200, lined up facing the crowd with about a 100-metre gap between them.

Eyewitnesses described the soldiers as cold-bloodedly opening fire on the unarmed Timorese without warning or shots in the air. Protesters screamed as they stampeded through the gate and among the tombstones, trying to reach the protection of the cemetery chapel.

The soldiers kept up sustained fire for more than two minutes, pumping thousands of rounds into the crowd, paused, and then fired in sporadic bursts.

None of the eyewitnesses who described what happened actually saw Bamadhaj shot. When he was found, he had dragged himself half a kilometre away from where the massacre took place. He was wounded in the right side of his chest.

According to a report drafted by a New Zealand diplomat who travelled to Dili, Bamadhaj was found by Anton Marti, the local representative of the International Committee of the Red Cross. Marti said Bamadhaj was lying on a deserted stretch of road, still conscious, bleeding heavily—and desperately waving his New Zealand passport.

Marti drove Bamadhaj towards the Dili General Hospital, but soldiers stopped his ambulance at road blocks several times before he reached medical help, and he had already lost a lot of blood.

Marti's ambulance had the familiar Red Cross insignia, but when he was stopped at one road block where he identified himself and explained he was carrying a wounded man, a soldier snapped at him: "Get out of here or we'll shoot you."

Marti then drove by another route and was again stopped outside a police station. Once more, Marti explained he had a badly wounded man in the vehicle and again he was barred from driving on to the hospital—or even getting out of the car.

After a long hold-up, Marti was told to drive to the military hospital.

"The delay was fatal," says Helen Todd, Bamadhaj's mother, a former New Zealand journalist now living in Malaysia. "Diplomats told me the shooting began soon after 7.50am. It seems likely that Mr Marti picked up Kamal around 8 o'clock.

"He was admitted to the hospital—by then unconscious and bleeding profusely—at 8.40am.

"Kamal was the first casualty to be admitted to the hospital and, according to the official medical report, he got immediate and professional treatment. But he died 20 minutes later."

Although eyewitnesses and global human rights groups believe at least 250 people died in the massacre, Indonesian authorities initially claimed an official death of 19 (although they earlier admitted to about 50).[14]

In an open letter to New Zealand Prime Minister Jim Bolger, Helen Todd said: "Deliberate firing by Indonesian military into a peaceful memorial procession in Dili ... and the systematic, brutal 'mopping up' action in the Santa Cruz cemetery—shown to a shocked world on videotape—have alerted us to a very different reality in East Timor."[15]

Indonesian government and military authorities expressed "regret" at the deaths and a National Investigation Commission was set up. However, the commission's preliminary report made available in January admitted a death toll of merely 50, with 91 wounded and at least 90 missing.[16]

But the Timorese resistance group Fretilin and its military wing Falintil was accused of instigating the events leading up to the "boiling point" when the shooting happened. No evidence was given and none of the foreign eyewitnesses to the massacre was interviewed.

In a "disorderly, wild and unruly atmosphere", said the seven-member commission's report, Major Gerhan Lantara, an intelligence officer, was stabbed, and a private was injured.

Shortly after the report was made public, Indonesia's armed forces chief, General Try Sutrisno, made the two generals in charge of East Timor scapegoats, recalling them and naming replacements. (Brigadier-General Theo Syafei took over from Brigadier-General Rudolf Samuel Warouw as military operational chief in Dili.)

Yet just one day after the massacre, General Sutrisno reportedly had called for political opponents of Indonesian rule in East Timor to be shot. The general, who visited New Zealand just one month before the massacre, claimed that people in the procession had "spread chaos" by unfurling slogans discrediting the government, and by shouting "many unacceptable things".

In retaliation, he said, the soldiers had fired shots in the air, "but they persisted. In the end, they had to be shot. These ill-bred people have to be shot—and we'll shoot them."[17]

Video footage and photographs of the shootings and the beatings that followed corroborate the testimony of eyewitnesses who said the procession and graveside ceremony were peaceful and that soldiers opened fire without warning or provocation.

Amnesty International, Asia Watch and other human rights organisations published detailed critiques of the "investigation" report. Describing the findings as "fatally flawed", Amnesty also said that other aspects of the Indonesian government and military response to the massacre had been inadequate and inappropriate:

East Timorese supporters and trade unionists at a Nuclear-Free and Independent Pacific (NFIP) rally in Port Vila.   DAVID ROBIE

> Rather than preventing future human rights violations and ensuring that those responsible are brought to justice, the response has been accompanied by further violations against East Timorese.[18]

At the time of writing, no members of Indonesia's security forces had been charged or brought before the courts over the killings and other later human rights violations. Yet more than 60 East Timorese [including the country's current Prime Minister, Deputy Prime Minister and several Members of Parliament] were imprisoned for perhaps no greater "crime" than that they had supported East Timor's self-determination.

The Santa Cruz massacre became the turning point in the global struggle for Timorese self-determination. In spite of the rampant media censorship within Indonesia and the diplomatic overtures for damage control in countries such as Australia and New Zealand, underground copies of Max Stahl's video evidence of the unprovoked slaughter began to circulate widely within Indonesia and internationally. An informed Indonesian view became increasingly critical of the military occupation and sceptical of the

Jakarta government lies about the repression. Links between Indonesian human rights movements and underground Timorese groups strengthened.

The Max Stahl massacre footage also had a growing impact on international civil society. As Stahl noted later, "Timor-Leste is the first country to have gained independence through an audiovisual war."[19] Solidarity movement websites began publishing galleries of atrocity images and there was heightened interest among the mainstream media. Kamal Bamadhaj's mother, Helen Todd, also won a lawsuit against an Indonesian general over the killing of her son and the US Court in Boston awarded US$14 million in damages. But General Panjaitan never turned up for the trial, and the damages were never paid. Filmmaker Annie Goldson made a documentary, *Punitive Damage*, about this case in 1999.[20]

Finally, in a remarkable about-face in Indonesian policy President B. J. Habibie declared in February 1999 his willingness to allow the United Nations to hold a referendum on independence for Timor-Leste.[21] Although many Timorese had hoped after a quarter of a century that Indonesia would relax its opposition to a "separate" East Timor state on its border, the sudden news was greeted with some apprehension. The referendum announcement provoked a wave of one-sided violence by Indonesian-armed militias. Twice postponed, the referendum finally took place on 30 August 1999 and the East Timorese people voted overwhelmingly in favour of independence.

However, Timorese supporters of independence became the targets of militia recruited by Indonesian troops to launch a rampage of "scorched earth" devastation over the "no" vote against special autonomy within the Indonesian republic (some believe this was an orchestrated warning against self-determination aspirations in Aceh and West Papua). Journalist Sander Thoenes was the only foreigner killed, in contrast to 1400 Timorese, but the Indonesians tried (and mostly succeeded) to scare foreigners away so that they "could conduct their massacres out of international view".[22] Pro-independence forces had observed the ceasefire which was part of the May 5 agreements, and Falintil guerrillas were in voluntary cantonment before and during the referendum, under orders from their commander Xanana not to respond to Indonesian/militia provocations. Violence was only perpetrated by one side—massacres and terrorism—but many media failed to report fully the Indonesian involvement.

Martial law was declared by the Habibie government without any serious attempt to restore stability. An Australian-led peacekeeping force, including troops from Britain, Fiji, Thailand and New Zealand, began arriving in September 1999 as part of the INTERFET operation. This paved the way for two and a half years of the UN Transitional Administration in East Timor

East Timorese citizens pay homage in 2013 to the memory of the martyrs who were killed by Indonesian troops in the Santa Cruz cemetery on 12 November 1991. The grave and bust in the middle distance mark the resting place of 15-year-old Sebastião Gomes, executed by soldiers almost a fortnight before the massacre.   DAVID ROBIE

(UNTAET) until independence in 2002 and then under the UN Mission of Support in East Timor (UNMISET), which provided a new peacekeeping force for three years. Little known was the role of Nelson Mandela, one of the world's most-loved statesmen who emerged from 27 years of imprisonment to negotiate the end of white minority rule in South Africa, and his "legacy to help the people of Timor-Leste".[23] As well as intervening with Indonesia to help the Timorese liberation, he also attempted to secure the release of Xanana Gusmão from prison in Indonesia in 1997.

At a War Reporting seminar at Massey University in Wellington in 2009, Lieutenant-Colonel Martin Dransfield, former commander of the Second Battalion in East Timor in 2000–2001, praised the relationship he had with journalists embedded with the peacekeepers: "My most vivid memory was with a journalist who was embedded with my team for a couple of days. We took time to brief him, and then gave him free range around the battalion. He produced some excellent articles ... In short, he wanted a story; we wanted to tell our story, so we both achieved what we wanted."[24]

Two years earlier, during the 2007 elections in Timor-Leste, I was a member of a media-monitoring mission organised and funded by the New Zealand Electoral Commission and led by Equal Employment Opportunities Commissioner Dr Judy McGregor, a former newspaper editor. We met some 125 journalists, media workers and advisers, and provided a 59-page report expressing our concern about human rights violations against journalists with a raft of recommendations for bolstering a free media. But we also praised the commitment and performance of the public broadcasters, Radio Timor-Leste (RTL) and Televisao Timor-Leste (TVTL), appealing for a more "positive and enabling regulatory environment" to support their national role in democracy.[25]

In November 2013, I returned to Timor-Leste while on sabbatical and worked as a volunteer with La`o Hamutuk (Timor-Leste Institute for Development Monitoring and Analysis) for a month. This was at a critical time politically with controversy over leaked documents exposing Australian espionage against Indonesia and Tmor-Leste.[26] La`o Hamutuk campaigners and analysts were focusing public debate over misguided use of Timor-Leste's limited oil and gas wealth and on whether the nation was making sufficient investment in education, health, agriculture and sustainable equitable development. This was to "reap the true benefits" of the oil revenues, as Irish academic Dr Gordon Peake put it in his perceptive book *Beloved Land: Stories, Struggles and Secrets from Timor-Leste.*[27] Revised projections have indicated Timor-Leste's oil and gas reserves are expected to run out by 2020—four years earlier than previously thought. At the time of writing, the Xanana government was defiantly seeking international arbitration to overturn the Certain Maritime Arrangements in the Timor Sea Treaty (CMATS) and to open the door to negotiations for a fair and just maritime border in the so-called Timor Gap in the face of Australian arrogance, intransigence and alleged espionage.[28]

In the national Independence Struggle Museum next door to the Timor-Leste National University (UNTL), a quote from a prominent Fretilin resistance leader, Konis Santana, is in pride of place as a warning to current political leaders not to squander the restoration of independence:

We trust that you will not turn your backs on the sacrifices made by your fallen brethren, that you will not pass over the blood shed by your slain comrades, that you will honour the heroic deaths of your kin. Let us turn their corpses into high-reaching blue mountains where the *lorikus*, who own the land, will continue to sing in praise of freedom.

Notes

1   David Robie (1994). Media hypocrisy on East Timor. *Pacific Journalism Review,* *1*(1): 97–98.

2   John Pilger (1994). *Death of a Nation: The Timor Conspiracy* [Video documentary]. London: johnpilger.com
   Available at http://johnpilger.com/videos/death-of-a-nation-the-timor-conspiracy

3   John Pilger (2004). *Tell Me No Lies: Investigative Journalism and its Triumphs.* London: Jonathan Cape, p. 174.

4   Geoffrey Gunn (1994). *A Critical Review of Western Journalism and Scholarship on East Timor.* Manila: Journal of Contemporary Asia Publishers.

5   James J. Fox and Dionisio Babo Soares (eds) (2003). *Out of the Ashes: Destruction and Reconstruction of East Timor.* Canberra: Australian National University Press.

6   East Timor Action Network (1995, June). World Court (ICJ) decides Timor Gap Case, No. 38. Retrieved on 13 January 2014, from www.etan.org/etanpdf/timordocs/timmas38%2095-06-30%20ICJ.pdf

7   Charles Scheiner, La'o Hamutuk (2013). Personal communication.

8   David Robie (1992, March/April). Terror in Timor. *New Zealand Monthly Review*, pp. 14–18.

9   Cited in Robie (1992), p. 14.

10   Tom Hyland (1991, October 28). Jakarta "sabotage Timor visit". *The Age.*

11   Jill Jolliffe (1978). *East Timor: Nationalism and Colonialism.* Brisbane: University of Queensland Press; (2009). *Balibo.* Sydney: Scribe Publications.

12   Max Stahl (1992, January 7). *In Cold Blood—The East Timor Massacre* [Video documentary]. ABC *Four Corners.* Available at http://trove.nla.gov.au/work/23407996?q&versionId=28347103

13   *Massacre: The story of East Timor* (2008, January 28). *Democracy Now!* A daily independent global news hour. Retrieved on 5 September 2013, from www.democracynow.org/2008/1/28/massacre_the_story_of_east_timor
   Video available on YouTube at www.youtube.com/watch?v=P4QiJ7l1jpo

14   Santa Cruz massacre (2013, September 4). Available at http://en.wikipedia.org/wiki/Santa_Cruz_massacre

15   Helen Todd (1992, March/April). "Time for NZ to change ... stop the killings and the terror". *New Zealand Monthly Review*, pp. 17–18.

16   ETAN (2000, May). Background on East Timor and US Policy. Retrieved on 5 September 2013, from http://etan.org/timor/BkgMnu.htm

17   Matthew Jardine (1999). *East Timor: Genocide in Paradise.* Monroe, Maine: Odonian Press, p. 17.

18   Associated Press (1992, February 5). Amnesty urges UN probe of Timor shootings. Retrieved on 5 September 2013, from www.apnewsarchive.com/1992/Amnesty-Urges-UN-Probe-of-Timor-Shootings-Calls-Indonesian-Inquiry-Flawed/id-0a18e7a6c33d7b5e77f34cb99e81d01a

19   Max Stahl (2013, December 2). Interview with the author, Dili. Authoritative documentaries by Stahl on Timor-Leste's path to restoration of independence and its aftermath include *Bloodshots* and *Justice Denied.* The Max Stahl Audiovisual Archive of Timor-Leste was declared a UNESCO Memory of the World institution in 2012.

20 Annie Goldson (2004). *Punitive Damage* [Video documentary]. Auckland. Available at www.nzonscreen.com/title/punitive-damage-1999

21 Clinton Fernandes (2012). *The Independence of East Timor.* London: Alpha Press.

22 Sander Thoenes (1999, September 21). Committee to Protect Journalists. Retrieved on 13 January 2014, from http://cpj.org/killed/1999/sander-thoenes. php .

23 Aboeprijadi Santoso (2013, July 22). Mandela, Indonesia and the liberation of Timor-Leste. *Jakarta Post.* Retrieved on 13 January 2014, from www. thejakartapost.com/news/2013/07/22/mandela-indonesia-and-liberation-timor-leste.html

24 Martin Dransfield (2010). "Embedded journalism": Some NZ military perspectives. *Pacific Journalism Review, 16*(1): 73.

25 Judy McGregor, Clive Lind, Shona Geary, Tapu Misa, David Robie and Walter Zweifel (2007). New Zealand Media Observation Mission Report: 2007 Timor-Leste. Wellington: New Zealand Electoral Commission, p. 53. Retrieved on 6 September 2013, from www.pmc.aut.ac.nz/research/new-zealand-media-mission-observation-report-2007-timor-leste-elections

26 Ramplin, Kimberley (2013, November 19). Should we be outraged that Australia spied on Indonesia? No. *The Guardian.* Retrieved n 13 January 2014, from www. theguardian.com/commentisfree/2013/nov/19/should-we-be-outraged-that-australia-spied-on-indonesia-no

27 Gordon Peake (2013). *Beloved Land: Stories, Struggles and Secrets from Timor-Leste.* Brunswick, Vic.: Scribe Publications, p. 186.

28 See La'o Hamutuk reference files and links at www.laohamutuk.org/Oil/Boundary/CMATSindex.htm

PART 5

Moruroa, mon amour

The bombed original *Rainbow Warrior* in the Marshall Islands in May 1985.   DAVID ROBIE

20

Climate change and
nuclear refugees, 1992

*In a sense the Marshall Islanders are the first victims of the Third World
War: they are the first culture in the history of [humanity] which has
been effectively destroyed by radiation.*
Filmmaker Dennis O'Rourke about the film *Half Life*

THIS morning—after the church service—one of the elders, John Salik,
stood at the northern tip of Han Island [and] whispered sacred words
into a handful of stones and cast them out to sea. Nicholas, the youth
tour leader, told us later that John inherited an ancestral power to
control the sea, though John wouldn't admit [it]. He definitely seemed
concerned; repeating to us throughout the morning that he hoped we
would have a safe trip. His fears are justified. The community called on
its strongest youth to represent them on the climate change awareness
tour. If anything happens to the boat, the community will lose its family
and its future leaders.[1]

By the end of the first decade of the 21st century, images of the Carteret
Islands off Bougainville had become iconic of an emerging age of so-
called "climate change refugees" or "environmental migrants". The above
comments were an excerpt from a daily blog written by Jennifer Redfearn
for the Pulitzer Center about the plight of the Carteret Islanders and their
flight to the unknown.

The banana boats, small single-engined motorboats, left the atoll mid-
morning carrying 17 young Carteret Islanders. We travelled in a boat
with 10 islanders and [more than] 12 bags. The open ocean no longer
resembled a smooth expanse of glass. Instead, wind swept across the
ocean creating ripples along the surface and swells that surged toward
the front of the boat.[2]

The more than 2700 islanders from this doomed group of seven tiny atolls off the coast of Papua New Guinea have become an icon for the fate of many communities globally threatened by climate change. Although they have struggled hard to stem the rising seawater, the islanders expect their atolls to be under water by 2015. The Pulitzer Center considers the Carteret Islands may become the first island chain to disappear in the impending decade, but other islands and coastal shores in other nations face a similar fate. The more remote Takū Atoll, more than 250 kilometres off the Bougainville coast, faces an even more serious plight.[3] According to statistics cited by the center one-tenth of the global population—634 million people—live in low-lying coastal areas; 75 percent of these people live in Asia, in the poorest pockets of the globe with limited resources.

Early in 2009, the Carteret Islanders embarked on the first forays of what has become a major evacuation to Bougainville, about 80 kilometres to the south. The decision to move has been forced on them because of worsening storm surges and king tides over recent years. These have contaminated the fresh-water supplies and ruined the islanders' staple banana and taro crops. The bleak outlook was a major focus of the 44th Pacific Islands Forum meeting in the Marshall Islands in September 2013. The island leaders threw down the gauntlet to the world's powers as "climate leaders" by signing the Majuro Declaration in a "game changer" strategy.[4]

As Adam Morton in the *Sydney Morning Herald* described their impending migration: "Fearing worse is to come—more frequent floods are expected to be the most visible signs of rising sea levels due to global warming—the islanders secured three blocks of coastal land. Some 1700 people are expected to relocate in the Tinputz area on mainland Bougainville over a five-year period from 2009."[5]

The story of our millennium

This remarkable operation was spearheaded by Ursula Rakova, an islander who pulled out of her job with Oxfam in Bougainville in 2006 to establish Tulele Peisa, an organisation that raises money and campaigns for social justice on behalf of her people. She was quoted by Morton, saying: "We have a feeling of anxiety, a feeling of uncertainty because we know that we will be losing our homes. It is our identity. It is our whole future at stake." A spate of emotive print, online, video, films and other media reports began to chronicle the first so-called climate change refugees. Among the many Fleet Street newspapers in Britain to devote resources to the coverage was the *Daily Telegraph*, whose online display featured staff writer Neil Tweedie (2009) and a series of reports proclaiming: "The sea is killing our

Takū village girls in a scene from the climate change documentary *There Once Was An Island*.   BRIAR MARCH

island paradise".[6] The coverage featured stories, pictures and interviews with islanders, videos and a blog diary as people left their ancestral islands. There were indications of a media "feeding frenzy" over the plight of the climate change refugees.

Ironically, *The Telegraph* and other media were beaten on the issue by almost two years by an earlier report filed by Australian-based journalist Richard Shears about the world's first climate change refugees. He noted then: "The Carteret Islanders have made what is possibly the smallest carbon footprint on the planet, yet they are the first to suffer the devastating effects of a wider, polluted world they know nothing about."[7] Heralding the end of the Carterets, Kevin Drum, writing in *Mother Jones*, said:

> Life, the [Carteret Islanders] hope, will be better for them here. On the Carterets, king tides have washed away their crops and rising sea levels poisoned those that remain with salt. The people have been forced to move.[8]

Perhaps even more poignant is the documentary film *There Once Was An Island: Te Henua e Nnoho* (director Briar March, 2010), about the Polynesian atoll of Takū, which was screened at the Creativity and

Climate Change conference in Suva in September 2010 and has since won many international awards. Like the Carterets, Takū Atoll is part of the Autonomous Region of Bougainville. The film portrays the "human face" of climate change in the Pacific. As the producers describe it:

> In this *verité*-style film, three intrepid characters, Teloo, Endar and Satty, allow us into their lives and culture and show us first hand the human impact of an environmental crisis. Two scientists, oceanographer John Hunter and geomorphologist Scott Smithers, investigate the situation with our characters and consider the impact of climate change on communities without access to resources or support.[9]

For me personally, the Carteret and Takū islanders' experiences strike a strong resonance. Almost three decades ago in May 1985, I was on board the environmental flagship *Rainbow Warrior* that was later bombed by French secret agents in a vain attempt to derail protests against French nuclear testing in the South Pacific. I had been on board for more than 10 weeks and had joined the ship in Hawai`i to cover a humanitarian voyage to the idyllic Rongelap Atoll in the Marshall Islands and transport the entire population to another barren, windswept island on Kwajalein Atoll, infamous for testing missiles as part of the so-called Star Wars strategy of the United States.

Nuclear refugees in the Pacific

The islanders were fleeing the demoralising health and social legacy of American nuclear testing on nearby Bikini Atoll, as told in Darlene Keju's biography *Don't Ever Whisper*.[10] My coverage of this momentous and emotional event was documented in my 1986 book *Eyes of Fire: The Last Voyage of the Rainbow Warrior*, and again in a later edition published in 2005 to mark the twentieth anniversary of the bombing.[11] It also featured in a photographic exhibition and a short documentary that I made with colleague Michael Fleck and Television New Zealand entitled *Nuclear Exodus: The Rongelap Evacuation*.[12] The people of Rongelap were dusted with radioactive fallout from a thermonuclear fireball codenamed Castle Bravo that drifted across the atoll on 1 March 1954. Since then the people had felt jinxed and their health had been contaminated by the radiation. As Australian filmmaker Dennis O'Rourke described it: "In a sense, the Marshall Islanders are the first victims of the Third World War."[13]

In 1989, a compelling documentary, *Niuklia Fri Pasifik* (Alister Barry and Phil Shingler) explored the nuclear-free and colonial issues of the Pacific

Rongelap Islanders boarding the *Rainbow Warrior* with their meagre possessions rescued from their village in May 1985 ready for the first of four voyages to Mejato Islet on the western rim of Kawajelein Atoll.   DAVID ROBIE

of the time. The NFIP movement was "at its peak", as Maire Leadbeater put it in her recent nuclear-free New Zealand history *Peace, Power and Politics*, after the third conference in newly independent Vanuatu in July 1983.[14] While the documentary certainly had an impact, by 1996 France had abandoned its nuclear testing programme in the South Pacific and nuclear and independence issues slipped from public consciousness.[15] As Shingler reflects:

> The nuclear-free issue has been off the political and media agenda for the past 25 years since we made the documentary. A commissioning editor told me after I pitched a doco-drama about the Black Brothers music group from West Papua in the early 1990s, "We've done the Pacific for this year!" I returned to the Solomon Islands in 1992 to make a film about coral reef conservation, *Rif Blong Yumi*, for Television Trust for the Environment in the United Kingdom but this only received non-broadcast distribution.[16]

GIVING PEACE A CHANCE
New Zealand Listener, 27 May 1989

MORUROA atoll and *la bombe* have long been challenges for independent Wellington filmmaker Alister Barry. As a 24-year-old student he embarked on the Danish-built peace schooner *Fri* to make *Mururoa 1973*, a dramatic documentary about protests against French nuclear testing in the South Pacific.

Several low-budget social issue films later, he had his sights on New Zealand's military links with the United States and the American nuclear strategy in the Pacific. But *Islands of the Empire*, a damning exposé which won him and his Vanguard Films partners Russell Campbell and Rod Prosser the 1985 Media Peace Prize, was never screened on New Zealand television. Not only was it rejected by state-owned Television New Zealand, but, because its sale to the National Film Library was blocked, the film was also effectively banned for a while from the nation's schools.

"After various appeals and consideration by the bureaucrats, in the end it was decided the programme didn't provide the military perspective on New Zealand's involvement with the nuclear strategy," recalls Barry. Much buck-passing between the Education Department (which was given "advice" from the Defence Ministry) and the then Education Minister, Russell Marshall, failed to break the deadlock.

Eventually a case was put up that the National Film Library isn't just a resource for schools or educational institutions alone, but also a library for the whole community—including more than 300 peace groups throughout the country. A compromise was reached: although the 16mm film wasn't bought for the library, a token three VHF video copies were.

Now the controversial *Islands* has inspired the making of a new television documentary, *Niuklia Fri Pasifik* (the title is drawn from Vanuatu pidgin language, Bislama). The 47-minute film tells the inside story of the birth and growth of the Nuclear Free and Independent Pacific (NFIP) movement from the first Suva conference in 1975 until the political negotiations that a decade later brought about the flawed Rarotonga Treaty, "banning" nuclear tests in the region.

"It tells an important story, a story of how little people, the little nations *can* make a difference," says producer Barry. Along with British co-producer Philip Shingler and New Zealand-born freelance director Lesley Stevens, he has pieced together a vibrant portrayal of how the anti-nuclear ideal influences the aspirations and the cultures of the Pacific.

About six months after *Islands* was completed, Barry received a letter from Shingler who had just seen it in Edinburgh. "We immediately dubbed it *Southern Front*," recalls Shingler, "because you could almost intercut sequences from our film *Northern Front* along with *Islands of the Empire*. It was extraordinary: here

Rongelap Islanders back on their atoll after evacuation by the *Rainbow Warrior* look at a photograph of their school before it was dismantled in May 1985. Published in the author's book *Eyes of Fire*.   CHARLES FINKBEINER

we focused on military influence, particularly US military influence in the North Atlantic, and there was Vanguard's film about US military influence in the South Pacific.

"I actually showed *Islands* to our commissioning editor at Channel 4. 'Oh yeah,' he said, 'that's a pretty interesting film, but it's a bit dated.' It ends in 1984 ... If you can come up with an idea that will bring the whole issue up to date, we'd be interested.'"

So Shingler sat down and wrote an outline for the three-part Pacific series which would look at the political, economic and strategic issues in the Pacific. When he eventually flew to Wellington in early 1987 to meet Barry, they narrowed their concept to a one-off film on the anti-nuclear theme because of the shortage of finance. The three-way funding was negotiated between the New Zealand Film Commission, TVNZ and Channel 4.

After a year of research and fundraising, the $180,000 Pacific Stories production was filmed in nine countries in 1988. It was completed in December in the modest Wellington studios of Vanguard Films. (The editing was done in a tiny hastily converted storeroom.)

A nine-minute longer version (entitled *A Nuclear-Free Pacific*) was screened in Britain in April 1989 at the first Festival of United Nations Theme Films at Eastbourne. The longer film is also being shown by SBS in Australia and by Channel 4 in Britain in June, possibly coinciding with the visit of Greenpeace's new Pacific peace ship *Rainbow Warrior II*.

When Sydney-based journalist Stevens was hired as director, she needed little encouragement: "Alister told me Phil is the 'miracle man'—and he is. Alister had been knocking at TVNZ and the Film Commission's door all these years, and then along came Phil Shingler and within three months they had money "falling around their ears".

"So there we had Alister, the researcher, we had Phil, the knocking-on-doors man, and a project with an incredible feeling from everybody involved that we were doing something we believed in."

Adds Shingler: "Yes, I feel with this one, it is the culmination of everything I've been doing in the last 10 years in television. I believe this is what I would call the first populist political documentary. One that looks at a wide general audience and tries to put out something in an entertaining way, using everything from music to dance to politics to volcanoes ...

"And gets the message across for a step back from the brink, a step towards disarmament, for as many countries as possible. It's our responsibility to do that."

Yet surely a programme about the making of the Rarotonga Treaty was a logical topic for TVNZ to produce itself? "Television dwells in the here and now—and the black hole next week," says Stevens. "That pressure is always there. So many ideas are dismissed simply from practicalities.

"The big problem for mainstream television is the research that has gone into this programme. Alister and Phil have the background and have done it over a year. Television doesn't put its resources into that kind of area; they believe they are unable to do that and still remain financially viable. It takes somebody who doesn't care whether or not they are financially viable, but is committed to making the film, to pour that kind of research into the project and get it together."

Barry believes *Niuklia Fri Pasifik* will make the New Zealand government uncomfortable by showing that its role in the making of the treaty doesn't match the "popular and politically useful" image that it has tried to build of itself as champion of the nuclear-free ideal. And the Australian government will also squirm.

One of the questions intriguing Barry as the film was being made was the motive of the Australian Prime Minister Bob Hawke and his government in promoting the treaty and pushing so hard for it. "On the one hand the Australian Labor Party came to power committed to taking nuclear disarmament initiatives at a time when Ronald Reagan was inventing Star Wars," says Barry. "On the other

Director Lesley Stevens interviews then Vanuatu Prime Minister Walter Lini for the 1989 documentary *Niuklia Fri Pasifik*.   DAVID ROBIE

hand, Hawke's foreign policy was one of continuing to try to involve the US in the regional, particularly Australian, defence."

Hawke was also prepared to take big political risks to achieve his goal, like supporting the abortive MX missile tests in the Tasman Sea. "Was Hawke's treaty initiative a genuine arms control initiative?" asks Barry. "Or was it a tactical move to frustrate and deflate the strong desire by so many nations of the region for a strong and effective nuclear-free treaty by leading the charge, but diverting it into a weak and toothless agreement?" When the filmmakers finally talked to Hawke he was remarkably frank.

They succeeded in interviewing almost all the significant political players— including three New Zealand prime ministers, Vanuatu's Father Walter Lini and former Papua New Guinea Prime Minister Michael Somare, who is now Foreign Minister. But there are two surprises.

Co-producer Alister Barry and cameraman Wayne Vinten filming a Vanuatu Independence Day rally in Port Vila for the 1989 documentary *Niuklia Fri Pasifik*.   DAVID ROBIE

Fiji's interim Prime Minister Ratu Kamisese Mara would have nothing to do with the documentary and the crew was not welcomed by Fiji authorities—in spite of Ratu Mara's key involvement in the years leading up to the treaty. (Critics of the film see the failure to address the significance of Fiji reversing its nuclear port ban in 1983 and the seizure of power by the military-backed regime as major flaws.) Prime Minister Solomon Mamaloni of the Solomon Islands, who was Opposition Leader when the filmmakers reached Honiara, was also a surprise non-starter.

A remarkable number of today's South Pacific leaders were involved in the formation of the NFIP movement in its early years. Lini, for example declares that his country, which has adopted a no-compromises anti-nuclear policy, still speaks for the majority of the people of the Pacific. "It is the governments of the South Pacific that have difficulty in signing a comprehensive nuclear-free Pacific treaty, not the people."

Some Pacific leaders, though, take a different view. Dennis Lulei, former Foreign Minister in the Solomon Islands, says the treaty is a giant step from nothing and "we've got it ... let's have a go at it."

But Solomon Islands trade unionist Joses Tuhanuku, who was among 80 delegates at the first NFIP conference in Suva in 1985 and has been elected to

Parliament as leader of his country's new Labour Party, disagrees: "I believed when I was a little kid, that the Soviet Union was just dying to invade the Solomon Islands," he recalls. "And therefore we needed the Americans to protect us against the Russians. And I also thought nuclear weapons ... were a good thing. The truth dawned upon me at the nuclear-free Pacific conference in Fiji."

Fiji Anti-Nuclear Action Group (FANG) campaigner Amelia Rokotuivuna agrees: "It was really a political birth, almost. We learnt about facts in the region we didn't even know." Adds Tonga's Bishop Finau: "Some Islanders were affected personally by the nuclear testing—and also their families. So they could speak very well and with emotion about the situation."

Much of the footage is visually dramatic—from the fiery volcanic explosions on Vanuatu's Mt Yasu to nuclear tests on Moruroa. A strong musical thread also runs through the film, featuring anti-nuclear rock groups such as New Zealand's Herbs and the Topp Twins, Australia's Midnight Oil and the Vanuatu string bands Huahere and Noisy Boys.

The filmmakers secretly interviewed Tahitian workers from Moruroa. One of the interviews reveals that the French authorities have been dumping radioactive waste in the Pacific, in defiance of international agreements. "When there are enough drums (of radioactive waste), the army puts the drums on a ship," says one worker, identified simply as "Tu".

"The drums are dumped into the ocean. One of the 'top brass' told us that one day these drums will leak. The drums will corrode and break open and the contamination will spread."

The Rarotonga Treaty specifically outlaws the dumping of nuclear waste at sea, but there has been no response by France over the allegation.

Perhaps the last words belong to the string band Huahere:

> Do you care Ronald Reagan
> About a chilly southern sky?
> We want peace.
> Nuclear-free the world will be;
> We'll make the world nuclear-free.

REGARDLESS of the fine print in the Nuclear-Free Pacific Treaty , reflects co-producer Alister Barry, the broader recognition of its existence has "endured and no doubt restrained various initiatives to encroach on the South Pacific region with nuclear technologies and waste":

In the same way as New Zealand's nuclear-free status has made it politically impossible for nuclear-powered vessels to come here, so, too, I think politicians in the South Pacific have felt politically constrained by the treaty. The film went to air in prime time to—one assumes—a large audience. There was no public reaction—no letters to the editor or letters to us, the filmmakers. This is a common experience of making programmes for television transmission. They seem to go out there but nothing bounces back.[17]

Phil Shingler, Barry and the rest of the team who had worked long and hard on the project were left to imagine that the film had indeed been effective in helping to "cement in viewers' minds the idea that we live in a nuclear-free zone". *Niuklia Fri Pasifik* was also shown on television in Australia, Japan, Jordan and the United Kingdom so their other objective— "that other citizens around the world might see what we had achieved in the South Pacific and imagine that something similar was possible in their own part of the globe"—was realised. "The size of the audience certainly reinforced for us that making documentaries was a worthwhile thing to do."

At the time we finished the film, I recall saying to Phil that this would probably be the biggest project we would ever work on. I imagine he thought I was talking nonsense, that this was just the beginning of decades of properly funded documentaries we would make for television. Sadly, my prediction has turned out to be true. I have continued to make serious documentaries for 25 years and have failed to get any television or Film Commission production funding. *Niuklia Fri Pasifik* was indeed the high point of both Phil and my careers as far as television was concerned. Since then all our films have been "no budget" productions.[18]

On 5 September 2013, the leaders of the Pacific Islands Forum (PIF) adopted the Majuro Declaration for Climate Leadership, calling for "urgent action to reduce greenhouse gas emissions" and for an "energy revolution".[19] Pacific communications coordinator Fenton Lutunatabua wrote in *The Huffington Post*: "The media has portrayed Pacific Islanders as helpless victms ready to drown with their islands or become refugees. The truth is, we are not drowning, we are fighting."[20]

Notes

1 Jennifer Redfearn (2009, January 16). Pulitzer Centre Untold Stories. The next wave: Climate change refugees in the South Pacific. Retrieved on 1 September 2010, from http://pulitzercenter.org/video/carteretislanders

2 Ibid.

3 See Briar March (2010). *There Once Was An Island: Te Henua e Nnoho* [Documentary feature film]. On The Level Productions. Retrieved from www.thereoncewasanisland.com

4 Al Jazeera (2013, September 6). Pacific islands hope to convince world to move on climate change. Retrieved on 10 September 2013, from http://america.aljazeera.com/articles/2013/9/6/pacific-islands-leadershopetoconvinceworldtomoveonclimatechange.html

5 Adam Morton (2009, July 29). First climate refugees start move to new island home. *Sydney Morning Herald*. Retrieved on 4 August 2010, from www.theage.com.au/national/first-climate-refugees-start-move-to-new-island-home-20090728-e06x.html

6 Neil Tweedie (2009, December 9). Carteret Islands: "The sea is killing our island paradise". *The Daily Telegraph*. Retrieved on 16 March 2011, from www.telegraph.co.uk/earth/carteret-islands/6771651/The-sea-is-killing-our-island-paradise.html

7 Richard Shears (2007, December 18). The world's first climate change refugees to leave island due to rising sea levels. *Daily Mail*. Retrieved on 4 August 2010, from www.dailymail.co.uk/news/article-503228/The-worlds-climate-change-refugees-leave-island-rising-sea-levels.html

8 Kevin Drum (2009, May 9). The end of the Carterets. *Mother Jones*. Retrieved on 1 September 2010, from http://motherjones.com/kevin-drum/2009/05/end-carterets

9 March (2010). *There Once Was An Island*. Available at http://www.thereoncewasanisland.com/about/

10 For a comprehensive and moving account of US nuclear testing in the Pacific and its aftermath, read Giff Johnson's biography of his wife Darlene Keju who died of cancer while campaigning for nuclear survivors, *Don't Ever Whisper: Darlene Keju: Pacific Health Pioneer, Champion for Nuclear Survivors* (2013). Majuro: "After Darlene's pride as a Pacific Islander was awakened in the late 1970s, she used her island cultural skills in combination with her modern, school-learned knowledge as a force for change in her home islands.", p. 381.

11 David Robie (2005). *Eyes of Fire: The Last Voyage of the Rainbow Warrior* [20th anniversary memorial edition]. Auckland: Asia Pacific Network.

12 David Robie, Chris Cooper and Michael Fleck (1987). *Nuclear Exodus: The Rongelap Evacuation* [Documentary film]. Television New Zealand. Available on YouTube at www.youtube.com/watch?v=Oq9fVlBwuJc

13 Dennis O'Rourke (1985). *Half Life* [Documentary]. Cited in Robie (2005), *Eyes of Fire*, p. 19.

14 Maire Leadbeater (2013). *Peace, Power and Politics: How New Zealand became nuclear free*. Dunedin: Otago University Press, p. 88.

15 *A Nuclear Free Pacific [Niuklia Fri Pasifik]* (1989). Alister Barry and Philip Shingler. Available at NZ On Screen www.nzonscreen.com/title/a-nuclear-free-pacific--niuklia-fri-pasifik-1988

16 Phil Shingler (2011, March 15). Personal communication.

17 Alister Barry (2011, March 18). Personal communication.

18 Ibid.

19. The Majuro Declaration for Climate Leadership (2013). www.majurodeclaration.org

20. Fenton Lutunatabua (2014, January 15). Pacific Warriors Declare: "We Are Not Drowning, We Are Fighting". Retrieved on 24 February 2014 from www.huffingtonpost.com

21

The *Rainbow Warrior*: Terrorism and justice, 2007

In a voice which I hope is as clear as possible, I answer first: "Guilty."
I hear Alain [Mafart] booming the same reply. Then there is an enormous
"brouhaha" in the courtroom. Those in attendance seem stunned.
French *Rainbow Warrior* saboteur Dominique Prieur in court

THE *Rainbow Warrior* affair in 1985, involving state terrorism by a friendly
nation, became iconic in New Zealand history because it highlighted New
Zealand opposition to nuclear testing in the Pacific on a global stage. It also
put the spotlight on solidarity with some smaller nations in the Pacific that
had courageously stood up to big power nuclear politics. "[Vanuatu Prime
Minister] Walter Lini in the 1980s was an inspirational leader [who] wanted
to see an independent and nuclear-free Tahiti," reflected Greenpeace New
Zealand executive director Bunny McDiarmid, a crew member at the
time of the bombing, about "kindred spirits".[1] "The Tahitians today face a
similar struggle as the Marshallese in getting access to information, justice,
recognition and compensation for the impacts of the French nuclear
testing programme." According to *Marshall Islands Journal* editor Giff
Johnson, "America shrouded its nuclear testing programme in Cold War
secrecy, aided by a compliant United Nations that ignored Marshall Islands
petitions complaining that the United States was violating the requirements
of its UN trusteeship."[2]

It was dubbed "Blunderwatergate". This was an apt epithet for the
Jacques Tati-like farce marking the sabotage of the *Rainbow Warrior* while
she was moored at Auckland's Marsden Wharf with twin bombs on the
night of 10 July 1985.[3] French officialdom bungled attempts to cover up the
murky trail leading back to the highest levels in Paris, even implicating
President François Mitterrand.[4] It was tragic too. The death of Portuguese-
born photojournalist Fernando Pereira that night—he drowned when he
clambered back on board to rescue his cameras before being caught by the
second bomb—was a devastating shock to the crew. With a stroke of luck,

the New Zealand police were able to arrest two of the 13 French agents operating in New Zealand as part of the state terrorist plot. But while media coverage of this affair has been intensive over the past three decades, one part of the saga has been relatively under-reported. New Zealand High Court closed-circuit television footage of the criminal proceedings showed the two French agents—Major Alain Mafart and Captain Dominique Prieur—pleading guilty to manslaughter after being charged with murder. During the next two decades, four separate attempts were made to gain legal access to the videotape for news and current affairs programmes. For the first three attempts, lawyers acting for Mafart and Prieur succeeded in blocking public release of the footage on privacy and administration of justice grounds.[5]

However, the fourth attempt, by public broadcaster Television New Zealand, was finally successful in the Court of Appeal and the footage was broadcast on 7 August 2006. A further appeal to the Supreme Court by the agents was dismissed. In December 2007, *Australian Journalism Review* published my case study of the 20-year struggle to broadcast this historic footage and a remarkable triumph of the public's right to know. Compiling this study was thanks to court records and extensive notes and records prepared by lawyers William Akel and Colin Amery.

THE RAINBOW WARRIOR, THE BOMBERS AND THE JUDICIARY

Australian Journalism Review, December 2007

Moruroa, Mon Amour, the celebrated and damning 1977 indictment of French nuclear colonialism in the Pacific, by the late Tahiti-based authors and campaigners Marie-Thérèse and Bengt Danielsson, was republished with new sections in 1986 under the title *Poisoned Reign*. At the time, French intransigence over nuclear testing and demands for independence in Tahiti was at a peak. The Greenpeace environmental campaign flagship *Rainbow Warrior* had been bombed by French secret agents the previous year. It seemed unlikely then that less than two decades later, nuclear testing would finally be abandoned in the South Pacific, and Tahiti's leading nuclear-free and pro-independence politician, Oscar Manutahi Temaru, would emerge as the territory's new President, ushering in a refreshing "new order" with a commitment to pan-Pacific relations.

In January 2006, then French President Jacques Chirac threatened to use nuclear weapons against any country that carried out a state-sponsored terrorist attack against it.[6] During his missile-rattling defence of a €3 billion-a-year nuclear

The original *Rainbow Warrior*, bombed by French secret agents in Waitemata Harbour, Auckland, 10 July 1985. JOHN MILLER

strike force, Chirac said the target was not "fanatical terrorists", but states that used "terrorist means" or "weapons of mass destruction" against France. The irony seemed lost on him that the only example of state-backed terrorism against New Zealand, codenamed Operation Satanic, had been committed by the French secret service on 10 July 1985. French authorities initially covered up the attack with a litany of lies and hypocrisy.[7]

Chirac made the threat at a naval base near Brest while addressing the crew of one of four nuclear submarines that carry almost 90 percent of France's nuclear warheads. It came a few months after documents published in France showed the *Rainbow Warrior* attack had been conducted with the "personal authorisation" of the late President François Mitterrand. On 10 July 2005, a *Le Monde* newspaper article published extracts from a 1986 handwritten account by Admiral Pierre Lacoste, former head of France's DGSE secret service.[8] Lacoste said he had asked the President for permission to embark on a plan to "neutralise" the *Rainbow Warrior* and would never have gone ahead without his authorisation.

> I asked the President if he gave me permission to put into action the neutralisation plan that I had studied on the request of Monsieur [Charles] Hernu [Defence Minister at the time]. He gave me his agreement while stressing the importance he placed on the nuclear tests.[9]

After being awarded by the International Arbitration Tribunal NZ$8 million from France in compensation for the attack, on 12 December 1987, Greenpeace finally towed the *Rainbow Warrior* to Matauri Bay and scuttled it to create a living reef off Motutapere, in the Cavalli Islands. Its namesake, *Rainbow Warrior II*, formerly the *Grampian Fame*, was launched in Hamburg on 10 July 1989, four years to the day after the bombing. On 15 July 1990, a memorial by Kerikeri sculptor Chris Booth was unveiled at Matauri Bay, featuring an arched creation incorporating the bombed ship's brass propeller.

An earlier compensation deal for New Zealand, mediated in 1986 by United Nations Secretary-General Javier Perez de Cuellar, awarded the government $13 million (US$7 million). The money was used for a nuclear-free projects fund and the Pacific Development and Conservation Trust. The agreement included an apology by France and the deportation of jailed secret agents Major Alain Mafart and Captain Dominique Prieur after they had served less than a year of their 10-year sentences for manslaughter and wilful damage of the bombed ship.

Mafart and Prieur, posing as a Swiss honeymooning couple, "Alain and Sophie Turenge", had been arrested on 12 July 1985, just two days after the bombing, as an exhaustive police investigation escalated. Police came close to arresting four more French suspects who crewed on an 11-metre sloop, *Ouvéa*, chartered in Nouméa, New Caledonia, to transport the explosives to New Zealand. Detectives flew to Norfolk Island in an attempt to retrieve incriminating forensic evidence. But without cooperation from Australian authorities, the secret agents were released and the *Ouvéa* and its crew subsequently vanished in the Coral Sea—three of the agents were believed to have been picked up by the nuclear-powered submarine *Rubis* and smuggled into French Polynesia.

Mafart and Prieur: "Club Med" celebrities
Alain Mafart and Dominique Prieur were a support team as part of Operation Satanic—they "were responsible for picking up and removing one of those

A chronology of key cases involving the *Rainbow Warrior*

July 10, 1985	*Rainbow Warrior* bombed in Waitemata Harbour; photographer Fernando Pereira drowned
July 12, 1985	French secret agents Alain Mafart and Dominique Prieur arrested as "Swiss honeymooning couple"
July 16, 1985	Three French secret agents on board the bomb supply yacht *Ouvéa* released by Australian authorities on Norfolk Island, set sail and disappear—apparently picked up by the French nuclear submarine *Rubis* in the Coral Sea
July 24, 1985	French secret agents Alain Mafart and Dominique Prieur charged with murder, arson and conspiracy to commit arson
September 23, 1985	French Prime Minister Laurent Fabius admits DGSE agents had sunk the *Rainbow Warrior* and they were acting under orders
November 4, 1985	Mafart and Prieur plead guilty to manslaughter in the High Court at Auckland
November 22, 1985	Mafart and Prieur sentenced to 10 years' imprisonment
April 23, 1986	High Court overturns ruling allowing NZBC to broadcast guilty plea tape
July 23, 1986	Mafart and Prieur transferred to Hao Atoll, French Polynesia
October 30, 1987	Law student Colin Amery seeks release of the "guilty" tape for thesis research
April 28, 1988	Amery unsuccessfully seeks release of the tape for a planned book
May 23, 2005	High Court rules in favour of unrestricted searching and copying of the tape
August 7, 2006	Television New Zealand broadcasts clips from the CCTV footage broadcast on *One News*
August 11, 2006	News archival CCTV footage withdrawn from TVNZ websites
September 26, 2006	Final appeal by the secret agents rejected by the court, finally freeing up unrestricted use of the CCTV footage

On board the *Rainbow Warrior* on 9 July 1985, the night before the bombing. David
Robie (second from left) chats to Charles Rara, a crew member delegated as an official
representative of the Vanuatu government, Niko Tangaroa (Atihaunui-a-Paparangi) and
Matiu Rata (Mana Motuhake Party).   JOHN MILLER

responsible for the placement of the explosive devices".[10] They were transferred
from New Zealand on 23 July 1986, to Uvea, Wallis and Futuna, en route to Hao
Atoll in French Polynesia, to serve three years in exile at a nuclear and military
base—regarded by some as a defence establishment "Club Med".[11] The pair were
attached for duties with the 57th Battalion of Pacific Support Command.

But the bombing scandal didn't end there. A campaigner who later studied law
and became a barrister with a penchant for human rights cases, Colin Amery, filed
a private prosecution of Mafart and Prieur in an attempt to prevent them leaving
New Zealand. He also made three attempts to gain access to the court footage
of the pair's guilty pleas. He recalled in his 1989 book *Ten Minutes to Midnight*
that legal issues raised by the *Rainbow Warrior* case were "totally novel" for New
Zealand. First, it was the country's first "head-on collision with international
terrorism". Second, New Zealand's counter-intelligence agency, the Security
Intelligence Service (SIS), "failed totally to uncover the espionage going on in its
midst".

Trying to pinpoint deficiencies within an organisation such as the SIS is
not an easy task for the researcher. He meets with a blank wall of official

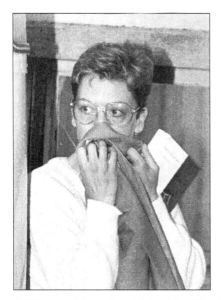

DGSE agents Major Alain Mafart (alias Alain Turenge) and Dominique Prieur (alias Sophie Turenge). The only Operation Satanic team members arrested and jailed for their role in the *Rainbow Warrior* bombing, they were convicted of manslaughter and wilful damage. They spent two decades waging a legal tug-of-war trying to suppress public exposure of the video images of their courtroom guilty pleas.   *EYES OF FIRE /AUCKLAND STAR*

silence when he uses the provisions of the *Official Information Act*, as I tried to do. The New Zealand Prime Minister who is also political head of the SIS pleaded s10 of the said Act which allows him to neither confirm nor deny the existence of a particular fact. Add to this the pleas under s6(a) and (b) which deal with withholding information to prejudice the security of defence of New Zealand and the wall of silence is complete.[12]

Amery concluded that the only alternative way to "get at the truth" would be through "a mole within the organisation who might be persuaded to turn Queen's evidence".[13] Incensed by the "seven-minute trial" in the High Court in Auckland, Amery filed his private prosecution against Mafart and Prieur, seeking, as he explained 21 years later in his autobiography *Always the Outsider*, to make the French agents serve the full time for their crime—"namely assisting in the murder of the photographer Fernando Pereira".[14] He also brought charges against Lieutenant-Colonel Louis-Pierre Dillais, the suspected ringleader of the French state terrorists involved in the sabotage operation. He accused the saboteurs under the *Crimes Act 1961* of wilfully damaging a boat, knowing danger was "likely to ensue",[15] an offence punishable by up to 14 years' imprisonment. Dillais surfaced two decades years later—exposed by a TVNZ current affairs programme as an arms dealer in Washington, DC.[16] He was chief executive of the US subsidiary of a Belgian arms manufacturer, FN Herstal. According to a *Guardian* report, FNH's office was "just down the road from the CIA" and the company's business in federal contracts turned over almost $US2.5 million in 2005 alone.[17] The report prompted a protest letter to the editor about the "act of horror" carried out by Dillais and his fellow plotters, pointing out that the ship "was not moored 'off' Auckland":

> [It] was in fact at one of the wharves [Marsden] in downtown Auckland, a few hundred metres from the main ferry terminal and the business centre. Not dissimilar in effect to someone trying to blow up HMS *Belfast* in the Pool of London.[18]

A hearing for Amery's Dillais case was set for the Auckland District Court for 10 October 1986. But like those for Mafart and Prieur, it never happened. The charge against Dillais "remains dormant and will probably sleep forever".[19] Amery recalled:

> This trial within a trial was almost over. The jury had been given very little of the true facts surrounding the case. This, despite a promise given by Mr Lange, the Prime Minister, on 5 November 1985 that police evidence gathered during the *Rainbow Warrior* Inquiry would be made public. He saw no reason at that time why the material gathered by the police should not be put into the public arena ... [T]he public still awaits for this promise to be fulfilled.[20]

Two days after the *Rainbow Warrior* was scuttled on 12 December 1987, Major Mafart was repatriated to a military hospital in Paris with a "serious stomach complaint".[21] French authorities smuggled him back to France (on a fake passport as a carpenter, Serge Quillan) in defiance of the terms of the United Nations agreement and in spite of protests from the Lange government.[22] Prieur had been repatriated back to France six months earlier. Colin Amery was particularly annoyed over the failure of the Lange government to be more determined in its opposition to French duplicity over the agents. He observed:

> Despite [Amery's] legal injunctions, the *Rainbow Warrior* sank to the bottom of Matauri Bay ... to become a permanent spectacle for scuba divers and a refuge for local marine life. The Lange government—and its chief helmsmen in particular—no doubt heaved a collective sigh of relief

when [she] hit Davey Jones' locker: a permanent memorial to the success of French state terrorism in Aotearoa waters.[23]

For Amery, many questions remained unanswered: "Our own home-grown anti-terrorist squad, the SIS, appear to have known nothing of the French plans to bomb the *Rainbow Warrior*, even though the *Ouvéa* crew members painted the town of Whangarei red in the week before."[24] Amery was a constant critic of Lange for the Prime Minister's perceived "surrender" to French pressure. Although Amery's two attempted prosecutions were not fully heard, the legal encounter propelled him into studying for a law degree and becoming a barrister.

> The two convicted criminals, [whom] the Chief Justice had said should not be allowed to return home as heroes, in the end did just that, each being rewarded with medals from the French government within the short space of one year.[25]

The disputed "visual images"

Documentary footage from the videotape of the criminal proceedings in which Mafart and Prieur pleaded guilty to manslaughter eluded the public domain for two decades. As detailed above, lawyers, media groups and law student Colin Amery, while writing a book about the *Rainbow Warrior* affair, made three unsuccessful attempts to gain legal access to the footage. Reflecting on what he regards as an abuse of the legal system by the French spies, Amery observed: "They really had no right to claim the privilege of privacy once their books were published and it was arrogant of them to persist."[26]

The fourth attempt to access the footage, by Television New Zealand,[27] was for a planned *Sunday* documentary marking the twentieth anniversary of the bombing—described by senior Simpson Grierson litigation partner William Akel as a "defining moment in New Zealand international affairs".[28] Justice Simon France, on 23 May 2005, in the High Court at Auckland, authorised the "searching and copying of the videotapes taken at the time of the committal and guilty plea" under the *Criminal Proceedings (Search of Court Records) Rules 1974*. Use from the copying was unrestricted. The judge explained when dismissing the privacy argument of the secret agents' lawyers:

> I have been most influenced by the significance of the event in New Zealand history, the essentially public nature of a plea, and the corresponding lack of privacy, and the reality that the very existence of the Search Rule discretion is because the respondents consented to the tape becoming part of the record. This seems to me to lessen unfairness issues.[29]

Writing in *The Independent*, Denise McNabb[30] described TVNZ's success as a "pyrrhic victory—a crucial tape is missing, showing the pair full frontal as they entered guilty pleas". Mafart and Prieur won leave to appeal to the Supreme Court in September 2005.[31] Although the phrase "videotapes" gives an impression of extensive footage, in fact TVNZ was seeking a brief segment of 1min 20sec comprising the images of Mafart and Prieur appearing in the Auckland courtroom and pleading guilty. This information was already in the public domain through news reports at the time, and both Mafart (1999) and Prieur (1995) had written about the events in their own books published in France. The disputed objects were the actual visual images of the guilty pleas.

At the time of the agents appearing in court, live recordings of proceedings were not permitted in the New Zealand justice system. However, in recent years New Zealand has become one of the Commonwealth's innovative jurisdictions in media use of courtroom video footage.

Mafart and Prieur were originally charged with murder. The committal proceedings were transferred to the High Court at Auckland because of more suitable facilities, but the two agents remained within the jurisdiction of the District Court. An estimated 150 journalists were expected to cover the hearing, and it was planned to provide closed-circuit television (CCTV) in an adjoining courtroom. One of the reasons for this procedure was to close the courtroom's upstairs gallery and allow the agents to "sit in a dock without a bullet-proof cage".[32] However, instead of the authorised CCTV system, a court-ordered closed-circuit video system was used. The contentious videotapes became part of the committal court record. Mafart, Prieur and their lawyers were not served with the court order and were not aware of it until five months later. Journalists were caught by surprise with the brief proceedings, which included charges being amended from murder to manslaughter, the taking of guilty pleas, and the reading of a summary of facts. The videotapes were collected by the Court Registrar and delivered to the judge in a sealed envelope.

Several weeks after the guilty pleas, BCNZ [Broadcasting Corporation of New Zealand] applied to the court for access to the videotapes. Although Mafart and Prieur objected, the tapes were handed over. But an interim injunction was upheld on appeal.[33] BCNZ's planned documentary at the 1986 Cannes film went ahead, stripped of the courtroom footage. At the time of these proceedings, the videotapes were considered by the High Court to be "documents" according to s182 of the Summary Proceedings Act 1957. They were transferred to the High Court as part of the committal record. The order included no leave to search, inspect or copy any part of the committal proceedings without the judge's ruling, and for the agents to be given 42 days' notice.

On 30 October 1987, Auckland barrister Colin Amery, then a law student researching a thesis on the *Rainbow Warrior* bombing, brought a case seeking access to the videotapes. Justice Thorp rejected the application.[34] The following year, on 28 April 1988, Justice Gault considered a revised application by Amery.[35] This was also turned down. Amery then filed a third application more than a decade later—linked to a planned documentary about his life—and on 1 March 2000, Justice Randerson rejected it.[36] Among the Search Rules principles cited by the judge:

> The principle purpose of the rules[37] is to ensure that, from the conclusion of the trial, with its necessary publicity, the privacy of the defendants will be protected by the court unless there is some sufficient reason for disclosing material on the file.[38]

Justice Randerson said the information was already in the public arena and "nothing new" would be added by granting the application. The argument that the public had a "right to see" was rejected as lacking in substance. The judge added that, in view of unsuccessful applications by the media and others about this section of the videotape, any new search application was "unpromising".

However, a judgment in 2000[39] overruled earlier High Court decisions that had identified the "protection of privacy" as the primary purpose of Search Rules. Mahanga was convicted of child murder and his trial was filmed by TVNZ.[40] One item of evidence was a videotaped interview of the accused, conducted by police. TVNZ recorded the showing of the videotape during the trial, but the result was poor quality. TVNZ then applied for access to the original videotape for use in a documentary. Although TVNZ was not successful in its appeal, the Court of Appeal reappraised searches of criminal records and ruled that privacy was no longer the primary consideration.[41] The judges held that the principles of open justice and freedom of expression were satisfied by the court being open to the public and by the media being able to report normally without restriction. But they also ruled that the application was governed by the Search Rules, which required a court to weigh the competing interests. Factors such as the principle of freedom of information, protection of individual privacy and protection of the administration of justice needed to be weighed up.

Privacy
In the Mafart and Prieur case, both secret agents had published books detailing their accounts of their involvement in the *Rainbow Warrior* bombing. These books undermined their argument for privacy. Dominique Prieur's book, *Agente Secrète*, written in collaboration with Jean-Marie Pontaut, was published in 1995, a decade after the sabotage. Her account said:

A little dazzled, I can make out the judge in front of me and the lawyers who are sitting on the side. I also notice, from the corner of my eye, in the first row, Joel [Prieur, her husband] to whom I make half a gesture. In the fog of the moment I don't pay any attention to the public or the journalists who are there. Daniel (Soulez-Larivière, her lawyer] will tell me later that there were 147 journalists who had come from around the world to cover the trial. However, only a dozen could actually be present at the hearing; the others follow the events from outside of the court room on a screen.

I had just put on the translation headphones when the Solicitor-General, Neazor (the prosecutor) rises to his feet. He announces that the prosecution has agreed to amend the charges. From now on we are only being charged with involuntary homicide (manslaughter) and "causing deliberate damage with explosives". Daniel [Soulez-Larivière] and Gerard Curry smile discreetly. The court clerk then turns to us and asks whether we wish to plead guilty or not guilty. There is immediate silence once again. I feel that everyone is staring at me, but I wait in turn for the translation, involuntarily raising the suspense. Then, in a voice which I hope is as clear as possible, I answer first:

"Guilty."

I hear Alain [Mafart] booming the same reply.

Then there is an enormous "brouhaha" in the courtroom. Those in attendance seem stupefied [stunned]. The judge, Ron Gilbert, who is presiding over the proceedings, silences the public with an authoritative gesture and the Solicitor-General reads a brief summary of the case. "The Crown's (the prosecution's) inquiries reveal that the accused had no other role than to support those who planted the bombs and whose identities have not been established," he explains. Victory! Daniel [Soulez-Larivière] has won! We will only be judged for manslaughter (involuntary homicide). We can hold out some hope. I look at Joel [Prieur] in triumph. But an internal voice reminds me that the sentence has not yet been imposed ... Too early to celebrate! [42]

Four years later, Alain Mafart (1999) also published a book giving his account, *Carnets secret d'un nageur de combat: du Rainbow Warrior aux glaces de l'Arctique*:[43]

... The hearing ... before the High Court is very brief. For us it is the main event since our arrest. The transfer [from prison to the court] takes place in a concert of sirens under the "protection" of heavily armed elite police. The prison van drops us off in a little cell that communicates directly with the courtroom via a spiral staircase. We are told to go up and enter, brutally, in the middle of the courtroom onto a stage. Silence is immediate and all eyes turn to us, the curious beasts that no one had yet seen. All these curious glances make me feel very uneasy. The courtroom is beautiful with dark and majestic wood panelling. I force myself to concentrate, trying to ignore the weighty public interest ...

In the first row of the public seating, behind us, I notice the head of Greenpeace, David McTaggart, and the head of the police enquiry, Allan Galbraith. French and international press reporters are present and are in such great numbers that the building had to be altered, with TV screens set up in neighbouring rooms so that all the members of the press could watch the spectacle. In front of us are our New Zealand lawyers. On the side, Joel Prieur, Dominique's husband, is seated next to Daniel [Soulez-Larivière]. This last person does not defend us officially, as he is not qualified at the New Zealand bar. He dominates the situation. In this auditorium no one suspects the strategy that he has concocted. The Court is declared open. Judge Ron Gilbert enters, looking extremely formal, wearing a robe and an Elizabethan-style wig. I have an impression of being a mutineer from the *Bounty* ... but that in this case the gallows would not be erected in the village square. Three courteous phrases are exchanged between [the judge] and our lawyers, the charges are read to us and the Court asks us whether we plead guilty or not guilty. Our replies are clear: "Guilty!" With that one word the trial is at an end.

There is total surprise among the journalists. As soon as they realise what has happened, they rush outside on their telephones all of a sudden, breaking the oppressive silence and solemnity of the courtroom. Against all expectation, they have just found out, dumbfounded, that the huge trial that was due to take place had, in some way, evaporated before their eyes—in one instant and without warning. They now knew that as far as the judicial phase was concerned, our affair was closed. On 4 November 1985 [*sic*], we knew the verdict: "Ten years", the judge, the Honourable Justice Davison, declared. Even if Maître Soulez-Larivière had forewarned me, it is still a massive blow: We had not avoided the maximum sentence, but at least I know, with the remission of sentences, that I would probably get away with only half of that time. I place all my hope in a vigorous effort by France to get us out of this black hole. [An] optimist by nature, I always believe that something positive can come out of the worst moments that a man can live. I will now be able to test, hour by hour, the validity of that principle.[44]

According to Justice Hammond in the Court of Appeal: "These passages, out of the mouths of the appellants themselves, are very significant. They do not portray humiliation in front of onlookers. If anything, there appears to have been vast relief and even a sense of 'victory' that the appellants would 'only be judged for manslaughter."[45]

When a "breach of privacy" is claimed to have happened, courts and statutes usually require that the intrusion must have impinged to an "unreasonable extent upon the personal affairs of the individual concerned".[46] Chief Justice Gleeson said: "The requirement that *disclosure or observation of information or conduct would be highly offensive* to a reasonable person of ordinary sensibilities is in many circumstances a useful practical test of what is private" (judge's emphasis added). Judge Hammond noted that one aspect of privacy was that "it was necessary to protect everybody from misinterpretation or misportrayals" by the media.[47] But this needed to be weighed up in relation to the French spies who did not seem to have been "afflicted by any concerns of that kind". Rather, it was more of a case of the agents "seeking to ... control the coverage".[48]

For Mafart and Prieur, lawyer Gerard Curry argued that there could well be harm in this case, due to the "constant 'repetition' of this rather iconic image over visual media"—perhaps around the world. Justice Hammond cited the example of a 10-second clip of the infamous head-butt by French football star Zinedine Zidane during the 2006 World Football Cup. The judge observed: "The visual media are not infrequently drawn to such things, like a moth to a candle."[49]

Freedom of information

In the judgment upholding the broadcast of the footage, Justice Hammond highlighted the historical significance of the *Rainbow Warrior* bombing and the importance of enduring images for a new generation of New Zealanders:

It is incontrovertible that this bombing was an extraordinary event in the history of New Zealand, and even internationally. It involved covert criminal activity by the security forces of one state on a friendly state's territory, and against the friendly state's interest. It is an event that has been, and will remain, important in New Zealand's history. As time passes, there will be new generations of New Zealanders who have not lived through the *Rainbow Warrior* affair and so will not have personal knowledge of it. Their knowledge of this important event in New Zealand's history will come through what they are told, through what they read and through what they see in the visual media.

A visual image of the kind at issue in this case may be a very powerful mechanism for conveying information about events. Who can forget the graphic force of the film images of the defendants in the dock at Nuremberg?[50]

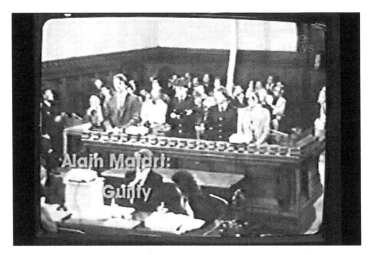

DGSE agent Major Alain Mafart pleads "guilty" in the High Court at Auckland to manslaughter over the *Rainbow Warrior* bombing on 10 July 1985. His pleading was filmed on the courtroom's CCTV cameras and eventually broadcast on television on 7 August 2006—almost two decades later.   TELEVISION NEW ZEALAND

Justice Hammond said there was a strong public interest in conveying the information in the visual image, not simply through the spoken or written word, but through the image itself. The footage was finally broadcast by Television New Zealand in news programmes on 7 August 2006. But the saga did not end there. Four days later, all footage stored on TVNZ's website was withdrawn when the spies made one last bid for an appeal to the Supreme Court.[51] The court dismissed the appeal application on September 26, ordering the pair to pay $2500 costs to TVNZ and permanently freeing up broadcast of the footage. TVNZ's then head of news and current affairs, Bill Ralston, said:

> This is a significant triumph for media freedom and hopefully demonstrates to the French (and any other government, corporate or individual) that the New Zealand media will not be intimidated into submission by legal stonewalling. Best of all, a whole new generation of New Zealanders will now get to be an eyewitness to a pivotal moment in our country's history.[52]

"Privacy" for state terrorism?

Infringement of privacy is one of the "fastest developing areas of media law".[53] But its boundaries are still far from clear and change has been fairly rapid. The rules apparently being developed by the courts parallel the "public disclosure of private facts" principles applied by the Broadcasting Standards Authority. The main difference is that the courts can award substantial damages for breaches of privacy and there is limited potential for an injunction to stop an unjustified breach of privacy. Steven Price summarises the general principles for the media in New Zealand as not disclosing private facts where both of the following tests apply:

- There is a reasonable expectation of privacy; and
- The disclosure is highly offensive to a reasonable person.

There is a defence if the facts are of public interest (meaning they are of legitimate concern to the public, not merely titillating). However, in the case of the *Rainbow Warrior* bombing, for the best part of two decades the courts surprisingly upheld privacy and administration of justice rights of the French secret agents, Mafart and Prieur, at the expense of the New Zealand public's right to know. It took the Mahanga case in 2000 to establish the legal principle that balancing competing interests should supersede the notion that court search rules were primarily about protection of privacy. The bombing was an iconic event of considerable historical importance in New Zealand dealing with state terrorism. While it is remarkable that privacy issues and judicial procedures weighed heavily for so many years in preventing the spies' guilty pleas footage being broadcast—especially when the agents had written about their court appearance and guilty pleas in their own books—it was a critical success for the functions of Fourth Estate scrutiny that this visual record eventually became part of the public domain. The issue was under-reported in the media, yet the campaign was vitally important. The public had every right to see full images of these guilty pleas from this example of state terrorism. The persistence of counsel William Akel—and also Colin Amery in earlier years—was vindicated when the Court of Appeal finally upheld the public's right to know about the *Rainbow Warrior* bombers.

ABOUT 13 French secret agents were believed to have been involved in the 1985 *Rainbow Warrior* bombing in New Zealand, but only two—Alain Mafart and Dominique Prieur—were brought to justice. In 1991, Swiss authorities detained Gerald Andries, one of four agents who crewed on board the yacht *Ouvéa*, which reportedly ferried the explosives to New Zealand from New Caledonia. Interpol had a warrant for their arrest. The National Party government of the time moved to extradite Andries, but dropped the case when France again applied trade pressure. Paris also argued that the 1986 agreement covered all its agents. Attorney-General Paul East stayed "all outstanding charges" and the *Rainbow Warrior* case

was closed. In October 2006, during the lead-up to the French presidential election, *Le Parisien* reported that French Socialist presidential candidate Ségolène Royal's brother, Gérard, had been named as a suspect as one of the two frogmen who planted limpet mines on the environmental ship.[54] Lawyer Colin Amery recalled later how the alleged field commander of Operation Satanique, Colonel Dillais (alias Jean-Louis Dormand),[55] was white water-rafting near Queenstown at the time of the bombing and was allowed with his fellow spies to get away "scot-free" by authorities.

> When I put this information [a receipt at Auckland's South Pacific Hotel during his stay from June 23–28 and a photo of him white-water rafting] to the Attorney-General on 3 June 1992, he denied there was sufficient evidence to prosecute Dormand. I then attempted to serve a summons on Dormand by sending a copy to the Minister of Defence in Paris on July 4 but, unfortunately, it was never acknowledged. This simply underlines the duplicity of the French.[56]

As Maire Leadbeater concluded in her 2013 study of the New Zealand peace movement, *Peace, Power and Politics*, the Operation Satanique debacle backfired on France and gave Greenpeace a "huge international profile": "There was a spin-off into the wider peace movement as the *Rainbow Warrior* affair had a multiplier effect on our image as a strong and resourceful movement lobbying and supporting our government to stand up to the nuclear powers."[57]

Notes

1   Bunny McDiarmid (2005). Preface. In David Robie, *Eyes of Fire: The Last Voyage of the Rainbow Warrior* [20th anniversary memorial edition]. Auckland: Asia Pacific Network, p. 9.

2   Giff Johnson (2013). *Don't Ever Whisper: Darlene Keju: Pacific Health Pioneer, Champion for Nuclear Survivors.* Majuro: Johnson, p. 9.

3   David Robie (2005). At the end of the sRainbow. *Waikato Times*, p. D4.

4   David Robie (2006). Revisiting French terrorism in the Pacific—*Rainbow Warrior* revelations. *Pacific Ecologist*, 12: 26–29.

5   See William Akel (2007). Privacy and the global media in the information age. *Pacific Journalism Review*, 13(1): 40–57; Mark Pearson (2007). *The Journalist's Guide to Media Law: Dealing with Legal and Ethical Issues* [3rd edition]. Crows Nest, NSW: Allen & Unwin; Steven Price (2007). *Media Minefield: A Journalists' Guide to Media Regulation in New Zealand.* Wellington: New Zealand Journalists Training Organisation, for evolution of general privacy principles in Australia and New Zealand.

6 Robie (2006). Revisiting French terrorism in the Pacific—*Rainbow Warrior* revelations.

7 See Colin Amery (2007). *Always the Outsider: An unconventional journey from spy to wandering poet to lawyer.* Christchurch: Hazard Press; Michael King (1986). *Death of the Rainbow Warrior.* Auckland: Penguin; Claude Lecomte (1985). *Coulez le Rainbow Warrior!* Paris: Messidor; David Robie (1989). *Blood on their Banner: Nationalist Struggles in the South Pacific.* London: Zed Books; Sydney: Pluto Press; David Robie (2005). *Eyes of Fire: The Last Voyage of the Rainbow Warrior* [20th anniversary memorial edition. Auckland: Asia Pacific Network; David Robie (2006). Revisiting French terrorism in the Pacific—*Rainbow Warrior* revelations. *Pacific Ecologist, 12*: 26–29; Michael Szabo (1991). *Making Waves: The Greenpeace New Zealand Story.* Auckland: Reed; *The Sunday Times* Insight Team (1986). *Rainbow Warrior: The French attempt to sink Greenpeace.* London: Arrow Books.

8 France's Mitterrand authorised bombing of Greenpeace boat: report (2005, July 10). Associated Press, archived on CommonDreams.org NewsCenter. Retrieved on 14 September 2007, from www.commondreams.org/headlines05/0710-03.htm

9 Ibid.

10 *R v Mafart and Prieur* [1985] 74 ILR 241 (*Rainbow Warrior* case). Summary of Facts (1985). Read to the Auckland District Court on November 4 by the Solicitor-General, Paul Neazor, QC.

11 Robie (2005). *Eyes of Fire*, p. 168.

12 Colin Amery (1989). *Ten Minutes to Midnight.* Auckland: Earl of Seacliffe Art Workshop, p. xi.

13 Ibid.

14 Amery (2007). *Always the Outsider*, p. 154.

15 Amery (1989). *Ten Minutes to Midnight*, p. 88.

16 *Sunday* (2005, June 26). "Operation Satanic". TVNZ. Retrieved on 6 November 2007, from http://www.tvnz.co.nz >> keyword sunday >> popular sunday stories

17 S. Goldenberg (2007, May 25). *Rainbow Warrior* ringleader heads firm selling arms to US government. *The Guardian.* Retrieved on 10 September 2007, from http://environment.guardian.co.uk/conservation/story/0,,2087879,00.html

18 L. Cooper (2007, May 26). *Rainbow Warrior* [Letter to the editor]. *Guardian Unlimited*, London, UK. Retrieved on 10 September 2007, from www.guardian.co.uk/letters/story/0,,2088659,00.html

19 Amery (1989). *Ten Minutes to Midnight*, p. 89.

20 Ibid.

21 D. Robie (1987, December 21). Mafart "smuggled out before NZ told". *The Dominion*, p. 1.

22 *Les Nouvelles de Tahiti* (1987, December 19).

23 Colin Amery (1988, March). *Rainbow Warrior* and the French. *The State Adversary*, p. 4.

24 Ibid.

25 Amery (2007). *Always the Outsider*, p. 156.

26 Colin Amery (2007, October 26). Personal email communication with the author.

27 Chris Cooke (2005). High Court application to access 1985 sentencing footage of bombers. Internal TVNZ, *Sunday*. Email dated February 14.

28 Denise McNabb (2005a, April 20). TVNZ fights for *Rainbow Warrior* film. *The Independent*, p. 1.

29 [2005] DCR 640, at [92].

30 Denise McNabb (2005b, May 25). TVNZ gets terrorist tapes. *The Independent*, p. 1.

31 Denise McNabb (2005c, September 28). Terrorists' last-ditch attempt at secrecy. *The Independent*, p. 4.

32 *Mafart & Prieur v TVNZ* [2006] CA92/05 [7 August 2006], at [18].

33 *Mafart v Gilbert* [1986] 1 NZLR 434 (CA).

34 *Amery v Mafart* [1988] 2 NZLR 747 (HC).

35 *Amery v Mafart* (No. 2) [1988] 2 NZLR 754 (HC), p. 762 at [8].

36 *Amery v Mafart* [2000] 3 NZLR 695 (HC).

37 Official Information Act 1982, s2(6)(a).

38 *Amery v Mafart* (No. 1) [1988] 2 NZLR 747 (HC), at p. 750.

39 *R v Mahanga* [2001] 1 NZLR 641.

40 See Amy Elvidge (2008). Trying Times: The right to a fair trial in the changing media environment. Unpublished Bachelor of Laws (Honours) thesis. Dunedin: University of Otago.

41 Cited in *Mafart & Prieur v TVNZ* [2006] CA CA92/05, at [40].

42 Dominique Prieur (with J-M. Pontaut) (1995). *Agente Secrète*. Paris: Fayard, pp. 187–89.

43 Alain Mafart (with J. Guisnel) (1999). *Carnets secret d'un nageur de combat: du Rainbow Warrior aux glaces de l'Arctique*. Paris: Albin Michel.

44 Ibid., p. 192.

45 *Mafart & Prieur v TVNZ* [2006] CA92/05, at [59].

46 *Australian Broadcasting Corporation v Lenah Games Meats* [2001] 208 CLR 199.

47 *Mafart & Prieur v TVNZ* [2006] CA92/05, at [61].

48 Ibid., at [63].

49 Ibid., at [65].

50 Ibid., at [68], [69].

51 TVNZ *Breakfast* (2006, August 8).

52 TVNZ wins *Rainbow Warrior* battle (2006, September 26). TVNZ. Retrieved on 6 November 2007, from http://tvnz.co.nz/view/page/836279.

53 Price (2007). *Media Minefield*, p. 257.

54 Kay Martin (2006, October 2). French frogman slips the net: Paper identifies bomber, but PM says the case will remain closed. *The Dominion Post*, p. 1. Retrieved on 14 September 2007, from http://io.knowledge-basket.co.nz.ezproxy.aut.ac.nz/iodnews/cma/cma.pl?id=28116-25

55 Greenpeace International (n.d.). A beret, a bottle of Beaujolais and a baguette. Archived at /www.greenpeace.org/international/en/about/history/the-bombing-of-the-rainbow-war/rainbow/

56 Colin Amery (2014, January 21). Communication with the author.

57 Maire Leadbeater (2013). *Peace, Power & Politics: How New Zealand Became Nuclear Free.* Dunedin: Otago University Press, p. 156.

PART 6

Media education

Papua New Guinean postgraduate student Henry Yamo (right) and West Papuan Benny
Wenda, 2013.   DEL ABCEDE/PMC

22

Shooting the messenger, 2002

*So much for the free media in this country—the debate always focuses
on freedom from government interference. What about freedom from
the big [private sector] boys on the block with their vested interests?*
Former Fiji Labour Senator `Atu Emberson-Bain

IN SPITE of the rhetoric about governments pressuring the media in Pacific
countries—yet this does happen all too frequently—I believe a greater
threat to press freedom sometimes comes from a small clique of self-
serving media veterans, many of whom are of expatriate *palagi* origin and
who have disproportionate influence.[1]

Every year, coinciding with the UNESCO World Press Freedom Day
(WPFD) on May 3, there are the usual platitudes and declarations about
"media freedom" in the Pacific. *The Fiji Times*, for example, complained in
an editorial about politicians with a "misguided theory" that Fiji was not
ready for a critical and aggressive media because of the traditional system
of values and its developing nation status.[2] Quite rightly, the newspaper
cited "countless examples of politicians in this country using the shoot-the-
messenger tactic to soften the impact of their blunders or lies". However,
in the next breath it reminded the public that then Information Minister
Josefa Vosanibola had dusted off plans to introduce new media legislation
based on a report by two British media consultants in 1996.

"Thankfully, the report is an independent outside view of the Fiji media,
which argues against curbing media independence."[3]

Unconvincing. Any journalists worth their salt should be resisting any
attempt by governments to hinder the media. The consultants' report was
merely an attempt by the Fiji Media Council to save its own vested interest.
In fact, one could argue that the industry itself opened up the thin end of
the wedge by collaborating in the first place with government attempts to
control media.

Media freedom as an issue in the Pacific has been defined in far too
narrow terms, as if Big Brother governments and politicians ignorant about
the role of media are the only problem. Of course, they're not. There are

many other issues that are vitally important in the region that impinge on media freedom yet are rarely mentioned—such as self-censorship, media ownership and convergence, poor qualifications and salaries for many journalists (which make them potentially open to undue influence and bribery) and lack of education:

> The litany of complaints against the media cannot always be dismissed out of hand. Concerns about unbalanced and unethical reporting, sensationalism, insensitivity, lack of depth and research in articles and a poor understanding of the issues are too frequent and too numerous. Another common complaint is that the media is loath to make retractions or correct mistakes. It has even been accused of bringing down a government or two.[4]

While the 1987 coups were a "watershed year" for the Fiji media (with one of the two daily newspapers closing, never to reopen because of censorship, and the other temporarily adopting self-censorship to survive), the media learned to be cautious in its reporting.[5] By the time the George Speight attempted coup happened in May 2000, many of the experienced journalists who had reported the 1987 political upheaval had left the country. Failing to get its own self-regulatory house in order: "A new generation of reporters found themselves in the frontline of another history-making episode. Again there are examples of courageous reporting, along with allegations that the media had fallen for the photogenic and quotable Speight, and his nationalistic message."[6]

By the time of the 2006 coup by Commodore Voreqe Bainimarama, the nationalist and indigenous paramountcy rhetoric had vanished. Instead, this coup was claimed to be a "'clean up' campaign against corruption and racism" that the military commander alleged had become entrenched under the leadership of elected Prime Minister Laisenia Qarase, a former banker who rose to political power after the Speight putsch due to Bainimarama's patronage.[7]

The Bainimarama regime was just as critical of the media as the ousted democratic governments. Self-censorship by the media was replaced by the longest sustained censorship regime of any Pacific country, imposed when the 1997 Constitution was abrogated at Easter 2009. Failure by the Fiji Media Council to get its own house in order led first to a deeply flawed media "review" by Hawai'i-based former Fiji academic Dr Jim Anthony arranged by the Fiji Human Rights Commission, and then the imposition of the notorious *Fiji Media Development Decree 2010*.[8] Two *Fiji Times* publishers (Evan Hannah in 2008 and Rex Gardner in January 2009) and the *Fiji Sun*'s Russell Hunter (in 2008) were deported. Although the Bainimarama regime never succeeded in closing *The Fiji Times* in a cat-and-mouse game, as it undoubtedly wished, the government did manage to force the Australian-based owner News Limited (a Rupert Murdoch subsidiary) to sell the newspaper to the local Motibhai Group in 2010. Chief editor Netani Rika, long a thorn in the side of the regime, and deputy editor Sophie Foster were also ousted and replaced with a more compliant editorship by Fred Wesley.

It was a refreshing change from the usual back-slapping and we-can-do-no-wrong rhetoric by media owners to hear comments from people such as the then Fiji Human Rights Commission director, Dr Shaista Shameem, and media and politics lecturer Dr Tarcisius Kabutaulaka at a University of the South Pacific seminar marking WPFD on 3 May 2002. Shameem wants a higher educational standard for Pacific journalists. In her view the region's journalists need to know far more about history, politics, sociology, philosophy and the sciences.[9]

"Anyone can learn the technical skills of journalism—that's the easy part," she says. "The hard part is to understand the worlds that you are writing about. My definition of a good journalist is someone with such in-depth understanding of the issues that the words, though simply written, virtually leap out from the page."

Solomon Islander Kabutaulaka, who has written widely as a columnist as well as critically examining the profession of journalism, raises the issue of media monopolies: "This raises the questions such as: Who controls or owns the media? Whose interests do they represent?" he asks. "In the world of globalisation and with the advent of the internet we must realise that a variety of media does not always mean a variety of sources."

Kabutaulaka also wonders whether Pacific media provide "adequate information that will enhance democracy". As he points out, "it is not an impartial medium. Rather, many [in the media] also have vested interests."

One of the problems in the region is that there is virtually no in-depth reportage of the media itself. While some sections of the media attempt valiantly to ensure power is accountable, there is little reflection about the power of the media. In fact, there is little media accountability to the public—nothing comparable to ABC Television's *Media Watch*, or TVNZ7's *Media7* (later TV3's *Media3*) and Radio New Zealand's *Mediawatch* to keep news organisations on their toes. Most media councils are rubber stamps for their media members with little proactive action. Most are "struggling for relevance" to the rapidly changing digital industry, according to a

PACMAS-funded review of national media councils in 2013.[10] "They are politically and financially challenged to continue to uphold their advocacy role for a plural, independent and professional media ... A new generation of graduates and younger media practitioners ... is challenging the ineffectiveness of media associations in several countries."[11] Much media dirty linen is rarely exposed, such as these examples at the time of the Speight coup:[12]

- The conduct of journalists such as a senior *Fiji Times* reporter whose paternity suit against former Prime Minister Sitiveni Rabuka reflected badly on the integrity of journalists and on her newspaper in particular. It is astounding that the newspaper editors tolerated her relationship for so long, but were only too happy to benefit from a series of questionable "scoops".

- Internet piracy was rampant with some local news organisations routinely downloading and publishing foreign copyright news and pictures. One regional "online" news service regularly takes stories from newspapers such as *The New Zealand Herald* and *Jakarta Post*, then on-passes them to its commercial newspaper members.

- The strident xenophobic tone of writers such as an *Islands Business* magazine's editor, perhaps a reflection of the entrenched racism that characterised Fiji during the Qarase period.[13]

- The role of former Fiji Journalism Institute (FJI) training coordinator Jo Nata, jailed for treason committed while acting as Speight's public relations spin doctor during the 2000 attempted coup. (He apologised to the people of Fiji in 2009.)

- The cloud over the institute itself, founded with Fiji media industry and government support in 1994, but a lack of accountability over a US$45,000 grant from UNESCO. Likewise, there has been a deafening silence since 2010 over allegations about the rorting of AusAID funds at the PNG Media Council. While the Fiji institute itself has long gone, the contextual issues remain the same.

- The Fiji media industry failed dismally in efforts to develop sustainable media training and undermined the University of the South Pacific regional journalism programme in the process. And some overseas aid donors are complicit in the charade. The

AusAID-funded PACMAS programme, for example, never directly supported the university-based journalism programmes, preferring instead to back their TVET media schools at a far lower standard and questionable professionalism.[14]

Issues such as these are barely raised in public, let alone discussed. In fact, the only serious post-Speight workshop on media reporting and accountability in the wake of the Stockholm syndrome controversy over journalists who allegedly became too close to the hostage-takers was never conducted by the industry itself.[15] It was left to the community standards lobby group Fiji Media Watch—which hosted a workshop run by *The Australian*'s respected Honiara-based correspondent Mary-Louise O'Callaghan in May 2001—to make an attempt.[16]

This chapter includes an extract from my address at the inaugural conference "Navigating the Future" of the Auckland-based Pacific Islands Media Association (PIMA)[17] later republished in *Pacific Journalism Review*.[18]

PACIFIC FREEDOM OF SPEECH

Pacific Journalism Review, June 2002

WHEN I arrived at my office at the University of the South Pacific on the morning of 12 September 2001 (Fiji time), I was oblivious to reality. I had dragged myself home to bed a few hours earlier, about 2am, after another long day working on our students' *Wansolwara Online* website coverage of the Fiji general election. One day after being sworn in as the country's fifth real prime minister, it seemed that Laisenia Qarase was playing another dirty trick on Mahendra Chaudhry's Labour Party, which had earned the constitutional right to be included in the multi-party government supposed to lead the country back to democracy.

Stepping into my office, I encountered a colleague. He looked wild-eyed, and he lamented: "It's the end of the world."

Naïvely, I replied, "Yes, how can legality and constitutionality be cast aside so blatantly yet again?"

But he said: "No, no, not Fiji politics. That's nothing. I mean New York: Terrorists have destroyed the financial heart of the Western world."

It was a chilling moment, comparable to how I felt as an 18-year-old forestry science trainee in a logging camp at Kaingaroa Forest the day President John F. Kennedy was assassinated on 22 November 1963.

"Young and brave": An *IPI Global Journalist* account of the USP student coverage of the George Speight attempted coup, 2000.

Over the next few hours, it seemed that half the Laucala campus descended on our newsroom to watch the latest BBC, TVNZ One and Fiji TV One coverage of the devastating tragedy.

While a handful of student journalists struggled to provide coverage of local angles such as the tightening of security around the US Embassy in Suva and shock among the Laucala intelligentsia, most students remained glued to the TV, stunned into immobility by the suicide jetliner terrorists.

Global jingoism and xenophobia followed, the assaults on Sikhs merely because they had an Arabian look, the attacks on mosques—in Fiji, copies of the Koran were burned—and the abuse directed towards Afghan refugees were par for the course.

Freedom of speech in the United States also quickly became a casualty of this new so-called "War on Terror". Columnists were fired for their critical views, television host Bill Maher was denounced by the White House, *Doonesbury* cartoonist Gary Trudeau dropped his "featherweight Bush" cartoons and so-called "unpatriotic" songs were dropped from radio playlists. Wrote Maureen Dowd of the *New York Times*:

Even as the White House preaches tolerance toward Muslims and Sikhs, it is practising intolerance, signalling that anyone who challenges the leaders of embattled America is cynical, political and—isn't this the subtext?—unpatriotic.[19]

But while much of the West lined up as political parrots alongside the United States, ready to exact a terrible vengeance, contrasting perspectives were apparent in many developing nations.

In the Pacific, for example, while many people empathised with the survivors of the terrible toll of 2996 lives—including the 19 hijackers—in New York and Washington, there was often a more critical view of the consequences of American foreign policy and a sense of dread about the future. Less than a week later, I asked my final-year students to compile some notes recalling the circumstances of when they heard the news and their responses.

One, a mature age student from Fiji who had worked for several years as a radio journalist, said:

> I was in bed and woke up about 2.30am. I have a habit of having the BBC running on radio and, half-asleep, I caught the news being broadcast. I pulled myself out of bed and tuned to BBC on Sky TV. The second plane had just hit the second tower, and I ended up staying up the rest of the night to watch the unfolding events.

On his impressions, he warned about scapegoats and the media:

> The relevance to us here in the Pacific is that terrorists can strike anywhere to get revenge. This conflict could evolve into war, and wars affect everyone. Americans already think Osama bin Laden is the terrorist ... Americans are looking to get someone quickly, and the media is leading the way.

Another mature student wrote:

> Good, they [the US] paid dearly for trying to intervene in Muslim countries ... Bin Laden is portrayed as the culprit ... The media is portraying the whole Muslim world as responsible, but actually this is not the case.

Recalled another:

> I was sleeping and my mother woke me up at 6.30am to tell me the news. I was shocked, and still sleepy, I thought my mother was doing one of

her practical jokes to get me out of bed … If there is World War III, it will have a big impact on the Pacific. America still has some form of control over various Pacific Island countries, and once again it will recruit Pacific Islanders. Pacific Islands are relatively weak and still trying to be developed.

Yet another:

I was at home having breakfast, listening to the news on Bula 100FM. My first reaction was disbelief, horror … Ethically, there is a need to remember the people involved and the amount of bloodshed and death. It would be necessary to censor material that would be emotionally upsetting.

One student was

really surprised to see TVNZ instead of the usual Chinese CCTV. The sound was mute so I couldn't really get was being said. I was about to turn it off when they showed the South Tower of the World Trade Center collapse. I thought it was a short piece from the movie *Independence Day*. Sad it may seem, but the first thing I thought about as a journalist was that reporters will have a field day … Phrases such as "historical day the world over" and "America under siege" popped up in my head as possible headlines. I got out my notebook and began writing down the number of people estimated to have died, the extent of the damage, and excerpts from President Bush's speech. Practically anything that involves the US also affects many people throughout the world.

Inevitably, some commentators began drawing parallels between the terrorism in New York in mid-September at one end of the continuum of hate and rogue businessman George Speight's brief terrorist rule in Fiji during 2000 at the other end. Politics associate professor Scott MacWilliam, for example, highlighted how terrorism becomes a political tool employed by a nation state to support its foreign and domestic policy objectives. He pointed out that many of the fundamentalist Muslim groups, which now carry out terrorism, were "nurtured, trained, financed and incorporated" into the Western security apparatus.[20] The media reported stories about how Taliban soldiers were trained in Scotland, and how terrorist pilots frequently gained advanced training at the most prestigious US flying schools. And also how the very suicide terrorists in the New York operation were in contact with US intelligence agents until just two weeks before the savagery was released on the Big Apple.

One might ask, what has this terrible urban graveyard created by fanaticism got to do directly with the South Pacific? In a sense, there is a disturbing relationship.

Freedom of speech in the Pacific: don't shoot the messenger

Many Pacific Islands neophyte journalists face a baptism of fire. It often takes raw courage to be a journalist in the Pacific. And it is also tough on the educators. **DAVID ROBIE** writes about the dilemmas after recently completing a decade of journalism education in the region

BARELY two-and-a-half years ago masked Fijian gunmen seized a consignment of books from the United States bound for the University of the South Pacific journalism program in Suva. The small cardboard box was stashed in a courier mail van hijacked by coup frontman George Speight's supporters hoping to find hard cash.

Two months later the carton was recovered by police from the ransacked Parliament and handed over to me; torn open but contents intact. Ironically, inside were six copies of Betty Medsger's *Winds of Change: Challenges Confronting Journalism Education*.

This was a poignant reminder of the realities facing Pacific media. Politics in the region are increasingly being determined by terrorism, particularly in Melanesia, such as in Fiji, Papua New established by media industry people that eventually closed under a cloud in 1999 about accountability over donor agency funding. Another Fijian journalist, Margaret Wise, recently sacked as chief-of-staff of *The Fiji Times*, has also been at the centre of debate over ethics and her paternity action against former coup leader and prime minister Sitiveni Rabuka.

Editorial headlines such as "Don't shoot the messenger" highlight the hypocrisy in the Fiji media when defending perceived threats to media freedom. There is little debate about the quality of the media itself and whether the Pacific gets the critical journalism that it deserves.

Other countries such as Australia and New Zealand have *Mediawatch*-style programmes on television and radio, and columns in newspapers that vigor-

Eyes of Fire, which was not popular with French colonial authorities.

Pacific media freedom in the *NZ Education Review*, December 2002.

Politics in the region is increasingly being determined by terrorism, particularly in Melanesia, such as in Fiji, Papua New Guinea and the Solomon Islands. And with this situation comes a greater demand on the region's media and journalists for more training and professionalism. Most journalists are young, relatively inexperienced and lowly paid.

Since George Speight's takeover of Parliament in May 2000, politics in Fiji have remained under the spectre of terrorism. While the Speight upheaval cost a relatively modest 15 lives—all indigenous Fijian—the fear of it happening again, and next time being perhaps even bloodier, made a mockery of the notion that there were "free and fair elections" in August 2001, as trumpeted by Commonwealth and United Nations observers.

Fiji politics today are driven by fear and a continuing threat to reinvoke terrorism if governments do not pursue a narrow particular direction—defined as ensuring "indigenous paramountcy". It would have been very interesting to see what would have happened if the country's first—and some say last—Indo-Fijian Prime Minister, Mahendra Chaudhry, had actually regained government in the election in spite of the $25 million (agricultural scam) vote-buying and scare-mongering tactics of the Laisenia Qarase regime. As independent journalist Ben Bohane remarked in an article questioning the loyalty of the military to the Constitution on the eve of the election and a court-martial:

Some weeks ago Chaudhry said that if he returned to power he would
"purge" the army of any rebels within its ranks. In such a confrontational
atmosphere, the fruits of reconciliation seem some way off yet and there is
real apprehension about the election outcome. As the army band trooped
off the parade ground with all the pomp of a colonial era brass band in full
swing, many of those watching hope it can keep playing the old anthems—
rather than the "Last Post" for any more soldiers killed by their own.[21]

Bohane was referring to the Special Forces killed when a mutiny on 2 November
2000 was ruthlessly crushed by the military, including the alleged beating to death
of four Counter Revolutionary Warfare Unit rebels taken prisoner.[22] This was an
extraordinarily sinister outcome given the proud reputation the Fiji military has
enjoyed as a United Nations peacemaker force.

Fiji is already a country prone to having coups and risks becoming consigned to
a fate of economic, political and legal instability—a "banana republic", as Chaudhry
called it during the election campaign. The political and judicial response to a
group of usurpers trying to seize control is crucial in determining whether or not
a country becomes a coup-prone nation.

Yet the options are simple. The coup cycle can be broken by a refusal to
recognise any unlawful regime by the courts established by the coup, and by
punishing the usurpers for treason. Sadly, this did not happen after Speight's
botched coup—key judges were alleged to have collaborated with the military and
the illegal abrogation of the Constitution.

Instead, Fiji now tends toward rewarding the usurpers and this will ultimately
destroy the social fabric and rule of law in the country. Fortunately, a judge had the
spine to bar Speight from taking his seat in Parliament when it convened for the
first time since the putsch.

When a prominent Indo-Fijian lawyer, feminist activist and onetime *Fiji Times*
columnist, Imrana Jalal, spoke out at a public seminar on the future of Fiji after the
polarised election on strategies to break the coup cycle, she talked of a need for
anti-coup provisions in the constitution. But she also called for visionary younger
leaders for a new Fiji who were not locked into communal thinking, and she urged
Indo-Fijians to change more than indigenous Fijians, saying "multiracial schools
are one key (not the only key) to multiracialism and integration". Fijian should be
compulsory in schools with Hindi as an optional subject.[23]

Some of her suggestions were perhaps worth closer consideration. However,
she was attacked in vitriolic terms by other Indo-Fijian community leaders and
politicians on radio and in the newspapers over the next few days. In one typical
letter to the editor she was accused of "blaming the victim". The writer went on to say:

She belongs to a class and circulates in a social circle that insulates her from the dehumanising experience of ordinary Indo-Fijians every time racism raises its ugly head in Fiji—and that is fairly frequently in recent times in case she hasn't noticed.[24]

The Fiji Times sprang to her defence. In an editorial, Imrana Jalal was described as a "welcome yet lonely voice in the wilderness of race relations".[25] The newspaper described the attacks on her as a pitiful indictment of her own community leaders and quite rightly pointed out that she had also called on the indigenous community to be more understanding of the views and needs of others.

However, the editorial headline "DON'T SHOOT THE MESSENGER" highlighted the hypocrisy over a paper only 10 months earlier that I had presented at the annual Journalism Education Association (JEA) conference in Mooloolaba, Queensland, in which I was critical of some of the reporting of Speight's coup. In the paper, titled "Coup coup land: The press and the putsch in Fiji", I also questioned the role of some elements of the media in the coverage of the year of the Labour-led People's Coalition government leading up to the coup, suggesting that this was a factor in the climate of destabilisation climaxing with Speight and his military henchman storming Parliament.[26]

My paper made a compelling case about issues of ethics, fairness and balance in reporting a conflict situation in the Pacific and it should have been debated. Instead, there was a howl of outrage by the very media executives who claim to be champions of a free press in the Pacific.

Clumsy attempts were made to gag me, or at least deflect public opinion. Nasty and abusive attacks were made against me on Commonwealth media email listservers, and an editorial deputation went from one foreign-owned newspaper to my university in a bullying and futile attempt to have me ousted.

Undoubtedly, in the Middle Ages I would have been burnt at the stake, or hung, drawn and quartered, for daring to criticise the vested interests in Pacific media.

As award-winning documentary-maker Senator `Atu Emberson-Bain said after Fiji Television declined to show her excellent documentary, *In the Name of Growth*, exposing the appalling exploitation of indigenous women workers by an indigenous-owned PAFCO (Pacific Fishing Company) tuna canning plant on Ovalau Island:

So much for the free (television) media in this country—the debate always focuses on freedom from government interference. What about freedom from the big (private sector) boys on the block with their vested interests?[27]

While Fiji TV turned down Emberson-Bain's programme on spurious grounds, SBS TV broadcast it in Australia and bought exclusive broadcast rights for four years. It was also nominated in the best documentary category at the 21st Annual Hawai'i International Film Festival.

After more than two decades reporting and teaching journalism in the region, unlike my colleagues Michael Field and Barbara Dreaver, I have never been barred from any Pacific country (although this happened to me with two African nations—Zaire, in 1973, and apartheid South Africa in 1972).

Nevertheless, I was twice arrested in 1987 by French military forces in New Caledonia, once at gunpoint near the east coast village of Canala. At the time I was covering the militarisation of indigenous Kanak villages in an attempt to suppress the struggle for independence. One of the problems was my book on the 1985 *Rainbow Warrior* bombing, *Eyes of Fire*, which was not popular with French colonial authorities.

But the real problem that I have encountered as a journalist and journalism educator is organisational attempts to censor or gag. One unfortunate example of this was in May 2000 during the Speight crisis in Fiji. This was a temporary 30-day closure of our *Pacific Journalism Online* news and training website without warning and initially without explanation by university authorities on May 29.[28] This happened the day after a mob of Speight's supporters attacked Fiji Television studios and put the station off air for two days. The final story posted on our website before we were suddenly pulled offline was a transcript of a controversial Fiji TV *Close-Up* programme discussing Speight and the media coverage of the crisis at that point.[29]

Political columnist Jone Dakuvula remarked:

George Speight is a two-day wonder who has just decided to champion indigenous rights for his own personal reasons in a matter of two days ... he has no real track record of fighting for indigenous rights.[30]

Two days later, the then Vice-Chancellor Esekia Solofa said in a media conference with our student reporters that the decision was made for "security reasons", but added the shut-down would be temporary. When I finally did get a meeting with university administrators to discuss reopening the website, they were more interested in trying (unsuccessfully) to censor our newspaper, *Wansolwara*, which had just gone to press.

But the University of Technology, Sydney, came to our rescue by hosting a website for our journalism students' Fiji coverage on their homepage.[31] This continued until August. Several international media freedom organisations, such as Reporters Sans Frontières, and other journalism schools protested to the

USP administration over our closure, with Associate Professor Chris Nash at the Australian Centre for Independent Journalism saying:

> The suggestion that journalism staff and students, and indeed any academics, might somehow desist from reporting, commenting and publishing on the current situation is akin to suggesting that doctors and nurses should turn their backs on wounded people in a conflict. It's unconscionable.[32]

However, my efforts at restoring the website and defending the student journalists' right to carry on their coverage of the coup was not popular with the administration. I received an extraordinary letter from then Vice-Chancellor Solofa, saying:

> The [Journalism] Programme "publications"— *Wansolwara* and the website [*Pacific Journalism Online*]—can be justified [for] one purpose only: to support a training function. That is, they provide a trial medium for practical skills training and for simulation work. They should not be regarded as a media outlet for students.[33]

Solofa seemed to have no understanding that student journalists learn about journalism by actively engaging in the craft. Merely writing classroom assignments isn't journalism. Covering the Fiji coup and the three months of intensive trauma that followed was the toughest call faced by the seven-year-old USP regional journalism programme.[34] But the delightful irony for me is that although we were chastised by our own senior administration for doing *real* instead of *simulated* journalism, Australian media judges awarded us the Dr Charles Stuart Prize at the Journalism Education Association of Australia's Ossie Awards for our coup coverage on our website *Pacific Journalism Online*.[35]

The Fiji crisis highlighted many dilemmas about culture and conflict. Customary obligations can be a burden on journalists. "Under pressure they can succumb to the demands of traditional loyalties," says former *Fiji Daily Post* editor Jale Moala. He wrote about the 2000 putsch:

> The problem that arose here was not so much one of reporters taking sides, as it may have seemed at the time, but the inability of many reporters to function objectively under the pressures of the crisis. A lack of leadership in newsrooms was one reason. One media organisation that came under early criticism was the state-owned Radio Fiji, which seemed to suffer from a combination of confusion over who was in power or who was going to end up in power, and lack of newsroom discipline and leadership—especially in the first two days of the hostage crisis.[36]

According to Michael Field—who has had the biggest share of bannings of any journalist in the Pacific, having being shut out of Kiribati, Nauru, Tonga, and even Fiji—the region is going through something of an unprecedented crackdown against journalists. For one of the most travelled and most aware journalists to be arbitrarily banned like this is an indictment of the region's politicians.

Journalists with long-standing experience and commitment to the Pacific should be encouraged, not gagged. Field, who is the most experienced journalist covering the South Pacific Forum, told one of our student reporters:

> What worries me, more than anything else, is that this is a signal against all journalists who work in the Pacific, that this degree of oppression and control and manipulation is now politically acceptable. It is important that we stop this kind of outrage, or the craft of journalism will be crushed in the Pacific.[37]

Our student journalists also faced victimisation over their reporting.

After publication of an edition of *Wansolwara*, one of our Samoan journalists, Vicky Lepou (now a journalism educator at the National University of Samoa), was subjected to a whispering campaign because of her front-page lead story about a joint Samoa and New Zealand probe into a sudden high failure rate among first-year students at USP.[38] Among reasons cited was uncertainty in the wake of the attempted coup. But some Samoan students harassed the reporter for having written the report, and the Samoan students' association patron denounced publication of the story.

The "shooting the messenger" syndrome always had more serious consequences in Papua New Guinea. Two University of Papua New Guinea student journalists gave testimony before a 2001 commission of inquiry examining the causes of the shooting to death of four young Papua New Guineans during the protests over structural adjustment.[39]

While I was at UPNG, the chief-of-staff, Kevin Pamba, and political reporter Jameson Bere of our training newspaper *Uni Tavur* were beaten up at night because of their front-page report on a political dispute between two national student leaders, both from the province of Enga. (Pamba later became a journalism lecturer in the Communication Arts Department at Divine Word University after working as business editor of *The National*.)

On another occasion, a student journalist had to go into hiding after he reported a funding scandal involving the then Miss UPNG winner. Miss UPNG's *wantoks* [comrades with shared language] led an angry protest march on the newspaper office trying to track down the reporter.

Rarely do Australian or New Zealand journalism schools encounter this degree of direct action or threats over stories. For many Pacific Islands journalists, it is a baptism of fire. Not only does truth hurt, it can sometimes lead to a brutal act of retribution. It often takes raw courage to be a journalist in the Pacific.

Another issue is allegations over bribes of journalists. Although such allegations rarely surface publicly, salaries for journalists in the Pacific are frequently so poor that it would be naïve not to accept that is likely to be a more serious problem than generally acknowledged.

In November 2000, our student journalists completed a salaries survey of the seven major news media organisations in Fiji and several were reluctant to cooperate. But nowhere was the starting salary, even for a graduate, higher than F$10,000 a year. Mostly, it was a lot lower. This then compared with about $15,000 for a secondary school teacher.

According to one senior editor, the starting salary for journalists at some major news media organisations in Fiji has not increased for more than a decade. Reporters work long hours for little pay.

> In fact, pay at *The Fiji Times* is still the same for cadet reporters as 12 years ago when I joined—$5500. No wonder staff turnover is so high in the industry. The enthusiasm evaporates very quickly because of the low pay, long hours.[40]

In September 2001, it was reported that journalists were handed envelopes with cash inside at the end of a recent news conference in Port Moresby. It was not disclosed how much and, according to the PNG Media Council, the journalists had handed the envelopes, with cash intact, to their editors. Council president Peter Aitsi revealed the episode while warning that news employees should not accept any benefits that might be seen as personal gain.[41]

Back in 1997, the PNG Media Council expressed concern at reports of political bribes being paid to "media collaborators" by politicians. The allegations arose out of a series of secretly taped videos allegedly showing politicians receiving bribe money from a former adviser to Prime Minister Bill Skate.

The videos were screened on ABC TV national news in Australia. Council chairperson Anna Solomon confirmed she had received a number of calls from concerned editors and media proprietors after the story broke. She said at the time:

> The Media Council would be extremely disappointed if these allegations are found to be true. The media in PNG prides itself on its integrity, courage and determination to root out corruption and to expose crooked politicians and business people. We are often called on to play the role of a de facto

political opposition to protect the interests of the grassroots people—a role we accept with deep conviction.[42]

Although Solomon called for a full inquiry into the allegations so the "rotten apples"—if they existed—could be removed, there was little progress. Unfortunately, these days the PNG Media Council has itself been under a corruption cloud.[43]

§

MANY challenges lie ahead in "navigating the future" of Pacific Islands media. In my experience, while there are a number of Pacific Islands media organisations and workshops around the region, rarely do they acknowledge the remarkable growth in the past few years of New Zealand-based Pacific media, both vernacular and English-language. Quality and informative programmes such as *Tagata Pasifika* on Television New Zealand and the Pacific Radio Network, and newspapers such as *Taimi 'o Tonga*, which is now based back in Tonga, are just some examples.

There is a need for an independent Pacific Islands journalists' network which nurtures and develops their needs and there is a need for more Pacific Islands journalists working in the mainstream media in Australia and New Zealand. This is especially so in this age of globalisation. The large attendance at the inaugural Pacific Islands Media Association (PIMA) conference at AUT University in Auckland in October 2001, and subequent conferences, was testimony to this. The establishment of the Apia-based Pasifika Media Association (PASIMA) resource website in 2010 is another example.[44]

However, more than a decade on, PIMA is now struggling to retain this leadership role in New Zealand and also needs to be more involved in the region in support of its sister and brother journalists. There is a vital need for a greater plurality of media voices and education if freedom of speech and the press are to flourish in the Pacific.

The late New Zealand High Commissioner to Fiji, Tia Barrett, made an important statement about indigenous issues and journalism at the University of the South Pacific journalism awards presentation in Suva during November 2000, which riled the military-installed regime:

What is difficult to accept in this dialogue on indigenous rights is the underlying assumption that those rights are pre-eminent over other more fundamental human rights. This just cannot be so, not in today's world ... Nowhere is it written in any holy scripture that because you are indigenous you have first rights over others in their daily rights. You

Media freedom Fiji-style, with regime leader Commodore Voreqe Bainimarama portrayed tinkering with the colonial legacy left by Britain in 1970 while keeping the press gagged.
MALCOLM EVANS/*PACIFIC JOURNALISM REVIEW*

should be respected and highly regarded as an indigenous person, but respect is earned not obtained on demand.[45]

As Tia Barrett said, information would make the difference in the process of cultural change for Pacific Islanders in the face of globalisation to improve people's lives. This is where the journalist plays a vitally important role, always bearing in mind the needs of the people and their thirst for knowledge.

Since the fourth coup on 5 December 2006 by Commodore Voreqe Bainimarama, press freedom has been on a downhill slide in Fiji culminating in the draconian *Fiji Media Industry Development Decree 2010*. Although formal military censorship virtually ended later at the start of 2012, Freedom House's annual media freedom report in 2013 said the harsh penalties under the decree—such as FJ$1000 fines or up to two years in jail for journalists and up to FJ$100,000 for organisations breaching the law— have "deterred most media from criticising the regime". Defenders of the

regime claim there is "freedom of the press" and it is the media editors who
are failing to take advantage of the freedom that they have. New director
of the Fiji Media Development Authority (MIDA), Matai Akauola, former
general manager of the Pacific Islands News Association (PINA), said in
a Radio Australia *Pacific Beat* interview: "In the last few years, we haven't
taken anyone to task, so that speaks for itself ... We even have clauses in
the new Constitution that have provisions for free media in Fiji. So for us
everything is open to the media ..."[46] But in February 2013 *The Fiji Times* was
fined FJ$300,000 and the editor given a suspended jail term for contempt
of court for a news report critical of the Fiji judiciary published by the New
Zealand *Sunday Star-Times* in 2011.[47] While this was not related to the
decree, the harsh penalty added to a "chilling" climate for media, echoed
by the experience of commentators on the ground such as US journalism
professor Robert Hooper who ran an investigative journalism course for
Fiji Television during 2012:

> I stressed the coverage of controversial stories on issues of national
> importance that, if produced, would be banned under Fiji's *Public
> Emergency Regulations* (PER) —an edict issued in April 2009 that placed
> censors in newsrooms—and the *Media Industry Development Decree
> 2010*, a vaguely worded law that criminalises anything government
> deems is "against the public interest or order". Under *PER*, overt
> censorship as well as self-censorship became routine at Fiji Television in
> 2009, in stark contrast to the openness and independence of the newly
> launched Fiji TV whose reporters I trained in the 1990s. Until *PER* was
> lifted in January 2012, military censors arrived at Fiji TV's newsroom
> daily at 2pm and 5pm to suppress stories deemed "political" or "critical
> of government". The arrest of reporters and confiscation of videotapes
> led swiftly to self-censorship in a demoralised newsroom.[48]

In October 2013, the regime banned foreign journalists, media trainers
and freelancers, and aid donors offering training from Fiji unless they
were registered and sought approval from the state-run MIDA.[49] The self-
censorship climate also impacted on academic freedom. At the University
of the South Pacific in 2011, one of its most eminent professors, economist
and former National Federation Party MP Dr Wadan Narsey, was gagged
and ultimately forced out of the academy.[50] Lamenting in one of his prolific
columns that the Fiji media was no longer a genuine watchdog, Narsey
added: "The real weakness in Fiji's media industry currently is that Fiji's
media owners are not 'dedicated independent media companies', but

corporate entities with much wider business interests which are far more valuable to the media owners than their profits from their media assets."[51] He was later gagged[52] from giving an address to journalism students on the UNESCO World Press Freedom Day event in 2013.[53]

In the inaugural UNESCO World Press Freedom Day lecture at AUT University on 3 May 2013, Professor Mark Pearson said that like teaching and nursing, a journalism career based on "truth-seeking and truth-telling in our societies had an element of a 'mission'" about it. "All societies need their 'Tusitalas'—their storytellers," he added.[54]

But he also warned that social media and blogging seemed to have "spawned an era of new super-pamphleteer—the ordinary citizen with the power to disseminate news and commentary" immediately. This raises the stakes for media accuracy, credibility and freedom.

"It would be an historic irony and a monumental shame," Pearson said, "if press freedom met its demise through the sheer pace of irresponsible truth-seeking and truth-telling today."[55]

Notes

1   Mat Oakley (2002, June 28). Robie's legacy outlasts critics. Fiji *Sunday Post/Pacnews/Pacific Media Watch*. Retrieved on 7 January 2014, from www.asiapac.org.fj/cafepacific/resources/aspac/fiji3006

2   David Robie (2002). Cited in an editorial, "Free media rhetoric", *Pacific Journalism Review*, 8(1): 5–9.

3   Ibid., p. 5.

4   Shailendra Singh (2002). Of croaking toads, liars and ratbags. *Wansolwara*, 7(4): 6.

5   Shailendra Singh and Biman Prasad (eds) (2008). Coups, media and democracy in Fiji [Editorial]. *Fijian Studies: A Journal of Contemporary Fiji*, 6(1 & 2): 1–8; see also David Robie (ed.) (2001). Crisis and coverage. *Pacific Journalism Review*, 7(1).

6   Ibid.

7   Singh and Prasad (eds) (2008). Coups, media and democracy in Fiji [Editorial], p. 3.

8   David Robie (2008, March 1). Fiji's "how to gag the media" report. Café Pacific. Retrieved on 13 April 2012, from http://cafepacific.blogspot.co.nz/2008/03/fiji-how-to-gag-media-report.html

9   Robie (2002). "Free media rhetoric" [Editorial], p. 6.

10 David Robie (2013, March 24). PACMAS report dodges the aid elephant in the room. *Café Pacific*. Retrieved on 20 September 2013, from http://cafepacific.blogspot.co.nz/2013/03/pacmas-media-report-dodges-aid-elephant.html

11 Ibid.

12 Robie (2002). "Free media rhetoric" [Editorial], pp. 6–9.

13 Philip Cass (2001, May 12). Opinion: response to Laisa Taga. *Pacific Islands Report*. Retrieved on 7 January 2014, from http://166.122.164.43/archive/2001/May/05-14-20.htm; Laisa Taga (2007, April 22). Different rules when it comes

to Fiji and Tonga. *Islands Business.* Retrieved on 7 January 2014, from http://uriohau.blogspot.co.nz/2007/04/different-rules-when-it-comes-to-fiji.html; Jese Sikivou (2001). Open letter to Laisa Taga. *Pacific Journalism Review* 7(1). Available at: www.pjreview.info/volume-7/issue-1

14 Robie (2002), pp. 7–8.

15 See Christine Gounder (2006). The Fiji 2000 coup: A media analysis. Unpublished Master of Communication Studies thesis. Auckland: Auckland University of Technology.

16 Robie (2002). "Free media rhetoric" [Editorial], p. 8.

17 David Robie (2001). Keynote address at the "Navigating the Future" conference at the Auckland University of Technology, Auckland, October 5–6.

18 David Robie (2002). [Pacific] freedom of speech. *Pacific Journalism Review,* 8(1): 10–119.

19 Linda Diebel (2001, October 3). Freedom of speech casualty of a new war: Journalists accuse the White House of intolerance. *Toronto Star Online.*

20 Scott MacWilliam (2001). 1997 Constitution is for the past not the future. Paper presented at the Parkinson Memorial Lectures, Suva: University of the South Pacific, September 19.

21 Ben Bohane (2001). Fiji military exorcise ghosts. *Pacific Journalism Review,* 7(1): 69–72.

22 Counter Revolutionary Warfare Unit court martial, Fiji (2000). Wikipedia. Retrieved on 20 September 2013, from http://en.wikipedia.org/wiki/Counter_Revolutionary_Warfare_Unit_Court_Martial,_Fiji

23 Imrana Jalal (2001). Building a fractured nation. A paper presented at the Parkinson Memorial Lectures, Suva: University of the South Pacific, September 19.

24 Angeli Devi (2001, September 24). Jalal under fire. [Letter to the editor]. *The Fiji Sun.*

25 Don't shoot the messenger [Editorial] (2001, September 22). *The Fiji Times,* p. 6.

26 David Robie (2000). Coup coup land: The press and the putsch in Fiji. Paper presented at the Journalism Education Association (JEA) conference, Mooloolaba, Queensland, December 5–8. Updated version published in *Asia-Pacific Media Educator,* Issue 10, January–July, pp. 148–162.

27 'Atu Emberson-Bain (2001, September 26). Personal communication with the author.

28 David Robie (2004). *Mekim Nius: South Pacific media, politics and education.* Suva: University of the South Pacific Book Centre.

29 The *Close-Up* TV script blamed for the raid on Fiji TV (2000, May 29). Pacific Media Watch. Retrieved on 7 January 2014, from www.pmw.c2o.org/docs00/TVfiji.html

30 Controversial *Close-Up* (2001). Transcript by Alison Ofotalau. *Pacific Journalism Review,* 7(1): 39–45.

31 University of the South Pacific Regional Journalism School (2000). Internet coup in Fiji 2000 archive. Available at: www.pmc.aut.ac.nz/articles/archive-internet-coup-fiji-2000

32 Australian Centre for Independent Journalism (ACIJ) (2000). Letter by the ACIJ Director to the USP Vice-Chancellor, June 13.

33 Esekia Solofa (2000, June 22). Letter to USP Journalism Coordinator.

34 Christine Gounder (2000, August). From trainees to professionals. And all it took was a coup. *CPU News*. London: Commonwealth Press Union, p. 7. Retrieved on 12 April 2012, from www.usp.ac.fj/journ/docs/news/cpunews.html

35 Frontline Reporters: USP student reportage of 2000 Fiji coup (2000). [Video] and winners of Dr Charles Stuart Prize for student journalism. Available on YouTube at: www.youtube.com/watch?v=4ShcdDD0ax8

36 Jale Moala (2001). Political reporting and editorial balance. Chapter in David Robie (ed.) (2001). *The Pacific Journalist: A Practical Guide*. Suva: University of the South Pacific Book Centre.

37 Noora Ali (2001, August 9). Banned journalist speaks out. *Wansolwara Online*. Retrieved on 12 April 2012, from usp.ac.fj/journ/docs/news/wansolnews/wansolo908011.html

38 Insight Report on the Media Industry: Fiji journalists underpaid (2000, November). *Wansolwara*, p. 7.

39 The Uni Tavur testimony (2001). *Pacific Journalism Review, 7*(1): 127–139.

40 SS, cited in David Robie (2001). *The Pacific Journalist: A Practical Guide*. Suva: University of the South Pacific Book Centre.

41 Warning as PNG journalists offered money at news conference (2001, September 5). *Pacific Islands Report*.

42 PNG Media Council shocked at bribery allegations (1997, November 27). Pacific Media Watch, Port Moresby. Retrieved on 12 April 2012, from http://166.122.164.43/archive/1997/December/12-04-09.html

43 Liam Fox (2011, June 3). PNG media council embroiled in fraud audit. ABC News. Retrieved on 20 September 2013, from www.abc.net.au/news/2011-06-03/png-media-council-embroiled-in-fraud-audit/2744952

44 Pasifika Media Association (PASIMA) website: http://pacificmedia.org

45 Tia Barrett (2000). Journalism and Indigenous Issues. Address by the New Zealand High Commissioner at the USP Journalism Awards, Suva, November 24. Retrieved on 12 November 2011, from www.usp.ac.fj/journ/docs/news/usp29awards00.html

46 Fiji: Media Industry Development Authority pleased with status quo (2014, January 10). Radio Australia, cited by Pacific Media Watch No. 8458. Retrieved on 7 January 2014, from www.pmc.aut.ac.nz/pacific-media-watch/fiji-media-industry-development-authority-pleased-status-quo-8458

47 Nanise Loanakadavu (2013, February 21). *Times* fined $300,000. *The Fiji Times Online*. Retrieved on 7 January 2014, from www.fijitimes.com/story.aspx?id=225792

48 Robert A. Hooper (2013). When the barking stopped: Censorship, self-censorship and spin in Fiji. *Pacific Journalism Review, 19*(1): 41–57, p. 44.

49 Anna Sovaraki (2013, October 10). Fiji Media Authority bans journalist training by foreign entities. *Fiji Sun*, cited by Pacific Media Watch No. 8429. Retrieved on 7 January 2014, from www.pmc.aut.ac.nz/pacific-media-watch/video-fiji-media-authority-bans-journalist-training-foreign-entities-8429

50 Acclaimed academic forced out of Fiji's USP (2011, August 18). *Coupfourpointfive*. Retrieved on 23 January 2014, from www.coupfourandahalf.com/2011/08/professor-wadan-narsey-forced-out-of.html

51 How media ownership in Fiji chokes the watchdog (2013, May 28). *Café Pacific*. Retrieved on 23 January 2013, from http://cafepacific.blogspot.co.nz/2013_05_01_archive.html

52 Ex-USP professor "gagged" over media freedom speech (2013). Pacific Media Watch No. 8290. Retrieved on 23 January 2014, from www.pmc.aut.ac.nz/pacific-media-watch/fiji-ex-usp-professor-narsey-gagged-over-media-freedom-speech-8290

53 Wadan Narsey (2013, May 24). Fiji Media ownership constricting media freedom: what should journalists do? [Gagged speech for the University of the South Pacific]. *República*. Retrieved on 23 January 2014, from http://narseyonfiji.wordpress.com/2013/05/24/iji-media-ownership-constricting-media-freedom-what-should-journalist-do-republika-24-may-2013-planned-speech-for-usp-journalism-students-celebration-of-unescos-world-press-freedom-day-usp/

54 Mark Pearson (2013). UNESCO World Press Freedom Day Lecture: Press freedom, social media and the citizen. *Pacific Journalism Review*, *19*(2): 215–227.

55 Ibid., p. 227.

23

Conflict reporting in the Pacific, 2010

Mainstream journalism has failed to communicate not only peace, but also human rights in ways that have the potential of illuminating the important nexus between them.
Media agenda-setting researcher and journalist Ibrahim Seaga Shaw

PEACE journalism is hardly a new concept, with Johan Galtung and Mari Ruge providing a key conceptual underpinning in 1965 and in later studies. However, while it flourished significantly in parts of the globe in the 1990s, notably the Philippines, albeit frequently referred to there as "conflict-sensitive journalism", it has only relatively recently become an approach seriously considered as applicable in a South Pacific context, especially in the wake of the Bougainville Civil War and the Solomon Islands ethnic conflict.[1] With other political upheavals such as four coups d'état in Fiji in two decades, paramilitary revolts in Vanuatu, riots in Tahiti and Tonga, protracted conflict in Papua New Guinea's Highlands, and the pro-independence insurrection in New Caledonia in the 1980s, conflict resolution poses challenges for the region's journalists and their education and training. In his 2013 memoir on his experience as being the first New Zealand diplomat to be declared persona non grata by any country, Michael Green was critical of media coverage of Fiji: "The quality of New Zealand media reporting and commentary on the [2006] coup and its implications was, by and large, disappointing. As a result, public debate around the issues raised by the coup was not well-informed."[2]

Peace journalism is one approach that can arguably make sense of a region that has become increasingly complex, politically strained and violent, yet the concept is generally eschewed by the legacy media as a threat to the core values of "traditional journalism" itself. As Australian investigative journalist John Pilger wrote in a foreword to a book reporting conflict from a peace perspective, "so-called mainstream journalism [is] committed almost exclusively to the interests of power, not people".[3]

This chapter, drawn from one of my articles in *The Journal of Pacific Studies*, examines conflict trends in the South Pacific, discusses the concept of peace journalism, and argues that journalists can take a more constructive approach to reporting conflict in the region. It is certainly not "soft" journalism as some have sought to misrepresent it; the approach in fact involves a higher level of committed and investigative journalism.[4]

WHY PEACE JOURNALISM HAS A CHANCE

The Journal of Pacific Studies, September 2010

THE STUDY of wars and news media portrayal and reportage of conflict has been well developed as an academic discipline, termed by some as "war journalism".[5] But the study of peace journalism lags far behind. While the Melanesian sub-region of the South Pacific, in particular, has been branded by some political analysts as an "arc of instability"[6] because of upheavals such as the four Fiji coups d'état since 1987, Solomon Islands ethnic conflict, the Bougainville Civil War and "*les Évènements*" in New Caledonia in the 1980s, journalism models deployed by the region's media have largely focused on "conflict" or "war" reporting as a predominant news value. There has been less reporting or even debate on process or alternative paradigms.

While a primary Australian view of the region projects a "more demanding and potentially dangerous neighbourhood",[7] New Zealand argues from a far more "Pacific" perspective that sees the region as perhaps less threatening.[8] However, an Australian media conflict perspective that eschews notions of peace journalism generally prevails.

Peace journalism: "Exposing truths on all sides"

War journalism often focuses on violence as its own cause and is less open to examining the deep structural origins of the conflict.[9] Heavy reliance on official sources leads to a general zero-sum analysis and deepens divisions. "Peace" is defined as victory plus ceasefire. It is of little consequence that the deeper causes of the conflict remain unresolved, condemned to resurface again later. After a period of violent conflict, such as during the decade-long Bougainville Civil War, war journalism concentrates on visible effects—those killed or wounded and damage to physical surroundings, not the impact on the people's health, psychology, sociology or culture. More than a decade after the end of the Bougainville war, the people are still recovering and rebuilding their lives in the autonomous region, emerging from under the shadow of a struggle popularised by New Zealand author Lloyd Jones in his 2006 novel *Mister Pip* (followed by a feature film in 2013).[10] War journalism also dehumanises the "enemy" and is "propaganda-oriented, elite-focused and victory-oriented, and tend[s] to concentrate on institutions (the 'controlled society')", as

Richard Keeble, John Tulloch and Florian Zollmann express it in a book advancing the theoretical framework for journalism and conflict resolution.[11]

In contrast, the notion of peace journalism offers a

"voice to all parties", focused on the invisible effects of violence (trauma and glory, damage to the social structures), aimed to expose "untruths on all sides", [is] "people-oriented", [gives] "a voice to the voiceless" and [is] solution-oriented.

According to Angela Romano,[12] drawing on Jake Lynch and Annabel McGoldrick,[13] at the simplest level:

Peace journalism relies on traditions of fact-based journalism, with close scrutiny of word and images. Journalists must avoid emotive and imprecise expressions, dichotomies of good versus bad, a focus on the victimhood and grievances or the abuses and misdemeanours of one side only, and the use of racial and cultural identities when they are not necessary. Journalists must attribute unsubstantiated claims to their sources rather than presenting them as facts, avoid focussing on the victimhood or causes of one party to the exclusion of [an] other, and seek diverse sources and viewpoints.[14]

In essence, much of this is good practice in traditional journalism but in times of conflict journalists don't "always scrupulously follow such ideals"[15] and there have been frequent examples of this in the South Pacific.[16] In a Fiji context, flawed news media responses to the George Speight attempted coup of 19 May 2000 illustrated this. As seasoned *Fiji Daily Post* editor Jale Moala noted later:

[That] coup polarised the races in Fiji, or so it seemed. And in seeming to do so, it created a situation in which many reporters found it difficult to focus on the issues from a totally impartial point of view as they were swept away by the euphoria of the moment and the tension and the emotion that charged the event. This was true of both indigenous Fijian and Indo-Fijian reporters alike.

Fear may have also played a role. As a result, the perpetrators of the terrorist action, led by George Speight, received publicity that at the time seemed to legitimise their actions and their existence.[17]

According to Canadian journalist and media development in conflict specialist Ross Howard, it doesn't take a war correspondent to recognise that journalism and news media can incite violent conflict. He offers several examples, including:

Kanak protesters during "*les Événements*" in New Caledonia in 1985.   DAVID ROBIE

In 1994, Radio Milles Collines in Rwanda incited genocide by employing metaphors and hate speech. Serbian state broadcasting during the 1995 and 1999 Balkan conflicts is almost equally infamous. Incompetent journalism and partisan news management can generate misinformation, which inflames xenophobia, ethnic hatred, class warfare and violent conflict in almost any fragile state. The anti-Thai violence in Cambodia in 2003, triggered entirely by partisan media, is [another] example. Radio Netherlands' website on counteracting hate media indicates that hate radio is currently operating on five continents.[18]

However, Howard also adds that less recognised is the potential for journalism to influence conflict resolution. Yet in recent years a range of literature has been developed critiquing the potential for media to promote "conflict resolution rather than war and violence"[19] and "human rights and social change".[20] Keeble, Tulloch and Zollmann, for example, cite a 17-point plan for practising peace journalism outlined by Lynch and McGoldrick,[21] who summarise by saying that peace journalism is when journalists use the insights of conflict analysis and transformation to "update the concepts of balance, fairness and accuracy in reporting".[22]

Howard argues that peace journalism can "inject context, an appreciation for root causes, and a new capacity to seek and analyse possible solutions, to the

Practising peace journalism

1.	Avoid concentrating always on what divides parties, on the differences between what each say they want. Instead, try asking questions which may reveal areas of common ground.
2.	Avoid focusing exclusively on the suffering, fears and grievances of only one party ... Instead, treat as equally newsworthy the suffering, fears and grievances of all parties.
3.	Avoid "victimising" language like "devastated", "defenceless", "pathetic", "tragedy" which only tells us what has been done to and could be done for a group of people by others. This is disempowering and limits the options for change. Instead, report on what has been done and could be done by the people.
4.	Avoid focusing exclusively on the human rights abuses, misdemeanours and wrongdoings of only one side. Instead, try to name all wrong-doers and treat allegations made by all the parties in a conflict equally seriously.

Source: Extracted from Lynch and McGoldrick's 17-point plan for practising peace journalism (cited by Keeble, Tulloch and Zollmann [2010, p. 3]).

otherwise daily repeating of violent incidents as news". For journalists and the news media in the South Pacific, there are growing opportunities for seeking alternative models that are more appropriate for the region's realities than Australian or New Zealand newsroom experience where peace journalism is rarely debated. The Philippines is one such notable example.

The Philippines: Peace journalism in a culture of impunity

One of the cradles of the development of peace journalism studies has been in the Philippines where advocates of the discipline have been forced to contend with both a culture of suspicion due to a protracted Maoist insurgency being waged by the New People's Army (NPA) against the authorities and a culture of impunity over the widespread murders of news workers. Suspicion and scepticism has led to peace journalism being branded as variously either a "left-wing" or "right-wing" manipulation and journalism educators have often been more comfortable using the term *conflict-sensitive journalism* instead.

Paradoxically, while having one of the "freest and least fettered" media systems in Asia, as cited by Jeanette Patindol,[23] the Philippines also ranks as one of the most dangerous countries for news media, after Iraq, because of the high death rate of local journalists. Journalists have been assassinated in the Philippines with impunity for almost a quarter-century—ever since the end of martial law and the flight of ousted dictator Ferdinand Marcos into exile in 1986. The media played a critical role in the People Power Revolution that led to the downfall of Marcos. In more than 23 years since democracy was restored, the National Union of Journalists of the Philippines (NUJP) recorded 136 killings of journalists, or an average of one killing every two months.[24] The NUJP and other groups monitoring media freedom noted "the killings have worsened under the Macapagal-Arroyo administration [until defeated at the polls in 2010 and replaced by President Benigno Aquino] as an average of one journalist got murdered every month from 2001 to 2009."[25]

The NUJP said in its year-end statement after the slaughter of 34 ambushed journalists that 2009 would be "forever remembered as a year of unprecedented tribulation for the Philippine press, with the November 23 massacre in Ampatuan town in Maguindanao [a province on the southern island of Mindanao] making its grisly mark in history as the worst ever attack on the media." The long-awaited start of the trial on 1 September 2010 was postponed after just one hour by Judge Jocelyn Solis Reyes, after a defence lawyer argued more time was needed to comment on pre-trial documents. A key witness for the prosecution was also murdered. Ampatuan town mayor Andal Ampatuan Jnr and 16 police officers, who allegedly served as members of the Ampatuan clan's private army in Maguindanao, in the southern Philippines, are accused. They face murder charges for the massacre of 58 people, including the journalists and media workers, who were travelling in a convoy with a political candidate running against Ampatuan Jnr for Governor of Maguindanao.

In the context of such killings of journalists, media educators have questioned how to advance peace journalism as a discipline when practitioners are faced with opposition, "not just from individuals and groups but from the entire media system itself":

> For peace journalism to be sustainable, those who have been trained in the field need to band together and engage in mutually helpful exchanges, building solidarity as they jointly work towards implementing peace journalism in the mainstream.[26]

This drive for solidarity led to the establishment of a movement of journalists, communication educators and industry professionals trained in "basic peace journalism" in Bacolod City, Philippines, in 2004 to establish a Peace and Conflict Journalism Network (PECOJON). Since then, this movement has spawned several national and international networks, with about 250 members in the Philippines and 165 members from 15 nations. But the rampant killings of news people, particularly radio reporters and talkback hosts, has led to a sustained debate about ethics and professionalism inthe Filipino media. Columnist Danny Arao raised a key question

Filipino journalists killed from 1986 to 2013

Year	Number killed	Presidents
1986	3	**Corazon Aquino** Total = 37
1987	10	
1988	7	
1989	4	
1990	8	
1991	5	
January – June 1992	0	
July – Dec 1992	6	**Fidel Ramos** Total = 19
1993	5	
1994	0	
1995	1	
1996	3	
1997	2	
January – June 1998	2	
July – Dec 1998	3	**Joseph Estrada** Total = 9
1999	2	
2000	3	
January 2001	1	
Feb – Dec 2001	3	**Gloria Macapagal-Arroyo** Total = 108
2002	2	
2003	7	
2004	15	
2005	11	
2006	12	
2007	6	
2008	7	
2009	39	
January – June 2010	5	
July – Dec 2010	4	**Benigno Aquino III** Total = 33
2011	8	
2012	7	
2013	14	

Filipino journalists killed under four democratic administrations since the Marcos dictatorship, 1986–2013.[27]

CENTER FOR MEDIA FREEDOM AND RESPONSIBILITY (CMFR)/DEL ABCEDE in his weekly commentary in *Asian Correspondent*: How should journalism be taught at a time when journalists are killed with impunity and the government remains hostile to press freedom? He sought answers to these three queries:

1. Should aspiring journalists be taught to practise "cold neutrality" in handling issues?

2. Is it right for a professor to encourage students to consistently follow the law?

3. Can professors and students just simply dismiss the media situation and just limit the classroom discussions to the theories related to journalistic writing, with special emphasis on grammar, syntax and diction?[28]

Arao also noted that the Philippines is said to be the freest press in Asia given the constitutional guarantees and laws protecting freedom of speech. But he also sounded a warning that there was "a difference between freedom *of* speech and freedom *after* speech" as journalists face dire consequences for exercising what is supposed to be their constitutional rights (my emphasis). "Cold neutrality," argues Arao, simply cannot be observed in a situation where the killings of journalists "become[s] the highest form of censorship". "The stakes are too high for journalists to practise indifference in the culture of impunity that gives rise to media repression," he added. While laws are necessary to maintain order in a society, there are laws that end up "muzzling the media instead of protecting them". According to the London-based International News Safety Institute (INSI) report *Killing The Messenger*, the Philippines was the third most dangerous country for journalists in 2013, behind Syria and Iraq. The total of 14 Filipino deaths, "which in past years has seen a mass shooting of reporters as well as individual assassinations, included five who lost lives in natural disasters."[29]

Killings of journalists inevitably encourages many other media people to embrace peace journalism, or to become "activists". Arao also argues that there should be no dichotomy in journalism between form and content because both are important. A critically important role of a journalist is to shape public opinion and therefore the ability to analyse is equally important to writing skills. Ideally, peace journalists move beyond presenting "just the facts" due to their awareness of how easily these facts can be "manipulated by narrow interests and unchallenged mythologies, especially from traditional elites".[30]

Reporting Pacific conflict

While reporting in the South Pacific in the past three decades, I covered the assassination of Pierre Declercq, secretary-general of the pro-independence

Armed conflicts in the South Pacific region, 1975–2013

Ongoing	Independence struggle in West Papua (Indonesia) (estimated deaths more than 100,000)
Ongoing	Tribal fighting in PNG's Southern Highlands and other provinces (several hundred deaths each year)
1980s	Independence struggle in New Caledonia (France) (more than 50 deaths)
1987, 2000, 2006	Four coups in Fiji (first two coups bloodless; at least 20 deaths in Speight coup in 2000; the Bainimarama coup in 2006, bloodless so far
1990s	Bougainville Civil War, or "war of independence" (more than 10,000 deaths)
1999–2006	Solomon Islands ethnic conflict (estimated 200 deaths)

Source: Adapted from Henderson (2005), p. 5.

Union Caledoniènne in New Caledonia (1981), the "Black Friday" rioting in Pape`ete (1983), the Hienghène massacre in New Caledonia (1984), the assassination of Kanak independence leader Éloï Machoro (1985), the bombing of the *Rainbow Warrior* by French secret agents (1985), military coups in Fiji (1987) and the start of the Bougainville Civil War (1989/1990). On assignment covering coups and conflict in the Philippines in 1988, I shared a room in Manila with former Protestant pastor Djoubelly Wea, the assassin who gunned down Kanak independence leaders Jean-Marie Tjibaou and Yéiwene Yéiwene for what he and other Kanak activists perceived to be a betrayal of the independence movement by their signing of the 1989 Matignon Accord. Wea himself was shot dead by one of Tjibaou's bodyguards.[31]

Subsequently as a journalism educator from 1993 (when I joined the University of Papua New Guinea after being an independent foreign correspondent for many years) onwards, the emphasis was more on what our student journalist newsroom focused on covering. Examples included the then ongoing Bougainville Civil War, including the Sandline mercenary crisis (1997) and the shooting of three students at UPNG (2001). Five years later, I was appointed to the University of the South Pacific, where the students covered the George Speight attempted coup in Fiji (May 2000) and other major news events on their website *Pacific Journalism Online* and in their newspaper *Wansolwara*.[32]

In a 2005 survey of violent conflict in the South Pacific, political analyst John Henderson found that one of the "more surprising" findings was that 10 political assassinations had happened in the region since 1981. The assassinations included New Caledonian independence leader Pierre Declercq (1981) and Belau president Haruo Remeliik (1985); Kanak independence leader Éloï Machoro (1985) as well as Jean-Marie Tjibaou and Yéiwene Yéiwene four years later (1989); Bougainville Premier Theodore Miriung (1996); Samoan cabinet minister and anti-corruption campaigner Luagalau Leva`ula Kamu (1999); West Papuan pro-independence leader Theys Hiyo Eluay (2001); and two leading Solomon Islands political figures, cabinet minister Augustine Geve (2002) and Peace Council member Frederick Soaki (2003). Henderson noted:

> In 2000, the Fiji military commander, Frank Bainimarama, narrowly escaped an attempt on his life. These findings suggest that political killings have become part of the region's pattern of political violence.[33]

The South Pacific's military and paramilitary forces have contributed to violence in the region, particularly in Melanesia. An estimated 120,000 Pacific Islanders have died in conflicts over the past quarter-century (plus another 200,000 when Timor-Leste is included). The major conflict in the region has been West Papua, often billed as the "forgotten war", yet this issue has been largely neglected by international media and the issue of state terrorism has rarely been addressed. Criticism of Pacific Islands regionalism projects often portrays this notion as a "by-product of the perceived security and other needs and ideologies of external powers".[34] West Papua is a critical example of this. In the early era of Pacific regionalism, the former Dutch colony of West Papua was the second largest entity until 1963.

Since then it has seen more conflict than the rest of the region put together. Indonesia obtained West Papua, against the wishes of the Papuan people, because the US and Australia saw more benefit to themselves in supporting Indonesia against West Papua. This is still the case, despite Indonesian forces having killed more than 100,000 Melanesians.[35] Since a security treaty was signed with Indonesia in November 2006, Australia has been becoming even more overtly involved in the repression of pro-independence activists.[36] The Indonesia and Australia Framework for Security Cooperation smoothed over a diplomatic rift caused when Australia granted 43 Papuans asylum early in 2006. Both nations agreed to respect each other's territorial integrity. The treaty recognises Indonesian sovereignty over Papua and commits both countries to suppressing independence activists. Since then, Australia has been involved in funding and training for an elite counter-terrorism force in Indonesia known as Densus 88, or Detachment 88, which is notorious for its brutal suppression of suspected pro-independence activists. In April 2013, the force was accused of killing 11 people and a further 20 disappeared after a combined military and police crackdown on the Free Papua Movement (OPM) in the Central Highlands, in an area dubbed the "Gaza Strip". This was denied by Indonesian authorities.[37]

"There's always been a background of violence in West Papua and the Indonesian military and the police in particular," says Professor Damien Kingsbury of Deakin University's School of International and Political Studies. "The anti-terror group [has] always taken a very strong line against what they perceive to be separatist sentiments by West Papuans. But the West Papuans themselves are really looking for a negotiated settlement to the problems of the province and they're pushing that agenda by engaging in things like the [banned *Morning Star*] flag-raising ceremonies to demonstrate their unhappiness."[38]

Allegations over the Australian involvement with Densus had been first raised over the assassination of a West Papuan leader, Mako Tabuni, of the non-violent KMPB on 14 June 2012. In an article in the Jayapura-based *Tabloid Jubi* newspaper, the University of Sydney's West Papua Project asked: "Is Australia funding Indonesian death squads? … Set up in the wake of the Bali terrorist bombings, Densus 88's mandate was to tackle the rise of domestic terrorism in Indonesia. Australian support might have been motivated by revenge as well—88 Australians were killed in the Bali attack" (out of a total of 202 deaths in the Kuta tourist district on 12 October 2002).[39]

Later, Densus 88 began operations in West Papua against the pro-independence movements. The ABC *7.30 Report* broadcast an investigation into Densus 88 that alleged there was "growing evidence that the squad is involved in torture and killings" against pro-independence activists.[40] "Detachment 88 is … trained in forensics, intelligence gathering, surveillance and law enforcement by the US, the UK and Australia," said reporter Hayden Cooper. "They've played a crucial role in Indonesia's counter-terrorism efforts. They're ruthless, often killing suspects. But their anti-terrorism mandate is now creeping into other areas, like policing West Papuan separatists."

While Australia and other Western nations have followed a policy actually supporting Indonesian suppression of protesters and movements seeking self-determination, New Zealand since the Lange Labour government took office in 1999 has been "focused on avoiding any disruption to New Zealand's relation-ship with Indonesia".[41] This policy is fairly similar to an accommodation that New Zealand practised in relation to Timor-Leste after it was invaded by the Indonesians in 1975.

A Pacific Media Watch research report on press freedom in the region, which included scathing sections on West Papua, warned that the Indonesian-ruled provinces posed the worst situation confronting journalists.[42] Describing the situation as a "media black spot" in *New Matilda* magazine, the report said

Media in Jayapura pictured in a photograph from a course in Safe Witness Journalism techniques developed by Sydney-based West Papua Media's editor Nick Chesterfield for both citizen journalists and media activists. The first such course was held in Papua New Guinea in 2013. WEST PAPUA MEDIA

the region was fraught with obstacles.[43] Nick Chesterfield, editor of West Papua Media, which has long provided the most consistent and in-depth reportage, detailed some of these issues:

> Jakarta still upholds its prohibition on all foreign journalists and media workers from entering either province in West Papua, unless pre-approved under a slow and bureaucratic process from the Ministry of Information. Even after approval, journalists are always accompanied by a minder from the Badan Intelijen Nasional (National Intelligence Body). Only three foreign journalists [were] allowed access to West Papua in 2011. Unsurprisingly, few journalists choose this official route, with many opting to travel into West Papua via unofficial means, a process unavailable to Jakarta-based correspondents under threat of immediate expulsion. Human rights workers regularly report that security forces harass and intimidate those seen talking to foreign journalists, though many still take the risk when a foreign journalist is present.[44]

Journalists committed to covering the Pacific region frequently find it frustrating working with news media that do not employ sufficient resources, or misread or interpret events simplistically and without sufficient depth. Vanuatu-based photojournalist Ben Bohane, for example, is in the vanguard of those who have brought an independent and critical perspective in the media . A curator's commentary for a Sydney exhibition of his work concluded: "The media maxim 'If it bleeds, it leads' may account for [an Australian and New Zealand] tendency to focus on eruptions in a perceived status quo rather than monitoring the sequence of events that precede or influence them."[45] Such tendencies equally apply to the New Zealand media. Although, at a policy level, New Zealand has a more nuanced stance, with a self-perception of being *part of* the Pacific rather than *in* the Pacific, as is the case with Australia.

Conflict-sensitive journalism education

Against this educational and training mediascape, how can notions of peace journalism or conflict-sensitive journalism take root? As Howard notes,[46] conventional journalism training and development "generally contains little or no reference to the wisdom of five decades of academic and professional study of conflict". He argues that conflict analysis theory and skills are still not considered mainstream journalism prerequisites or practices. However, Howard also cites examples of the gradual development of journalism training courses that are indeed recognising "conflict-sensitive journalism" as a methodology. While such training includes core journalism values and skills, this approach includes an introduction to conflict analysis, the concept of conflict and most common causes, the forms of violence by which conflict is played out, and some insights into the techniques of resolution.

On an optimistic note, Howard suggests these added capabilities developed through education and training lead to a "better story selection and much more insightful writing and broadcasting".[47] And he adds: "At best, they substantially expand a stressed community's dialogue and possibly offer glimpses of common ground."

Filipino columnist Danny Arao, in answer to his questions raised earlier in this chapter, suggests that "cold neutrality" actually becomes "counterproductive" to the shaping of public opinion when it is considered that a journalist is "expected to analyse and not just present data".[48] He argues that the challenge for student journalists over pressing social issues is to acquire the "necessary skills and knowledge of articulating their analysis in a manner that can be understood by their audiences". He says that in order for the teaching of journalism to be effective, the profession should "remain critical of the forces that perpetuate media repression".

Peace journalism or conflict-sensitive journalism education and training ought to provide a context for journalists to ensure that both sides are included in any reports. The reporting would also include people who condemn the violence and offer solutions. Blame would not be levelled at any ethnicity, nor would combatants be repeatedly identified by their ethnicity. But the reporting would constantly seek to explain the deeper underlying causes of the conflict. This approach to journalism surely could offer some hope for conflict resolution in the Pacific and a more peaceful future.

¶

MOST peace journalism research has focused on the representation of conflict in the corporate news media. Instead of championing the case for marginal reforms in corporate media, such scholars argue that peace journalism should concentrate on "the tradition of radical journalism [openly] committed to progressive social change".[49] According to Robert A. Hackett, "alternative media" represent a "challenger paradigm" to the objectivity regime, as its own structural underpinnings erode, one that opens up new "vistas" for peace journalism by offering new insights and horizons.[50] The table opposite shows the key differences between war and peace journalism.

The editors of *Expanding Peace Journalism*[51] question whether the practices of peace journalism, "if embedded more widely in public communication processes and institutions, make a significant difference to conflict cycles"? While mainstream media generally "sides with official rhetoric and policy stances", argues Ibrahim Shaw, developing a human rights journalism is also an expansion of the peace paradigm.[52]

Notes

1 Tarcisius Kabutaulaka (2001). *Beyond Ethnicity: The Political Economy of the Guadalcanal Crisis in Solomon Islands*. Suva: SSGM Working Paper; Jon Fraenkel (2004). *The Manipulation of Custom: From Uprising to Intervention in the Solomon Islands*. Wellington: Victoria University Press/Pandanus.
2 Michael Green (2013). *Persona Non Grata: Breaking the Bond—Fiji and New Zealand 2004–2007*. Auckland: Dunmore Publishing, p. 11.
3 John Pilger (2010). Foreword. In Richard Lance Keeble, John Tulloch and Florian Zollmann (eds). *Peace Journalism, War and Conflict Resolution*. London: Peter Lang.
4 David Robie (2010). Conflict reporting in the South Pacific: Why peace journalism has a chance. *The Journal of Pacific Studies*, 32(2): 221–240.
5 Richard Keeble, John Tulloch and Florian Zollmann (eds) (2010). Introduction: Why Peace Journalism Matters. In Keeble, Tulloch and Zollmann (eds) (2010), *Peace Journalism, War and Conflict Resolution*, pp. 1–12.
6 See Alfred Deakin Lectures (2001). The arc of instability: Australia's role in the Asia-Pacific. Radio National. Available online at www.abc.net.au/rn/deakin/content/

Differences between "war" and "peace" journalism

War Journalism	Peace Journalism
1. War/violence oriented: reactive/first-zero sum/win-lose focus	1. Peace/conflict oriented: prevention/win-win focus
2. Propaganda/deceit oriented: exposes "their" untruths/lies and covers up "ours"	2. Truth oriented: exposes all untruths on all sides
3. Elite oriented: focuses on "those" evil-doer and "our" victims/friend (good), enemy (bad)	3. People oriented: names all victims of conflict
4. Victory oriented: peace = victory + ceasefire	4. Solution oriented: peace = Long term resolution of grievances

Source: Adapted from Galtung (2006) , p. 1, and Shaw (2011) , p. 109.

session_2.html. Paul Dibb (2002, October 23). Does Asia matter to Australia's defence policy? Public lecture at the National Institute for Asia and the Pacific; Stewart Firth (2005). A new era in security. In J. Henderson and G. Watson (eds), *Securing a Peaceful Pacific*. Christchurch: Canterbury University Press, pp. 91–98.

7   Paul Dibb (2002). Does Asia matter to Australia's defence policy?; David Hegarty (2005). New modes of security management. In Henderson and Watson (eds), *Securing a Peaceful Pacific*, pp. 53–61.

8   Colin James (2006). From the Pacific: A New Zealand perspective on Australia's strategic role. Paper presented at the Australian Strategic Policy Institute's Global Forces conference, September 26–27.

9   Johan Galtung and Richard Vincent (1992). *Global Glasnost: Toward a New World and Information Order?* Creskill, NJ: Hampton Press.

10 *Mister Pip* trailer (2013). [Feature film]. Available at www.youtube.com/watch?v=tRn3gr8Pt_0

11 Keeble, Tulloch and Zollmann (eds) (2010). *Peace Journalism, War and Conflict Resolution*.

12 Angela Romano (ed.) (2010). *International Journalism and Democracy: Civic Engagement Models from Around the World*. London: Routledge.

13 Jake Lynch and Annabel McGoldrick (2005). *Peace Journalism*. Stroud, UK: Hawthorn Press.

14 Romano (ed.) (2010), p. 27.

15 Ibid.

16 Michael Field (2005). *Speight of Violence: Inside Fiji's 2000 Coup*. Auckland: Reed; Jale Moala (2001). Political reporting and editorial balance. In David Robie (ed.) (2001), *The Pacific Journalist: A Practical Guide*. Suva: University of the South Pacific Book Centre; David Robie (2001). Coup coup land: The press and the putsch in Fiji. *Asia Pacific Media Educator, 10*: 148–162; Brian Woodley (2000, June 8–14). Courage under fire. *The Weekend Australian* media section, p. 6.

17 Moala (2001). Political reporting and editorial balance, p. 125.

18 Ross Howard (2009). The case for conflict sensitive journalism. Center for Journalism Ethics, School of Journalism and Mass Communication, University of Wisconsin-Madison. Retrieved on 11 September 2013, from www.journalismethics.info/global_journalism_ethics/conflict_sensitivity_in_ practice.htm

19 Keeble, Tulloch and Zollmann (eds) (2010). *Peace Journalism, War and Conflict Resolution*, p. 2.

20 Ibrahim S. Shaw, Jake Lynch and Robert A. Hackett (eds) (2011). *Expanding Peace Journalism: Comparative and Critical Approaches*. Sydney, NSW: Sydney University Press.

21 Lynch and McGoldrick (2005). *Peace Journalism*.

22 Ibid., p. 5.

23 Jeanette Patindol (2010). Building a peace journalists' network from the ground: The Philippine experience. In Keeble, Tulloch and Zollmann (eds) (2010), *Peace Journalism, War and Conflict Resolution*, p. 194.

24 Danny Arao (2010). Teaching journalism amid the culture of impunity. *Asian Correspondent*. Retrieved on 11 September 2013, from http://asiancorrespondent. com/danny-arao-blog/teaching-journalism-amid-the-culture-of-impunity

25 Ibid.

26 Patindol (2010). Peace network, p. 193.

27 Filipino journalists killed during President Benigno Aquino III's term of office from July 2010 to December 2013 only:

> July 2010 – December 2010: Jul 3: Jose Daguio, Tabuk (radio); Jul 9: Miguel Belen, Iriga City (radio); Aug 1: Edilberto Cruz, Cabanatua City (print); Dec 10: Edison Flameniano Sr, Zamboanga del Sur (print).
>
> January – December 2011: Jan 24: Gerardo Ortega, Palawan (radio); Mar 24: Maria Len Flores Sumera, Malabon, Metro Manila (radio); Jun 13: Romeo Olea, Iriga City (radio); Aug 22: Neil Jimena, Silay City, Negros (radio); Oct 11: Johnson Pascual, Santiago City, Isabela (radio & print); Oct 14: Roy Gallego, Agusan del Sur (radio); Nov 11: Alfredo Velarde, Gen Santos City (print); Dec 15: Antonio Silangon, December 15, Bohol (print).
>
> January – December 2012: Jan 5: Christopher Guarin, Gen Santos City (radio & print); Apr 8: Aldion Layao, Davao City (radio); Apr 30: Rommel

Palma, Koronadal (media worker); May 8: Nestor Libaton, Mati City, Davao (radio); May 8: Michael Calanasan, San Pablo, Laguna (print & radio); Sep 1: Eddie Apostol, Kidapawan (radio); Nov 8: Julius Cauzo, Cabanatuan City, (radio).

January – December 2013: Jan 3: Edgardo Adajar, San Pablo, Laguna (radio); Apr 22: Mario Vendiola Baylosis, Zamboanga (radio); Jun 2: Miguelito Rueras, Masbate (radio); Jul 28: Richard Kho, Quezon City, Metro Manila (print); Jul 30: Bonifacio Loreto, Quezon City, Metro Manila (print); Aug 1: Mario Sy, Gen Santos City (photojournalist); Aug 29: Fernando Solijon, Iligan City (radio); Sep 4: Vergel Bico, Calapan City (print); Sep 14: Jesus Tabanao, (radio); Nov 8: Ronald Vinas, Tacloban (radio); Nov 8: Allan Medino, Tacloban (media worker); Nov 8: Archie Globio, Tacloban (radio); Nov 8: Malou Realino, Tacloban (radio); Nov 29: Joas Digos, Bukidnon (radio); Dec 5: Michael Diaz Milo, Tandag City, Surigao (radio); Dec 6: Jhonavin Villaba, Iloilo (radio); Dec 11: Rogelio Butalid, Tagum City (radio).

28 Arao (2010). Teaching journalism.
29 Philippines 3rd most dangerous country for journalists – INSI report (2013, February 19). GMA News.
30 Howard (2009). Conflict sensitive journalism.
31 David Robie (1989). *Blood on their Banner: Nationalist Struggles in the South Pacific*. London: Zed Books; Sydney: Pluto Press, p. 280.
32 David Robie (2004). *Mekim Nius: South Pacific media, politics and education.* Suva: University of the South Pacific Book Centre.
33 John Henderson (2005). Introduction: Pacific conflict—how much and why? In Henderson and Watson (eds), *Securing a Peaceful Pacific*, p. 8.
34 Ron Crocombe (2005). Regionalism and the reduction of conflict. In Henderson and Watson (eds), *Securing a Peaceful Pacific*, p. 8.
35 Ibid., p. 55.
36 Mark Forbes (2006, November 8). We'll help Indonesia go nuclear. *The Sydney Morning Herald*. Retrieved on 11 September 2013, from www.smh.com.au/news/national/well-help-indonesia-go-nuclear/2006/11/07/1162661684698.html
37 Peter Lloyd (2013, May 24). Indonesian counter-terrorist unit accused of mass killing in disputed Papua province. ABC News. Retrieved on 11 September 2013, from www.abc.net.au/news/2013-05-24/indonesian-counter-terrorist-unit-accuse-mass-killing-papua/4712070
38 Ibid.
39 West Papua Project, University of Sydney (2012). Is Australia funding Indonesian death squads? Densus 88 in West Papua. *Tabloid Jubi*. Retrieved on 11 September 2013, from http://tabloidjubi.com/z/index.php/english/19588-is-australia-funding-indonesian-death-squads-densus-88-in-west-papua
40 Hayden Cooper and Lisa Main (2012, August 28). Australia faces link to West Papua torture. ABC *7.30 Report*. Retrieved on 11 September 2013, from www.abc.net.au/7.30/content/2012/s3578010.htm
41 Maire Leadbeater (2005). Expediency, hypocrisy, policy. In Henderson and Watson (eds), *Securing a Peaceful Pacific*, p. 495.

42 Alex Perrottet and David Robie (2011). Pacific media freedom 2011: A status report. *Pacific Journalism Review, 17*(2): 147–186.

43 Alex Perrottet and David Robie (2011, October 24). Papua a media black spot. *New Matilda*. Retrieved from

44 Nick Chesterfield (2011). West Papua. In Alex Perrottet and David Robie, Pacific media freedom 2011. A status report, p. 178.

45 Bec Dean (2006). Bohane's portrayal of spirit and war in Melanesia. *Pacific Journalism Review, 12*(2): 157–160.

46 Howard (2009). Conflict sensitive journalism.

47 Ibid.

48 Arao (2010). Teaching journalism.

49 Richard Keeble (2010). Peace journalism as political practice: A new, radical look at the theory. In Keeble, Tulloch and Zollman (eds) (2010), *Peace Journalism, War and Conflict Resolution*, p. 50.

50 Robert A. Hackett (2011). New vistas for peace journalism: Alternative media and communication rights. In Shaw, Lynch and Hackett (eds) (2011), *Expanding Peace Journalism*, p. 54.

51 Shaw, Lynch and Hackett (eds) (2011). *Expanding Peace Journalism*, p. 28.

52 Ibid., p. 97.

24

Changing paradigms in Pacific journalism, 2013

I learnt long ago that the best gift you can bring to Islanders are your stories ... Not trinkets or promises. There is a notion here of wan solwara (one ocean)—that is the sea that links us all even if we come from different Pacific islands; whitefella or blackfella, we are all Pacific islanders.

Photojournalist Ben Bohane in The Black Islands

SOUTH Pacific media face a challenge of developing forms of journalism that contribute to the national ethos by mobilising change from passive communities to those seeking change. Instead of news values that have often led international media to exclude a range of perspectives, such a notion would promote deliberation by journalists to enable the participation of all community stakeholders. Deliberative journalism is issue-based and includes diverse and even unpopular views about the community good and encourages an expression of plurality.

In a Pacific context, this resonates more with news media in some developed countries that have a free but conflicted press such as in India, Indonesia and the Philippines. This has far more relevance in the Pacific than a "monocultural" Western news model as typified by Australia and New Zealand. Early in the millennium, I examined notions of the Fourth Estate in the South Pacific. These were applied through a "Four Worlds" news values prism in the global South that included the status of indigenous minorities in dominant nation states.[1] This chapter explores how that has been modified over the past decade and its implications for media and democracy in the Pacific.

Related to these issues is a fundamental rethink of journalism's rights and responsibilities in law and political philosophy which derive from the concept of "the public right to know" in democratic theory. As Professor Chris Nash acknowledged in a paper in *Pacific Journalism Review* arguing for greater recognition by universities of journalism practice as a research discipline, journalism historically is linked as a corollary to universal freedom of expression in a democracy: "Internationally, most nation states define [journalism] as a practice by adherence to professional codes of ethics relating to truth, and regulate its role and practice through legal instruments such as Bills of Rights, statutes and the common law, and in civil jurisprudence."[2]

An Australian media researcher found many journalists covering the first three Fiji coups between 1987 and 2000 were too reliant on elite sources to provide a good understanding of the complex crises, and the pattern arguably continued for the fourth coup by Commodore Voreqe Bainimarama in 2006. This reliance increased the likelihood of reinforcing the status quo and provided a "limited version of reality".[3]

Anthony Mason, then a doctoral candidate from Canberra University,[4] wrote his analysis in a review paper for a regional research journal, marking the twentieth anniversary of the original coup by Lieutenant-Colonel Sitiveni Rabuka on 14 May 1987. Dr Mason argued that it was critical for Australia and New Zealand to gain a deeper understanding of troubled societies "on our doorstep" such as Fiji, Papua New Guinea, Solomon Islands and Tonga.

> The media can definitely contribute to improving the broader level of understanding. The front line journalists have a lot of freedom to cover the story the way they want to, but the impact of their stories—of their expertise, their understanding and their contacts—is swamped by the coverage from home and elsewhere.[5]

Mason reported on some of his findings from interviews with 15 Australian and New Zealand journalists and a content analysis of three broadsheet newspapers, *The Australian, The Canberra Times* and *The Sydney Morning Herald*. Another researcher, Fiji-born Christine Gounder of New Zealand's AUT University, reported findings showing that it was difficult for many Fijian journalists to remain professional in their jobs because of strong cultural or ethnicity ties with supporters of failed businessman George Speight. Gounder, who interviewed 13 Fiji journalists and four foreign reporters, said many Fijian journalists suffered from the so-called Stockholm syndrome—where captives identify with their captors.[6] These were reporters who had stayed for long periods in Parliament with the rebels where they held Indo-Fijian prime minister Mahendra Chaudhry and his multiracial cabinet at gunpoint for 56 days.

> Many experienced journalists and editors have migrated, taking with them the institutional knowledge and leaving behind a mostly inexperienced and young newsroom.[7]

Investigative journalist and media advocate Kunda Dixit, editor-in-chief of the *Nepali Times*, in Auckland in 2010. He urges media practitioners to consider their profession more critically.   DAVID ROBIE

In Timor-Leste, the *Jornal Naçional Diaro* was one of the smallest and youngest of the country's three daily newspapers, but it was also one of the brightest and gutsiest. It was selling around 600 copies a day, had barely more than a dozen young reporters and operated out of a derelict former Indonesian police station in the port city of Dili. Getting to a reporting job depended on a tired fleet of five small motorbikes parked in the paper's front yard. The newspaper used to have eight machines, but three were stolen in raids at the height of the country's factional bloodshed in May 2006. Young editor-in-chief José Gabriel fiercely defended the independence of the paper, which boasted then president and Nobel peace laureate Dr José Ramos-Horta on the contributors' masthead.[8]

The author with student journalists from the University of Papua New Guinea. Many in this 1998 photograph have made a name for themselves as journalists, including Gorethy Kenneth (centre front row with her arms folded), a star Bougainville bureau reporter and now chief-of-staff on the *PNG Post-Courier*.   *UNI TAVUR*

After a flurry of creative challenges to the Fiji military-backed regime as it entrenched its power post-2006, the news media was forced to face the harsh reality of life after a censorship crackdown in mid-2009. Leading editors and journalists opted to be cautious following the regime's gag and threats but authorities warned that they would be shut down if they stepped out of line. Not tolerating any dissent since martial law was declared on 10 April 2009, the regime ordered so-called "*sulu*-censors"—named because of the traditional Fijian kilt-like garment some officials wear—and police into newsrooms to check stories and broadcasts. The regime expelled three foreign journalists, detained two local reporters and questioned many more. It also forced the eventual sale of Fiji's oldest and most influential newspaper, *The Fiji Times*, founded on 4 September 1869. Retired former *Times* editor Vijendra Kumar refused to be pessimistic in an article he wrote for *Pacific Scoop*: "During its 141-year-long history, *The Fiji Times* has changed hands at least five times and has been none the worse for it ... And so it will continue."[9] Along with global media freedom and human rights groups such as the Paris-based Reporters Sans Frontières and the London-based Amnesty International, the Auckland-based Pacific Media Centre called on Bainimarama's regime to "end this

Orwellian era of ruthless censorship and intimidation".[10] But while censorship remained until the *Public Emergency Regulations* were scrapped at the start of 2012, some journalists and civic leaders argued Fiji media coverage should be broadened out to focus on other issues.[11] Since the lifting of formal censorship, a climate of self-censorship and media timidity has prevailed, even prompting the regime itself to call for more vigorous reporting.

Globalisation and development journalism

Development should lead to human progress, but this is not always the case. Journalists are a "crucial link in the feedback loop", ensuring that improvements in the quality of life can be sustained and do not permanently damage nature and the human environment.[12] Authors such as one-time Inter Press Service journalist Kunda Dixit have warned against the cost of globalisation for developing countries of the global South, such as in the Pacific. He calls this rapacious process sweeping the world today "gobble-isation", and says "there is a danger that free trade will worsen the balance of payments deficits, accumulate debts, and force poor countries to set things right by accelerated exploitation of their forests, marine and mineral resources".[13] According to Dixit, this "massive haemorrhaging of wealth has already bled many countries dry" and ruined their environment.

> In addition, languages, indigenous cultures, oral testimony are vanishing forever, obliterated by a "monoculture" spread by the globalisation of the economy and communications. The more tangible signs of crises are alarms over ozone depletion, global warming, rainforest loss and fishless seas—the results of the dizzying acceleration of human technological advancement in the past century. It is called "development", but where is it taking us?[14]

If journalists are serious about tackling the major issues confronting the Pacific such as climate change, exploitation of the forests and mines, and depletion of the fisheries, they will need to "look at the theory and practice of their profession far more critically", argues Dixit in his republished edition of the classic *Dateline Earth*.[15] They need to be far more receptive about new ideas and being non-conformist.

> Traditional journalism schools teach you to look for the counterpoint to make stories interesting. They tell you that it is the controversy, the disagreement, which gives the story its tension. Most reportage then sounds like a quarrel, opposites pitted against each other, even when

the point of argument may be minor and the two sides are in overall agreement. The technique of press interviews is to provoke the head of the Olympics drugs testing committee to make a nasty remark, and play that back to [the] chief swimming coach of the Chinese team and ask him to comment. The next day's headline is ready-made: "CHINA BLASTS OLYMPIC COMMITTEE".

Conflict is the adrenaline of a macho media. But this kind of "on the one hand this, on the other hand that" reporting can be an obstacle in spreading clarity about global problems. Readers and audiences worldwide are fed a mainstream viewpoint on issues like global poverty, conflict-free trade and environmental degradation by reporters that stick to the status-quo perspective to give the semblance that they are "objective".[16]

According to Australian journalism educator Angela Romano, corporate and mainstream journalism often "provides technically accurate but kneejerk reports about the specific facts about any dramatic event or issue that rises to the reporters' attention".[17] Romano's book *International Journalism and Democracy* argues for a "more sophisticated" understanding by journalists of the consequences of their work. It also offers a strong case about the role of deliberative journalism in a democracy, which encourages "greater consideration of the subtle nuances of the visible facts" and how seemingly obscure details make up a more rounded and greater picture of unfolding trends and issues.[18] Romano is concerned about

journalists' propensity to overlook topics until they reach the scorching point of crisis. For example, in many countries, hunger and starvation do not become big media issues until there is a famine ... It is usually harder to write compelling reports about issues that are simmering. It requires more talent and effort to recognise the issues that may be leading to a potential calamity, to find the compelling features of the story, and to be inventive in developing new storytelling strategies to best tell these tales.[19]

As a philosophy, deliberative journalism involves some "subjectivity", but in a sense it is more objective than mainstream reporting when it is "attached to the process of democratic deliberation", and involves robust reporting and analysis of public issues rather than focusing on any particular "side" or outcome.[20] It involves reporting the daily news as *issues* rather than as *events* for citizens to make a judgement and is well suited to geopolitical reporting.

Romano notes that while liberal Western media are "structurally impaired" in facilitating an "authentic deliberative discourse", the rhetoric about "neutral news" does not match the fact that media reflect the "outlooks of eloquent political elites".[21] While a common criticism of deliberative journalism models is that they are perceived to "potentially threaten" journalistic standards of objectivity, in fact the opposite applies.[22] Deliberative journalism requires a reflection on how high standards of objectivity might be balanced with fairness and ethical considerations.[23] A good example of this is some case studies on cultural diversity and race relations published in *The Authentic Voice: The Best Reporting on Race and Ethnicity*, which "delivered solid, fundamental journalism and fused voice, context and complexity into one authentic piece".[24] Levi Obijiofor and Folker Hanusch have explored how journalists in collectivist cultures are more likely to value role perceptions "such as 'setting the political agenda', 'influencing public opinion' and 'advocating for social change' than their counterparts in individualist cultures".[25] The authors also cited research indicating a link between journalists supporting interventionist roles in nations regarded as "more hierarchical and tradition-oriented".

Deliberative journalism involves empowerment, often a subversive concept in conservative societies. It involves providing information that enables people to make choices for change. Deliberative models include notions such as public journalism, development journalism, peace journalism and even "human rights" journalism.[26] Development journalism in a nutshell is about going beyond the "who, what, when, where" of basic inverted pyramid journalism; it is usually more concerned with the "how, why" and "what now" questions addressed by journalists.[27] Some simply describe it as "good journalism".[28] As a media genre, development journalism peaked at the height of the UNESCO debates for a New World Information and Communication Order (NWICO) in the 1970s. The debates were "used by Third World countries to argue for a more positive portrayal" of developing countries by Western news organisations such as Associated Press (AP), United Press International (UPI) of the United States, France's Agence France-Presse and Reuters of the United Kingdom.

According to a Malaysian media academic who settled in Australia, *Asia Pacific Media Educator* editor Eric Loo, "development journalism was understood and linked by Western journalists to a biased reporting approach focused on positive developments as opposed to the conventional focus on conflict, such as failed government projects and policies".[29] In fact, the term development journalism is often used to refer to two different types of journalism,[30] although Dixit and others argue that there is a wider range of definitions. One ideal of development journalism, or *critical development journalism* as I describe it, has a parallel with investigative journalism, but it focuses on the condition of developing nations and ways of improving this. With this approach, journalists are often encouraged to travel to remote areas, interact with the citizens of the country and report back on critical projects. Proposed government projects are put under the spotlight and they are analysed to see whether they really would help communities. People are usually at the centre of this storytelling. And often the journalist comes up with proposed or potential solutions and actions.

> The main essence of investigative reporting is "why". Development journalism attempts to highlight the "what, why and how" of the process of events. The basic philosophy of investigative journalism is to unveil the secrecy, to expose. But development journalism has to be alive to the realities of the situation and has to tail, study and report the process of socio-economic, cultural, political, educational changes in the country.[31]

Another form of development journalism, one usually denigrated and misrepresented as the only approach by Western journalists, involves government participation in the mass media. On the positive side, this means that important information can be distributed throughout the nation. Governments can educate their citizens and seek support for major development projects. However, the downside means that state authorities can also capture the idea of "development" to stifle free speech and restrict social justice.[32]

Both forms of development journalism are used in the South Pacific.[33] Ironically, this is not always understood or accepted by the news media in the effort to replicate Western media practices. In many respects, the challenges facing the South Pacific media have more in common with countries such as India and the Philippines—two nations that pioneered development journalism in its more positive forms—than in Australia and New Zealand. Development journalism also needs to be considered in the context of comparative news values, as outlined in the next section.

News value models

While the winds of change swept through Third World or developing nations (usually now referred to as the global South) in the post-Second World War rush to decolonisation in the 1960s and 1970s, similar transitional ideological shifts later applied to "Fourth World" nations in the 1980s and 1990s. First World nations were the industrialised Western countries and Second World nations were the totalitarian remnants of the Soviet-era Marxist bloc—such as China, Cuba and Vietnam—and also other dictatorships such as the right-wing regimes of El Salvador and Guatemala.[34] In an attempt to provide a more constructive analysis of comparative news values, Jack Lule developed a "Three Worlds" news model in the late 1980s showing that a "dramatic difference" in global news values was a "function of political, economic and philosophical developments of the past three centuries".[35] However, by the 1990s the appropriateness of this media model had become somewhat outdated in a globalised world. Obijiofor and Hanusch are among many who have critiqued Siebert et al's "Four Theories" model, highlighting a view that the analysis was "loaded with the propaganda elements of the time" supporting an expansionist US model of "privately owned-for-profit media".[36] In post-Cold War politics in an era of the so-called "War on Terror", news value definition boundaries became blurred and it was no longer possible to slot some countries into three simplistic typologies of West ("objectivity"), East ("collective agitator") and Third World ("nation-building"). Globalisation, the dramatic evolution of digital media technologies, and declining definitions of geopolitics in North versus South terms call for more sophisticated models.

While several other models addressing global geopolitics and media-scapes have emerged, such as *The World News Prism*'s author William Hachten's five concepts—authoritarian, Western, communist, revolutionary and developmental—none have been completely compelling and few provide an adequate model to include Fourth World media communities.[37] This latter category refers to indigenous and ethnic minorities and their media, which have been absorbed within larger, dominant states. They never really fit Lule's "Three Worlds" framework and are now among the more distinct groups resisting globalisation.

In the mid-1990s, while teaching journalism at the University of Papua New Guinea, I modified Lule's model into a "Four Worlds" news values approach, which could be more readily applied to independent Pacific post-colonial states and indigenous minorities amid economic and socio-political developmental and media transition.[38] This model was also used at the University of the South Pacific journalism school when relating to multiethnic Pacific communities, and resonates in New Zealand in the context of indigenous iwi (tribal) radio broadcasting and the evolution of indigenous media such as the national Māori Television Service (MTS).

Professor Emeritus Peter Russell, while writing about aboriginal nation-alism in Canada, defined Fourth World communities (or First Nations) as "indigenous peoples residing in developed nations, but living in Third World conditions":

The Four Worlds news values matrix

First World	Second World	Third World	Fourth World
Objectivity Examples: Australia, New Zealand, Canada, European Union nations, UK, USA	**Collective agitator** Examples: China, Cuba, Vietnam	**Nation-building** Examples: Cook Islands, Fiji, India, Papua New Guinea, Philippines	**Self-determination** Examples: Koori, Māori Iwi, First Nations, Sami, Cordillera, Lumad peoples
1. Timeliness News is now	**1. Ideological significance** News is politically correct ideology	**1. Development news is progress** News is growth, news is new dams, news is new buildings	**1. Independent voice** News spearheads a political view challenging the mainstream media perspective
2. Proximity News is near	**2. Party concerns** 'The one party state (ie communist) is news what it does, what it thinks and what it does not think.'	**2. National integration** 'News is positive achievement, pride and unity.'	**2. Language** News is in the first language of the cultural minority
3. Personality News is prominent or interesting people, celebrities, politicians, royalty, sports heroes and heroines, hip hop artists and movie stars	**3. Social responsibility** News is responsible to society in the 'Second World'	**3. Social responsibility** News is responsible	**3. Culture** News is reaffirming distinct cultural identity
4. Unusual, Odd events News is quirky, weird, bizarre, oddities, outside the norm	**4. Education** News is instruction, news teaches, news preaches	**4. Education** News teaches, news passes on knowledge	**4. Education** News is teaching in own language language 'nests' Example: Te Reo Māori, Maohi, Bislama, Tok Pisin
5. Human interest	**5. Human interest** Similar to First World but with an ideological touch	**5. Other values** News similar to First World, human interest, people, etc.	**5. Solidarity** News supports other indigenous minorities
6. Conflict	**6. Disaster**	**6. Conflict**	**6. Conflict** Crises interpreted through an indigenous prism
7. Disaster		**7. Disaster**	**7. Disaster**
			8. Environmental news News reaffirms cultural and traditional values; focus on community response

Source: Robie (2013) (adapted from his earlier model, (2001), p. 13).[44]

Although cultural traditions maintain a significant place in indigenous communities, it is contended that technological advancements have resulted in the increased proficiency of indigenous political skills; ironically, the colonised are overcoming the political mechanisms instituted by the colonisers.[39]

However, unlike Third World (global South) nations, Fourth World communities "cannot separate from imperial power because of their location within the boundaries of the imperialist nation". This means that indigenous peoples must either obtain equal access to the political and economic opportunities of the democratic society, or continue to struggle for political autonomy.[40] According to the United Nations Declaration on the Rights of Indigenous Peoples, Part IV Article 17 declares that "indigenous peoples have the right to establish their own media and in their own languages".[41] The media play an important role in that struggle and thus news values applied by indigenous media are often at variance with those of the West (First World), East (Second World remnants) and developing nations (Third World/global South) in a globalised world. Such media conditions are particularly appropriate for indigenous First Nation minorities in Australia and New Zealand and the Philippines (such as the Cordillera peoples of Luzon or the Lumad of Mindanao). They also apply in Bougainville, especially during the 10-year civil war waged by island tribes against the state of Papua New Guinea.

Photojournalist Ben Bohane, who chronicled the Bougainville war and many conflicts in the western Pacific, examined the role of culture in political developments and media representations in research in the mid-2000s, concluding that for media to be able to play its Fourth Estate role in the region it must be able to "read and interpret the indicators". He compared the role of the Bougainville Revolutionary Army (BRA) with the so-called "Taukei Movement" in the 1987 Rabuka coups and George Speight attempted coup in Fiji in 2000, and the four-decade-long struggle for independence by the West Papuans against Indonesian rule.[42] He considered that the failure of Western journalists to comprehend the role of *kastom* (custom), traditional movements and spiritual beliefs eroded meaningful Western reportage in the region. This was also a subject of Bohane's evocative ethnographic image collection published in Vanuatu in 2013, *The Black Islands*.[43]

Much of the political and journalistic discourse analysing the troubles of Melanesia have centred on a diagnosis incorporating political

The five-legged tanoa media model

'PACIFIC WAY'
tradition

First Estate
The Executive

Second Estate
Parliament

Fifth Estate
Cultural Hegemony

Third Estate
The Judiciary

Fourth Estate
The Press

Source: Robie (2013). The talanoa and the tribal paradigm.[46]

corruption, poor management, lack of "good governance", urbanisation, breakdown of "traditional values" and respect for chiefs, blaming the *"wantok"* [one language] system of tribal loyalties, unemployment and poor education.

Many of these elements alone, or in combination, have certainly played a role in destabilising Melanesian nations. However, while each nation faces different circumstances and the simmering conflicts in each case stem from different causes, there is one area that is often overlooked when examining the conflicts of Melanesia. This has proved to be a significant catalyst.

This catalyst is the role played by *kastom* and so-called "cult" movements in these societies. In order to have a better understanding of the social and political turmoil prevalent in contemporary Melanesian societies, it is instructive to have an understanding of the belief systems that exist.[45]

In the context of the South Pacific, and particularly Fiji in the wake of four coups, there is a notion of a "fifth estate", a traditional cultural pillar, which is a counterbalance to all other forms of power, including the news media, or Fourth Estate.[47] My model based on a five-legged *tanoa*, or kava bowl used for ceremonial and informal dialogue, seeks to integrate this "custom" factor into journalism with a particular reference to the Pacific

Talanoa journalism matrix

Mainstream Journalism Western	Talanoa Journalism Pacific
Élite-source oriented	Grassroots source oriented
Hard news description	Hard news with context, cultural interpretations
Objective, detached, uninvolved stance	Reflexive stance
Solutions not an issue	Possible solutions for identified problems
Top-down mainstream vertical public opinion	Grassroots, citizen public opinion, horizontal views
Emphasises individualist achievement	Emphasises community achievement
Unfettered free media focused on conflict	Free media, but balanced with social responsibility
Consumer, business orientation	Public interest, civil society, community empowerment focus
Entertainment or sensational angles	Focus on positive outcomes for wider community
Focus on crime, disaster and deviant behaviour	Focus on socio-economic development, community needs, wellbeing and progress
Normative mainstream ethical codes	Community ethics with recognition of indigenous, diversity, cultural values

regional tradition of *talanoa* or debate. It adds a fifth leg of "cultural" thinking to the more rational and orthodox Fourth Estate approach. Instead of limiting the "four estates" of power notion debated by media analysts to the traditional executive, parliament and judiciary plus the media (fourth) branches, it introduces "indigenous tradition or *kastom*, to use a Tok Pisin term", as a critical agency.[48] In a more detailed rationale for this model in an article in *Australian Journalism Review*, I have argued that "understanding the role of this customary 'prop' is critical in a successful talanoa approach" to journalism and writing from a cross-cultural perspective.[49] Comparative characteristics of this notion of talanoa journalism and its representative tanoa are shown in this matrix.

"Self-determination" and the media
"Objectivity" is espoused as a dominant ideal for First World media. However, the notions of "collective agitator" and "nation building" are more important for the Second and Third Worlds respectively. News values reflect timeliness, proximity and personality for the First World in contrast to "ideological significance", "party concerns" and "social responsibility" for the (totalitarian) Second World. Third World news values prioritise "development", "national integration" and "social responsibility".[50] And for the Fourth World, an "independent [political] voice", "language", "culture", "education" and "solidarity" become the mantra.[51] Education is also important for the Second and Third Worlds, but is not given so much emphasis with First World media values.

Both Australia and New Zealand have a thriving indigenous media that apply Fourth World news values in a "self-determination" frame, although news editors may not necessarily define it in quite those terms. In the case of New Zealand, there are currently 21 Māori or iwi (tribal) radio stations. They are all bilingual—Māori and English—but are required to broadcast a minimum of 30 percent of airtime in Te Reo Māori (language) to qualify for state funding assistance. No iwi newspapers have survived and just one Māori newspaper remains, *Te Māori News*, which is bilingual.

However, two established Māori magazines, *Mana* (www.manaonline. co.nz) and *Tu Mai* (www.tumaimagazine.com), are flourishing and the Māori Television Service (www.maoritelevision.com) was launched in 2004, overcoming widespread mainstream media and conservative political opposition. Today it is widely regarded as New Zealand's de facto public broadcaster and programmes such as its award-winning current affairs flagship *Native Affairs* (www.maoritelevision.com/tv/shows/native-affairs) are without peer.

Geopolitical analysis reporting triangle model

Source: Manning, cited by Robie (2013). "Four Worlds" news
values revisited.

In Māori media, many of the Fourth World news values are objectives,
such as "promotion of language, cultural revival, education, collective
inspiration, portraying positive images of individuals and success stories in
hapu and iwi".[52] Author and journalist Carol Archie says self-determination
issues are discussed regularly—such as the Treaty of Waitangi guarantee of
tino rangatiratanga (Māori self-determination), constitutional change and
land issues.

In the South Pacific, few examples of genuinely Fourth World media
exist. Many major daily newspapers are foreign-owned and tend to mirror
First World and Third World news values. Until 2010, News Limited, for
example, owned both the major daily newspapers in both Fiji and Papua
New Guinea—*The Fiji Times* and *PNG Post-Courier*. (The sale of the *Fiji
Times* to the local trading company Motibhai was forced in September
2010 under the regime's *Fiji Media Industry Development Decree*, which
restricted foreign ownership to 10 percent.) The Malaysian logging group
Rimbunan Hijau owns *The National*, the second daily in Papua New Guinea,
which has now overtaken the *Post-Courier* with the largest circulation.

Wantok Niuspepa is an example of Fourth World media in Papua New Guinea. It is a national weekly published by the ecumenical church enterprise Word Publishing in Tok Pisin. Unique in the South Pacific, *Wantok* was founded in 1970 through the extraordinary and visionary efforts of the late Father Frank Mihalic.[53] It became an icon of national development and the contribution that good journalism can make to national education at the grassroots level.

In Fiji, the leading surviving Fijian language weekly newspaper is *Nai Lalakai*, founded in 1962 by *The Fiji Times* group. Although much of what *Nai Lalakai* publishes is actually different from its parent daily, it is still fairly conservative, unlike the "self-determination" Fourth World style of *Wantok*.[54]

Among other Fourth World publications are the feisty *Taimi 'o Tonga*, published by Kalafi Moala, who has campaigned for almost two decades for democracy in the kingdom of Tonga—14 years of this living in exile; and the radical newsletter *Ko 'e Kele 'a*, published by pro-democracy Tongan Member of Parliament 'Akilisi Pohiva. In his 2002 book *Island Kingdom Strikes Back*, Moala documented the struggle for democracy, including his jailing in 1996 for contempt of Parliament—and his imprisonment was ruled unconstitutional and illegal by the Supreme Court.[55] (However, in his later 2009 book *Tonga: In Search of the Friendly Islands*, he argued that the reforms would not produce the desired social outcome "without a truly spiritual reformation" in every aspect of Tongan life).[56] Both the *Taimi 'o Tonga* and *Kele'a* have at times displayed the traditions of a radical and revolutionary press published within countries in transition from authoritarian to development and free press models. According to Moala, his development vision for the Pacific includes the "common people" having greater control over the media rather than being "hijacked by island government policies allied with elitist and corporate financial interests".[57]

Western journalists ought to "explore ways of combining their privilege of free comment with respect for minorities and the integrity of public discourse", argues Loo. "One way is to consider the alternative development journalism approach to reporting, in which the social and cultural cohesion of the people takes priority over news commercialism."[58]

Among successful journalists who have established a reputation for reportage with a development critical edge that often demonstrates the "processes" and "community power" referred to by Loo is Television New Zealand Pacific correspondent Barbara Dreaver, born and raised in Kiribati. Since starting her own newspaper in the Cook Islands, she has managed considerable "legwork" around the region that has uncovered many

Differences between "**orthodox**" and "development" journalism

Orthodox (Western) Journalism	Community And Development Journalism
Mainstream-source oriented	User-source oriented
Reports on random events (What)	Reports on causes processes leading up to events (What, How and Why)
Dominant news value	Development news value
Balance in terms of neutrality; dispassionate observer	Balance tips towards grassroots
Occasionally provides possible solutions to problems without consultation with people	Elicits alternative solutions to problems identified by the people
Formation of public opinion is vertical – from dominant mainstream group to grassroots	Moulding of public opinion is horizontal – views of grassroots and those affected by policies given priority
Highlights individual achievements and accomplishments	Highlights community power as source of self-reliant community
Follows prescribed and tested rules and procedures in journalism	Tries out new methods and procedures – takes risks, thus has more ways of information-gathering and reporting
Right to information without hindrance or censorship; free press	Aware of conflict between reporter's needs and government's needs to protect sensitive negotiations and developments; socially responsible press
Deals mainly with crimes, law and order, disasters, deviant and dramatic events	Deals mainly with socio-economic development, desirable attitudes, values and basic needs of community security and belonging
Profit maximisation, popular appeal	Runs risk of low readership; less popular
Factual reporting, objective, consumption-oriented	Interpretative reporting, subjective, growth-oriented
Awareness and entertainment	Understanding, attitude and behavioural change

Source: Adapted from Eric Loo, p.5.[61]

The author with researchers and development advocates of La'o Hamutuk in Dili, Timor-Leste, in December 2013. From left: Alexandra Arnassalon, Celestino Gusmao, Juvinal Dias, Charles Scheiner (obscured), Adilsonio da Costa Junior, Maximus Tahu and Ines Martins.

LA'O HAMUTUK

remarkable stories. In a 2007 interview with the *Listener*, she revealed that her favourite story was a report exposing a US-based baby-smuggling ring in Samoa: "It was a real punt when I went across but we got the goodies. It was the only time I'd ever cried on a story."[59] She also talked about the growing global interest in the Pacific.

> The US is worried about the Pacific, because it's their border. And in the War on Terror, such as it is, you can see why they're worried—the Pacific is weak in terms of security. And they may be only little countries, but they've each got a vote, as Japan with the whaling knows. I feel sorry for the whales too but it's all very well criticising Tuvalu and Kiribati for supporting Japan, but Japan gave them the money that they really, *really* [original emphasis] needed.[60]

Japan offered aid to small Pacific nations in return for their vote to end a moratorium on commercial whaling. Tongan publisher Kalafi Moala advocates major reform for media systems in the Pacific to address development, saying that to train journalists and then send them to work is like "sending in soldiers to a war zone without a mission".[62] He has been impressed with Tongan-language community broadcasters in San Francisco, where he used to live with his wife and family, and their contribution to Fourth World development. Moala sees three major media development problems facing the Pacific:

1. An inevitable bias in news coverage because most major media operations in the region have been government-owned or controlled: "Island journalists sometimes play servant to corrupt policies developed without public participation."

2. Media business and commercial interests have usurped the traditional role of information: "They may be entertained, horrified, titillated and stressed—but not informed."

3. Globalisation has impacted on media to such an extent that less is being done to make media appropriate for indigenous and local socio-political contexts: "Instead, the social-cultural contexts are being progressively adapted to fit the 'one shoe' of a globalised media."

Tougher scrutiny

Deliberative and critical development journalism have an essential role to play in the future of the South Pacific region and a new generation of educated journalists has responsibility to provide this for their people. Pacific Islanders are no longer people confined to microstates scattered across the vast Pacific Ocean. They are peoples who have migrated around the globe in diaspora. Small nations such as the Cook Islands, Niue, Samoa, Tonga and Tuvalu have a greater part of their population living as migrants in Australia, New Zealand and the United States or elsewhere. Pacific journalists now have a greater task than ever in encouraging "democratisation" of the region and informed insights into development, social justice and peace issues facing island states. Deliberative journalists ought to also forge more productive links with non-governmental organisations, some of which have overtaken the media as being watchdogs on power. A good example of such an NGO is La`o Hamutuk, the Timor-Leste Institute for Development Monitoring and Analysis (www.laohamutuk.org). The robust investigations being done by this independent agency's researchers on so-called "resource curse" development over the country's oil and gas industry, land reform and agricultural production are vastly better than what journalists are doing. Yet some media are reluctant to use the research because they see La`o Hamutuk as a rival media outlet.[63]

Some of the region's journalists warn about allowing politicians' slogans such as "cultural sensitivity" being used as a smokescreen for the abuse of power and violations of human rights. The deliberative journalist seeks to expose the truth and report on alternatives and solutions.

"To use the guise of cultural sensitivity as a cover to protect oneself from criticism is an insult to that culture, for the implication is that culture does not condone transparency, honesty, order and proper management of affairs," argues Kalafi Moala. "Corrupt and dishonest politicians and bureaucrats have often reacted to media scrutiny by throwing up a pretentious cover of cultural taboos and insensitivities as excuses to avoid being scrutinised."[64]

Critical deliberative journalism also means a tougher scrutiny of the region's institutions and dynamics of governance. Answers are needed for the questions: Why, how and what now? Journalists need to become part of the solution rather than being part of the problem.

Notes

1 Adapted from David Robie (2013). "Four Worlds" news values revisited: A deliberative journalism paradigm for Pacific media. *Pacific Journalism Review, 19*(2): 84–110.
2 Chris Nash (2013). Journalism as a research discipline. *Pacific Journalism Review, 19*(2): 123–135.
3 Anthony Mason, cited in David Robie (2007, May 14). Researchers call for deeper understanding from coup reporters. *Asia Media*, UCLA Asia Institute. Retrieved on 3 August 2012, from www.asiamedia.ucla.edu/article.asp?parentid=69873
4 Anthony Mason (2009). Australian coverage of the Fiji coups of 1987 and 2000: Sources, practice and representation. Unpublished doctoral thesis, Faculty of Arts and Design. Canberra, ACT: University of Canberra.
5 Anthony Mason (2007). Elite sources, journalistic practice and the status quo. *Pacific Journalism Review, 13*(1): 107–123, p. 121.
6 Christine Gounder (2006). The Fiji 2000 coup: A media analysis. Unpublished Master of Communication Studies thesis. Auckland: AUT University.
7 Christine Gounder, cited in Robie (2007, May 14), Researchers call.
8 David Robie (2007, August 7). Growing pains in Timor-Leste. *Asia Media*, UCLA Asia Institute. Retrieved on 3 August 2012, from www.asiamedia.ucla.edu/article.asp?parentid=75294
9 Vijendra Kumar (2010, September 27). Fiji: The best of the *Times*. *Pacific Scoop*. Retrieved on 7 January 2014, from http://pacific.scoop.co.nz/2010/09/fiji-the-best-of-the-times/
10 David Robie (2009, May 8). Too much pressure. *Asia Media*, UCLA Asia Institute. Retrieved on 3 August 2012, from www.asiamedia.ucla.edu/article.asp?parentid=108200

11 Shailendra Singh (2012). Investigative journalism: Challenges, perils, rewards in seven Pacific Island countries. *Pacific Journalism Review, 18*(1): 83–104.

12 Kunda Dixit (2010). *Dateline Earth: Journalism as if the Planet Mattered* [2nd edition]. Bangkok: Inter Press Foundation, p. 112.

13 Ibid., p. 125.

14 Ibid., p. 83.

15 Ibid., p. 53.

16 Ibid., p. 55.

17 Angela Romano (2013). *International Journalism and Democracy: Civic Engagement Models from Around the World* [2nd edition]. London: Routledge, p. 231.

18 Ibid., p. 231.

19 Ibid., p. 235.

20 Ibid., p. 232.

21 Ibid., p. 11.

22 Angela Romano (1998). Normative theories of development journalism: State versus practitioner perspectives in Indonesia. *Australian Journalism Review, 20*(2): 60–87.

23 Romano (2013), p. 235.

24 Arlene Notoro Morgan, Alice Pifer and Keith Woods (2006). *The Authentic Voice: The Best Reporting on Race and Ethnicity.* New York: Columbia University Press, p. xv.

25 Levi Obijiofor and Folker Hanusch (2011). *Journalism Across Cultures: An Introduction.* Houndmills, UK: Palgrave Macmillan, p. 59.

26 See Ibrahim S. Shaw (2011). "Human rights journalism": A critical conceptual framework of a complementary strand of peace journalism. In Ibrahim S. Shaw, Jake Lynch and Robert A. Hackett (eds). *Expanding Peace Journalism: Comparative and Critical Approaches.* Sydney, NSW: Sydney University Press, pp. 96–121.

27 David Robie (2008). Media and development in the Pacific: Reporting the why, how and what now. In Shailendra Singh and Biman Prasad (eds) (2008). *Media and Development: Issues and Challenges in the Pacific Islands.* Suva: University of the South Pacific; Auckland: Pacific Media Centre, pp. 11–26, p. 12.

28 Jean-Marc Fleury (2004). Development journalism or just good journalism? *BBC World Online.* Retrieved on 10 June 2004, from www.bbc.co.uk/worldservice/trust/2015/story/2004/06/040609_jean_marc_fleury.shtml

29 Eric Loo (1994). Teaching development journalism in the reporting of cultural diversity. *Australian Journalism Review, 16*(2): 1–10, p. 2.

30 S. E. Smith (2007). What is development journalism? Retrieved on 4 June 2007, from www.wisegeek.com/what-is-development-journalism.htm

31 P. Sinha (1981). The ASEAN journalist. Cited by Loo (1994), Teaching development journalism, p. 3.

32 Alex Perrottet and David Robie (2011). Pacific media freedom 2011: A status report. *Pacific Journalism Review, 17*(2): 147–186.

33 Robie (2008). Media and development, p. 13.

34 Arnold de Beer and John C. Merrill (eds) (2008). *Global Journalism: Topical Issues and Media Systems* [5th edition]. Boston: Pearson Education Inc.; Obijiofor

and Hanusch (2011). *Journalism Across Cultures*; Dixit (2010). *Dateline Earth*; Wilbur Schramm (1964). *Mass Media and National Development: The Role of Information in the Developing Countries*. UNESCO/Stanford University Press; Fred Siebert, Wilbur Schramm and Theodore Peterson (1956). *Four Theories of the Press*. Urbana and Chicago: University of Illinois Press; John Street (2001). *Mass Media, Politics and Democracy*. London: Palgrave.

35 Jack Lule (1987). News values of Three Worlds. In A. L. Hester and J. To Wai Lan (eds) (1987). *Handbook for Third World Journalists*. Athens, Georgia: Center for International Mass Communication, Training and Research, Henry W. Grady School of Journalism and Mass Communication, University of Georgia, pp. 23–46.

36 Obijiofor and Hanusch (2011). *Journalism Across Cultures*, p. 16.

37 William Hachten (1981). *The World News Prism: Changing Media, Clashing Ideologies*. Ames: Iowa State University Press; cited in Obijiofor and Hanusch (2011), *Journalism Across Cultures*, p. 17.

38 David Robie (1995). *Nius Bilong Pasifik: Mass Media in the Pacific*. Port Moresby: University of Papua New Guinea Press, p. 11.

39 Peter H. Russell (1996, November–December). Aboriginal nationalism—prospects for decolonisation. *Pacifica Review*, 8(2): 57–67.

40 Robie (1995). *Nius Bilong Pasifik*, p. 11.

41 As cited by Haunani-Kay Trask (1999). *From a Native Daughter: Colonialism and Sovereignty in Hawai'i*. Honolulu: University of Hawai'i Press.

42 Ben Bohane (2006). Blackfella armies: Kastom and conflict in contemporary Melanesia, 1994–2006. Unpublished Masteßr of Arts (Journalism) thesis. Wollongong, NSW: University of Wollongong.

43 Ben Bohane (2013). *The Black Islands: Spirit and War in Melanesia*. Port Vila, Vanuatu: Waka Press.

44 David Robie (2013). "Four Worlds" news values revisited: A deliberative journalism paradigm for Pacific media. *Pacific Journalism Review*, 19(1): 84–110.

45 Bohane (2006). *Blackfella armies*, pp. 3–4.

46 David Robie (2013). The talanoa and the tribal paradigm: Reflections on cross-cultural reporting in the Pacific. *Australian Journalism Review*, 35(1): 43–58.

47 Ibid., pp. 51–52.

48 Ibid., p. 52.

49 Ibid., pp. 52–53.

50 Lule (1987). News values of Three Worlds, pp. 23–46; Murray Masterton (1996). *Asian Values in Journalism*. Singapore: Asian Media, Information and Communication Centre (AMIC), p. 48.

51 David Robie (2001). *The Pacific Journalist: A Practical Guide*. Suva: University of the South Pacific Book Centre, p. 13.

52 Carol Archie (2007). *Pou Kōrero: A Journalists' Guide to Māori and Current Affairs*. Wellington: New Zealand Journalists Training Organisation, p. 62.

53 See Philip Cass (2011). Fr Francis Mihalic and *Wantok* niuspepa in Papua New Guinea. *Pacific Journalism Review*, 17(1): 210–226; David Robie (2004). *Mekim Nius: South Pacific media, politics and education*. Suva: University of the South Pacific Book Centre, pp. 151–58.

54 Paul Geraghty (2005). Literacy and the media in the Fiji Islands. *Pacific Journalism Review, 11*(1): 48–57.

55 Kalafi Moala (2002). *Island Kingdom Strikes Back: The Story of an Independent Island Newspaper—Taimi `o Tonga.* Auckland: Pacmedia Publishers.

56 Kalafi Moala (2009). *Tonga: In Search of the Friendly Islands.* Kealakekua, Hawai'i: Pasifika Foundation Press; Auckland: Pacific Media Centre.

57 Kalafi Moala (2005). The case for Pacific media reform to reflect island communities. *Pacific Journalism Review, 11*(1): 26–35, p. 27.

58 Loo (1994). Teaching development journalism, p. 5.

59 Sarah Barnett (2007, August 11). Barbara Dreaver [Profile]. *New Zealand Listener,* Issue 3509, p. 12. Retrieved on 3 August 2012, from www.listener.co.nz/commentary/barbara-dreaver/

60 Ibid.

61 Loo (1994). Teaching development journalism, p. 5.

62 Moala (2005). Pacific media reform, p. 27.

63 David Robie (2013, December 16). Taking on the challenge of Timor-Leste's media transition. Pacific Media Centre Online. Retrieved on 7 January 2014, from www.pmc.aut.ac.nz/articles/taking-challenge-timor-lestes-media-transition

64 Moala (2005). p. 34.

Epilogue

ONE OF Fiji's best investigative journalists and media trainers ended up as a spin doctor and henchman for wannabe dictator George Speight. Like his mentor, he is now languishing in jail for life for treason.

Some newshounds in Papua New Guinea have pursued political careers thanks to their media training, but most have failed to make the cut in national politics.

A leading publisher in Tonga was forced to put his newspaper on the line in a dramatic attempt to overturn a constitutional gag on the media. He won—probably hastening the pro-democracy trend in the royal fiefdom's 2010 general election.

The editor of the government-owned newspaper in Samoa runs a relentless and bitter "holier than thou" democracy campaign against the "gutless" media in Fiji that he regards as too soft on the military-backed regime. Yet the editor-in-chief of the rival independent newspaper accuses him of being a state propagandist in a nation that has been ruled by one party for three decades.

Media intersects with the raw edge of politics in the South Pacific, as countries are plunged into turbulent times and face the spectre of terrorism. A decade-long civil war on Bougainville, four coups in Fiji (if the ill-fated George Speight putsch is counted), ethnic conflict in the Solomon Islands, factional feuding in Vanuatu and political assassinations in Samoa have all been part of the volatile mix in recent years.

While teaching journalism in Australia, New Zealand and other Western countries involves briefing students how to report on local business, development, health, politics and law courts free of the perils of defamation and contempt, in Pacific media schools one also needs to focus on a range of other challenging issues—such as reporting blasphemy, sedition, treason and how to deal with physical threats and bribery.[1]

At times, it takes raw courage to be a neophyte journalist in the Pacific. At the University of Papua New Guinea, at a time when it still had the region's best journalism school, two senior reporters were ambushed and beaten by a war party from a Highlands province after the local award-winning training newspaper, *Uni Tavur*, featured the campus warriors' home affiliation in an unflattering front-page report on politics.

On another occasion, a student journalist slipped into hiding when ominous "wanted" posters with his name and picture were plastered around campus because of his report exposing corruption over an annual Miss UPNG beauty pageant.

Also, at the University of Papua New Guinea in the mid-1990s, trainee reporters covered five campus-related murders over two years as part of their weekly assignments, including the slaying of a lecturer by off-duty police officers.

In July 2001, four students were shot dead in protests against the Papua New Guinean government over unpopular World Bank structural adjustment policies. Two young women, *Uni Tavur* reporters Wanita Wakus ad Estella Cheung, wrote inspiring accounts of the shootings and gave evidence at a subsequent commission of inquiry.

At the University of the South Pacific—a unique regional institution owned by a dozen Pacific nations—a team of students covered the Speight rebellion in 2000, when Fiji's elected government was held at gunpoint for 56 days, for their newspaper, *Wansolwara*, and website, *Pacific Journalism Online.* Nervous campus administrators closed the website after the military under Commodore Voreqe Bainimarama declared martial law for a 48-hour period.

But the students carried on filing reports for a special coup website established by the Australian Centre for Independent Journalism (ACIJ) at the University of Technology, Sydney. They scooped that year's Ossie Awards, the student media awards named after the late foreign correspondent Osmar "Ossie" White and open to entrants from Australia, New Zealand and the Pacific.

Although three long-established journalism schools at university level exist in the Pacific—UPNG in Port Moresby and Divine Word University at Madang in Papua New Guinea, and USP in Fiji—along with a second tier of trade school-level programmes supported by AusAID, most journalists in the region still have little solid training (apart from Papua New Guinea where 81 percent have formal qualifications).

During my decade teaching journalism in Fiji and Papua New Guinea, I found many bright young graduates will work for a year or so as journalists then leave for other, more highly paid, media-related jobs using the double major degrees they gained to get into journalism. This continual loss of staff makes it very difficult to achieve stable and consistent editorial standards and policies.

Poorly paid journalists are potentially more readily tempted by "envelope" journalism—the bribery and other inducements used by unscrupulous politicians and other powerful figures. Financial hardship and lack of training are an unhealthy mix for media in a democracy.

Media organisations themselves are too dependent on donors in the region for the limited training that does go on, and this makes them captive to the donors' agendas. For example, under the mantra of "good governance", AusAID (now Australian Aid) has since 1996 financed a Pacific Media Initiative (PMI) project and its various multi-million-dollar successors, the Pacific Media and Communications Facility (PMCF) and now the Port Vila-based Pacific Media Assistance Scheme (PACMAS).[2] Many view both the early ventures as band-aid projects out of step with journalism training and education in Australia and New Zealand, although the PACMAS version is undoubtedly an improvement. AusAID has contributed little to the main university-based journalism schools—the best hope for sustainable media training and education in the region.

But even the universities are under threat. Once a campus-based stand-alone journalism school with a discrete journalism degree and a proud record since established with New Zealand at independence in 1975, the University of Papua New Guinea programme is now a mere shadow of what it once was.

One consultant, Dr Eric Loo, said the restored reputation at UPNG "rests on the revival of *Uni Tavur* and recommissioning of Campus 98.5FM radio".[3] And the credibility of the regional University of the South Pacific journalism programme took a severe beating in 2012 when the acting head, a Canadian, scrapped Pacific content from the course and stumbled from one controversy to the next. Eventually, he was dumped by the university itself in the wake of a series of complaints from students, including the widely respected news editor from New Caledonia's Radio Djiido.[4] According to US journalism professor and attorney Robert Hooper on an investigative journalism training contract with Fiji Television, "after 16 years away from Fiji, my heart sank when I returned to USP and found the Journalism Programme in disarray".[5] Criticising the suppression of an award-deserving documentary, *Recycle*, made by one of his student journalists about USP's environmental policy, Hooper wrote: "In a pervasive climate of censorship and suppression of press freedom, even investigative journalism that uncovers significant issues at a local university can be viewed as controversial."[6]

Even in Timor-Leste, there is severe criticism of media education and training strategies. Award-winning José Belo, arguably his country's finest investigative journalist and president of the Timor-Leste Press Union, is highly critical of "wasted" journalism aid projects totalling more than US$5 million. A "journalism in transition" conference in Dili in October 2013 attempted to strengthen the self-regulatory status of the news industry "in response to the so-called international aid, particularly from the United States and Australia, which has been misused in the name of journalism in this country".[7] The good news was that there was a united stand on a new code of ethics.

Attempts to establish journalist unions have been largely unsuccessful, except for a brief period of support and training by the International Federation of Journalists (IFJ) in the early 1990s. Once funding ended, the commitment and energy of local organisers dissipated.

The most disturbing trend in the digital age is electronic martial law—a new law in the Philippines that criminalises e-libel in an extreme action to protect privacy. The Supreme Court in Manila ruled in December 2012 to temporarily suspend this law and then extended it until further notice in February 2013. However, in February 2014, the Supreme Court ruled that the law was indeed constitutional, "effectively expanding the country's 80-year-old libel law into the digital domain".[8] Ironically, this marked almost to the day the 28th anniversary of the "People Power" revolt that ousted the Marcos dictatorship. The Philippine Internet Freedom Alliance and many other groups have called for a complete repeal of the law as being unconstitutional.

This *Cybercrime Prevention Act* is like something out of the Tom Cruise futuristic movie *Minority Report.* An offender can be imprisoned for up to 12 years without parole and the law is clearly a violation of Article 19 of the International Covenant on Civil and Political Rights. And truth is not recognised as a defence. In March 2014, the indictment of two journalists, Alan Morison and Chutima Sidasathian, for criminal libel under a similar *Computer Crime Act* in Thailand "may spell doom" for the online news website Phuketwan.[9] It would be disastrous if any South Pacific country, such as Fiji, wanted to impose a copycat decree and gag cyberspace.

In the Philippines at least 206 journalists have been murdered since 1986—34 of them in the Ampatuan massacre in Mindanao in 2009. Four years later nobody has been convicted for these atrocities. The Philippines is a far more dangerous place for the media under democracy than it was under the Marcos dictatorship. There is a culture of impunity.

West Papua is the most critical front line for defending media freedom in the South Pacific at present. The West Papua Freedom Flotilla in September 2013 focused unprecedented global attention on human rights and freedom of expression in the Indonesian-rule region.[10] A flotilla of small boats from Australia defied Indonesian military threats with Aboriginal leaders meeting Papuans for a "sacred" cultural exchange at an undisclosed border location on the Papuan mainland.

Australia's shameful human rights violations and suppression of information about asylum seekers is another media freedom issue.

Journalism must fundamentally change in the Pacific to cope with the political and industry chaos. Just as much as it needs to reach across an increasingly globalised world, it needs to strike a renewed bond with its communities—trust, participation, engagement and empowerment are essential. In the 2013 book *Rethinking Journalism*, editors Chris Peters and Marcel Broesma pointed to climate change as an apt metaphor for the challenges journalism faces: "Climate change scientists can point to a number of problematic indicators: rising sea levels, unstable temperature patterns, the deteriorating ozone layer, retreating glaciers ..."[11] Yet, the editors argue, any proposed solution demands a fundamental reconceptualisation of our relationship to the environment. Likewise, journalism must fundamentally change its relationship with our audience.

Deliberative and critical development journalism have an essential role to play in the future of the South Pacific region. So does peace journalism, or conflict-sensitive journalism—another form of investigative and deliberative journalism—and human rights journalism. And a new generation of educated journalists has a responsibility to provide this for the people.

Pacific journalists now have a greater task than ever in encouraging "democratisation" of the region and informed insights into development, environment along with climate change, and peace challenges facing island states. The deliberative journalist seeks to expose the truth and report on alternatives and solutions. Journalists need to become part of the democratic solution rather than being part of the problem.

Pacific political leaders finally picked up the challenge over climate change at the 2013 Pacific Islands Forum in the Marshall Islands. Now Pacific journalists need to follow this lead and target climate change as a top priority for the media and education.

Finally, some good news in Fiji as it approaches the 2014 elections with the founding of a new magazine, *República*, whose editor Ricardo Morris makes precisely these pledges over truth to power. In the very first edition, The República Manifesto declared:

> We aim to regain some of the vibrancy of a free media, to act as a mirror on society without fear or favour. The Pacific—and Fiji—has not been immune to the ethical lapses ... common ... around the world, so we anticipate being held to the same high standards we expect of our leaders and those we criticise.[12]

Notes
1   David Robie (2005). Pacific solutions. *The Walkley Magazine*, No. 33: 36–37.
2   David Robie (2008). Changing paradigms in media education aid in the Pacific. In Evangelia Papoutsaki and Usha Sundar Harris, *South Pacific Islands Communication: Regional Perspectives, Local Issues*. Singapore, Suva and Auckland: Asian Media Information & Communication Centre (AMIC), pp. 59–81.
3   Eric Loo (2010, February 24). Preliminary review of Bachelor of Journalism UPMNG, p.3.
4   See Graham Davis (2013, December 11). Splutterings from the edge. *Grubsheet*. Retrieved on 7 January 2013, from www.grubsheet.com.au/splutterings-from-the-edge/; Robert A. Hooper (2013). When the barking stopped: Censorship, self-censorship and spin in Fiji. *Pacific Journalism Review, 19*(1): 41–57. Available at www.pjreview.info/articles/when-barking-stopped-censorship-self-censorship-and-spin-fiji-840; David Robie (2013, February 3). The lies of Marc Edge, "counterpropagandist". *Café Pacific*. Retrieved on 7 January 2014, from http://cafepacific.blogspot.co.nz/2013/02/the-lies-of-marc-edge.html
5   Hooper (2013). When the barking stopped: Censorship, self-censorship and spin in Fiji, p. 49.
6   Ibid., p. 51.
7   David Robie (2013, December 16). Taking on the challenge of Timor-Leste's media in transition. Pacific Media Centre Online. Retrieved on 7 January 2014, from www.pmc.aut.ac.nz/articles/taking-challenge-timor-lestes-media-transition
8   Freedom won, freedoms lost; black Tuesday on EDSA anniv (2014, March 3). The PCIJ Blog, Philippines Center for Investigative Journalism. Retrieved on 9 March 2014, from http://pcij.org/blog/2014/02/25/freedom-won-freedom-lost-black-tuesday-on-edsa-anniv
9   Journos face indictment under Thailand's cybercrime law (March, 7). The PCIJ Blog, Philippines Center for Investigative Journalism. Retrieved on 9 March 2014, from http://pcij.org/blog/2014/03/07/journos-face-indictment-under-thailands-cybercrime-law
10 Marni Cordell (2013, September 18). Freedom Flotilla contacts say military threats have forced them into hiding. *The Guardian*. Retrieved on 7 January 2014, http://www.theguardian.com/world/2013/sep/18/west-papua-freedom-flotilla-threats
11 Chris Peters and Marcel Broersma (eds) (2013). *Rethinking Journalism: Trust and Participation in a Transformed News Landscape*. London: Routledge, p. 3.
12 Ricardo Morris (2012, September). The *República* Manifesto. *República,* p. 5.

Select bibliography

Archie, Carol (2007). *Pou Kōrero: A Journalists' Guide to Māori and Current Affairs*. Wellington: New Zealand Journalists' Training Organisation.

Barber, Benjamin J. (1992). *Jihad vs. McWorld: Terrorism's Challenge to Democracy*. London: Ballantyne Books; New York, NY: Times Books.

Bohane, Ben (2013). *The Black Islands: Spirit and War in Melanesia*. Port Vila: Waka Books.

Bourne, Richard (1995). *News on a Knife Edge: Gemini Journalism and a Global Agenda*. London: John Libbey.

Brown, Dee (1971). *Bury My Heart at Wounded Knee: An Indian History of the American West*. London: Picador.

Burchett, George and Shimmin, Nick (eds) (2007). *Rebel journalism: The Writings of Wilfred Burchett*. Melbourne: Cambridge University Press.

Chomsky, Noam (2006). *Failed States: The Abuse of Power and the Assault on Democracy*. New York: Metropolitan Books.

Clements, Kevin (ed.) (1993). *Peace and Security in the Asia Pacific Region*. Tokyo: United Nations University Press; Palmerston North: Dunmore Press.

Connell, John (1987). *New Caledonia or Kanaky? The Political History of a French Colony*. Canberra, ACT: Research School of Pacific Studies, Australian National University.

Danielsson, Bengt and Marie-Thérèse (1977). *Moruroa, Mon Amour: The French Nuclear Tests in the Pacific*. London: Penguin Books.

Danielsson, Bengt and Marie-Thérèse (1986). *Poisoned Reign: French Nuclear Colonialism in the Pacific*. Ringwood, Vic.: Penguin Books.

Dean, Eddie, and Rotova, Stan (1988). *Rabuka: No Other Way: His own story of the Fijian coup*. Sydney: Doubleday.

Dixit, Kunda (2010). *Dateline Earth: Journalism as if the Planet Mattered* [2nd edition]. Bangkok: IPS Asia-Pacific.

Fernandes, Clinton (2012). *The Independence of East Timor*. London: Alpha Books.

Firth, Stewart (1987). *Nuclear Playground*. Sydney: Allen & Unwin.

Firth, Stewart (2011). *Australia in International Politics: An Introduction to Australian Foreign Policy* [3rd edition]. Sydney: Allen & Unwin.

Forde, Susan (2011). *Challenging the News: The Journalism of Alternative and Community Media*. London: Palgrave Macmillan.

Fraenkel, Jon, Firth, Stewart and Lal, Brij V. (eds) (2009). *The 2006 Military Takeover in Fiji: A Coup to End All Coups?* Canberra: Australian National University.

Freedman, Des and Thussu, Daya K. (eds) (2012). *Media and Terrorism: Global Perspectives*. London: Sage.

Gibson, Neville (2007). *Final Deadline: The Last Days of the Rand Daily Mail.* Cape Town: David Philip Books.

Green, Michael (2013). *Persona Non Grata: Breaking the Bond – Fiji and New Zealand 2004-2007.* Auckland: Dunmore Publishing

Hannis, Grant (ed.) (2014). *Intro: A Beginner's Guide to Journalism in 21st Century Aotearoa/New Zealand* Wellington: New Zealand Journalists' Training Organisation

International Committee of The Red Cross (ICRC). (2009). *Under the Protection of the Palm: Wars of dignity in the Pacific.* Suva: Fiji.

Johnson, Giff (2013). *Don't Ever Whisper—Darlene Keju: Pacific Health Pioneer, Champion for Nuclear Survivors.* Majuro: Johnson.

Keeble, Lance, Tulloch, John and Zollmann, Florian (eds) (2010). *Peace Journalism, War and Conflict Resolution.* London: Peter Lang.

King, Michael (1986). *Death of the Rainbow Warrior.* Auckland: Penguin Books.

King, Peter, Elslie, Jim, and Webb-Gannon, Chris (eds) (2011). *Comprehending West Papua* [Monograph]. Sydney: Centre for Peace and Conflict Studies, University of Sydney.

Lal, Brij, with Michael Pretes (eds.) (2008). *Coup: Reflections on the Political Crisis in Fiji.* Canberra: Australian National University E-Press.

Lal, Brij (2011). *Islands of Turmoil: Elections and Politics in Fiji.* Canberra: Australian National University.

Lange, David (1990). *Nuclear Free: The New Zealand Way.* Auckland: Penguin Books.

Leadbeater, Maire (2006). *Negligent Neighbour: New Zealand's complicity in the invasion and occupation of Timor-Leste.* Nelson: Craig Potton Publishing.

Leadbeater, Maire (2013). *Peace, Power & Politics: How New Zealand Became Nuclear Free.* Dunedin: Otago University Press.

Levine, Stephen (ed.) (2009). *Pacific Ways: Government and Politics in the Pacific Islands.* Wellington: Victoria University Press.

Maclellan, Nic; Chesnaux, Jean et al. (1988). *After Mururoa: France in the South Pacific.* Melbourne: Ocean Press.

McCoy, Alfred W. (2009). *Policing America's Empire: The United States, the Philippines and the Rise of the Surveillance State.* Madison: University of Wisconsin Press.

McKnight, David (2012). *Rupert Murdoch: An Investigation of Political Power.* Sydney: Allen & Unwin.

Magubane, Peter (1978). *Magubane's South Africa.* London: Secker & Warburg.

Maniaty, Tony (2009). *Shooting Balibo: Blood and Memory in East Timor.* Camberwell, Vic.: Viking.

Merrill, John C. (1996). *Existential Journalism.* Ames, Iowa: Iowa State University.

Moala, Kalafi (2002). *Island Kingdom Strikes Back: The Story of an Independent Island Newspaper—Taimi `o Tonga.* Auckland: Pacmedia Publishers.

Moala, Kalafi (2009). *Tonga: In Search of the Friendly Islands.* Kealakekua, Hawai'i: Pasifika Foundation Press; Auckland: Pacific Media Centre.

PACMAS (2013). Regional State of Media and Communication Report. Port Villa: Australia Aid.

Peake, Gordon (2013). *Beloved Land : Stories, Struggles and Secrets from Timor-Leste.* Brunswick, Vic.: Scribe Publications.

Perrottet, Alex, and Robie, David (2011). Pacific Press Freedom 2011: A status report. *Pacific Journalism Review*, 17(2).

Peters, Chris and Broersma, Marcel (eds) (2013). *Rethinking Journalism: Trust and Participation in a Transformed News Landscape.* London and New York: Routledge.

O'Callaghan, Mary-Louise (1999). *Enemies Within: Papua New Guinea, Australia and the Sandline Crisis: The Inside Story.* Sydney: Doubleday.

Obijiofor, Levi and Hanusch, Folker (2011). *Journalism Across Cultures: An Introduction.* London: Palgrave Macmillan.

Pilger, John (2004). *Tell Me No Lies: Investigative Journalism and its Triumphs.* London: Jonathan Cape.

Projects in Asian Journalism (2006). *Blood on Their Hands: Infanticide in India and Other Stories.* Manila: Konrad Adenauer Asian Centre for Journalism.

Ratuva, Sitiveni (2011). *Politics of Preferential Development: Trans-global study of Affirmative Action and Ethnic Conflict in Fiji, Malaysia and South Africa.* Canberra: Australian National University.

Robertson, Robert and Tamanisau, Akosita (1988). *Fiji: Shattered Coups.* Sydney: Pluto Press.

Robertson, Robert and Sutherland, William (2002). *Government by the Gun: The Unfinished Business of Fiji's 2000 Coup.* Sydney: Pluto Press.

Robie, David (1986). *Eyes of Fire: The Last Voyage of the Rainbow Warrior.* Auckland: Linden Books; (2005). [20th anniversary memorial edition]. Auckland: Asia-Pacific Network.

Robie, David (1989). *Och Världen Blundar ... Kampen för frihet i Stilla Havet [And the World Closed its Eyes—Campaign for a free South Pacific].* [Swedish trans. Margareta Eklöf]. Hoganas, Sweden: Wiken Books.

Robie, David (1989). *Blood on their Banner: Nationalist Struggles in the South Pacific.* London: Zed Books; Sydney: Pluto Press.

Robie, David (ed.) (1992). *Tu Galala: Social Change in the Pacific.* Wellington: Bridget Williams Books.

Robie David (ed.) (1995). *Nius Bilong Pasifik: Mass Media in the Pacific.* Port Moresby: University of PNG Press.

Robie, David (ed.) (2001). *The Pacific Journalist: A Practical Guide.* Suva: University of the South Pacific Book Centre.

Robie, David (2004). *Mekim Nius: South Pacific media, politics and education.* Suva: University of the South Pacific Book Centre.

Robie, David and Singh, Shailendra (eds) (2013). "Media and democracy in the Pacific" edition. *Pacific Journalism Review*, 19(1).

Robie, James (1867). *The Representative Radicals of Edinburgh.* Edinburgh: W. P. Nimmo.

Sharpham, John (2000). *Rabuka of Fiji: The Authorised Biography of Major-General Sitiveni Rabuka.* Rockhampton, Qld: Central Queensland University Press.

Shaw, Ibrahim S., Lynch, Jake and Hackett, Robert A. (eds) (2011). *Expanding Peace Journalism: Comparative and Critical Approaches.* Sydney, NSW: Sydney University Press.

Singh, Shailendra and Prasad, Biman (eds) (2008). *Media and Development: Issues and Challenges in the Pacific Islands.* Suva: Fiji Institute of Applied Studies; Auckland: Pacific Media Centre.

Singh, Shailendra and Prasad, Biman (eds) (2008). Coups, media and democracy in Fiji [Editorial]. *Fijian Studies: A Journal of Contemporary Fiji*, 6(1 & 2): 1–8.

Szabo, Michael, and Greenpeace New Zealand (1991). *Making Waves.* Auckland: Reed Books.

Trask, Haunani-Kay (1999). *From a Native Daughter: Colonialism and Sovereignty in Hawai'i* [Revised edition]. Honolulu: University of Hawai'i Press.

West, Richard (1972). *River of Tears: The Rise of the Rio Tinto-Zinc Mining Corporation.* London: Earth Island Ltd.

Index

V

Vakatora, Tomasi 117
Vanguard Films 251
Van Peteghem, Bruno 65
Vanuatu 147, 148
Vayadimoin, Jean-Luc 73
Veitata, Taniela "Big Dan" 110, 117, 120
Vernaudon, Emile 89
Vietnam War 19
Vigilantes 144
Vinten, Wayne 254
Volavola, Mosese 115
Vosanibola, Josefa 281

W

Walters, Vernon 114
Wansolwara and *Wansolwara Online* 285,
    292–294, 345
Wapae, Edward 58
Ward, Martin 198–200
Warren, Christopher 157
Watson, Rupert 174, 182
Watson, Tom 4
Wea, (Pastor) Djubelly 108
Wenner, Chris 234–235, 237–238
Wesley, Fred 283
West Papua 143–148, 312–314, 347
West, Richard 195, 204
Whelan, Ellen 189
Wilkes, Owen 29
Wilson, Barry 153–154
Wingti, Paias 202
Women 146–148
Women's International League for Peace and
    Freedom (WILPF) 29
Wong, Sam 130
World Health Organization (WHO) 147, 185
World Press Freedom Day (WPFD) 281, 299

Y

Yabaki, (Reverend) Akuila 123
Yéiwene, Yéiwene 57, 64, 74, 106

Z

Zaire 39–40
Zoning 144
Zubiri, Jose Ma. R. Jr 182

About the Author

Professor David Robie is director of AUT University's Pacific Media Centre. For more than two decades he focused on reporting the Asia-Pacific region. He has covered and researched post-colonial coups, indigenous struggles for independence, and environmental and developmental issues. Formerly he was head of journalism at both the universities of Papua New Guinea and the South Pacific. David is founding editor of *Pacific Journalism Review*, convenor of Pacific Media Watch and editor of the independent Pacific Scoop news website. He has written several books on the region's politics and media, including *Mekim Nius: South Pacific politics, media and education*, and a book about the bombing of the *Rainbow Warrior*. David also publishes the media freedom and transparency blog *Café Pacific*. He was Australian Press Council Fellow in 1999 and was awarded the Pacific Islands Media Association Press Freedom Award in 2005 for his services to Pacific journalism education and media freedom.

www.cafepacific.blogspot.com

Printed in Australia
AUOC02n0700090414
260585AU00001B/1/P

9 781877 484254